Phantom of the Opera

A SOCIAL HISTORY OF THE WORLD'S MOST POPULAR MUSICAL

Kathleen Kendall-Tackett, PhD

Praeclarus Press, LLC

www.PraeclarusPress.com

Praeclarus Press, LLC
2504 Sweetgum Lane
Amarillo, Texas 79124 USA
806-367-9950
www.PraeclarusPress.com

DISCLAIMER

The author disclaims all warranties, whether expressed or implied, including any warranty as the quality, accuracy, safety, or suitability of this information for any particular purpose.

ISBN: 978-1-946665-07-2

Cover Design: Ken Tackett
Developmental Editing: Kathleen Kendall-Tackett
Copyediting: Chris Tackett
Book Layout & Design: Nelly Murariu

Take a deformed ghost, a virginal beauty, her rather drippy suitor, and a collapsing chandelier. Add lashings of lush romantic music, and there you have it. The most successful stage show in history, with songs you can't get out of your head—even if you try.

BBC, *Behind the Mask* (part 1)

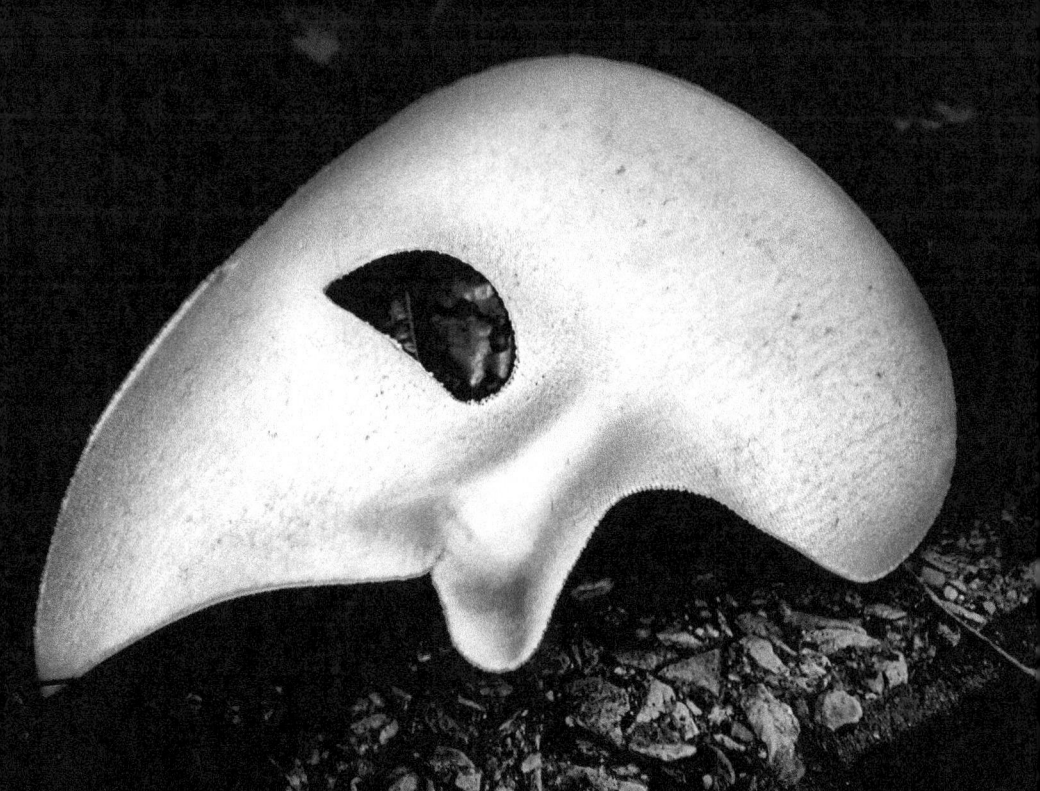

Contents

Chapter 4

Working with Lloyd Webber: The Good, the Bad, and the Ugly 35

Chapter 5

Lloyd Webber and the Critics 45

Chapter 6

Composer and Muse: Story of a Marriage 55

SECTION II
PHANTOM ON FILM   111

Chapter 10

Phantom Goes from Stage to Film   113

Chapter 11

Changes in the Story from Stage to Film   127

How to Use This Book

Writing about music is inherently challenging. I can describe it, but it's often difficult for you, as reader, to fully grasp the nuances, even with a piece as well known as *The Phantom of the Opera*. To address this limitation, I have provided links to YouTube videos throughout the book. The photos are YouTube thumbnails. You can access these by typing in the link. Or you can use a barcode scanner app on your cell phone. This is, admittedly, an older technology—and not ideal. But it provides you way to listen along with the passages I'm describing. If you don't already have a barcode scanner on your phone, you can download one for free from the App Store for iPhones or Google Play for Android devices.

Preface

The day after the 2016 U.S. Presidential election, Andrew Lloyd Webber appeared on a talk show and joked about writing *Trump: The Musical.* It was all in good fun. The election results shocked pundits in the U.S. and around the world. I was in London during the election, and it was all anyone could talk about. The article with Lloyd Webber's interview even had a picture of Lloyd Webber and Trump together, probably back in the 1980s. Life was good. They were kings of their respective empires, and they actually have quite a bit in common.

- ♦ Both have been wildly successful in business and amassed huge fortunes.

- ♦ Both have been married three times, and disposed of their first two wives with calloused alacrity. They both left their first wives for their second wives, and in a few years, dispatched their second wives via press release. (Six years for Lloyd Webber, 9 years for Trump.)

- ♦ Both are members of the ruling class: Trump as President of the U.S., Lloyd Webber as a Baron and member of the House of Lords.

- ♦ Both vote conservative, but more for fiscal rather than social reasons.

- ♦ Both starred in their own reality TV shows demonstrating their talents in their respective industries.

- ♦ Both are distained by the cultural elite, who generally regard them as "tacky," despite myriad professional accomplishments and vast fortunes.

- ♦ Both are loved by the general public, who defy the cultural elite and like them anyway.

Lloyd Webber even lives in Trump Tower in New York, and in the 1990s was called "the Donald Trump of Musicals." But whereas Trump revels in the populist appeal, Lloyd Webber is embarrassed by it. Popular appeal brings success and a lot of money, but Lloyd Webber wants to be accepted by the cultural elite—something that continues to elude him.

During the run-up to the presidential election, Trump asked Lloyd Webber if he could come to the opening of Lloyd Webber's new show, *The School of Rock*, which was opening in New York. Lloyd Webber asked him not to, saying that his presence would take attention away from the young stars of the show. That is one possible explanation. A darker explanation is that Lloyd Webber didn't wish to be associated with Trump, a pariah among the social elite, or be seen to be friends with him.

The similarities in the lives of Lloyd Webber and Trump give this social history a particularly contemporary ring. The social history of *The Phantom of the Opera* demonstrates, in rather stark terms, how the cultural elite, in the terms of theater critics, political pundits, and the media in general, are often remarkably out of touch with what the average person thinks. This blindness lost an election, and it shows up over and over again in the life of Andrew Lloyd Webber; he has created record-breaking hits where critics screamed "flop."

Both Trump and Lloyd Webber have been able to capture the loyalty of this large constituency in a way that simply baffles the small percentage who consider themselves the gatekeepers of public opinion. More people are now openly asking why these people, the so-called elite, get to decide what is good.

Populism is now sweeping the U.S. and Europe. We are in the decade of the "every man." In the end, history will judge the merit of this movement, as well as the enduring legacy of both Trump and Lloyd Webber—men with astonishing populist appeal.

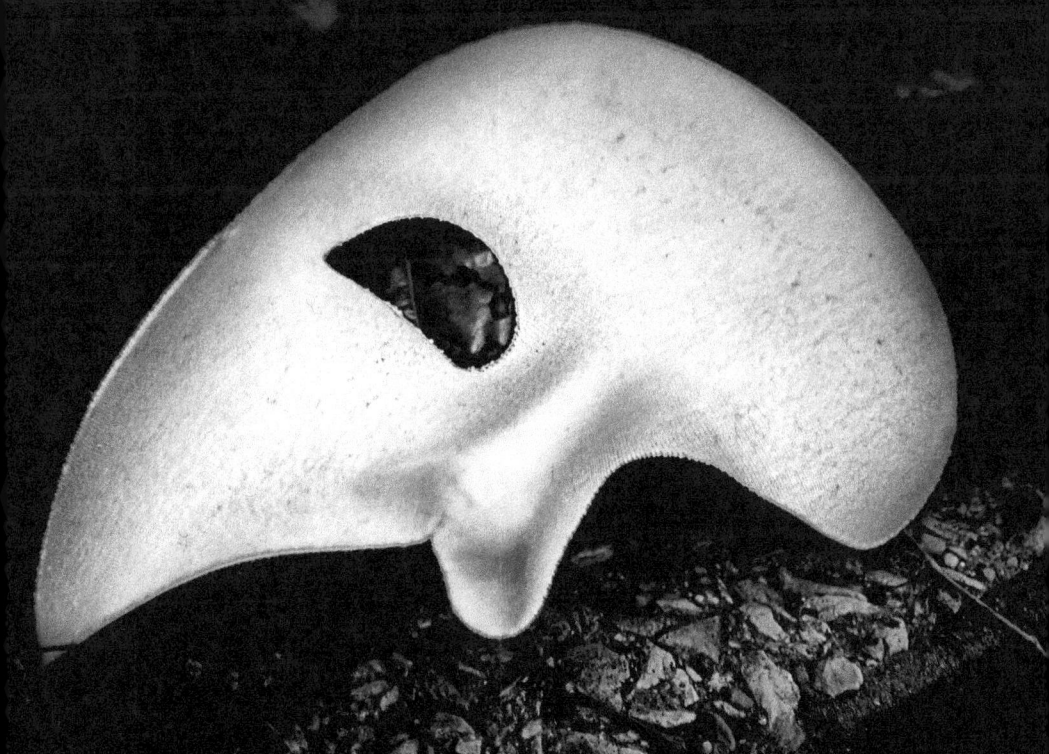

SECTION I
The Show that Started It All

CHAPTER 1

Introduction

On October 9, 1986, the final curtain came down on the opening night performance of Andrew Lloyd Webber's *The Phantom of the Opera.* The audience responded with a stunning 10-minute ovation. It was clearly a good sign. Michael Crawford, who played the Phantom in the original cast, recalled the audience reaction.

> It was astonishing. It was just astonishing. Then the reviews started to come in the next morning. I'd never read or heard anything like it. I spent more time in tears that day, after all the years you've been acting that you were reading such things about a show you were in was the most thrilling moment of my life (*Behind the Mask*, part 8).

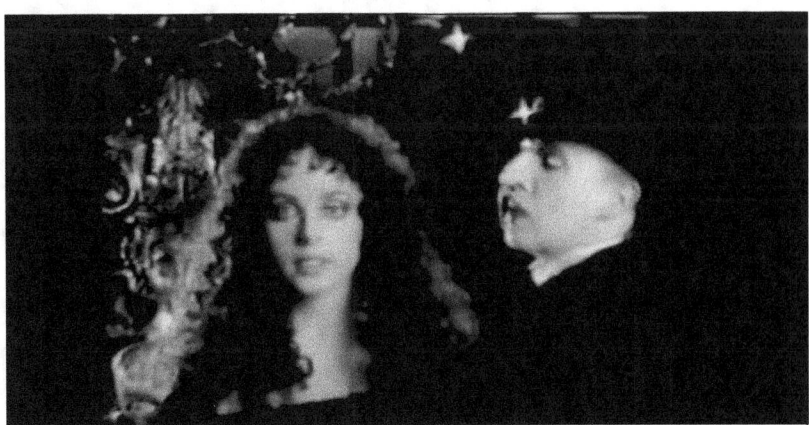

Michael Crawford owned the role of Phantom. In this music video, he sings Music of the Night to Sarah Brightman.
https://www.youtube.com/watch?v=oZDcSrODALQ

In fact, the road leading up to the first night had been quite rocky. Rumors had abounded for weeks, and even months, leading up to the opening night, with headlines forecasting the show's impending demise. Director Hal Prince had been fired and then rehired. There were mechanical difficulties with the sets. And no production would be complete without a star throwing tantrums and terrorizing the production staff. Michael Crawford was prone to bursts of temper, and was often known as "Joan Crawford" to people who worked with him.

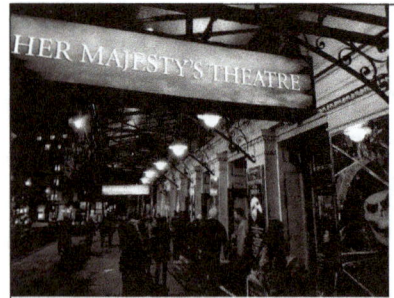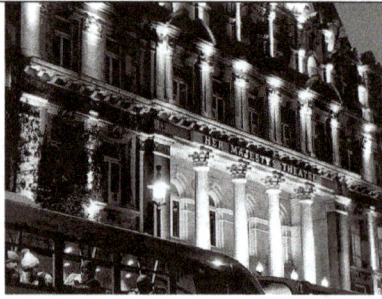

Phantom has been going strong at
Her Majesty's Theatre in London for more than 30 years.

There were many amusing technical difficulties. Prince wanted to include radio-controlled rats. Cameron Macintosh, *Phantom's* producer, said, "Hal was fixated with rats with red eyes. He'd drag these fucking rats backwards and forwards, across the stage. We were hysterical." Set designer Maria Bjornson also wanted a mechanical white horse on stage. According to Macintosh, "the thing went sideways, it went backwards. You could see the ass-end of the horse." Prince also wanted to use live doves, but gave up when they kept flying into the house. Stage manager, Alan Hatton made reference to these. "I think they started shitting on people's heads, so it wasn't very nice." The crew started calling it "Phantom of the Menagerie" *(Behind the Mask,* part 6).

Even the famous boat that Phantom punts away in was having problems. It was radio-controlled and on the same frequency as the local fire brigade. When the fire brigade used their radios, the boat easily went astray. According to Macintosh, the weeks before the show opened "like a root canal, only not as enjoyable. ... and until it came together, it was ghastly." Even up to a week before the opening, it wasn't working; "it was noisy. It was clunky. And I thought 'how are they going to get it together'" (*Behind the Mask*, part 7).

When the show finally opened, Webber and Macintosh couldn't take the pressure, and went down the street in a pub for a "jar" on opening night. They came back to hear the rousing standing ovation. Clearly, Lloyd Webber had another hit, but at the time, no one predicted that this show would break every record in theater history and go on to be the longest running musical of all time. Even 31 years out, it plays to full houses every night in both London and New York. It has won over 70 major theater awards. *The Phantom of the Opera* has been translated into 15 languages and played to audiences in 35 countries, totaling 140 million people and grossing $6 billion. Lloyd Webber described it this way:

> I know for a certainty that I'll never have anything as big as *The Phantom* again cause it would be very hard to see how a musical ever could be. I mean, when you look back over it all, it is extraordinary because, I mean, new productions keep opening all the time. I mean I wish I could explain it because if I could explain it, I'd write another one. But I can't, and I haven't (*Behind the Mask*, part 9).

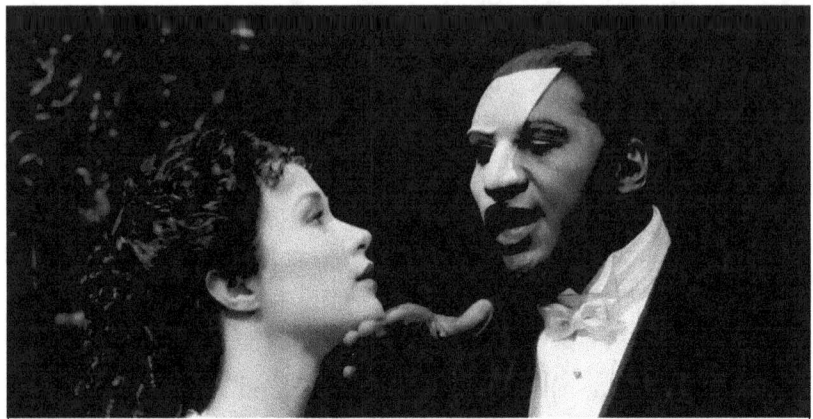

Norm Lewis made recent history by being Broadway's first Black Phantom, seen here with Sierra Boggess. He's amazing in this part and it's surprising that it took so long to happen. https://www.youtube.com/watch?v=lCAdkACAH78

Phantom Goes Global

For a show with English people pretending to be French people in the late 1800s, it translates surprisingly well into other different cultures. Here, you can see the splashy premiere in Russia.

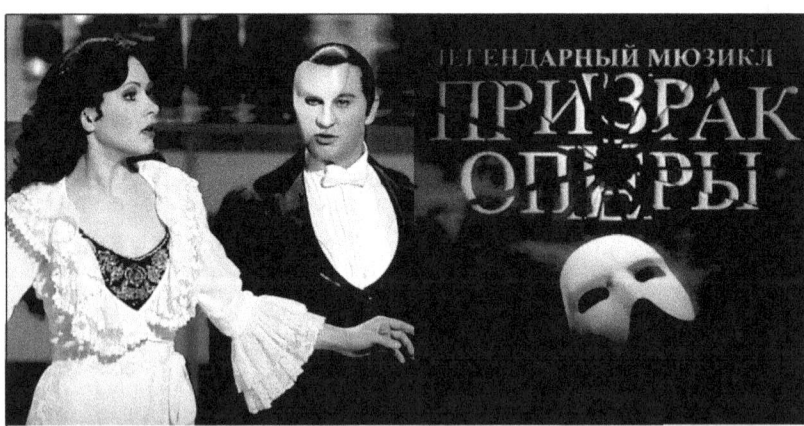

The lavish launch of the Russian *Phantom*.

https://www.youtube.com/watch?v=l6SWE1gqFF4

Even in Chinese, it is quite recognizable. The singers may be Chinese people pretending to be English people pretending to be French people, but they are clearly the Phantom and Christine.

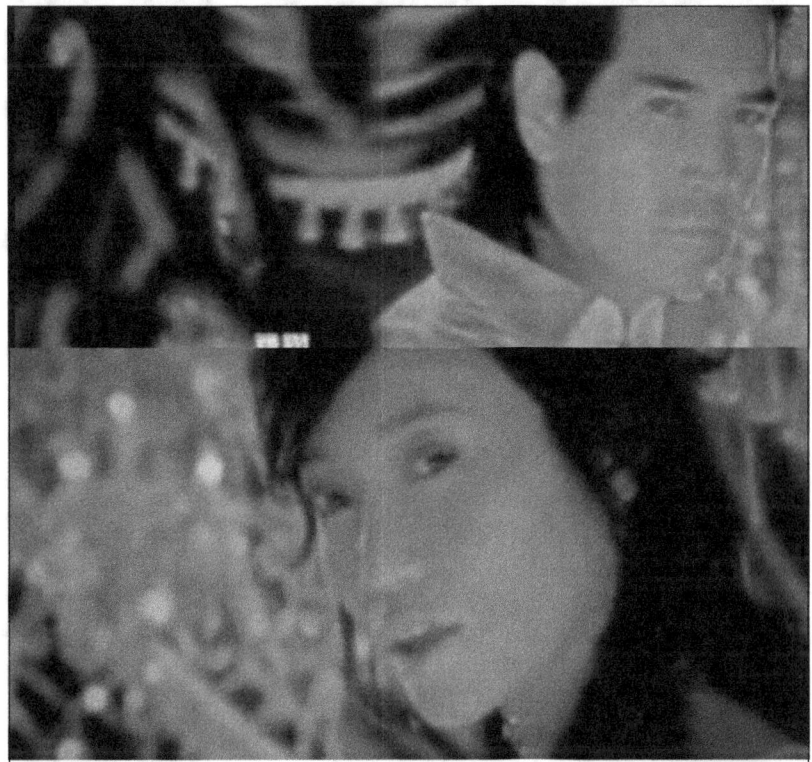

The Chinese version of *Phantom* is surprisingly recognizable as Phantom and Christine. https://www.youtube.com/watch?v=3AQJzxKTocs&list=RDeY_Xs3sXQDg&index=42

The Next Generation of *Phantom* Fans

Younger generations have embraced *Phantom* as well. Rock violinist Lindsey Stirling developed a video medley of *Phantom* songs that have been seen by more than 41 million viewers on YouTube.

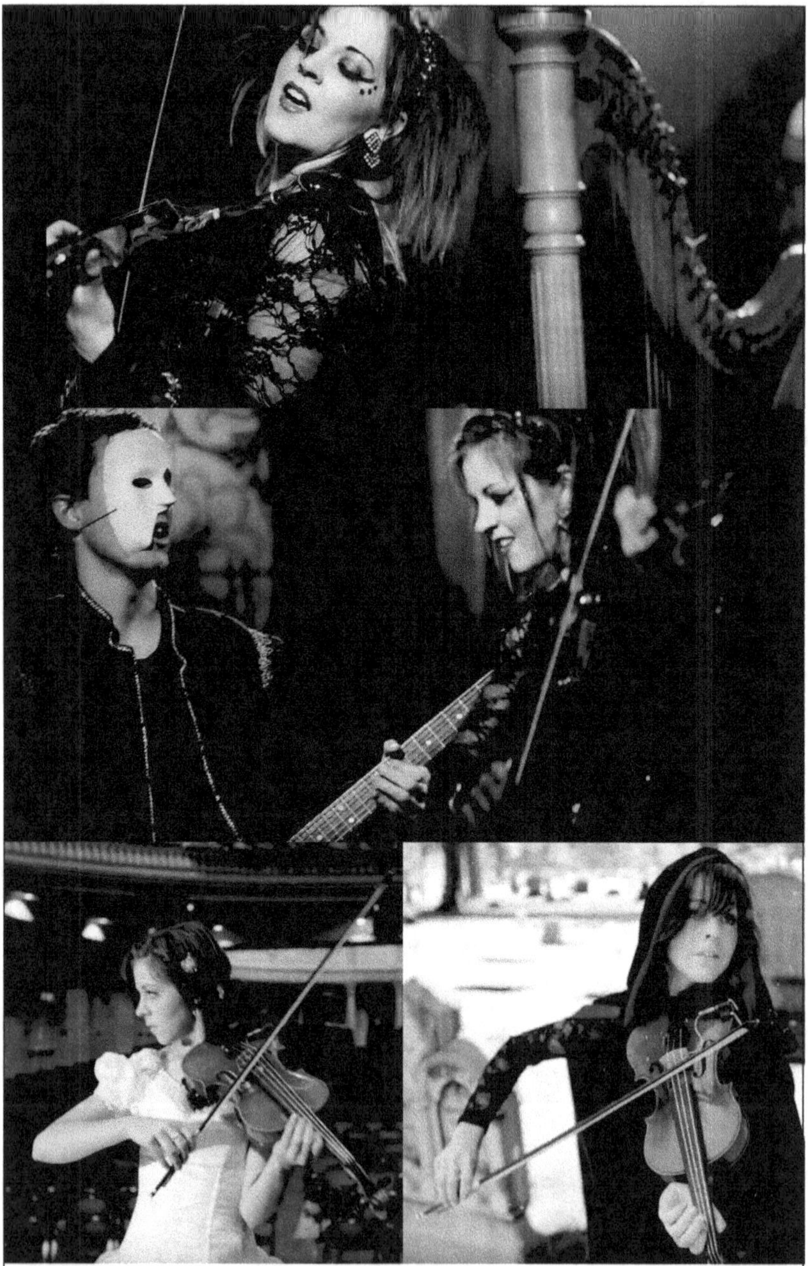

Lindsey Stirling's medley of *Phantom* tunes
has been seen by more than 41 million viewers.
http://www.youtube.com/watch?v=TCL94-MsxY-
c&list=RDeY_Xs3sXQDg&index=26

The Finnish symphonic metal group, Nightwish, have also produced a version that is very popular with its young fans, judging by the enraptured audience members singing along, ensuring another generation of *Phantom* fans.

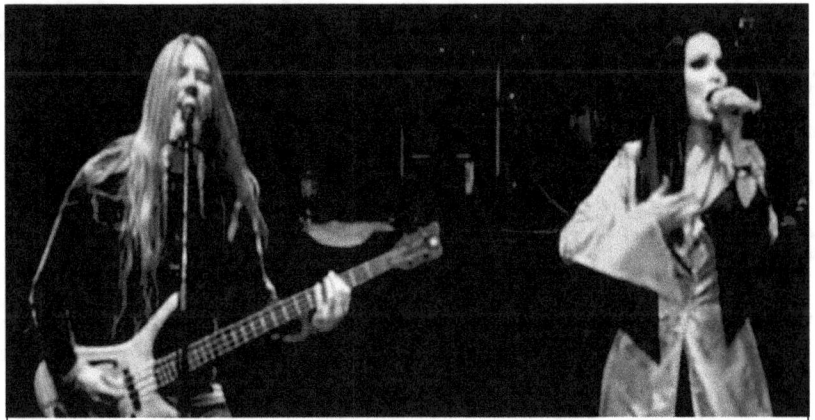

The symphonic metal band, Nightwish, sings their popular version of *Phantom*. https://www.youtube.com/watch?v=zccEDofeEqQKESstudio

Phantom Was Also Good for Its Stars

Phantom also launched spectacular solo careers for its two original stars, Michael Crawford and Sarah Brightman. Michael Crawford, the original Phantom, described the influence of *Phantom* on his life like this:

> *Phantom* has completely changed my life. It was the most wonderful thing that ever happened to me ... I knew the richness of it. It wasn't something that I took for granted and you look back on it and say, "those were the days." I knew they were the days when I was doing it (*Behind the Mask*, part 9).

We have to ask: what is it about this show?

The Social Context of *Phantom*

The BBC documentary, *Behind the Mask*, placed part of *Phantom's* popularity in context of the times in which it was created. Life in 1986 Britain was grim; the economy was in the tank and unemployment was high. Novelist Kathy Lette noted that England "was the most grimy, gloomy place. It was like a whole nation of Eeyores" (*Behind the Mask*, part 1). And then, here comes this lavish, big production musical that was pure escape. By 1986, "there was a new appetite for sex, glamour, and escapism. And *Phantom* caught the mood" (*Behind the Mask*, part 8). Lloyd Webber biographer, Michael Coveney (1999) reiterates *Phantom's* role in bringing wonderful costumes, glamour, designs, and sex back to London theater after they had been missing for a very long time.

Director Hal Prince also talked about the romance of the story, and likened it to the musical, *South Pacific*, a favorite of both Prince and Lloyd Webber. The romance of *Phantom* was what ultimately drew Prince to this show. He noted that many in the audience wished that Christine had ended up with Phantom.

> ... when Andrew first played for me All I Ask of You ... I felt surrounded by something ... larger than life and extremely romantic. And that hasn't happened to me in a really long time (20/20 *Phantom* Strikes Broadway, 2010).

Phantom Beat Them All

The social context of the late 1980s could explain *Phantom's* early success, but what about now? Why is this musical still so popular? We hear a phrase like that—longest running musical of all time—and really don't take in the significance of it. Think about it. *Phantom* has eclipsed *The Sound of Music*, *My Fair Lady*, *The King and I*, *Cabaret*, and so many others. It even eclipsed *Les Miserables*, its closest competitor. Said another way, *Phantom* topped the complete works of Rodgers and Hammerstein,

Lerner and Lowe, Cole Porter, Jerome Kern, George Gershwin, and even the previous works of Andrew Lloyd Webber. *Phantom* was to become Lloyd Webber's biggest single hit, in an impressive career that included a great number of record-breaking hit shows. *Phantom* bested them all. Although Lloyd Webber has written seven musicals since then, he has never replicated the success of *Phantom*.

The success of the stage show is interesting, with plenty of backstory. But that is not what drew me to this story; it was what happened next.

CHAPTER 2

A Social History of
The Phantom of the Opera

I came upon this story largely by accident. I rarely go to the theater. Like 40 million others who purchased the CD with *Phantom's* original cast, I enjoyed the music, and finally had a chance to see a live performance in 1997 at the Kennedy Center in Washington DC. I enjoyed it too, but then walked out of the theater and went on with my life.

Another 8 years passed, and I finally got around to watching the *Phantom* movie. I had heard nothing about it, but rented it along with three others to watch over the long Thanksgiving weekend. It totally surprised me. I loved it. Why hadn't I heard anything about it? I didn't know anything about the actors, director, or production. That's not terribly surprising. I was living in a tiny town in New Hampshire at the time. I don't follow the machinations of the entertainment industry, and, generally don't care. It's a very different world from the one I live in.

Being curious, I went online and was stunned by what I found. The controversy around the movie had been going on for *years*. I remember thinking, "*Who has time for this?*" I was amazed that people were so worked up over a movie. I found myself drawn to this story. Who were these people? The people who hated the movie the most were the stage play's most avid fans (sometimes calling themselves "Phans"). As a psychologist, I'm always fascinated by human behavior, and this little subculture was *interesting*. I knew then that this story would make a good book.

Several years later, when I finally decided that I would write a book about *The Phantom of the Opera*, most of my friends were astonished. I live in the academic world. A book about *Phantom* didn't seem quite "serious" enough. In the end, however, I could not resist this story. Lloyd Webber's *Phantom* is the biggest entertainment venture of all time. I wanted to tell the story of the people who built it.

When it came down to it, many of the tools I use in my academic life came in handy for this project. In telling this story, I read through hundreds of interviews, articles, blog posts, and websites. My best data source was the huge library of interviews and video clips on YouTube. The principals could tell their own unfiltered stories, and I could watch their body language while they talked. In addition, the three biographies on Andrew Lloyd Webber (Coveney, 1999; Snelson, 2004; Walsh, 1989) were very helpful, as were the three books written specifically about *The Phantom of the Opera* (Film Companion, 2004; Heatley, 2011; Perry, 1986), the original novel (Leroux, 1987), and Forsyth's sequel, *The Phantom of Manhattan* (Forsyth, 2007).

One thing I love about academic research is when data surprise me. I may approach a data set with hypotheses, but then I dig deeper and find something completely different. That's what happened here. I approached this project with some preconceptions, only to have them completely overturned by the data. That's when I knew I was on the right track.

My journey to write this book started with the movie controversy, but I discovered there was so much more to the story. What follows in this chapter is a brief summary of what I found. I'll go into more detail in subsequent chapters.

The Film Controversy

Lloyd Webber and Schumacher first talked about a film version of *Phantom* in 1988. Protesters launched websites and letter-writing campaigns, particularly over the casting of the Phantom role. They wanted Michael Crawford to be the Phantom, the role he created on stage.

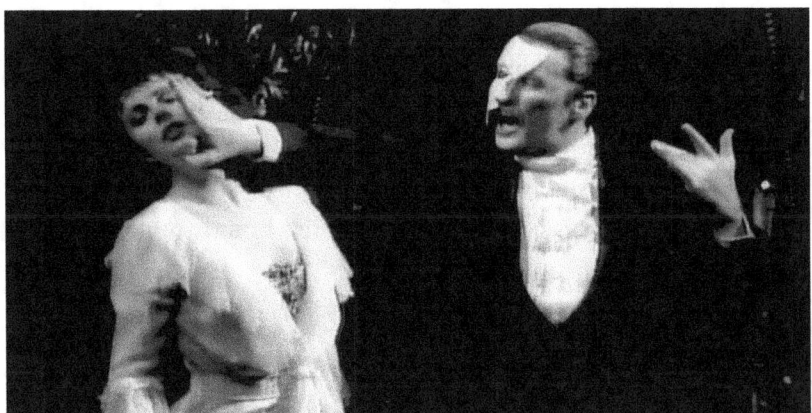

Fans lobbied hard to have Michael Crawford, who origi-
nated the role, play the in movie-version of *Phantom*.
https://www.youtube.com/watch?v=xByDWnibbBE

Several other actors were considered, including Antonio Banderas.
Actually, he wouldn't have been a bad choice, having played Che in
the movie version of *Evita*. He was short-listed.

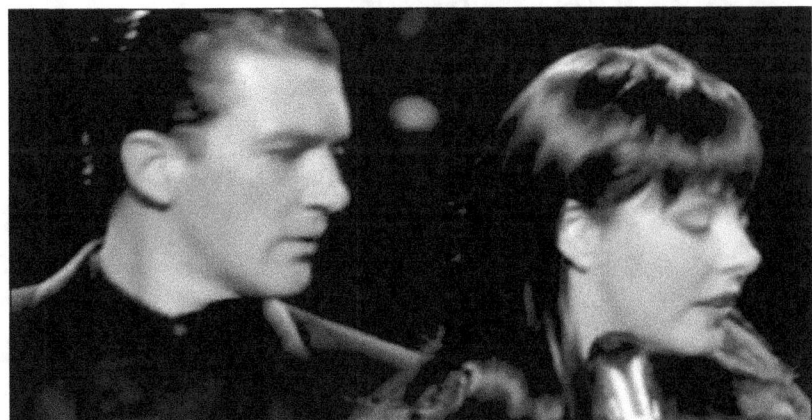

Antonio Banderas was short-listed to play the *Phantom* in the
movie version. Here he performs the title song with Sarah
Brightman. http://www.youtube.com/watch?v=l71jSwn6etw

The movie stalled out following Lloyd Webber and Sarah Brightman's divorce. In 2004, the movie project was up and running again. By then, Lloyd Webber had purchased the rights back from Warner Brothers, and now had complete creative control over his project. Lloyd Webber's production company, The Really Useful Group, provided all the financing. The question on everyone's mind was, "who would play the Phantom?" A few possibilities were considered, and then Lloyd Webber surprised everyone.

Gerard Butler as Phantom

Fans were apoplectic when the then-unknown actor, Gerard Butler, was cast. It made no sense at all. Gerard Butler was an actor, not a singer, and an admittedly strange choice for this key role. Lloyd Webber and director Joel Schumacher both knew it and thought it actually added to the role. Fans interpreted this choice as a deliberate thumb in their eye. In response, Schumacher and Lloyd Webber asserted their right to cast whomever they wanted in their movie.

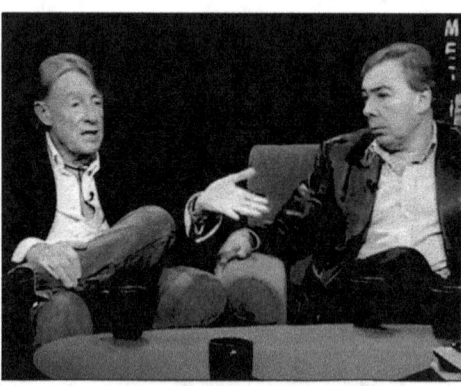

Joel Schumacher and Andrew Lloyd Webber describe decisions they made for the movie version of *Phantom* on Theater Talk. https://www.youtube.com/watch?v=FVrmARNTIVA

Schumacher as Director

The choice of director also made fans go ballistic. Joel Schumacher, director of *Batman and Robin*, was best known for adding nipples to Batman costumes—a comment that comes up with surprising frequency in movie reviews. Schumacher was feisty and defiant when questioned about his choice of Phantom, taunting people who challenged his choice. In a rare nod to propriety, he pointed out that it was not seemly for the then 60ish Michael Crawford to be groping a 16-year-old Christine. Good point, that. Schumacher further enraged fans with his announcement that he was going for a "younger, hotter" *Phantom.* The Phantom may be hideously deformed, and living under the Paris Opera House, but that's okay as long as he's "hot." In the end, a 34-year-old Butler got to grope 16-year-old Christine. Somewhat better, but still felonious.

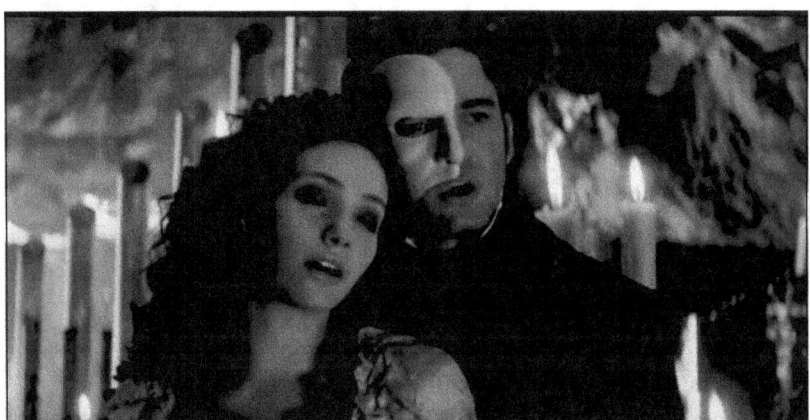

The choice of Gerard Butler enraged the Phans.
https://www.youtube.com/watch?v=77umP7IRxD4The Phantom of the Opera

The critics, by and large, were downright venomous. One critic said he half expected a gondola from the *Pirates of the Caribbean* ride to appear. Another said he expected Christine to leave those two "warbling losers" and run off with the "first cute guy from the audience." Noted film critic, Roger Ebert, liked the movie, but hated the *Phantom* musical itself (Ebert, 2004).

When the negative reviews poured in, the letter-writing fans could hardly contain their glee. Each review was lovingly posted on their sites, and webmasters didn't even try to hide their "we told you so's."

Critics vs. the Public

In contrast, the audience reaction was positive. It's not the first time that critics were out of sync with the general public. Nor would it be the last.

I wanted to write about this story back in 2005, as I was absolutely fascinated by all these quirky characters (the fans, the cast, the director, Lloyd Webber). Unfortunately, I didn't have the resources to do it properly, so I put the project aside and went on to other things.

I'm so glad I waited because eventually, Lloyd Webber produced a sequel.

The Sequel: Should Love Die?

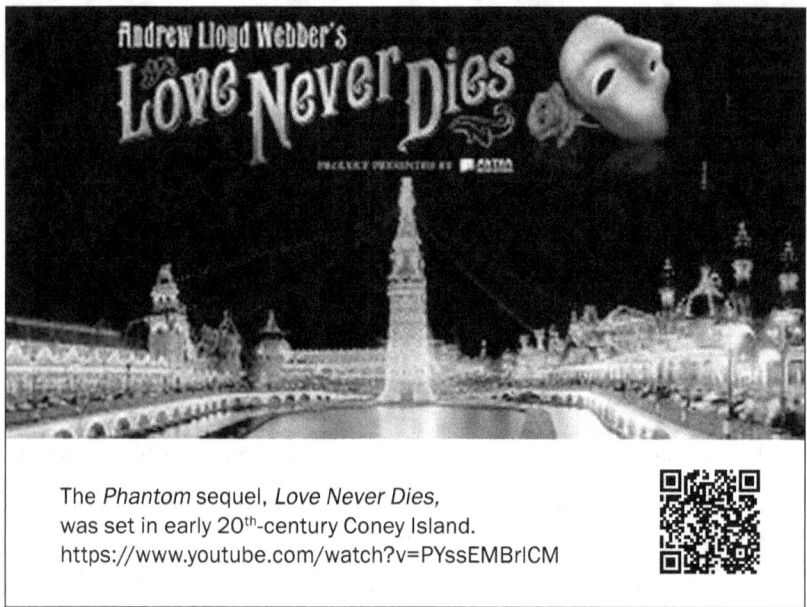

The *Phantom* sequel, *Love Never Dies,*
was set in early 20th-century Coney Island.
https://www.youtube.com/watch?v=PYssEMBrICM

Andrew Lloyd Webber was determined to produce a sequel to *Phantom*—a story in which the Phantom gets the girl. The sequel was eventually called *Love Never Dies*, and was another project that was years in the making. Lloyd Webber's clout was such that he persuaded a respected novelist, Frederick "Freddie" Forsyth, to write a sequel. The result was a novella called *The Phantom of Manhattan* (Forsyth, 2007), widely acknowledged to be a serious piece of crap. It even ended up on a "Books I Regret Reading" list.

Lloyd Webber and his crew changed the story so much from the original novella that almost none of the story elements remained. Along the way, the characters became unrecognizable. Hence, the seeds of its destruction were sown.

The controversy over the film was minor compared to the controversy that surrounded *Love Never Dies*. Twelve people with a Facebook page and website effectively challenged Andrew Lloyd Webber, a man with almost unlimited financial resources and clout in the theater world—and prevailed. They named their website and Facebook page Love Should Die, and launched a campaign.

Social media marked a fundamental shift in the relationship between critics and fans. Suddenly, the "rabble" had a say. Creators and critics suddenly found themselves on the same side—and they were not amused. *They* were the experts. Fans were just supposed to buy tickets and show up.

The people behind Love Should Die were *Phantom* fans who thought that the sequel, with its silly storyline, was sacrilege, and they wanted to make sure it didn't happen. It did, of course, and Lloyd Webber threw all his considerable resources behind it. However, that was not enough. *Love Never Dies* closed after an 18-month run, but not before it lost £5 million pounds.

If *Love Never Dies* had been a good show, Love Should Die would not have succeeded. Unfortunately, in its first two iterations, it was not a good show. It was long and gloomy, poorly lit. The characters of the Phantom, Christine, and particularly, Raoul, went through major personality changes that were never explained. Even the climactic death scene was too long, according to critics, with one saying, "die already." Clearly not the reaction Lloyd Webber was going for.

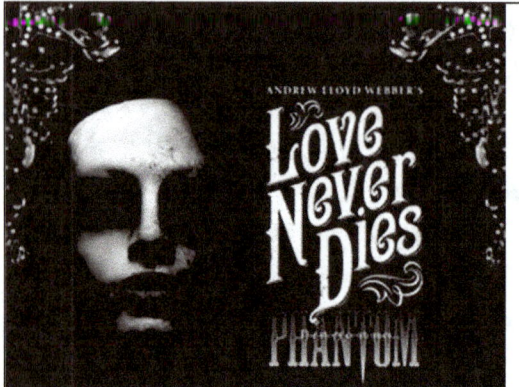

The original graphics for *Love Never Dies* were ripe for parody, and the West End Whingers (2010) did just that. Unfortunately, the name "Paint Never Dries" was to stick. It contributed to the demise of the first two versions of the show on the West End.

Lloyd Webber was immensely sad over the closing of his show, considering it some of his best work to date. The closure made him finally open to feedback. His team moved the entire production to Australia, recast it, edited it quite a bit, and designed all new sets. The result was quite good. It still has major plot holes (e.g., how does a single kiss result in a love child?), but the music is excellent.

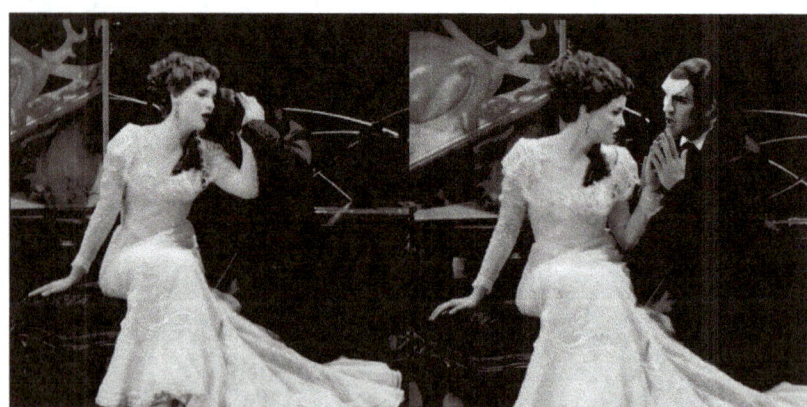

The Australian version of *Love Never Dies* was a significant improvement across the board. *Beneath the Moonless sky* is the song where the Phantom reveals himself to Christine for the first time in 10 years. It is one of the pivotal scenes of the show. https://www.youtube.com/watch?v=r7GaFyD1r1w

The process of how that third version came to be tells us much about Lloyd Webber's creative process. There are many video clips from all three productions. By studying them, we can see the changes. It gives us an awesome opportunity to see, in detail, how a musical is made.

The Man Behind the Music

We cannot talk about the social history of *Phantom* without considering its creator, Andrew Lloyd Webber. Lloyd Webber has broken every record in the theater, including several of his own. He has made more money than anyone in the theater—ever. Even his critics, and they are legion, admit that his productivity and number of honors are unprecedented. He has changed the face of musical theater. He is an impresario who cares deeply about the craft, and is truly without peer. And yet, he can make a statement like this, after his musical, *Stephen Ward*, closed following a 4-month run.

> I haven't had a hit in 20 years. I've written six musicals in that time. I'm resigned now to the fact that anything I do probably, nobody is going to like (BBC News, 2014).

Granted, Lloyd Webber was having a rough night. However, reading this statement reminded me of what a biographer once said about Richard Nixon. Even though Nixon had achieved the highest levels of political success, including winning the presidency—twice—he was convinced that he had experienced nothing but failure, and that everyone was out to get him.

I've often observed that fame is a double-edged sword. It can bring money, adulation, and clout. People who are famous often long to have control over what they create. Lloyd Webber has achieved that, but it doesn't seem to bring happiness or contentment. The bar for what constitutes success keeps moving. So, you can make a statement about how "no one" likes what you write, even with a personal fortune approaching a £ billion.

Sarah Brightman

Also central to the social history of *Phantom* is Lloyd Webber's brief marriage to Sarah Brightman. Brightman and Lloyd Webber's relationship was born in scandal. Lloyd Webber left his wife and young children for her after "falling in love with her voice." Oddly, most male biographers place the blame squarely on Brightman's shoulders. According to biographer, Michael Coveney, Lloyd Webber just couldn't help himself as Brightman was "sex on two legs." *Sex on two legs?* (BBC also called Michael Crawford "sex on legs." Apparently, there was a lot of that going around.) The "homewrecker" moniker followed Brightman for years, and it colored the way people judged her talent and her performance in *Phantom*. Even years later, in an interview for the BBC documentary, *Behind the Mask*, critic Howard Kissel said this.

> She wouldn't have got the part if she were not married to the composer. She's not all that attractive. Her voice, I don't think, is a very attractive voice. It's kind of thin, with very little support. She was okay. She was fine. And no one was unaware of why she was there (*Behind the Mask*, part 9).

After only 6 years of marriage, Lloyd Webber discarded Brightman—by press release—and announced his new "friend," who became Mrs. Lloyd Webber 3. Given critics' general animosity towards Brightman, being cast off could have finished her career. It didn't. Her rebirth as a highly successful solo artist is an inspiring story in and of itself.

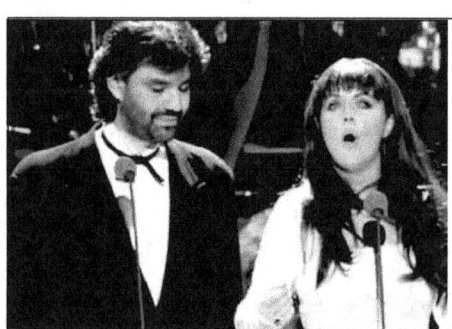

Brightman's mega-hit, Time to Say Goodbye, with Andrea Bocelli, cemented her position as an international superstar. https://www.youtube.com/watch?v=LWQbu-J24Wzg

What Happened to Michael Crawford?

Michael Crawford's story following *Phantom* is also inspiring. I was curious why he appeared on stage for the 25th anniversary, but didn't sing. Brightman did. Crawford's lack of singing was notable, and it turns out that he had been very ill. As he reported in 2011, Michael Crawford had been battling an illness called myalgic encephalophy (ME), and finally was able to return to the stage in the Lloyd Webber production of *The Wizard of Oz*. He said, "I was so ill I thought my career was over" (Wigg, 2011).

The cause of this illness was a strange one. It was all attributed to the fat suit he had designed to play the overweight Count Fosco in *Woman in White*. The fat suit caused him to sweat profusely. The water he was drinking was not enough to replace the lost minerals, so he became vulnerable to a virus. He became more and more fatigued until he had to pull out of the show. He eventually moved to a small house in Auckland, New Zealand, where he re-discovered life at a slower pace.

It took him four years to feel well enough to work again, but by then, he really didn't want to. After spending time with his grandchildren, however, he decided to accept Lloyd Webber's offer to perform in *The Wizard of Oz*. His grandchildren had never seen him on stage before. He decided to do it for them (Wigg, 2011). He needed to save his voice, so he couldn't sing at the 25th anniversary, having just returned from being out sick. Crawford made a successful comeback, despite feeling like he would never sing again.

Summary

The social history of *The Phantom of the Opera* is a story of people—the people who made it and the people whose lives were touched by it. It is a story of a scandalous divorce, famous marriage, and a Svengali-like relationship between a composer and his gifted young protégé. It is a tale of fans so caught up in the original stage production that they would have no other version be made. It is a story of the creative process, how it is often iterative, and how constraints often encourage, rather than discourage, creativity. It is a story of a composer who has achieved every type of honor, is famous and very rich, but is convinced that no one likes what he writes. It is also a story of the love-hate relationship that exists between creator, fans, and critics, and Lloyd Webber's public distain for the people who have made him rich. In short, the social history of *The Phantom of the Opera* is a rich and complex tale that includes a wide cast of characters. It tells us much about the art world, the creative process, and the people who continue to fill the seats. I hope you enjoy your journey into the "strange, new world" that is *The Phantom of the Opera* subculture.

CHAPTER 3

Revered and Reviled
A Primer on Andrew Lloyd Webber

The story of Andrew Lloyd Webber is at the heart of the social history of *The Phantom of the Opera*. In many ways, Lloyd Webber looms larger than life. No single person who has contributed more significantly to the GNP of the UK in recent years than him. He has elevated that status of the British musical (typically considered an American art form) around the world. Through his various productions, he employs thousands of people. His shows ran so long that they broke all existing records, first with *Cats*, and then with *Phantom*. Lloyd Webber biographer, Michael Coveney (1999), noted that only two people could reach the ticket-buying public in the late 1990s: Lloyd Webber and Cameron Macintosh (who produced *Phantom*, and also produced *Les Miserables*). Lloyd Webber wanted to make money, but also change the way things were done in musical theater. He's been very successful in meeting both goals.

Lloyd Webber is the son of a music professor and pianist, who grew up with modest means in London. He studied for one year at Oxford before dropping out to work on *Jesus Christ Superstar* with Tim Rice. The rest, as they say, is history.

A Partial List of Honors

Lloyd Webber has won many honors. Most normal people, even many accomplished people, would be pleased with one or two of these honors and awards. Lloyd Webber has them all. His work has swept across the worlds of classical and pop music, musical theater, movies, and recordings. He's had multiple gold and platinum records, and Top-10 singles on both pop and classical charts. His original cast album of *Phantom* was the bestselling cast album of all time.

Almost on the EGOT List

There's an interesting category of folks at the highest echelons of honors. It's a list called EGOT, which stands for Emmy, Grammy, Oscar, and Tony. This list includes only 12 people in the world, both living and dead. Lloyd Webber misses this list by one. He hasn't won an Emmy—yet. There are two composers on that list of 12: Lloyd Webber's hero, Richard Rodgers, and Marvin Hamlisch (Hamlisch has also received a Pulitzer Prize). Lloyd Webber has also received Kennedy Center Honors, a Golden Globe, 5 Laurence Olivier awards, and 14 Ivor Novellos.

Lloyd Webber's accomplishments do not end there.

- ◆ In 1991, Andrew Lloyd Webber was the first and only composer to have six productions running at one time in the West End.

- ◆ He had three musicals running in London and New York simultaneously: in 1988, 1990, and 1994.

- ◆ He owns seven London theatres, including the Theatre Royal, Drury Lane, and the London Palladium.

To acknowledge his contributions to both the arts and the UK, he was knighted by the Queen in 1992, becoming Sir Andrew Lloyd Webber. In 1997, he was made a Lord of the Realm, and is now "Lord Lloyd-Webber of Sydmonton."

Accomplished, But Not Necessarily Happy

Accomplishment alone does not automatically lead to happiness. Despite all the fame, honor, and wealth, friends and family do not describe him as particularly happy. Some of that may have to do with his relentless drive. Lloyd Webber never seems to feel that he's done enough. He's only as good as his current show. According to his brother, Julian, Lloyd Webber wanted to be the best there ever was in musical theater. On the opening night of *Jesus Christ Superstar*, Julian recalled a conversation Lloyd Webber had with his aunt, who asked Lloyd Webber if he was pleased. Lloyd Webber replied that he would not feel like a success until music stores were selling "the Greatest Hits of Andrew Lloyd Webber," and that he was like his hero, Richard Rodgers (Coveney, 1999, p. 78). Biographer, Michael Coveney, described Lloyd Webber as "complex" and a "victim of his own personality," and that he's driven to prove himself. Lloyd Webber is happiest when he's alone in a room with a piano (Coveney, 1999).

Artistic Control

One thing that most artists aspire to is having control over their work. Lloyd Webber made a concerted effort to buy back the rights of his earlier shows and to have control over them. Many artists would sympathize with these goals. Lloyd Webber's production company, The Really Useful Group, has been in and out his hands (it went public and he subsequently bought it back). Artistic control is a dominant theme in his story.

Artistic control has allowed him to be creative in his choice of topics. His instincts have proven correct in many cases where he has cast someone unlikely in a role (e.g., such as Michael Crawford as the Phantom), or he picks subject matter that no one thinks will make a good musical (e.g., the poems of T.S. Elliot about cats). A downside to having complete artistic control, however, means there are no

27

checks and balances in the system, which has led to some creative missteps. Lloyd Webber was inspired by the children's series, *Thomas the Tank Engine*, to create the musical *Starlight Express*. Think two hours of roller-skating singers moving all about the theater. Lloyd Webber also seemed oblivious to the sexual and racial politics of his story (e.g., the cabooses were also female and the engines hooked up with them). Frank Rich, a consistent critic of Lloyd Webber's, noted that *Starlight* was supposed to be a musical for children who loved trains. Rich described emerging from a production of *Starlight* "two numbing hours later." The story was supposed to be one that children might also enjoy, yet Rich found the story rife with noise, misogyny, and "Orwellian special effects. ... *Starlight Express* is a perfect gift for the kid who have everything, except parents" (cited in Walsh, 1989, p. 165).

Flies in the Face of Convention

Lloyd Webber's desire to do whatever he wants was first apparent in *Jesus Christ Superstar*. The music is undeniably catchy, but the theology is unbelievably bad. Judas is the hero? Jesus didn't know the consequences of his "fame?" What? More importantly, they ignored the pivotal belief in Christianity: the resurrection. Without that, there is no Christianity. They laughed when leading Christians, such as Billy Graham, denounced their work. That made Lloyd Webber and Tim Rice seem edgy and anti-establishment. Lloyd Webber and Rice stuck their thumb in the eye of Christians, then seemed surprised by pushback. (I dare say that if the topic had been another religion, rather than Christianity, the reaction would not have been as sanguine.) It's not the genre that offends; it's what they did with the story.

Critics have noted Lloyd Webber's tendency to defy social norms from the beginning. John Simon of *New York Magazine*, called *Evita* an "artfully produced monument to human indecency." He referred to Lloyd Webber and Tim Rice as "two amoral, barely talented whippersnappers, and their knowing or duped accomplices" (Simon 2005, p. 148). When Rice first approached Lloyd Webber with the story idea for *Evita*, Lloyd

Webber said that he had no desire to write another musical about someone who was obscure, had a meteoric rise, only to die at the age of 33! *Evita* and *Jesus?* Many would be offended with the conflating of those two life stories.

Regardless of pushback, Lloyd Webber's approach seemed to work well for many years. Eventually, however, the public appeared to tire of his creative choices. That was apparent in the controversy around the film version of *Phantom* (although it eventually did well). Where it really backfired was in the sequel to *Phantom, Love Never Dies*, which I'll describe in detail in Section III. As early as 2008, *Phantom* fans gave Lloyd Webber very clear feedback about the story, which Lloyd Webber ignored. Yes, the ultimate decisions were his. But if you defy feedback, and ignore your audience, don't be surprised when there's pushback, and the show eventually flops.

Lloyd Webber said he hasn't had a hit in more than 20 years, though he continues to produce work. From a creative standpoint, that's admirable. He's following his artistic impulses. On the other hand, he's not found the audience he once had.

Lloyd Webber's Personal Life

Lloyd Webber has also been criticized for his personal life, particularly his two well-publicized divorces. He cast off his first two wives via press release, while announcing his next wife waiting in the wings. His callous behaviors did not go unnoticed. He has re-established relationships with both ex-wives, but I suspect that has more to do with them than with him. His personal relationships, particularly his second marriage, are particularly relevant to the story of *Phantom*.

In addition, Lloyd Webber is not above throwing his weight around. When he falls out with someone, he leaks information to the press, and has his staff cyberbully people who disagree with him on his social media pages. That someone with his level of fame and wealth is not a nice person is not really news. That's true for many famous people. With Lloyd Webber, it's a remarkably persistent theme.

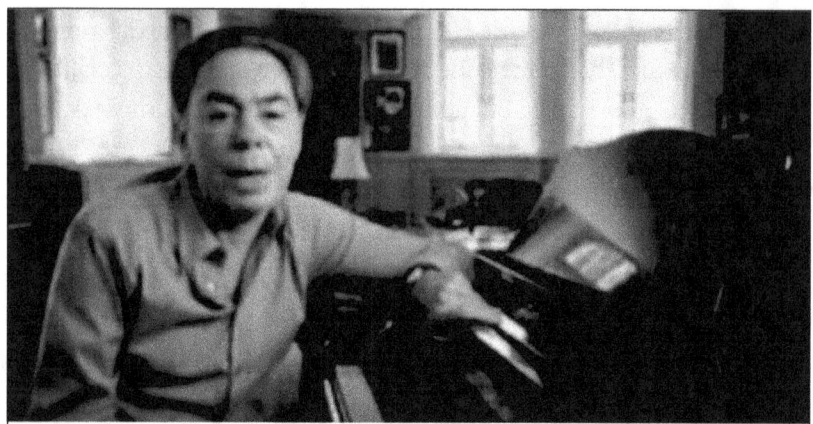

Lloyd Webber is most comfortable sitting behind his piano. Here he is being interviewed for the BBC documentary, *Behind the Mask*. https://www.youtube.com/watch?v=EmPwlfJxSjw

His lifestyle also provokes a certain amount of venom. He indulges his taste for wine, and when he sold half his wine collection, it fetched over £3 million. He's also quite a foodie, and is willing to try all manner of strange things to eat. He breeds horses and collects houses. Having a lifestyle of the rich and famous makes people jealous. More concerning is that his level of privilege puts him out of touch with the ordinary people who buy tickets to his shows.

"Plagiarist" and "Misogynist"

On Lloyd Webber's Wikipedia page, I was surprised to see the words "plagiarist" and "misogynist" in the text. Usually, Wikipedia articles tend to be positive, or at least neutral. Seeing these two inflammatory words gives some sense of how controversial Lloyd Webber is. We'll examine both of those claims in some detail in subsequent chapters.

Life Since *Phantom*

Phantom will likely be Lloyd Webber's biggest single hit. Lloyd Webber has continued to produce work, but at nowhere near the same level of success. *Aspects of Love*, his show following on the heels of *Phantom*, was a reasonable success in London, but bombed in New York. *Sunset Boulevard*, his biggest hit since *Phantom*, was a critical success, but didn't have the staying power of *Phantom* (or *Cats*). It opened to a $30 million-dollar advance, and had good word of mouth, but the Really Useful Group found out that there was limit to *Sunset's* appeal. Biographer Michael Coveney describes how the Really Useful Group's belief that *Sunset* would be another *Phantom* was "seriously misguided," even though many considered it one of Lloyd Webber's best shows. After 9 months, it "hit a wall and dropped away," proving that good word of mouth was not enough to sustain it (Coveney, 1999, p. 259).

Lloyd Webber's underperforming musicals since *Phantom* include *The Beautiful Game*, *The Woman in White*, and *Love Never Dies*. *Stephen Ward* was another creative misstep. The subject of *Stephen Ward* was a political and sex scandal in Britain in the 1960s. Based on a true story, the protagonist of the musical, Stephen Ward, was framed in a political sex scandal, and eventually killed himself. That plot hardly says, "fun evening out at the theater," though the topic might have worked better as a play. *Stephen Ward* also featured an orgy (set to music). Lloyd Webber predicted that it might not find an audience. It didn't. *Stephen Ward* closed after only 4 months (BBC News, 2014).

Despite these rebuffs, Lloyd Webber keeps working away, even when he knows his work may fail. He's starred in his own reality TV show, and cast musicals that way. I admire his persistence and dedication to his craft. He keeps at it even when he doesn't need the money. He works because he loves it, as he shares in this interview with the *CBS Morning News* when launching the 25th anniversary of *Phantom* on Broadway. He also manages to take a dig at his most dedicated fans, including the correspondent who was interviewing him, calling them "crazy" (CBS Morning News, 2012).

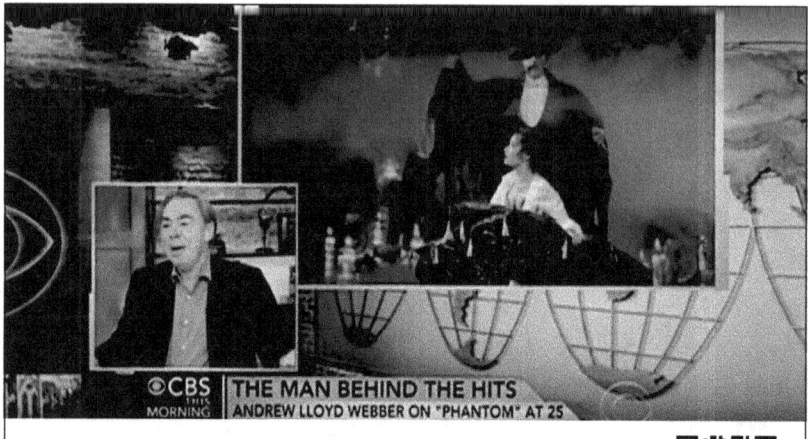

THE MAN BEHIND THE HITS
ANDREW LLOYD WEBBER ON "PHANTOM" AT 25

Lloyd Webber's interview celebrating the 25th anniversary of *Phantom*. https://www.youtube.com/watch?v=LgKljgaCL4Y

CBS: What makes it possible for you to do this that resonates so with the public?

ALW: I'm just very lucky really. I love musical theater. And I'm very lucky that I've been able to make a career out of it.

CBS: Speaking of repeat fans

ALW: There are a lot of people who, they're crazy, I think. They've changed their names to Christine Daae. It's all a bit strange to me. *The Phantom* has been extraordinary, and I've been very, very lucky.

CBS: Does that make it your favorite?

ALW: You know, I'm always asked which one is my favorite, and you know they're a bit like your kids. It's hard to pick one.

CBS: Have you ever failed? Failed wildly?

ALW: Oh yes, *Love Never Dies* in London didn't work. But I have to say it worked very, very well in Australia.

There's a fine line between success and failure in musical theater and it's terribly small sometimes. ...

CBS: Well yes, you do. And the movie helped make it even more famous. Well what's the difference? What's that fine edge?

ALW: Put it another way. If Maria Bjornson hadn't done the wonderful designs for *The Phantom of the Opera*, we might not be here talking about it. I always remember something Hal Prince said to me when I was just starting out. It was before he agreed to direct *Evita*. "You can't listen to music if you can't look at it." And what he meant is that if the design of a show isn't right, it ruins something.

CBS: Your friends say you're a workaholic. Are you a workaholic?

ALW: I love what I do. That's the thing. One of things I do enjoy doing, which we've been doing back in Britain, is casting on television. It's great fun.

CBS: This is reality television.

ALW: Yes, it is. But we've found some fantastic people.

CBS: And you like the casting of it.

ALW: Well, I love working with young people.

CBS: You write such beautiful love songs. Are you a hopeless romantic?

ALW: I'm a romantic, yes. I care very much. Well, let me put it another way. I find it very difficult to write about a character I don't care about. The most difficult role I had to write about was *Evita*.

CBS: You don't like her?

ALW: No, I don't like her. But I found a way of doing it.

Andrew Lloyd Webber has accomplished amazing things, but balance his accomplishments with things he's done to other people. Lloyd Webber is someone with complete power to whatever the hell he wants, which has led to some dismal behavior.

In subsequent chapters, we'll learn more about the man who changed musical theater forever, but did many unkind things to collaborators, stars, and those closest to him. I'll also describe his career-long love/hate relationship with the press, and his uncomfortable relationship with his fans. In summary, Lloyd Webber is not always nice, but he's created musicals that continue to speak to people around the world.

CHAPTER 4

Working with Lloyd Webber
The Good, the Bad, and the Ugly

L loyd Webber has had many successful collaborations during his long career, but he regrets not having "a long-term writing partner like [Richard] Rodgers had with either Hart or Hammerstein." He thought the Tim Rice might be that partner, but Lloyd Webber's father was the first one who thought that that relationship might not go the distance (Spenser, 2013). The problem wasn't entirely Tim Rice. Lloyd Webber's behavior also significantly contributed to the demise of that partnership, as I describe in Chapter 9.

According to biographers, collaborating with Lloyd Webber enhanced—or even made—the careers some people, such as choreographers Arlene Phillips, Anthony van Laast, and Gillian Lynne. For others, however, collaborating with Lloyd Webber was fraught with challenges. In addition, when Lloyd Webber feels that others used him to "feather their own nests," he retaliates in a way that is "swift and merciless" (Coveney, 1999, p. 320).

"Difficult"

Lloyd Webber's personality has been examined and discussed in great detail, and he's known for being difficult. That's not particularly surprising. Many people in the upper echelons of business, science, academe, entertainment, and other fields are often difficult. Biographer

Coveney attributes Lloyd Webber's personality to his drive and artistic temperament, often making things excessively complicated (Coveney, 1999). He can be "your best friend and your worst enemy, the nicest guy in the world and the nastiest" (Coveney, 1999, p. 319). David Mason, Lloyd Webber's friend, once compared him to Rasputin. Lloyd Webber yelled and screamed. Mason said, "Well, Andrew, you are," and he said, "I know, but I don't want to read it in the bloody papers!" (cited in Coveney, 1999, p. 319). Not surprisingly, his personality traits have impacted his long-term relationships.

Aloof, Rude, and Has a Temper

The parts of his personality that have come under particular scrutiny are his temper, aloofness, and rudeness. Lloyd Webber apologists have attributed his aloofness to his British reserve, which he used to keep his distance from others, especially as he got more famous. But this behavior doesn't just apply to his fans. His relationships with people close to him, such as Sarah Brightman or his father, have been described as cool or dispassionate. His temper, on the other hand, has been described as his only visible emotion. It was likely to erupt whenever he felt "pressed or criticized" (Walsh, 1989, pp. 173-174). Lloyd Webber was often unfavorably compared to his early collaborator, Tim Rice. Rice was good looking and easy going, and more adroit in handling the press.

Walsh describes how Lloyd Webber was so powerful that few felt they could challenge him. He frightened those outside his small inner circle, and once his temper explodes, people scurry for cover (Walsh, 1989, p. 210). Lloyd Webber, when angry, was compared to a cat. His whole body would go rigid, and he'd spit out his words, terrifying everyone. In contrast, Rice was described as easygoing and friendly, someone you would gladly share a pint with, and possibly discuss some cricket.

Cameron Macintosh and Maria Bjornson

Lloyd Webber has had a highly successful and long-term collaboration with producer Cameron Macintosh, but as with others in Lloyd Webber's life, his relationship with Macintosh is also complicated. Macintosh described his relationship with Lloyd Webber in positive terms, saying he's "the most talented man he will ever work with," and describing their partnership as a "marvelous marriage" (Coveney, 1999, p. 135).

Set designer, the late Maria Bjornson, however, described Macintosh's and Lloyd Webber's relationship as more complex. They were more like frenemies, with a "competitive animosity" between them.

Lloyd Webber has also spoken positively of the late Maria Bjornson on many occasions, and she spoke highly of him, describing him as "very generous," and saying, "Andrew said after the showing [of her sets for *Phantom*] that if his music was as good as my set, we were going to be all right" (Coveney, 1999, p. 183).

His Personal Assistant, Biddy Hayward

No one bears the brunt of Lloyd Webber's volatile personality more than his personal assistants. For his assistants, Lloyd Webber is Miranda Priestly, and they were expected to make their lives all about him. Biddy Hayward was Lloyd Webber's personal assistant for 10 years. According to Walsh, Hayward's job got worse in the wake of the success of *Cats*. Lloyd Webber was now a public figure and Hayward was expected to be on call 24/7. Lloyd Webber was no more adroit at handling the press than during his *Jesus Christ Superstar* days, and his rising fame made him a bully, especially to people who couldn't fight back. "In sum, he was a personal assistant's nightmare" (Walsh, 1989, p. 154).

Hayward later became an executive in his production company. She eventually left with six of Lloyd Webber's employees in tow.

Depending on your point of view, she pulled off a spectacular coup or perpetrated supreme act of treachery, when she took several other employees from the Really Useful Group with her to start her own firm.

Sacking Stars

Lloyd Webber didn't limit his bullying to his underlings. He has bullied and behaved badly towards his stars as well. This is by no means a complete list, but here are a few examples.

Steve Harley

Cockney Rebels star, Steve Harley, was originally slated to play the Phantom. He auditioned 9 months before the opening. His agent called him and told him he had the part. Harley made the promotional video with Sarah Brightman of the title song. The contracts were signed, the posters printed, but Lloyd Webber wouldn't announce it to the press. Harley kept asking about it, but Lloyd Webber told Harley to trust him to know when the time was right (*Behind the Mask*, part 3).

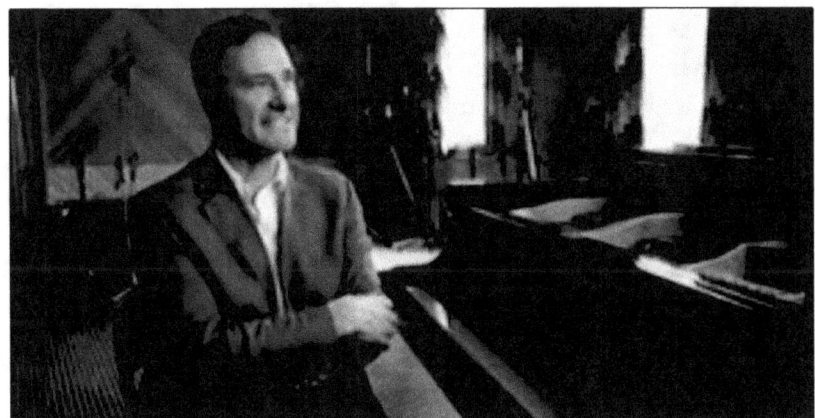

Steve Harley was originally slated to play the Phantom, but was dropped without explanation after Lloyd Webber happened to hear Michael Crawford at a singing lesson. https://www.youtube.com/watch?v=jgxXSK8nLSo

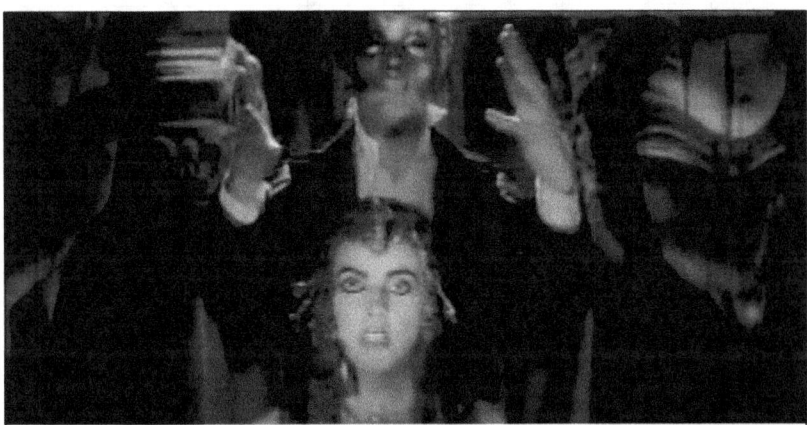

Steve Harley was featured in a promotional video singing a very campy version of *The Phantom of the Opera*. https://www.youtube.com/watch?v=AHtLc7JctLc

By chance, Lloyd Webber had accompanied Brightman to her singing lesson and heard Michael Crawford, also there for his lesson. He knew he had his Phantom. Steve Harley was dropped without ever knowing why or what he did wrong. (The answer was nothing, really. Lloyd Webber simply found someone whom he liked better.) Harley was sent away with £20,000, and *Phantom* went on to become the most famous musical of all time. That had to be a bitter pill for Harley to swallow. Lloyd Webber attempted to placate Harley in the press, claiming that he would writing another musical just for him. That, unfortunately, turned out to be "moonshine" (Walsh, 1989, p. 203).

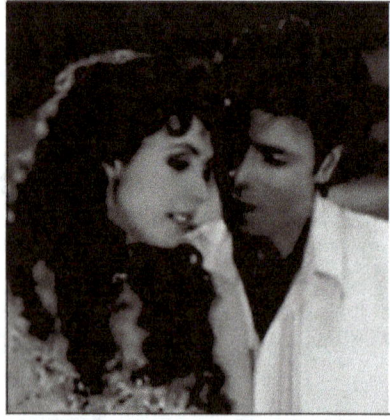

Pop-star, Cliff Richard, also recorded a promotional video for *Phantom* with Sarah Brightman, singing *All I Ask of You*. They sound good together, but the cinematography is unintentionally hilarious. (I especially like the tidal wave behind their heads. Run, run!)

 https://www.youtube.com/watch?v=gQi-TaRZSOEE

Patti Lupone and Faye Dunaway

History was to repeat itself with casting of the lead role of Norma Desmond in his production of *Sunset Boulevard*. Patti LuPone created the role in London and was ready to re-create it on Broadway. Glenn Close starred in the role in the L.A. production. In the end, Close was given the role on Broadway, not LuPone. It caused all manner of hard feelings. Lloyd Webber did not help himself with his attitude: as one of his biographers stated, "he never apologizes." Lloyd Webber said LuPone had been "quite difficult with everybody." There was eventually a settlement of a million dollars. Lloyd Webber sent flowers, but "not an apology, leading LuPone to declare that Lloyd Webber had no feelings and was major bad karma" (Coveney, 1999, p. 248).

Lloyd Webber also had a run-in with Faye Dunaway, also cast as Norma Desmond. When director, Trevor Nunn, felt that she would not be ready, they decided to close the show. The salvoes between Lloyd Webber and Dunaway's attorneys when back and forth. Lloyd Webber then released a confidential letter to the press that claimed that he was "acting in her own best interests and protecting her from a critics' roasting" (Coveney, 1999, p. 249). Dunaway responded with a 37-page lawsuit. She stated that she hoped she was the last "in a long line of artists who have come to this man's productions in good faith and have suffered great personal and professional injury at his hands" (Coveney, 1999, p. 250). The Really Useful Group hit back with a 123-page court document, also leaked to the press, describing the difficulties of the "aging actress."

Lyricists

Charles Hart

Charles Hart was a young, unemployed lyricist who was plucked from obscurity and given a chance to write some lyrics for *Phantom*. Richard Stilgoe had already written lyrics for *Phantom*, but Lloyd Webber thought they were too comic. He gave Hart the chance to come up with some new lyrics. Hart knew nothing about the plot of the show and was only given a recording of a melody and asked to write lyrics for it. The song was Think of Me. Hart got the gig, and Stilgoe, essentially, got the sack, again without knowing what he had done wrong. Hart's lyrics became a key part of the success of the show.

Given his key role, it's surprising (or not) that Lloyd Webber has treated Hart rather poorly following the success of *Phantom*. Hart made a great deal of money, and that's good. But he's been excluded from Lloyd Webber's circle, dropped from internal email lists, and even excluded from the bash celebrating the 10th anniversary of *Phantom* in New York. *Variety* wrote up a 29-page anniversary section, and Hart's name was not listed, even once, in the text, congratulatory messages, advertisements, or editorials (Coveney, 1999, p. 346).

For Hart, working on *Phantom* was a mixed blessing. On the plus side, it shot him to instant stardom and made him rich. On the negative side, he's found himself adrift, not unlike people who win the lottery. Hart describes the pressure he felt to "live up to something," and that his world was feeling increasingly lonely (Coveney, 1999, pp. 228-230). He was brought in to help spruce up the lyrics for *Love Never Dies*, and made many significant improvements, so he's still got the touch.

Don Black

Don Black is another lyricist who worked with Lloyd Webber. Although his collaboration was positive, he had some interesting insights about Lloyd Webber, describing him as "bizarre." He also described him as "sensational." "He's out there on his own. Who else is there like this?" (Coveneny, 1999, p. 116).

Tim Rice and Trevor Nunn

Two of Lloyd Webber's longest collaborations were with Tim Rice and Trevor Nunn. Both relationships led to great success for all involved. Rice was Lloyd Webber's collaborator on *Jesus Christ Superstar, Joseph and the Amazing Technicolor Dreamcoat*, and *Evita*. Nunn collaborated on *Cats, Starlight Express, Aspects of Love*, and briefly, on *Phantom*. For Lloyd Webber, Rice, Nunn, and Cameron Macintosh were all important in his creative life, and at different times, good friends. Maria Bjornson commented on Lloyd Webber's relationship between Lloyd Webber, Nunn, Rice, and Macintosh. She noted that he was obsessed with them, and were his "intellectual lovers." They were his mentors, but he also "loved or hated each of them at any given time" (Coveney, 1999, pp. 183-184).

Unfortunately, their relationships, especially with Nunn and Rice, also ended badly. I will describe the reasons why for this in more detail in Chapter 9. Lloyd Webber talked about his relationship with Rice in a 2011 interview. Interestingly, he doesn't mention the things biographers described as happening between them, but focuses on their relative obsession (or lack of obsession) with musicals. His take on why his partnerships with Rice and Nunn ended seems miles apart from Nunn and Rice's versions. In this interview, for the 25th anniversary of *Phantom*, Lloyd Webber describes why he thinks his relationship with Rice fell apart.

> I suppose the difference is that I'm obsessed with theatre, and for Tim it's something that he does enjoy doing, is very good at, but it isn't his whole life like it is with me.
>
> The natural rhythm of our partnership fell apart because I never could figure out quite how dramatically you did the story of *Chess*, which was his baby, so he went off and did it with Bjorn [Ulvaeus and Benny Andersson, of Abba]. Bloody good songs it had in it, too. Of course, then *Cats* happened [a musical to poems by TS Eliot], and that, by definition, didn't need a lyricist.
>
> That, I think, would be the biggest regret. I'm one of those people who likes the security of working with people they have worked with before (Spenser, 2013).

Why Doesn't He Have a Long-Term Partner?

Ultimately, Lloyd Webber's lack of long-term partnership seems to come down to this: he doesn't need one. He works with people as long as they are useful to him. Once they are not, he casts them off without a second glance. With *Cats*, he proved he didn't need Rice. Nor did he need outside financing. And he didn't need critics' approval to be a popular success. Lloyd Webber characterized his split from Rice as "taking control of his artistic destiny."

Lloyd Webber's power was such that during the stage production of *Phantom*, he hired Hal Prince and then fired him, bringing on Trevor Nunn. When it looked like the other show Nunn was directing, *Les Miserables*, was going to be a flop, Nunn was fired and Hal Prince returned (instead of telling him to piss off). This incident, perhaps more than any other, demonstrated Lloyd Webber's power in the world of musical theater. Without even an apology, he played fast and loose with the two most famous theater directors in the English-speaking world, and made them do his bidding. (Of course, *Les Miserables* went on to be the second-longest running show of all time. I hope that that was some consolation to Nunn.)

It's amazing to me that Lloyd Webber is surprised and disappointed that no one works with him long-term. He treats people badly. Many of his collaborators hung in far longer than they probably should have. The more pertinent question was why did they stay as long as they did?

CHAPTER 5
Lloyd Webber and the Critics

L loyd Webber has had record-breaking success throughout his long career. Yet, critics seem to think of his work as a piñata: they all line up to take a whack at it. It's amazing that someone could survive the kind of thrashing Lloyd Webber has endured. He has, but it has taken its toll. While he has been called "critic proof," Lloyd Webber seems to still crave the approval of the "cognoscenti" (Walsh, 1989, p. 285).

Some critics genuinely dislike his music. Others dislike him. Still others dislike the public for *liking his work*. In short, critics hate the composer, his music, and the fans, whom they view as tasteless rabble. On top of it, Lloyd Webber makes a great deal of money (Snelson, 2004; Walsh, 1989). Even so, Lloyd Webber's lack of critics' approval even scared off some investors when the Really Useful Group went public, as music professor, John Snelson describes.

> This paralleled the growing split between an institutional academic distaste for the man and his works, and the individual support from the ticket buyers in theaterland. ... Invoking the images of critical disdain, mass appeal, and personal wealth that have so frequently coincided in Lloyd Webber, the West End producer Thelma Hold later said: "The British have never been generous about success. The spirit of envy is alive and well in the arts, as it is everywhere else."

Joe Queenan, in his book *Red Lobster, White Trash, and the Blue Lagoon* (1998) describes what he calls "the fiendishly vapid world of Andrew Lloyd Webber" (p. 5), and also describes the schism between the cultural elite and everyone else. According to Queenan, Lloyd Webber defines the rift between high and low culture. He noted that when a work is popular, it guarantees the contempt of the critics "who take themselves more seriously than the work they review." He describes the response as "sanctioned sneering, knee-jerk knocking and politically correct lip-curling," with a dash of "metropolitan cultural snobbery" that surrounds light entertainment.

Let's unpack what Queenan said.

◆ Lloyd Webber's work is popular, therefore it is bad.

◆ "Critics take themselves more seriously than the work they review." Enough said there.

◆ There's a "culture of contempt" for the general public demonstrated by "sanctioned sneering, knee-jerk knocking, and politically correct lip-curling."

Commercial vs. Artistic Success

Underlying much of this critical vituperation is the belief that if something is a commercial success, it can't be artistically valid. Which is better? To be profitable, but iffy artistically? Or to be so "arty" that you close in a few weeks, after losing lots of money? When discussing the issue of commercial vs. artistic success, Lloyd Webber is often compared with fellow composer, Stephen Sondheim. A friend of mine (a musical theater major) told me her professors frequently said Sondheim=good; Lloyd Webber=bad. Many in the theater world seem to share that view. Sondheim has the intellectual respectability that Lloyd Webber has craved, but never seemed to get. Conversely, Sondheim had the critical respectability, and was reasonably successful, but never had the level of commercial success that Lloyd Webber enjoyed.

According to director Hal Prince, it needn't come down to Sondheim vs. Lloyd Webber. Prince has worked with both Sondheim and Lloyd Webber, and has championed them both. Prince attributed Lloyd Webber's low critical repute to jealousy, "And it's too damn bad" (Walsh, 1989, p. 219).

Prince may be right. Some of this ire may be a simple matter of old-fashioned jealousy. Biographer Coveney cites the example of Jonathan Coe, author of *The Dwarves of Death*, and his rant about Lloyd Webber, his music, and all the tacky people who love him. Coe claims that the musical ideas that Lloyd Webber uses were "common currency among composers" 50 to 70 years ago, claiming "dull minds think alike, and anybody with half an ear for melody could churn this stuff out." The audiences are also a problem. "And then the audience laps it up. They love it. I just cannot get this phenomenon" (cited in Coveney, 1999, p. 272). Coe, the author of this screed, spoke to a reporter from the *Guardian*, and couldn't explain why he was so angry. And yet, he did: Lloyd Webber had too much money! He was also mad because he felt that many writers, musicians, and "people like me" are better, but not as rich. Coveney's response was funny and to the point.

> Dream on, baby. What is sad about this, apart from the arrogance, is the sheer weight of material envy, rather than intelligent analysis, informing his attitude (Coveney, 1999, p. 273).

Lloyd Webber's friend, Sir David Frost, no stranger to criticism himself, notes that Lloyd Webber has overcome the burden of harsh criticism by working out that "it's better to be Andrew Lloyd Webber than be stuck on the outside looking at Andrew Lloyd Webber" (cited in Coveney, 1999, p. 327).

Critics vs. *Phantom*

Although a runaway popular success, the critical response to *Phantom*, particularly when it opened in New York, was harsh. The big knives were out. John Simon, in *New York*, said that *Phantom* was only deficient in the "book, music, and lyrics" (cited in Walsh, 1989, p. 207). Critics were downright *offended* that people actually liked this stuff. Their dislike of Lloyd Webber and his fans once again reflects the schism between the general public and the cultural elite. Peter Conrad of *The Observer* described "the stupefyingly banal tunelet" in *Phantom*, claiming that

Lloyd Webber only listens to himself, which Conrad described as his vision of "aural hell" (cited Walsh, 1989, p. 272).

Michael Feingold of *The Village Voice* described the *Phantom* score as "unapologetic derivativeness." Feingold's comments, reflecting his populist touch, describe his views on both Lloyd Webber and "the semi-educated middle-class." Showing his efficiency with the English language, in a mere paragraph, Feingold manages to pander to the "educated world," slap the fans, and state that Lloyd Webber is pathetic, a fake, a second-hand music peddler, and plagiarizes his music.

> Yes, yes, I know. The semi-educated middle-class world loves Andrew Lloyd Webber best of all theater composers ... Nevertheless, the educated world knows by now that [he] is not a real composer ... I don't accuse him of plagiarism; he never quotes more than 3 ½ bars of anyone else's work verbatim (cited in Walsh, 1989, p. 207).

The issue of populism vs. distain regarding *Phantom* has also been a topic of academic study. A recent issue of the *Cambridge Opera Journal* described *Phantom* as occurring within the "political, economic, and cultural context of the Thatcher/Reagan era." They claimed that the "conservative-leaning" tabloids in Britain took "nationalist pride" in Lloyd Webber's success. However, "others"

> ... on both sides of the Atlantic claimed that *Phantom* was tasteless and crassly commercial, a musical manifestation of a new Gilded Age. Broader issues regarding the relationship between the government and "elite" culture also affected the critical response. For some, *Phantom* forged a path for a new kind of populist opera that could survive and thrive without government subsidy, while less sympathetic critics heard *Phantom's* "puerile" operatics as sophomoric jibes against an art form they esteemed (Winker, 2014).

It's interesting that the critics also seemed to be mad that Phantom could survive (and thrive!) without some type of government subsidy. It goes back to "it makes money, therefore, it is bad."

Biographer Michael Walsh (1989) describes and comments upon the inflammatory rhetoric of Frank Rich's review of *Phantom*. Other reviews could be bad, but Rich's review was the one that mattered to both the public and the theater world. The news was not good. Rich did predict *Phantom's* success, but only because theater goers had so little taste. Rich wasn't known as the "Butcher of Broadway" for nothing. This review also reflects the view of New York City vs. "the Boondocks" (aka, the rest of the world). He did note that theater goers would likely have a good time at *Phantom*, and that "Only a terminal prig would let the avalanche of pre-opening publicity poison his enjoyment of this show..." But as Walsh summarized, Rich then went on to prove that he was that terminal prig. He called *Phantom* "long on pop professionalism and melody, impoverished of artistic personality and passion."

> *The Phantom of the Opera* is as much victory of dynamic stagecraft over musical kitsch as it is a triumph of merchandising *Über alles* ... Mr. Lloyd Webber has again written a score so generic that most of the songs could be reordered and redistributed among the characters (indeed, among other Lloyd Webber musicals) without altering the show's story or meaning (cited in Walsh, 1989, pp. 207-208).

Walsh's commentary on Rich's review is interesting, and also puts his comments in a context.

> Thus, did the country's most influential drama critic prosecute the case of the Broadway Establishment vs. Lloyd Webber. Spray painted with gratuitously inflammatory phrases (in a paper as solicitous of its heavily Jewish readership as *The New York Times*, the Nazi-era locution "*Über alles*" was especially provocative; cited in Walsh, 1989, pp. 208).

Walsh described Rich's review "trip to the woodshed," and that Rich referred to Lloyd Webber as "the Demon Composer of Broadway."

Rich predicted that *Phantom* would be Lloyd Webber's most popular musical, but that its popularity would wane by the end of the

Reagan-era, the so-called era of glitz and greed. Walsh described that Rich's view reflected his American perspective. The Reagan era may have been drawing to a close, but in Britain the Thatcher-era was still going strong (Walsh, 1989).

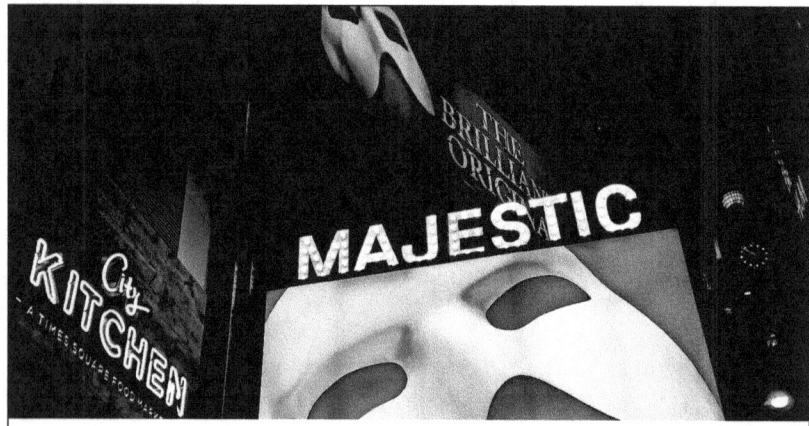

Phantom continues to run at New York's Majestic Theater.

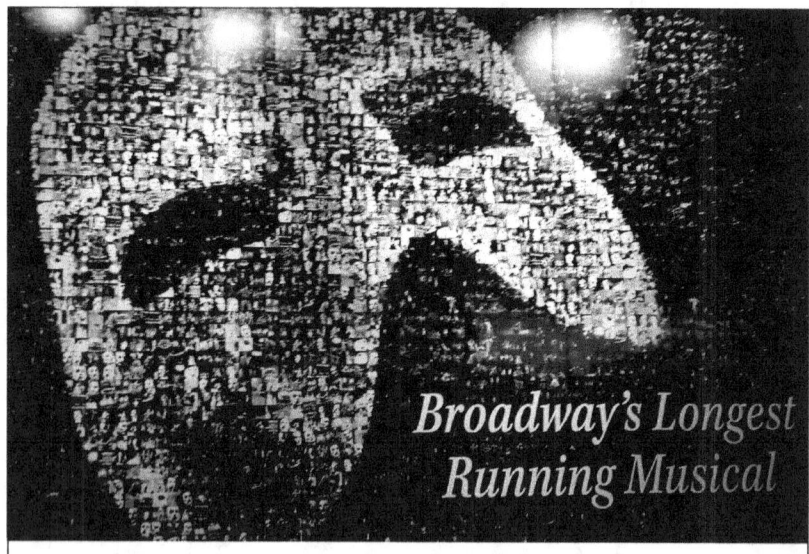

Phantom went on to be Broadway's longest-running musical despite being thrashed by the critics in New York.

Critiques of Other Lloyd Webber Musicals

Starlight Express

Critics also disliked other Lloyd Webber productions. According to Walsh, critics really got the ball rolling in their reviews of *Starlight Express*. Prior to that show, Lloyd Webber's one major flop to date, *Jeeves*, hadn't really hurt his reputation, but the failure of *Starlight Express* did. Lloyd Webber was suddenly "not just fair game, but big game. He was no longer invincible" (Walsh, 1989, p. 164). Unfortunately, Lloyd Webber responded to the negative reviews of *Starlight* by blaming his director, Trevor Nunn. Lloyd Webber's program notes for the American production of *Starlight* described how *Starlight* was original conceptualized as being a concert for schools, but Nunn "had other ideas." Although the show was successful in London, "something of the joy and sense of pure fun that was the original intention seemed to get lost." This is where Lloyd Webber, as Walsh describes, threw Nunn under the bus.

> It was, in short, all Trevor's fault. The Nunns of the world had made him do it. This admission was all the ammo the American critics needed. They sacked *Starlight Express* like the Wild Bunch robbing a Wells Fargo Bank train (Walsh, 1989, pp. 164-165).

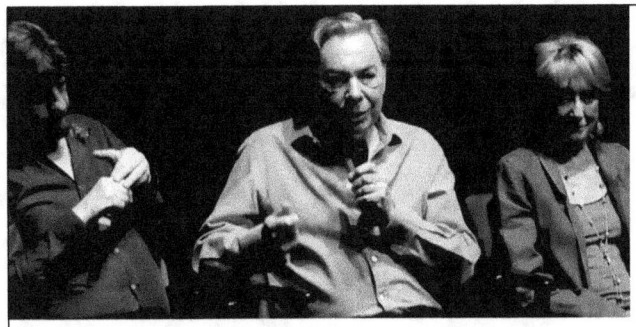

Trevor Nunn, Lloyd Webber, and Gillian Lynne in a 2014 interview about *Cats*.
https://www.youtube.com/watch?v=_m3NqP5gvnQ

Aspects of Love

The show immediately following *Phantom* was *Aspects of Love. Aspects* has a few excellent songs, such as Seeing Is Believing, but it has the vilest plot of anything Lloyd Webber had done to date. It's a classic tale of everyone sleeping with everyone, which doesn't sound a lot like "love." Rather, it sounds like "poor impulse control." That was not enough to offend critics, who are quite used to plots like that. But the particularly repulsive plotline has a young man sleeping with Rose, a woman a few years older than him, at the beginning of the show. She decides that she'd rather shack up with his rich uncle. By the end of the show, the original young man is trying to bed Rose's teenaged daughter! When this show was workshopped at Sydmonton, audience members from the UK rolled with this plot. American members were more dubious. Critical response was similar. Once *Aspects* got to the U.S., critics, who were frustrated that no one listened to their reviews of *Phantom*, came out in force.

Frank Rich said that "Though *Aspects of Love* purports to deal with romance in many naughty guise" it was boring, and "generates about as much heated passion as a visit to the bank." Clive Barnes noted that "Lloyd Webber has never done well in *The New York Times*," but that was nothing compared to the "storm of civilized and urbane invective against *Aspects of Love*." Charles Bremner also noted that the New York critics "wielded their axes" with "a glee that, to some in the composer's camp, smacked of anti-British prejudice" (cited in Walsh, 1989, p. 165). *Aspects* closed after 761 performances. For anyone but Lloyd Webber, this would have been a hit. For Lloyd Webber, it was not.

What Should the Response Be to Critics?

It takes a certain personal hardiness to stand up to this kind of public bashing. Fortunately, the popular success of Lloyd Webber shows, particularly *Phantom*, buffered some of it. At the end of the day, many artists choose to ignore the critics. They almost have to. Interestingly, *Boston Globe* critic Frank Stark, at the age of 81, gives similar advice to a young director in his blog post on Notes to a Young Director. Stark summarizes his views of critics and tells the young director to protect himself from their opinions.

> Critics wound so much, and so easily, because every syllable they utter is a critique of each and every one of those selves exposing themselves onstage like fish in a barrel waiting to be targets. And not one of you fish can ever fight back.

> Every critic who has ever been criticized immediately hides behind the "Hey, mine is only One Humble Opinion here!" dodge, but they never notice when attacked that their voices, through the megaphone of something like *The Globe*, reach thousands of gullible ears, and most of those readers read reviewers, so they don't have to have opinions of their own.

Stark also points out that critics often have quite large egos, calling it "Elephantiasis of the Ego," but often are so busy sharing their opinions that they don't tell audiences what the show is actually about.

> ...The critics are all so busy monging opinions they have no time to think anymore.

And in the end, it comes down to what the audiences think, something I think Lloyd Webber would wholeheartedly agree with.

> So, none of what they said is important to YOU, and I'm serious about protecting yourself from critics. I know how much who and what you are is invested in everything you do. And I know the bubble reputation is important to a young director, even in the critics' mouths. Yes, they are important, but what none of them says is one tenth as important as the word from any of your friends who work in the business, any one of whom knows infinitely more about what you've made, and how, than any one-night egomaniacs can ever know. Trust your friends. And your audiences

> And opinion-mongers be damned! (Stark, n.d.).

CHAPTER 6

Composer and Muse
Story of a Marriage

The story of Lloyd Webber's *The Phantom of the Opera* is intimately tied to his marriage to Sarah Brightman. Many reporters over the years have noted the parallels between their relationship and that of the story they created. In real life, Brightman was Lloyd Webber's muse, and with her, he created his greatest score, as musicologist John Snelson (2004) describes.

> Andrew Lloyd Webber couldn't have been unaware of the parallels between his second marriage and the most opulently romantic of his musicals, *The Phantom of the Opera*. A less-than-handsome maestro woos a young, unknown singer... and sets about transforming her into a star. He writes the ambitious *Requiem*, giving his new bride one of his most melting melodies. Then he casts her in a magnum opus, *Phantom*, and won't allow his musical to come to America unless Actors' Equity relents and lets his leading lady sing and act the part he has written especially—only—for her. *The Phantom* would have applauded such romantic hubris (Snelson, 2004, e-page).

Lloyd Webber and Brightman's marriage ended after only six years. Of course, no one really knows what happens in marriage except the two people who are involved, but both Brightman and Lloyd Webber have given numerous interviews since the split, so it's possible to piece together at least part of the story. Lloyd Webber and Brightman have an ongoing personal and professional relationship. However, while they have managed to find a way to continue to work together, it's not always harmoniously.

The Beginning

Sarah Brightman was a 20-year-old singer who auditioned for the part of Jemima in *Cats*. Before that, she had been a singer and dancer with the pop group Hot Gossip, which had one hit: a very-late-70s-style single, I Lost My Heart to a Starship Trooper. There is nothing particularly memorable about the song or the video, but the tune is undeniably catchy. And while they do briefly mimic some live sex acts, they are fully clothed while doing it. It's a typical mindless big-haired, uni-tarded, late-1970s dance video. (I particularly like the bit with the barbells.)

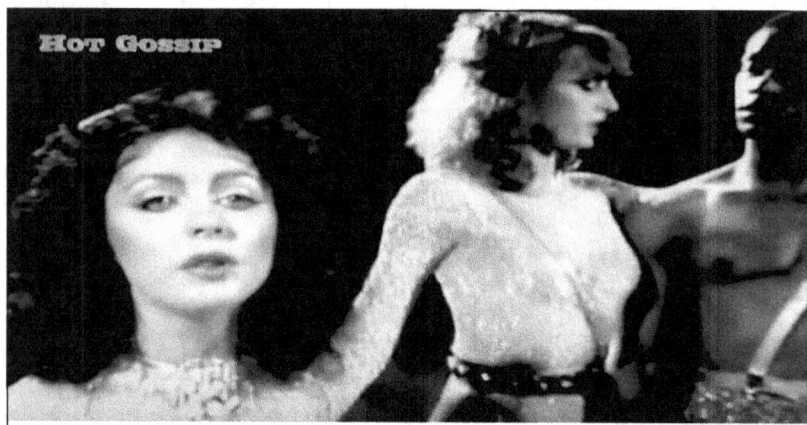

Sarah Brightman's first hit was with the group Hot Gossip:
I Lost My Heart to a Starship Trooper.
https://www.youtube.com/watch?v=kgW9I7CR1WQ

Lloyd Webber was not taken with Brightman until he went to see her in *Nightingale*, a children's opera. He was drawn there by rave reviews. Lloyd Webber was reportedly "bewitched" and asked her to dinner, as Brightman describes years after their breakup in an interview on Loose Women ITV.

> **Interviewer:** Because you were in *Cats* for a year, weren't you?
> And he didn't really notice you at all.

SB: That's right. And I went and sang in a little children's opera called *Nightingale*. And he went to see a performance and took me to dinner afterwards. But we'd always got on very well because we were interested in the *Sound of Music*, which of course he's done, and I had started a little record company, I'd put a single out, a medley of pieces from the *Sound of Music*. And we like the same composers. We like Rachmaninoff and Puccini. And we could talk about lots of things. There was always something between us.

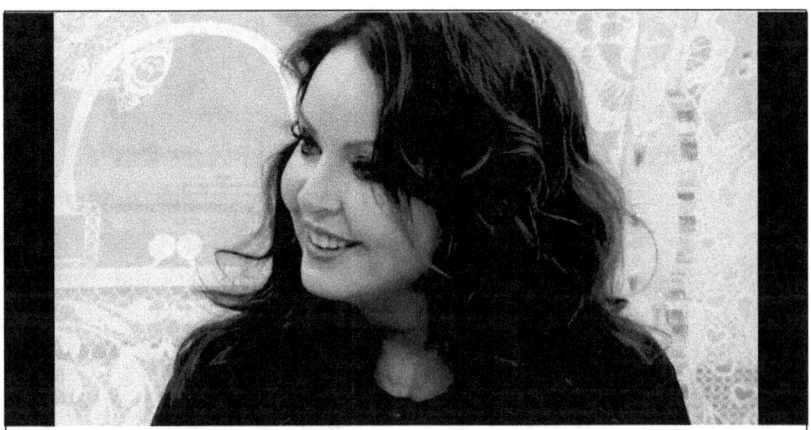

Sarah Brightman on Loose Women ITV.
https://www.youtube.com/watch?v=qNCAsOEcjig

Lloyd Webber, age 32, was soon smitten and they began a relationship. But as the BBC so coyly states, "There was one tiny problem. They were both already married" (*Behind the Mask*, part 1).

Oh. That.

I'm amazed at how casual the BBC was. Lloyd Webber had two young children when he began his affair and then left his first wife, also named Sarah. The implications of the split for Sarah One (as she became known in the press) must have been horrific. Not only did she lose her husband, but she was kicked out of their family home at Sydmonton. After being discarded, Sarah One then had to see Lloyd Webber and Brightman all over town as a West-End power couple. We hear little about her in the press, but according to Lloyd Webber's biographers, his first wife had been exemplary, expertly handling the demands of sudden wealth and fame, and handling things for Lloyd Webber on the home front (Coveney, 1999). In contrast, Lloyd Webber was drawn to Brightman because of her voice.

Lloyd Webber, flush with success from *Cats*, was discovering that there were certain perks associated with fame, including women being interested in him. He also started feeling dissatisfied in his marriage, though none of his friends suspected that anything was wrong. According to Walsh,

> Sarah [#1] had been the best helpmeet a man could want, functioning as wife, mother, lover, and majordomo. She had spent months in the hospital bearing their two children. During the *This is Your Life* program, she had beamed with pride at the celebration of her husband's work, and at the end of the show Imogen and Nicholas had been brought out to cuddle with their daddy. If Andrew was an unhappy husband, he did not let on. Besides, what fueled him was success, not sex, and so far he had resisted all temptation to fool around in a profession in which fooling around came with the territory (Walsh, 1989, pp. 119).

In contrast to Sarah One, Brightman was forbidden fruit, "ripe and luscious. There was about her more than a whiff of forbidden sexuality" (Walsh, 1989, p. 119). Lloyd Webber is portrayed as "flattened," being "helpless to resist" her, with another reference to forbidden fruit, this time, with a smell of musk. "She was a free spirit, and emitted the musky smell of forbidden fruit" (Walsh, 1989, p. 146).

Not exactly.

According to biographer Micheal Coveney (1999), Brightman and Lloyd Webber's friendship grew when he started *dating her*. He even took Brightman on holiday to Italy, later claiming that his relationship with Brightman "just happened." It didn't become public until he decided to openly bring her to the first night party of his show, *Daisy Pulls It Off*. He actually talked to the press about it (*Behind the Mask*, part 1, 2008). Meanwhile, his wife, wanting to be spared the humiliation of public acknowledgement of her husband's affair, and knowing that the blow was coming, took her widowed mother home for a simple dinner (Walsh, 1989, p. 155).

Shortly after, Lloyd Webber issued a public statement: "I want to record that my affection for Sarah is still very great, but unhappily we will be seeking a divorce in the near future. Sarah Brightman and I have known each other professionally for several years. Only recently has our relationship developed" (Walsh, 1989, p. 155).

History was to repeat itself just a few short years later, when Brightman became the discarded wife.

Once he was finished with his first wife, Lloyd Webber behaved with appalling callousness. Fortunately, one of their friends offered her refuge. Long-time friend Peter Brown invited Sarah One and her children to stay at his New York apartment. Brown reported that Lloyd Webber was furious with Brown for harboring a woman Lloyd Webber claimed "took him to the cleaners." Brown said, "fuck you, she's my friend as well" (Coveney, 1999, p. 147).

Lloyd Webber was a multi-millionaire at the time. Given his personal fortune, he hardly got "taken to the cleaners." In many states in the U.S., he would owe her half. Instead, he paid a very small fraction of total fortune, not even amounting to £1 million. The final settlement totaled £750,000 in cash and property. This included the house on West Eaton Place, plus £300,000 in trust for his children. He later also purchased them a house in Oxfordshire (Walsh, 1989, p. 156).

Brightman was also married, but she had married at a very young age and then moved back in with her parents. She was still technically married, but not living with her husband. She also divorced her husband.

The Backlash

The BBC might have been casual about their divorces, but the theater world and the general public were not, with most of the backlash directed at Brightman.

> Fleet Street, that last bastion of middle-class sensibility, went wild. In Britain, successful men simply didn't ditch their long-suffering wives—they had met when she was 16, for God's sake. It was all very well to keep "a bit on the side" (as the army officers had sung in *Evita*), but to move her to the center... It was too much.

I'm not sure how his first wife would have felt about that: just keep Brightman as a mistress.

> On that day was born the image of Brightman the Jezebel homewrecker, the sexy showgirl who had broken up the Lloyd Webbers' happy family. Her past was picked over and amplified; reporters were shocked—*shocked!*—to discover that she had once danced in fishnets with the racially mixed Hot Gossip troupe.

It's interesting that so much was made of this video. It is suggestive, but it's typical of the genre.

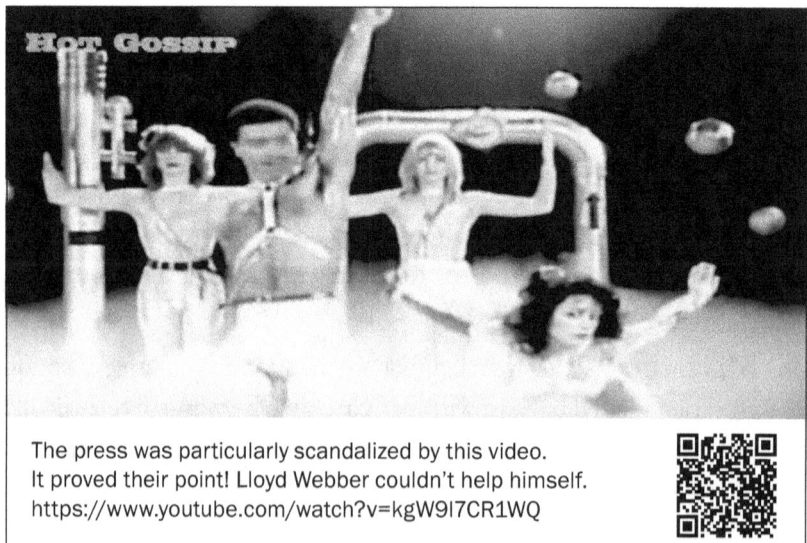

The press was particularly scandalized by this video.
It proved their point! Lloyd Webber couldn't help himself.
https://www.youtube.com/watch?v=kgW9I7CR1WQ

From then on, Andrew and Sarah, or "Sarah II," as she was immediately dubbed, became media staples, their comings and goings watched, their trash pawed through, their rows breathlessly reported or vividly imagined. They became, in short, modern celebrities (Walsh, 1989, p. 155).

Even the cartoonists got involved, portraying Lloyd Webber as a cat with a saucer of cream. He's finally gotten the "dollybird of his dreams" (Walsh, 1989, p. 155). Lloyd Webber's third wife, whom he left Brightman for, said he should have gotten his obsession out of his system "by having a short, sharp affair" (Walsh, 1989, p. 155). Given Mrs. Lloyd Webber #3's role in the break-up of Brightman's marriage, something about that comment seems quite off.

The Wedding

On Lloyd Webber's 36th birthday, Lloyd Webber married Brightman at the local magistrate's office in Kingsclere. Lloyd Webber's final divorce decree had come through two days earlier. The Queen would be at the gala preview premiere of *Starlight Express* and Lloyd Webber wanted to introduce Brightman to the Queen as his wife (Walsh, 1989). Brightman and Lloyd Webber continued to be targets for the press. Brightman once noted, "Do you realize that, after Charles and Diana, Andrew and I are the most famous couple in the world" (Walsh, 1989, p. 145)? Be careful what you wish for. That story did not end well either.

An Alternate Interpretation of Events

Before I researched this story, I assumed that biographers' interpretation of these events was accurate: that Brightman instigated the relationship. However, upon reading this more closely, it occurred to me that there may be another way to look at it. The male biographers of Lloyd Webber all blame Brightman, the "sexy showgirl" (Walsh,

1989, p. 146). However, if you look at pictures of Brightman at that time, she's not nearly as pretty as she is now, so the "sex vixen" image really doesn't fly.

Not only that, it takes two people to wreck a home. Lloyd Webber was the one with the real power in the relationship. He was 12 years older than her (she was a mere 20), and the most powerful figure in musical theater. He was rich and famous, with his own production company. There was nothing he couldn't have. He had outlasted all his competitors. To say that *she* was the one with all the control is absurd. Biographer Michael Walsh describes Lloyd Webber's power this way.

> His commanding position allowed him to do almost anything he wished, and with his wealth he could afford to do almost anything. There was nothing standing in the way of the realization of his vision, nothing at all: no director he couldn't hire or fire, no producer he couldn't dominate, no cast he couldn't handpick; just put his name on the poster and watch the paying customers line up ... he had outlasted, or would outlast, them all. The only thing he couldn't do was fail (Walsh, 1989, p. 230).

All Brightman did was perform in an opera. Lloyd Webber is the one who asked her out. *He's* the one who decided to date her when he was already married. He needs to take some responsibility for his own behavior.

When Lloyd Webber came into Brightman's life, in true Svengali fashion, he set about transforming her. He drilled and groomed her. She was expected to train as a member of the *corps de ballet*. She had to sing and act. The parallels between the Phantom and Christine are apparent. Yet, amazingly, Lloyd Webber somehow escaped the majority of the blame for the breakup of his first marriage.

The backlash went on for years against Brightman, even once *Phantom* was a huge hit. There was still the belief that she didn't deserve to be in that part, that Lloyd-Webber created a star vehicle for his mistress/wife, and that she wouldn't have gotten the role otherwise. Lloyd Webber often countered in interviews that she had had to audition and had to beat out stiff competition to get the part of Christine. That was rubbish too. I find it interesting that in a profession that tends to be rather liberal about sexuality, it wasn't *adultery* that really offended them. It was *nepotism.*

The Fight with American Equity

In the book for the 25th anniversary, Lloyd-Webber describes the fight he had with American Equity (the actors' union) over allowing Brightman to be in the starring role of *Phantom* when they moved the play to New York. That attitude of "she wouldn't have gotten this part without sleeping with the composer" still existed even after she had proven herself—and then some—during the run on London's West End. Lloyd Webber threatened to pull the entire production, and not bring it to the U.S., unless Equity relented. Equity claimed that Brightman did not have sufficient experience to play this part—the part she created—and that it should go to an American actress. Lloyd Webber finally prevailed, but the New York theater community exacted its revenge. Brightman was the only one in *Phantom* not nominated for a Tony Award. When Lloyd Webber won his award for best play, he defiantly held it up and said "this one's for Sarah."

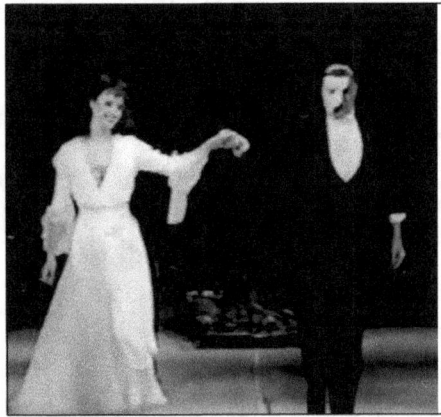

Crawford and Brightman's brilliant performance at the 1988 Tony Awards. https://www.youtube.com/watch?v=oZDcSrODALQ

What Happened to Sarah One?

Two years after her split with Lloyd Webber, Sarah One married Jeremy Norris, a magazine management executive. Their wedding was on the same weekend as Lloyd Webber's Sydmonton Festival. His friend and collaborator, Tim Rice, went to the wedding rather than the festival. Eventually, Sarah One was able to form a post-divorce relationship with Lloyd Webber, something she credits to her second husband.

> For me, lots has also happened in the 14 years since [her split with Lloyd Webber]. In particular, my marriage to Jeremy, and the happiness and stability he has brought into the children's lives, have been an enormous source of pleasure and contentment, enabling me to forge a richly satisfying and private way of life. Jeremy has also been immensely successful in his important role as stepfather while, at the same time, ensuring that the children, and indeed all of us, have a healthy and continuing relationship with Andrew (Coveney, 1999, p. 147).

In surreal fashion, several years after the breakup, Lloyd Webber brought his two families together at the premiere of *Aspects of Love*. Lloyd Webber and Brightman sat at a table with his first wife, now Sarah Norris, and their children. Jeremy Norris opted out of the "one big happy family photo." The next day, the photos were in nearly every tabloid. *The Sun* featured Lloyd Webber saying, "How Love Changes Everything for Me" (Walsh, 1989, p. 230).

Dark Clouds on the Horizon for Brightman

Lloyd Webber had fallen for Brightman because of her voice. She became his muse, his protégé, his star—someone he worked with. But then Lloyd Webber started to miss someone to mind his home, have his children, and take care of *him*. In other words, what he had before. It didn't bode well. Michael Coveney (1999) described how he started growing wistful for his first wife. He bought her a home in Oxfordshire, and took her and the children on a road trip to see *Evita*. He even considered re-proposing to her, but she was already remarried.

In the meantime, Lloyd Webber continued to manage Brightman's career. After starring in *Phantom* in London and New York, Lloyd Webber decided that Brightman should go out on tour rather than being in a musical. This would get her away from the critics, and allow her more freedom. Unfortunately, Brightman's tour schedule, instigated by Lloyd Webber, was one of things that contributed to the breakup of her marriage.

CHAPTER 7

Was Phantom Created with Sarah Brightman in Mind?

A common consensus among historians of *Phantom* was that Brightman had a critical role in the its creation. This belief has been widely accepted. For example, the BBC notes, "with his muse by his side, he set off writing the score of his life" (*Behind the Mask*, part 2, 2008). Musicologist Snelson (2004) reiterates this belief.

> Acting as his muse through her clear soprano voice, Brightman herself performed in the next two of Lloyd Webber's works. [*Requiem* and *Phantom*]

> The next work for Brightman was *The Phantom of the Opera*, a musical setting of Gaston Leroux's famous novel which brought renewed lyricism to Lloyd Webber's style.

Brightman's role was also acknowledged in the companion volume for 25th anniversary—a book published by Lloyd Webber's production company, the Really Useful Group. It said the following:

> Andrew Lloyd Webber had never tried to hide the fact that he had his then wife, Sarah Brightman, in mind when he was writing the role of Christine Daae. Her selection was still subject to rigorous auditioning, however. The demands of the role were high, and Brightman's physical frailty, which made her ideal for the role, called for use of an alternate of comparable quality (Heatley, 2011, p. 51).

The Initial Idea

The initial idea for Lloyd Webber's version of *Phantom* came almost by chance. Lloyd Webber was stuck in New York on a rainy day and happened upon a copy of Gaston LeRoux's novel, *The Phantom of the Opera*. He was surprised that the movie versions bore little resemblance to the book. He also found the story to be quite confused: was it a horror novel? A detective novel? He described the story as "hokum." The story redeemed itself in a little footnote: The Phantom's corpse had been discovered still wearing Christine's ring. Lloyd Webber recognized the story was a great romance. "*Phantom*, it seemed to him, should not be a cheap horror show, but a serious piece about repressed sexuality" (Walsh, 1989, p. 177).

> This was it, the opera plot he had always wanted. ... it gave him a perfect excuse to cast Sarah Brightman with her high, pure, virginal soprano voice as the heroine, Christine (Walsh, 1989, p. 176).

Lloyd Webber had already written the *Requiem* for Brightman's voice, including the popular Pie Jesu. Yet, he was still anxious to write something that would showcase her voice.

> This show would be Lloyd Webber's own wedding Mass with Sarah Two (Walsh, 1989, p. 172).

Brightman Changed the Way He Wrote

Brightman described the process of creation of the role in more detail in her interview to the BBC. According to her account, Lloyd Webber had never written for a soprano before, so he kept asking her, "can you do this?" Brightman noted that she "was around to try things out." The role seemed custom designed for her voice. Cameron Macintosh said she was "the muse of this story" (*Behind the Mask*, part 2, 2008). Current Christines even look like Brightman in the 1980s, with her long, curly hair. Brightman concurred in a 1997 interview. She noted that *Phantom* was written with her voice in mind, but was never meant to be just for her.

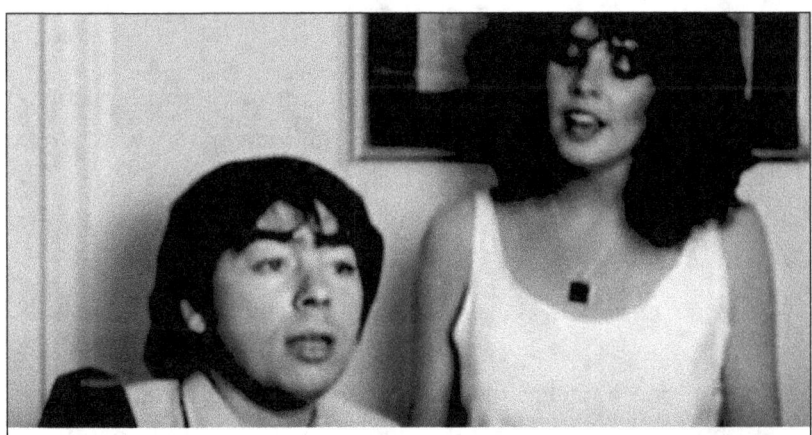

Lloyd Webber composing with Brightman by his side.
https://www.youtube.com/watch?v=g_Bhz0aymx

Christine is a difficult part. She's on stage for most of the show. In the companion volume for the 25th anniversary, Lloyd Webber talked about the role of Christine.

> The role of Christine is one of the most demanding I have ever written. It involves not only being able to sing music covering an enormous range for a considerable length of time, but also demands that the artist can dance *en pointe*. My Christine is a member of the *Corps de Ballet*. The Phantom believes in her voice because it represents a new sound of music, purer than a conventional soprano (Heatley, 2011, p. 51).

What biographers seem particularly impressed by is that *Phantom* came shortly on the heels of the vapid score for *Starlight Express*. They considered that Lloyd Webber's music had taken a quantum leap in quality, and credited Brightman's influence for much of that. For example, Walsh noted that,

From the key structure alone, it is clear that Lloyd Webber himself considered *Phantom* his most important score. ... When one takes into account that *Phantom* is also Lloyd Webber's theatrical successor to *Starlight Express*, its quality is even more astounding (1999, p. 202).

Musicologist John Snelson (2004) makes a similar comparison between *Phantom* and *Starlight Express*. The qualities of Brightman's voice changed the way Lloyd Webber wrote music. He wanted to write music that would highlight what she could do. His music became more romantic and story-driven.

Such a change was provoked by his second wife, Sarah Brightman, whose voice—large range, flexible technique, bright tone, and clear diction—provided the catalyst for Lloyd Webber to begin writing in a more expansive and romantic idiom, first with *Requiem* in 1985 and then with *The Phantom of the Opera* in 1986 (2004, e-page).

Brightman's voice allowed him to write in a different way.

Phantom's change of direction was made more marked by the elevation of Sarah Brightman not only to center stage, but to the center of the very concept. Inspired by her vocal qualities, Lloyd Webber broke into a warmer and more romantic musical vein, and returned to some of the thematic devices that he had begun to experiment with in *Jesus Christ Superstar* and *Evita*, but from which he had been sidetracked by the essentially revue-like formats of *Cats* and *Starlight Express* (2004, e-page).

The story of *Phantom* also seemed to have some similarity to Lloyd Webber's life.

The show, and his own romantic pursuit of Sarah Brightman, seem linked, given that he said, "*The Phantom* is really about this man's obsession with this girl, and nothing will stop him from getting *to* her."

The effect of writing for Sarah Brightman's voice spilled over into the other characters, and the singing range of the Phantom especially seems to have been written to match hers as Christine, and then parodied in Carlotta (2004, e-page).

Was the Storyline Autobiographical?

More than one reviewer noted that there was something strangely autobiographical about storyline. For example, the BBC, in its documentary, *Behind the Mask*, notes the following:

Had it not been for a real-life love affair, *Phantom* may have never been created in the first place. How did a show about a man obsessed with a beautiful, young singer, written by a man obsessed with a beautiful young singer become the biggest blockbuster in theatre history (*Behind the Mask*, part 1, 2008)?

Similarly, David Shannon of *Today* wrote:

Andrew Lloyd Webber's new musical is, he says, "About a man who is hideously ugly who falls hopelessly in love with this girl and is only able to express himself through music." Only those of a very cruel frame of mind would suggest the musical was at all autobiographical (cited in Walsh, 1989, p. 204).

Biographer Walsh made a similar point about the similarities in the story and Lloyd Webber's own life (Walsh, 1989, p. 166).

He had been looking to write a work for Sarah to sing ... where a lovelorn composer was wooing a beautiful young soprano with a new opera he was writing just for her. And any relation to any person, living or dead, was purely coincidental.

Phantom set designer, the late Maria Bjornson, also sensed something crucial to Lloyd Webber's anguish that is so prevalent in *Phantom*.

I also know about being single and about unrequited love. And I think Andrew knows about that. I think that is absolutely how he felt about Sarah. She never gave him the whole of herself and I'm sure that is what also bred this need to write this musical. If they had been truly happy, we would never have had *Phantom* (p. 184).

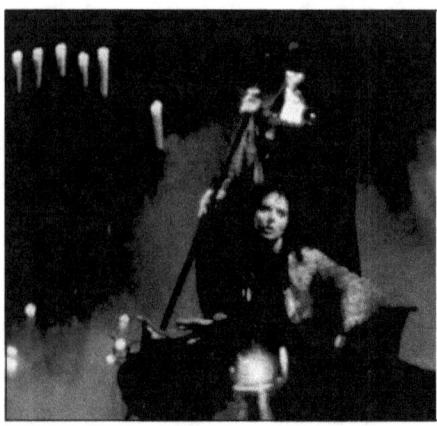

Lloyd Webber wrote something very different when writing for Brightman. https://www.youtube.com/watch?v=oZDcSrODALQ

The Backlash

Lloyd Webber's intention to write for Brightman was quite clear to everyone in their orbit. Many viewed it as a blatant attempt to boost his wife's career. This made them an easy target for ridicule. Not everyone was happy about her role, but it was widely acknowledged. People in the theater world thought that it was unfair that she had this inside track.

> In writing the show, Lloyd Webber had already partly cast it, for Christine was specifically written for Brightman. By this time, the Lloyd Webber's marriage was a routine subject for newspapers, and the fact that Lloyd Webber had written the show for Sarah touched off a frenzy of "investigative" marital reporting (Walsh, 1989, p. 202).

With the constant pressure, Lloyd Webber's nerves frayed. Choreographer Gillian Lynne reported that he went into a meltdown before the opening, turning various shades of red and purple, threatening to withdraw his score. "He'd stacked everything on making this show for Sarah, and it's very few times a writer will put his own heart, and love, on the table."

Brightman starring in *Phantom* night after night added fuel to the already blazing fire. The pressure was on Brightman, knowing the knives were out. Brightman said "I got the part. I auditioned for it, so you couldn't say I didn't get it." In many ways, they were victims of their own success.

> With their love story played out nightly on stage, the cast album shooting up the charts to Number One, and his wealth multiplying by the minute, Andrew and Sarah came under more press scrutiny than ever. I think that it's from around this time that the backlash sets in, the tone of envious jeering and childish rudeness that characterizes quite a lot of press comment on Lloyd Webber from the late 1980s (Walsh, 1989, p. 187).

The backlash didn't end once *Phantom* was a hit. If anything, it intensified once it came to New York in 1988. As I described in the previous chapter American Equity, the actors' union, refused to allow Brightman to repeat her role in the U.S. Brightman was also under intense pressure, so much so that she underwent surgery for stomach ulcers.

> Lloyd Webber was furious. He had written the piece with Sarah's voice and dancing ability in mind, and who was Equity to tell him who he could or could not have in his show (Walsh, 1989, p. 206)?

Bill Henry, writing for *Time*, had nothing nice to say about Brightman. In fact, his comment was one that seemed to particularly rankle.

> Brightman's Maypole figure, long nose, and prominent overbite do not aid in explaining why both men adore her. But these deficiencies might be overcome if she displayed the least hint of star quality, or even stage presence, instead of acting *like Minnie Mouse on Quaaludes* [emphasis added] (cited in Walsh, 1989, p. 207).

The snubs went on. *Phantom* triumphed at the Tony Awards, including getting the Tony for Best Musical, but did not win for best score. That went to Stephen Sondheim for *Into the Woods*. Brightman was not even nominated.

At the time of the 25th anniversary, Lloyd Webber reflected on the backlash in *Phantom's* early days in his Foreword to the 25th anniversary volume. It's interesting to note that although Brightman bore the brunt of the negative press, Lloyd Webber still interprets it as mainly about him. He also managed to take a swipe at the bloggers he believed were responsible for the negative press for the *Phantom* sequel, *Love Never Dies* (more about this in Section III).

> Although it's true that *Phantom* is the only show I have ever been involved with that was entirely unchanged during previews, I wish I could say I truly had the best time of my life during those heady days.
>
> Two years before I had married Sarah Brightman, the ex-Hot Gossip girl who had a huge hit with Starship Trooper. Notwithstanding that she had fantastic reviews for the Charlie Strouse opera *Nightingale* at the Lyric Theatre, Hammersmith, everyone was ready to snipe and say that she only got the role of Christine because she was my wife. When in previews she got ill and missed a performance, the chattering started big time. I shudder to think what would have happened if the Net had been around with its malicious and often fake or professional bloggers.
>
> Big opening nights, even when you feel sure you have the public with you, are when you feel your most vulnerable, the night that you want your closest loved ones around you. But when your loved one is a woman who is perceived by even some of your closest friends to have broken a marriage, and she is playing the leading role in your new musical (having previously been a kitten in the world's then biggest musical, *Cats*), *goodness knows I felt alone and frightened* whilst all

around were celebrating. I couldn't even bear to sit through the show. Cameron brought me back to the theater to see the curtain calls.

So when I read the first review, that of the late Jack Tinker of the *Daily Mail*, in which he said that he could think of no other actress than Sarah who could have premiered the role, frankly, I cried. I had to wake Sarah up to show her. Jack, in those days, was the most powerful and respected critic of musicals. His continued support for Sarah and the show is something I will always cherish.

Of course, the only Achilles heel that we had on our move to Broadway was Sarah. *It was such a blindingly easy way to get to me.* There was the refusal of American Equity to allow the girl without whom there would have been no *Phantom* to play the role on Broadway. And, of course, the hurtful fact that she was the only major ingredient of the show not to be nominated for a Tony. *I felt Sarah's slight as if it were directed at me.* Jack Tinker continued his championing of Sarah when he wrote after the Tonys that Sarah was the real Tony Award winner with a performance like precious porcelain (Heatley, 2011, pp 7-9) [emphasis added].

Lloyd Webber reiterated many of these points in an interview following the 25th anniversary performance. Lloyd Webber again called her "my angel of music." They hugged her tightly on stage and Brightman's performance of *The Phantom of the Opera* brought him to tears (Nathan, 2011).

He told the *Daily Mail* that musical's premiere in London, he was more fearful for Miss Brightman than to critical reaction to the show, admitting: "It is hard for me, there are loads of memories …

And everybody was slightly thinking 'why is she in the show?' It must be because she is Mrs. Lloyd Webber.

The answer is that she was in the show because she was the right person to be in the show at the time. I was much more worried on opening night about her, not about my show at all. I was concerned about whether she was going to get through it.

She was the angel of music, Sarah always will be, she has a wonderful quality as Christine, she's like porcelain ... it's lovely to have Sarah back again and in lovely voice."

After Their Breakup

After they separated, Lloyd Webber announced that he would be postponing the *Phantom* movie, but he assured the public that Brightman would still have the starring role, the part he wrote "just for her." Years after their divorce, Brightman also reiterates that the role was written for her.

> **Loose Women:** I know Andrew Lloyd Webber, your ex-husband, pretty well, and he played *Love Never Dies* to me when he'd written it. And it must be so incredible to be married to someone who wrote a musical especially for you.
>
> **SB:** It was a lovely thing. It's funny, at the time, you don't realize that because it's all happening in the present and you're just going with it. But when I look back on that time, and knowing him ... there was always something between us that was sweet (Sarah Brightman on Loose Women ITV, 2013).

Yet Lloyd Webber Denies It

Despite these many statements, when asked about it in an interview for the TV show, 40 Years of Andrew Lloyd Webber, Lloyd Webber denied he wrote *Phantom* for Brightman. Michael Ball interviewed him. Lloyd Webber's answer clearly stunned him. Ball and Brightman both starred in *Aspects of Love.*

MB: At the time, was it was your most personal show, because you'd written it for Sarah?

ALW: Kind of. Everybody thinks that, but what in actual fact happened was that Sarah was asked to do it as kind of a jokey version. It eventually came to Stratford East. And Cameron Macintosh and I thought it might be kind of fun to produce it. It was written by a guy called Ken Hill. And it used real opera, and it was this kind of jokey, larky thing. And I didn't really think that it was for me at all. So six months passed and I found the book in a second hand bookstore in New York, and it was completely different, and I thought I could do something with that. So then Sarah was, obviously, a very important part of it. I never, ever like writing for a specific person. Even though she was the one.

MB: Damn.

ALW: I just find it very inhibiting. ... I had no idea that *Phantom* was going to be a huge global success. I thought it was going to work, but I had no idea about its extent (Ball & Lloyd Webber, 2013).

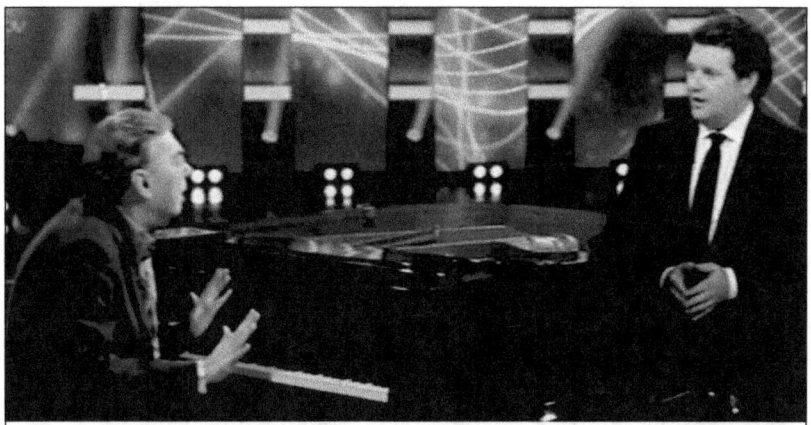

Lloyd Webber and Ball on 40 Years of Andrew Lloyd Webber.
https://www.youtube.com/watch?v=dPw67_2dfiY

It's hard to know what to make of Lloyd Webber's answer. In the excerpt cited above with Lloyd Webber's discussion of *Phantom's* early days and the backlash against it, he acknowledged Brightman's pivotal role in *Phantom's* creation.

> There was the refusal of American Equity to allow *the girl without whom there would have been no Phantom to play the role on Broadway* (Lloyd Webber cited in Heatley, 2011).

Lloyd Webber prevailed in a court case because he described the process of creating *Phantom* at his piano, with Brightman by his side (see Chapter 10). If she wasn't involved in its creation, why was she there? If she wasn't participating, that factoid would be immensely boring, and she would have probably been distracting as he tried to compose. The more probable explanation was that she was there to help.

Yes, he alone is the one who really knows what is going on in his mind. But he described Brightman's role, under oath, in a court of law. Further, Brightman, the other half of this equation, states that the role of Christine Daae (and *The Requiem*) were written for her, as she describes on her website.

> Brightman starred as Chistine Daae in Lloyd Webber's adaptation of *The Phantom of the Opera* on October 1986. Once again, the role of Christine was written specifically for her (Brightman, n.d.).

The same statement is also on her Wikipedia page.

> Brightman starred as Christine Daae in Lloyd Webber's adaptation of *The Phantom of the Opera*. The role of Christine was written specifically for her (Wikipedia, 2017a).

Lloyd Webber's denial of Brightman's role in his most famous part is likely a product of their ongoing complicated relationship.

CHAPTER 8

Life After Lloyd Webber
Brightman Reborn

After a mere six years of marriage, Brightman was cast off for another woman. It was history repeating itself. As with virtually every other aspect of their relationship, it played out on a public stage. Brightman found out about her divorce when Lloyd Webber's publicist faxed a release to the press. He announced that not only was he divorcing Brightman, but that the new Mrs. Andrew Lloyd Webber was waiting in the wings. His release announced his "special relationship" with 27-year-old Madeleine Gurdon, known as "Gurtie." She was a member of the horsey set and trafficked in the same circles as Princess Anne. On the day his divorce was final from Brightman, Lloyd Webber announced his engagement to Gurtie. Oddly, none of the "homewrecker" moniker stuck to Gurtie. A year later, she was Lady Lloyd Webber.

Brightman, in the meantime, loyally went off to try to boost the box office performance of Lloyd Webber's ailing show, *Aspects of Love*, in New York. Lloyd Webber declared that Brightman, still in her late 20s, was now old enough to play Rose Vibert, the middle-aged woman who loses in love. In his press release, Lloyd Webber indicated that his admiration for Brightman "as an artist is undimmed." Apparently, it was Brightman as a person that he couldn't stand.

Lloyd Webber and Brightman's breakup could have destroyed Brightman—but it didn't. Instead, she became the bestselling soprano in the world, has sold more than 30 million records, and has made so much money that she offered to return Lloyd Webber's £6 million divorce settlement. He refused. She says she may give it charity.

The Divorce Was a Complete Surprise

The breakup seems to have caught Brightman totally by surprise. According to an unnamed friend:

> I don't think Sarah was expecting the whole thing to be over. From what I understand, there have been lots of problems, and she thought Andrew would issue a statement acknowledging that. She didn't realize he would publicly humiliate her in the way he did. She's behaving very well, but it is anybody's guess as to what is going on (Gliatto, 1990).

As with his previous divorce, Lloyd Webber's settlement was chintzy. Lloyd Webber's net worth, at the time of the split, was estimated at $526 million, with royalties on *Phantom* of $175,000/day. The cast album, with most of the tracks sung by Brightman, sold around 40 million copies. Yet, Brightman's settlement was around $9 million (or £6 million). The British public also still thought of Brightman as a "Jezebel," and that reputation continued to follow her (Walsh, 1989, pp. 214-215).

Why Did They Break Up?

Some theories about the breakup include that Brightman did not fit into Lloyd Webber's increasingly country, upper-crust lifestyle, with its love of horses and gentry. There was also speculation that Brightman didn't want to have children. Really, the main issue seems to have been that Brightman *worked* (even if it was in his show), and she wasn't around to take care of *him* (Walsh, 1989, pp. 214-215). Lloyd Webber also said that "she had played around a wee bit," even as he announced his adultery in a press release. The rumors about Brightman were never confirmed.

So, the sentiment seemed to be that Brightman was the "slutty sex vixen" who lured hapless Lloyd Webber away from his happy home, insisted on working in her chosen field, and wasn't around to take care of him. This criticism seems spectacularly unfair. I'm sure that there was also a faction that felt she "got what she deserved" when she was cast off. Even as late as 2008, Brightman was referred to as Andrew Lloyd Webber's "big-eyed, toothy toy girl" (Paton, 2008). There was surprisingly little blow-back on Lloyd Webber, or Gurtie, for the breakup of Lloyd Webber and Brightman's marriage.

The real issue seems to be what Lloyd Webber wanted in a relationship. Ross, who interviewed Brightman in 1997, abandoned all pretense of objectivity and characterized Brightman as a "rubbish" wife. Her evidence for this observation was Brightman's apparent lack of desire for children. Ross made the snarky remark, supposedly summarizing Brightman's view on children: "plus, of course, they'd rather get in the way." Brightman seems to have also internalized this negative view of herself, but also indicated that she wanted to work.

> I can't be a wife. I'm not that sort of person. Wives have to compromise all the time. I knew I had a Gift and had to follow that Gift. I wrapped myself in cotton wool and did what I knew I had to do. I tried to do both, but couldn't make it work (Ross, 1997).

This negative view of Brightman is quite retro, and not in a good way. Are we really still having a problem with a working wife? No one seems to make negative comments about Lloyd Webber's single-minded focus on his work. Arlene Phillips commented about Brightman's focus on her work, and how she used to come in early when she was in Hot Gossip so she could warm up and practice, and that rehearsals and singing lessons came before other things, regardless of its importance, that was happening in her life with Andrew (cited in Walsh, 1989, p. 215). She *rehearses* and that makes her a bad woman?

Lloyd Webber in 2011, following the 25th anniversary, was ungallant enough to say that Brightman should never get married again because she wasn't "the marrying kind." Strange thing to say about someone who has already been married twice.

It was clear pretty quickly that she was not someone who was going to make a huge home. Sarah is a gypsy. She shouldn't marry anyone because she's not the marrying sort. Her world is performing, traveling. She wants to get around, always did, and I have to say she's achieved in spades everything she wanted to and more (Nathan, 2011).

Keep in mind that during their marriage, Lloyd Webber controlled pretty much every aspect of Brightman's life. He told her which shows she would sing in, and he moved her from London to New York, and then decided that she should go on tour rather than perform in musicals. And then he decided that they should have kids. He wasn't prepared to be with someone who had a career of her own. Even the fact that *Phantom* was taking off and doing well, largely due to her efforts, seemed to be held against her, with Lloyd Webber complaining that he had no one to have dinner with (Walsh, 1989, p. 217).

The Issue of Children

Let's circle back to the issue of children. Brightman has been characterized as "selfish." There are a couple of things to say there. First, women have the right to choose whether they have children. Perhaps she was being realistic about having children, knowing she'd probably have little help when it came to raising them with Lloyd Webber. Maybe she refused because she was still in her 20s and wanted to do something professionally before having children. Maybe she didn't want Lloyd Webber to be in control of this one small area of her life. Lloyd Webber wanted Brightman to be the type of wife he had before. Yet, he was attracted to Brightman primarily because she was so different than his first wife.

Second, Brightman, as it turns out, actually did want children and went to great lengths to have them with her long-time partner, Frank Peterson. She had two miscarriages, an ectopic pregnancy, and four rounds of in vitro fertilization (IVF). In the end, she was unable to have children, as she described.

If motherhood had happened, it would have been lovely. I am extremely good with my nieces, so I think I'd have been a good mother. I tried everything to have a baby—including IVF—but it wasn't to be (World Entertainment News Network, 2007).

Lloyd Webber's desire to have children seems to be more about his desire to atone for abandoning his first two children when he went off with Brightman. His friend, Peter Brown, said that Madeleine was "the best thing that ever happened to him" and "an enormously good influence. With Madeleine, he got another chance to be a father. He was working so much that he ignored his first two children when they were growing up" (cited in Coveney, 1999, p. 323).

Walsh described how Lloyd Webber wanted to have "another shot" at having small children. "He loved small children and he had a lot to share with them" (Walsh, 1989, p. 215).

Interestingly, Lloyd Webber was not around when his fifth child was born. He was at the opening of his *Jeeves* reboot—in Scarborough. His wife was left alone to labor and give birth. Did he run right home after the show? No. *He went on holiday.*

As Isabella was being born, I stayed up there several weeks and had a lovely time looking at buildings in Whitby and other remote parts of Yorkshire during the day, while Alan was slogging away in the theatre. We met up in the evenings and reviewed what was happening. It was a lovely time, like a holiday (cited in Coveney, 1999, p. 336).

What Happened to Brightman?

Lloyd Webber, and his Svengali-like influence, cast such a large shadow that Brightman had to leave the UK to re-establish herself in her own right. The British public was in a time warp. Brightman was forever "that fabulous singer who married the rich bloke" (Craig, 2008). *The Daily Mail*, in a 2008 article, described her rebirth as a performer.

And, boy, has she worked hard at it, in all sorts of surprising directions, with a thrilling range of musical moods on *Symphony* and the release next month of her film-acting debut in the musical thriller, *Repo! The Genetic Opera* (Paton, 2008).

Post-split, Brightman went first to New York to star in *Aspects of Love*. Brightman described how she was very much in Lloyd Webber's shadow throughout their marriage and their divorce.

> I was quite middle-aged when I was younger. I always felt older than my years, maybe because I was married to someone older. I think it's typical of women when they love someone that they move themselves into that person's life and go with that (Paton, 2008).

The move to America turned out to be good for her. It gave her a chance to start again.

> ... it was a painful time. The end of a marriage always is. Our time together was a very positive and creative phase for me. With hindsight, moving to America afterwards was a good thing. I started again and won success in a country where I was an unknown. On a personal level, though, I had to practically rebuild myself ... (Craig, 2008).

Brightman later moved to Germany and began to forge her own career, moving even further out of Lloyd Webber's shadow.

> When I moved from Britain to Germany at the beginning of the 1990s, all my friends were involved with techno, and suddenly I was being introduced to younger types of music and a different way of doing things. ... And I'm having a lot of fun now (Paton, 2008).

On her website, Brightman also described her moves to first America, then Germany, and her growing independence during this time.

> By 1990, Brightman played the lead in Lloyd Webber's *Aspects of Love*, opposite Michael Ball, before transferring to Broadway.

Perhaps the most poignant declaration of independence came in the form of her second solo album from this period, an eclectic but personal collection of folk-rock songs that she hand-picked. It was a departure from musical theater, and indeed, a departure from Lloyd Webber himself. More tellingly, the album bore a most prescient title: *As I Came of Age* (Brightman, n.d.).

"Friends Forever"

Brightman's star has continued to rise in the time since her divorce from Lloyd Webber. Her concerts in the U.S. have sold more than Elton John and The Rolling Stones. She's performed at the opening ceremony of the Olympic Games—twice (the only artist to do so).

In 1997, Brightman's duet with Andrei Bocelli, Time to Say Goodbye, was a huge international hit, and went platinum five times. She even made a triumphal return to the UK. At a sell-out concert at Albert Hall, Lloyd Webber was in the audience. She invited him to join her on stage.

> Sarah beckoned on a sheepish-looking man in shirt-sleeves to play the piano. "I'm so glad you could come," she gushed. "I only live round the corner, so I'd not much excuse" (Coveney, 1999, p. 231).

Brightman sang a Lloyd Webber and Don Black song for the Barcelona Olympics, *Amigos para Siempre* (Friends Forever), which Coveney noted, "summed up her new relationship with Andrew" (p. 232). She performed Lloyd Webber's music all over the world, and recorded two albums of his greatest hits. She then struck out on her own (Coveney, 1999, p. 230).

Lloyd Webber's star, in contrast to Brightman's, has dimmed somewhat. Yes, he has won some wonderful awards: a knighthood and a barony. He's written other musicals. But he's never again achieved the success he had with Brightman and *Phantom*. In fact, he's had several notable failures. He's still making money, but has had less artistic success.

Brightman has been gracious about the man who cast her aside in every interview I've come across. She may say different things in private, but has not publicly badmouthed him. A brilliant moment occurred when Brightman, the cast-off wife, was the one who presented Lloyd Webber's Kennedy Center Honors. Her speech was downright kind.

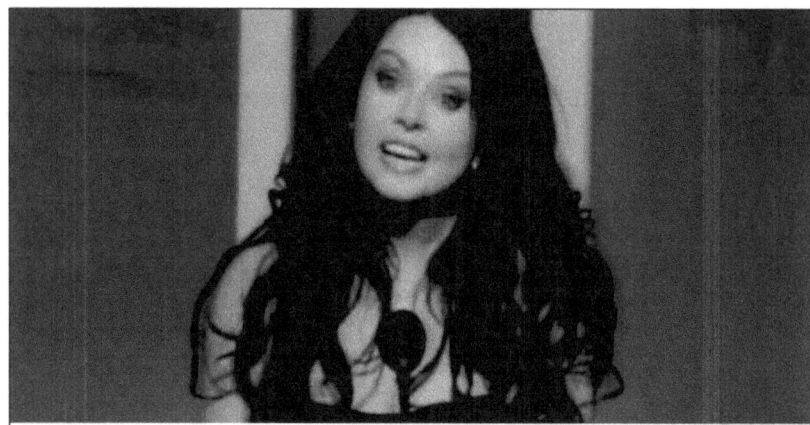

Brightman presenting Lloyd Webber his Kennedy Center Honors. https://www.youtube.com/watch?v=sTQ4CZxyQxs&list=RDR2HrHFbEy5w&index=16

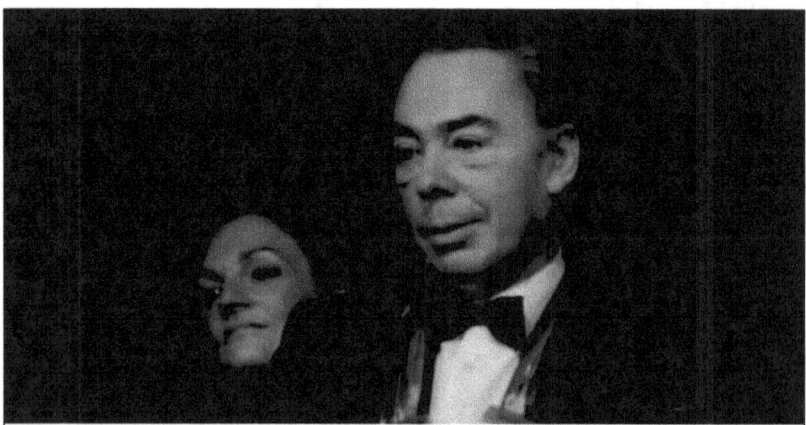

Lloyd Webber looks more dyspeptic than usual during her speech, probably worried about what she would say.

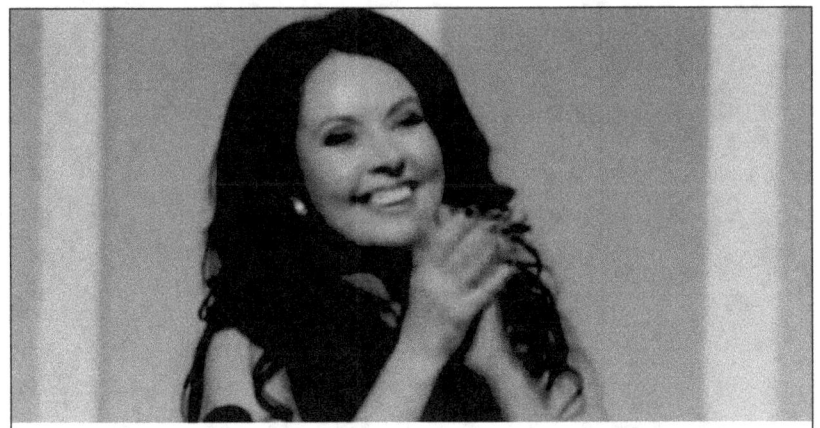

Brightman cheers him on during a standing ovation.

I have been privileged to know Andrew now for 26 years. And have seen many sides to this complex and unique man. I have seen the searching and brilliant mind that has found hit shows in the pages of the Old Testament or the poems of T.S. Eliot. He is by terms, and Andrew don't kill me for saying this, funny, boyish, self-effacing, adorable, passionate, complicated, exasperating, lovable, explosive, demanding, innovative, and often extremely outrageous.

When he is composing, it only looks as if he is in the room with you. In reality, he is in some exotic place far, far away, where there is only him and the notes. But when he comes back, he brings with him music that is exciting, moving, and beautiful. That is why tonight, and every night, people around the world are going to see Andrew Lloyd Webber shows, and will continue to do so, long after this curtain has come down, long after all of us here have made our final curtain call, because his music of the night is music for all time (Brightman, 2006/2011).

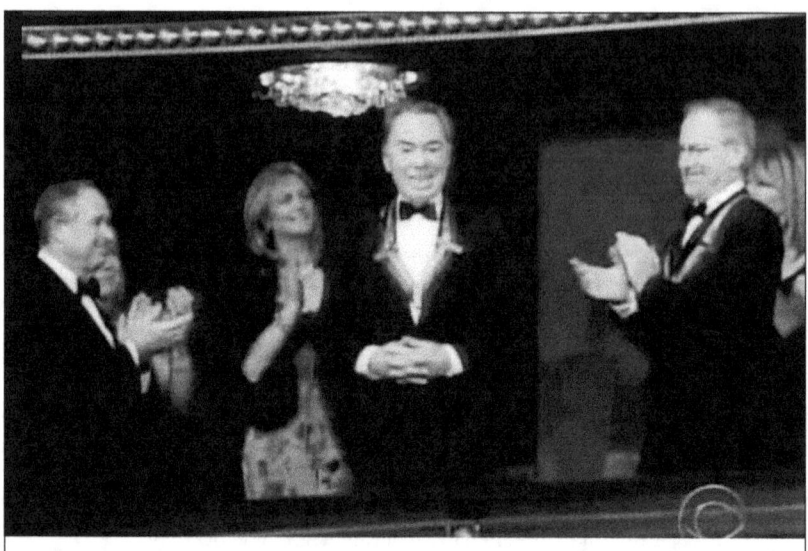

Lloyd Webber is genuinely pleased to receive a standing ovation for his life's work. Fellow honoree, Steven Spielberg, is on his right. https://www.youtube.com/watch?v=sTQ4CZxyQxs

Lloyd Webber has not always been kind in return. Some think that he delayed the *Phantom* movie so that she couldn't be in it. And as a result of their divorce, she had to leave the UK to get away from his influence.

In a rather blue interview with Lloyd Webber on the Jonathan Ross show, Ross referenced comment Brightman had made in an earlier interview on his show. He mentioned that Brightman said Lloyd Webber was "very well-endowed." I wasn't sure I had heard that correctly and went back found her original interview. Brightman was (oddly) defending Lloyd Webber when she made the comment, and told Ross about why she found Lloyd Webber attractive. She indicated that she would not have gone into musical theater were it not for her relationship with Lloyd Webber, and has not returned to that world, even though there have probably been many opportunities for her to do so. This interview says a lot about their ongoing relationship.

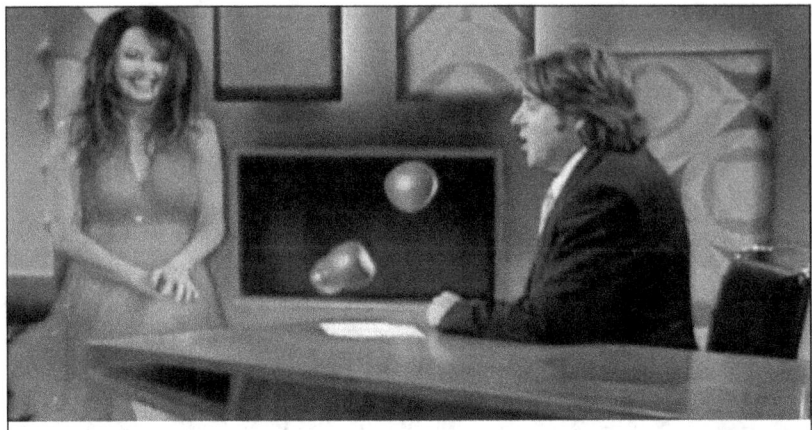

Sarah Brightman on the Jonathan Ross show.
https://www.youtube.com/watch?v=F4dQPNWBMzk

Jonathan Ross: Did you enjoy *Phantom* or did you get tired of it even if it's a real crowd pleaser?

SB: You become tired, because they're quite tough, especially when you're doing the 6 or 8 performances a week. It's been a long time ago, for me. You have to hold focus with your audience and explain your story to them. You have to be the story, be the character. No, you don't get tired of that within the performance at all. You just carry through.

JR: I've never seen *Phantom of the Opera*.

SB: No. You're like me. I don't get to see musicals very much.

JR: I went to see *Cats* once. I didn't enjoy it. It wasn't when you were in it. It was in New York.

SB: But I wouldn't have minded if I was in it. I ended up in musical theater because I needed a job. I've only been in three musicals. ...

JR: I feel very sorry for him [Lloyd Webber]. He's doing very well, obviously, he's done well for himself. But he always gets held up as a bloke who looks weird ... and people have made jokes about him being ugly. I've made jokes. But I've seen him in person and he doesn't look too bad.

SB: He doesn't look bad at all. He's got the most beautiful eyes. When I first met him, he was much, much younger, he had this amazing face. Gorgeous. And he still has that look about him, although he's much, much older. And he's really great with women. When he talks to women, he makes them feel really good and happy about themselves, and engages in conversation, which is wonderful.

JR: Let's say he's going to make a move, what kind of technique did he use on you?

SB: He's just gentle and lovely, and very appreciative of the person he's talking to.

JR: Of your company.

SB: Yes.

JR: And when does he make his move?

SB: Stop it. He's not like that. Maybe that's what you would do. ...

JR: Andrew Lloyd Webber, I met him a couple of weeks ago, and was interviewing him on a radio show that I do, and I asked him a question about something, and I think he thought I'd asked him something else. And he was then saying that you had gone on record to say he was fabulously well-endowed.

SB: [Sigh]

JR: But what a nice thing to say about a former partner because normally people are somewhat dismissive of those they've been with in the past. But to actually big 'im up, so to speak, is a nice thing to do.

SB: It wasn't done on purpose. Or it hadn't been calculated. I was just put in a situation where I thought "this isn't nice," and "there are great things about this guy." And apart from that, but that's the thing that came out.

JR: Well, all men are happy to have that spoken about.

SB: He wasn't happy. I had his lawyers on the phone the next morning.

JR: Hold on. So you said he was packin' the big load, and then he got his lawyers to follow up.

SB: Yes. They phoned. And they were very embarrassed and I said, "Look, this is ridiculous. Don't be so silly," and put the phone down. But then a week later, the whole the British female population were looking at him differently. And he changed his tune and it was fine. It was alright.

JR: Andrew Lunchbox Webber

SB: Stop it. You're just jealous.

JR: I'm not jealous. I'm enormous. I am. I'm very well-endowed.

SB: That's very lucky. That's not bad, I have to say.

Lloyd Webber was on Ross' show after this interview. When asked about it, Lloyd Webber responded with filthy double entendre: "Sarah always had a big mouth." The audience did not miss his double meaning and responded with howls and cheers. He was probably mad about what she said earlier, and made a highly salacious and mean-spirited response back.

Their Ongoing Relationship

As for how they have continued to work together since their break up, Brightman continues to respond with grace.

We can be at war, but when the beauty of art is revealed, it overrides the personal stuff. If it's good, everyone wants to work on it. That's it. ... And we just got on with it, fine (SB talks Lloyd Webber marriage & more, 2013).

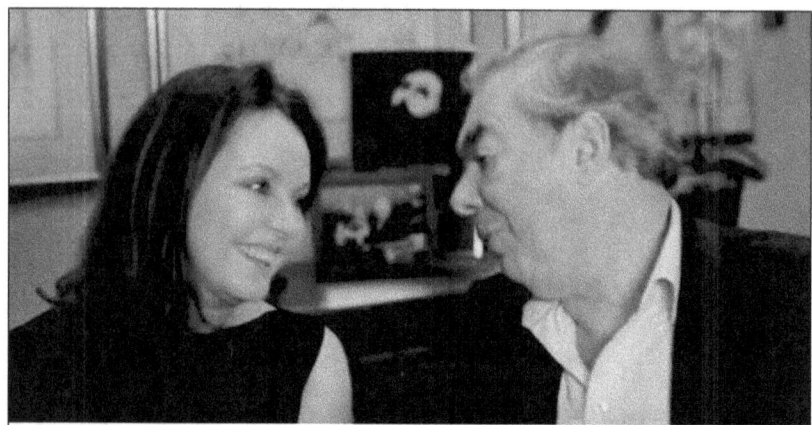

Sarah Brightman and Andrew Lloyd Webber in their first interview together since their split in celebration of the 25th anniversary of *Phantom*. https://www.youtube.com/watch?v=aRdkbMzJJDA

However complex their relationship remains, Brightman and Lloyd Webber continue to be bound together, professionally and personally, as Brightman describes in her BBC interview in the documentary, *Behind the Mask*.

> When I look back on it, and I'm with Andrew and we're out for lunch or having a laugh or a drink, or whatever, it was amazing time, incredibly creative, in fact, incredibly positive things came out of it, so for all the little negative things that happened, we're all still standing, we're all still successful, we're all still friends (*Behind the Mask*, part 8).

Their Legacy Lives On

In 2015, the first Andrew Lloyd Webber Foundation Sarah Brightman Music Scholarships were awarded. These scholarships support students in postgraduate studies at the Royal Northern College of Music in the two-year Master of Music Program.

CHAPTER 9

Does Andrew Lloyd Webber Plagiarize His Work?

Charges of plagiarism have dogged Lloyd Webber for decades. Plagiarism is the most serious charge that can be leveled at any writer. Any composer with Lloyd Webber's level of success is bound to have people who claim that he (or she) stole their work. Most of these claims are proven groundless, but they take up a lot of time and energy for everyone involved. For Lloyd Webber, however, claims of plagiarism have been remarkably persistent. They are even on his Wikipedia page.

Musical Genius?

Or Plagiarist?

YouTube videos like this point out musical similarities. But is it plagiarism?
https://www.youtube.com/watch?v=wW5wwi4ahLc

Biographer Michael Walsh describes how two key people have assiduously defended Lloyd Webber against charges of borrowing the melodies of others. David Cullen, Lloyd Webber's long-time orchestrator, said,

> Andrew has this terrific melodic gift, and I do very much resent people criticizing him for borrowing and stealing (cited in Walsh, 1989, p. 268).

His brother, Julian Lloyd Webber, a concert cellist, also weighed in.

> It's impossible to avoid quoting other bits of tunes when writing tonal music. But Andrew's become so neurotic about this now that he gets everything checked out. You can hardly blame him when obscure people from Denver, Colorado, keep coming out and saying they wrote the same tune as his years before (cited in Walsh, 1989, p. 268).

Musicologist John Snelson (2004) also makes a similar point.

> Lloyd Webber's path to reconciling the creation of a personal musical space with the retention of a sense of cultural continuity has been to reshape the past to his own ends; it is an aesthetic of cultural collage and comment. The use of such musical references, re-readings, and reworkings shows a broader continuum of possibilities than the simple dichotomy of originality vs. plagiarism suggests (e-page).

Drawing from Classical Music

Some have claimed that the melodies of several Lloyd Webber songs were similar to classical music pieces. Most of these pieces have been in the public domain for many years, so "borrowing" their melodies is not plagiarism, nor is it legally wrong. In fact, many popular songs have been riffs off of melodies taken from classical pieces. Lloyd Webber certainly isn't the first to be inspired by classical music.

There are many examples of popular composers borrowing from classical music. Musicologist John Snelson (2004) describes how borrowing from the works of others was common practice in the 19th and 20th century. "In bringing into being a 'new' work there is inevitably an influence from what gone before ... the creative process and its evaluation are most commonly seen to exist within the framework of their identification with the past."

> Musical cognates have been cited across such a broad range of composers as Mendelssohn, ... Brahms, ... Sondheim, ...

94

Ravel, Gershwin, Rodgers, ... Vaughan Williams, J.S. Bach, Stravinsky, and frequently, Prokofiev and Puccini. Clearly Lloyd Webber's relationship with past musical repertory is an important one, and often so self-evident as to make covert borrowing unlikely. ... What increasingly emerges in studying his works is a core feature of resynthesizing existing materials to create new musical drama through changed juxtapositions.

Of significance for Lloyd Webber, in particular, is the trend to create rock versions of an art repertory works in the classic rock of the late 1960s and the 1970s.

Snelson described how 2 to 5 bars of I'd Be Surprisingly Good for You from *Evita* matches 2 to 5 bars of the Beatles' Yesterday, but with substantially different rhythm. He also noted that the Lloyd Webber/ Rice single 1969 borrows from Beethoven's *Für Elise*, and Down Through the Summer borrows from the opening phrases of the second movement of Dvorak's New World Symphony. A few other examples have been more contentious.

Mendelssohn's Violin Concerto E minor v. I Don't Know How to Love Him

One oft-cited example of Lloyd Webber's borrowing from classical music was the Mendelssohn Violin Concerto in E minor and I Don't Know How to Love Him from *Jesus Christ Superstar*. Composer Jack Androdanovic offered his analysis.

From a musical standpoint, the resemblance between the pop melody and the concerto is so obvious and continues through such an extended passage (some seven bars) that any claim to coincidence is untenable.

However, Lloyd Webber's version made it a new work.

But the effect of the reworking has provided Lloyd Webber with a significant and effective number for his repertory, and the Mendelssohn source is easily overshadowed by the resulting pop-folk ballad.

95

Alexandrovics went into much greater detail about the technical aspects of the similarities.

> If we look at the melodic intervals, we can see there are some very stark similarities.
>
> ♦ Both melodies begin on the third of accompanying tonic chord (Mendelsohn has modulated to C major. I Don't Know How to Love Him is in D major).
>
> ♦ They both rise a semitone before descending. Each pattern of descent is slightly different until both melodies leap to a major sixth above the tonic. This is a B in the case of Mendelsohn, and an A in Webber.
>
> ♦ They both then slide down a major second to finish the phrase. Differing patterns of descent then occur, yet both melodies then move to two held notes, this time holding the third above the tonic before sliding down a major second [bullets added].

Although similar, even if his use was deliberate, it's not illegal.

> It is now obvious to me that these melodies are much more similar than I imagined before careful analysis. Webber himself has never commented upon this, and the music of Mendelsohn is in the public domain, which means using its melodies is legal (Alexandrovics, n.d.).

So how does an existing piece get incorporated into a new work? Musicologist Snelson (2004) explains.

> There are many ways in which a musical element from an existing piece of repertory can become incorporated into a new work. It may be through sheer coincidence: such things do happen, especially when there are similarities of musical vocabulary and thought. This is even more likely when a style imposes limitations on a range of music: for example, the choice of a strophic, twelve-bar blues as the basis for a pop song immediately draws certain boundaries (e-page).

Snelson noted that David Whelton, then managing director of the Philharmonia Orchestra in London, defended Lloyd Webber from charges of plagiarism, noting that he metamorphizes melodies and makes them his own.

> [It is] unfair to argue that the tunes are not his own. ... In every age you have tonal composers whose own ideas must have an awareness of the ideas of others. As Elgar said of the process: "It is in the air, all around me" (cited in Snelson, 2004, e-page).

That may be true. When it comes to copyright infringement, however, "In the air, all around me" is not likely going to be much of a legal defense.

What Does the Law Say?
Copyright Infringement v. Fair Use

What about "borrowing" from music that is not public domain, where copyright laws are still in force? Most of the biographers that have discussed the plagiarism issue are either theater critics or musicologists. They are not necessarily familiar with some of the ins and outs of copyright law. I'm not an attorney, but I am an editor, and I have to work with U.S. copyright law every day. It's helpful to consider the allegations of plagiarism against Lloyd Webber in light of the laws pertaining to fair use. In other words, in some situations, it's fair use (i.e., not plagiarism) to use a portion of someone's work. However, the line for what is acceptable vs. copyright infringement is often quite blurry.

A Short History of Copyright Law

Copyright law has an interesting history in the U.S. It was considered so important to the new Republic that it was drafted even before the Bill of Rights. The reason for this? The Founding Fathers felt that it was essential that people engaged in creative enterprises be allowed to profit from their works. If these works were not protected, people would have no incentive to do creative things, and this would ultimately hamper the growth of the fledgling country. (It probably didn't hurt that at least two of the Founders, Jefferson and Franklin, were writers and amateur inventors.)

Inherent in the copyright laws was something called public domain, which set a limit to how long a creative work would be protected under copyright law. After a period of 70 years after the death of the creator, the copyright would transfer and the work would be considered public domain, which meant that it was then free to use without obtaining permission from the original author.

U.S. copyright law ensures that authors' expressions are protected. That means if someone uses a composer's exact melody or sequence of notes, then that person needs permission to use more than what can be considered fair use. According to the fair-use rule, authors may make limited use of others' material without permission. But the guidelines for what constitutes fair use are much vaguer than you might suspect. Indeed, fair use is considered an "affirmative defense," meaning that the burden of proof is on the person using someone's work to demonstrate that his or her use of another composer's materials falls within these guidelines.

Four Guidelines for Fair Use

There are four guidelines that determine whether something falls under fair use. I'll briefly describe each of these (Kendall-Tackett, 2005).

Is the Work Transformative?

Transformative means that it adds to or extends the existing work (e.g., a comment, criticism, or parody of the original). This can often be a key factor that overrides other considerations. If the new work merely substitutes for the original, then it is less likely to be considered fair use.

What is the Nature of the Prior Work?

Unpublished work has more protection than published work. This means that someone cannot use unpublished work without the author's express permission. Using someone's unpublished materials without permission, and simply citing them, is not fair use. Authors should always be able to publish their work first. If the publication of their materials denies the author them that opportunity, then that use infringes on their copyright.

What is the Amount and Substantiality of the Material Used?

How much can you quote without permission? As an example from writing, the American Psychological Association, in an attempt to provide some rough guidelines, allows authors to cite 400 words in single-text extracts, or 800 words in a series of text extracts, without permission (American Psychological Association, 2010). However, that guideline does not apply to every publisher, and requirements for obtaining permission vary between publishers and other copyright holders.

The nature of the work also influences what someone is allowed to use without permission. If it's a large proportion of a short work (e.g., song lyric or poem), or it's key, then even a few bars of a song, or a few lines of a poem, may not be fair use. That why in discussing copyright infringement in music, even a few bars can be considered plagiarism. Even in longer works, if the part that copied is the critical heart of the work, then it may not be fair use.

Will the Use of the New Work Impact the Market Value of the Original Work?

If the work has commercial value, will the new work impact potential sales for the copyright holder? This guideline includes not only the economic impact of use of the material, but the impact if others were to do the same. Copyright may also apply to any derivative work, or a work that is so similar to the original that it could impact the sale of the original (e.g., writing a play with a plot highly similar to a recently published novel).

Summary

Fair use allows some latitude in using other people's work, but it is a fuzzy boundary. If in doubt, and the work is not public domain, authors need to ask permission from the copyright holder. Even with permission, authors of new works must acknowledge the copyright holder with the name of the copyright holder, the name of the publication, year of publication, and the wording "Used with permission."

Lloyd Webber v. Composers: Cases that Went to Court

Although many have accused Lloyd Webber of plagiarism, only two cases against Lloyd Webber went to court: one in the U.S. and one in UK. In both cases, Lloyd Webber prevailed. Below is a brief summary of those cases.

Brett v. Lloyd Webber

John Brett (Brett v. Lloyd Webber, cited in Snelson, 2004) claimed that the *Phantom* theme song and Angel of Music were taken from copies of tapes he had sent to Tim Rice and Elaine Paige on July 29 and August 7, 1985. The case was dropped because the songs had been played at Lloyd Webber's music festival, Sydmonton, on July 5th of the same year, demonstrating that the songs were already written by the time Rice and Paige received the tapes.

Repp v. Lloyd Webber

A more serious case was the lawsuit filed by Ray Repp. Repp claimed that Lloyd Webber plagiarized the *Phantom* theme from a hymn he wrote in

1978. Repp's case had more substance than Brett's. Repp claimed that the melody from the *Phantom* theme had been taken from a song he wrote called Till You. Repp's case lasted nearly a decade and came to court in 1998. Lloyd Webber went to court and described how he composed the melody with Brightman by his side (Walsh, 1989, p. 271).

The jury eventually concluded that Repp's performances of his work, and its distribution on cassette, were on such a limited scale (at religious conventions and Catholic churches) that Lloyd Webber was unlikely to have heard it. Nevertheless, expert testimony acknowledged its similarity, as Snelson describes.

> Expert musicologist evidence presented for Repp made a convincing case for the similarities of melodic motifs, rhythms, and phrase structure; yet "substantial similarity" was not in itself proof of infringement (knowing or otherwise) of copyright (Snelson, 2004, e-page).

Even though Lloyd Webber prevailed, both cases highlight the difficulties inherent in deciding whether material has been plagiarized. Nonetheless, these cases show the legal shades of gray. In Repp v. Lloyd Webber, it all came down to access. Lloyd Webber couldn't have plagiarized the work because he was unlikely to have heard it (Snelson, 2004).

Girl of the Golden West v. **Music of the Night**

Surprisingly, the estate of Giacomo Puccini brought a case that did have merit. The estate claimed that Lloyd Webber borrowed the melody for Music of the Night from Puccini's opera, *La Fanciulla del West* (*Girl of the Golden West*). The disputed melody is *Quello che Tacete*, sung by the character Johnson at the end of the first act. Given the age of piece, I'm surprised that it wasn't in public domain. Apparently, it wasn't, and the estate claimed copyright infringement. The case was settled out of court for an undisclosed amount.

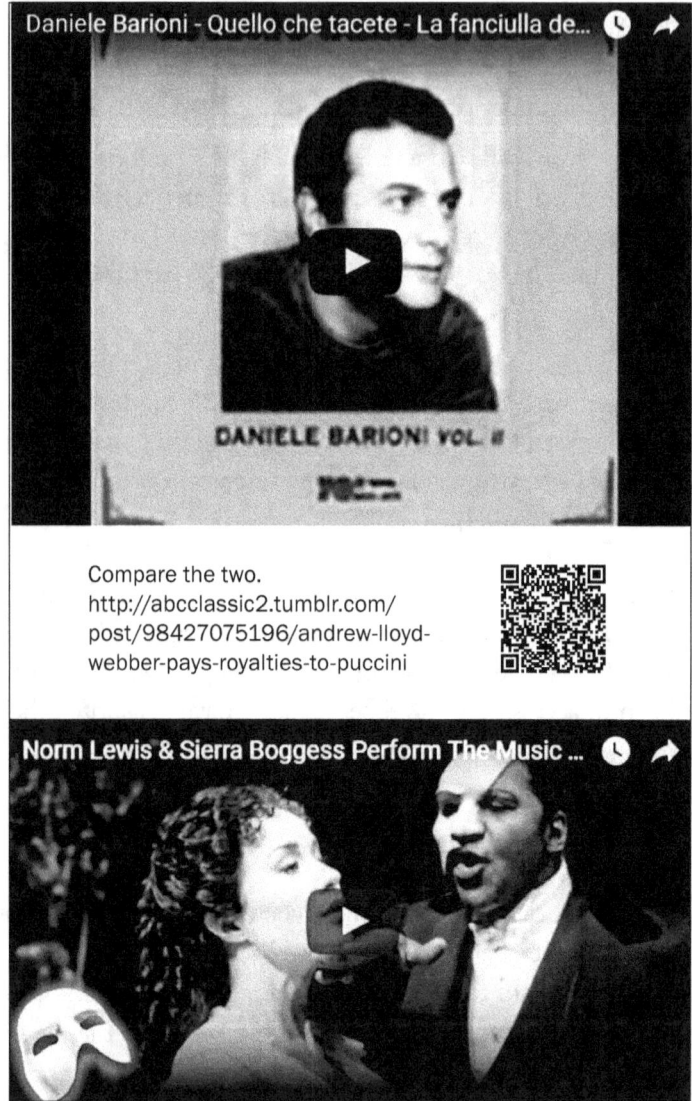

In this very homemade video, you can also hear the similarities in the melodies. The unnamed singer is excellent.

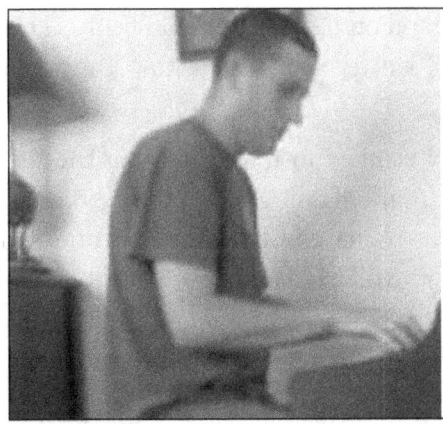

A homemade video plays both melodies side by side. https://www.youtube.com/watch?v=fx1KNRCijCY

Lloyd Webber is a huge Puccini fan. He had likely heard this work sometime in his life, and the melody may have popped into his head as he was working on *Phantom*. A composer on BroadwayWorld.com notes a similar possibility, and states that just because something is similar doesn't mean that it was consciously plagiarized (ClapYo'Hands, 2011).

> ... there are only a certain amount of melodies humans can write before similarities appear. Lloyd Webber, of course, could have had this happen to him, but by the time The Music of the Night was heard by the Puccini estate and challenged, it has already become an instant hit. Why would Lloyd Webber even try and change it when *The Phantom of the Opera* was already taking off so quickly?

Phantom Theme v. Echoes

Although biographers discuss the Brett and Repp cases, none mentions Pink Floyd's song, Echoes, which was published in 1971. This is the most compelling case in terms of copyright infringement. Like the *Phantom* theme, Echoes is a series of ascending and descending chromatic scales. Echoes is clearly similar to the opening bars of *The Phantom of the Opera* theme. You can hear both on the YouTube video

103

at the beginning of this chapter and on the YouTube clip below. The opening phrase is 10 bars that are repeated throughout the song. Wikipedia describes it like this.

> Roger Waters has repeatedly claimed in interviews that the signature descending/ascending half-tone chord progression from *Phantom's* title song was plagiarised from the bass line of a track on the 1971 Pink Floyd album *Meddle* called Echoes (Wikipedia, 2017c).

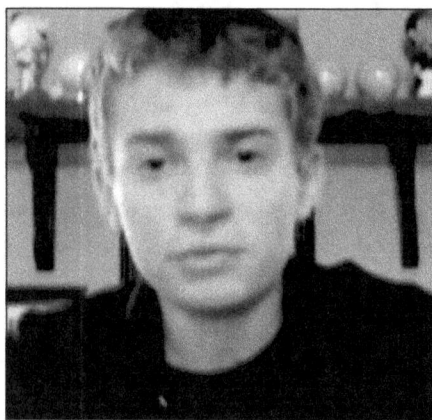

A young YouTuber, Giggan1, offered a detailed comparison of Echoes v. the *Phantom* Theme, including playing them side by side. He makes a good case about the similarities between the two. https://www.youtube.com/watch?v=xkx4ia6Th1A

Some academics have weighed in, including composer Jack Alexandrovics, who described the opening theme as the most recognizable musical motif of the entire musical. Getting into some of the technical detail, he noted:

♦ Echoes is written in C Sharp Minor, and the riff begins on the tonic chord. *Phantom of the Opera* is in B Flat minor, and also begins on the tonic chord. Putting tempo differences aside, the C Sharp Minor and B Flat Minor Chords respectively hold for a relative equivalent beat.

♦ In the final beat(s) of the bar, a descending chromatic four-note pattern plays, beginning on the tonic note, and finishing a major third below (A major chord in Echoes, and a G flat major in *Phantom*). In this part, the two pieces slightly differ, as the Guitar in Echoes continues from the descending pattern into a run of notes.

♦ The bass guitar and organ, however, continue the pattern, playing the A Major chord for 3 beats before ascending again back up the chromatic scale to the C Sharp Minor tonic. *Phantom of the Opera* follows suit, excluding the guitar passage. It holds the G Flat for the equivalent amount of beats before once again ascending to the tonic [bullets added].

This is exactly the kind of evidence musicologists would provide in a court case. His conclusion?

It seems undoubtable to me that this is a conscious use of someone else's work. Of course, it has never been admitted by Webber, and this is the required testimony to learn the absolute truth.

While Alexandrovics thought use of Mendelssohn was fair use, he came to the opposite conclusion regarding *Phantom*.

I take an opposite approach, however, to *Phantom*, purely on the grounds that its similarity is so obvious, and its function in each work so integral and well-known, that it deserves credit to the original author. Although both pieces do take different directions after the ostinato has played, both are repeated consistently and resonate in the audience's mind till long after they are first presented, and eventually become completely associated with whichever version the audience member has heard, something like this again could—and should—be potentially amended by admitting appropriation of an idea, or considered an act of paying "homage" to a great progressive rock piece along with compositional credits and potential compensation due to the immense revenue it has earned (Alexandrovics, n.d.).

Roger Waters, composer of Echoes, also weighed in in an interview.

... I couldn't believe it when I heard it. ... It's the same structure and it's the same notes and it's the same everything. Bastard. It probably is actionable. It really is! But I think that life's too short to bother with suing Andrew f**king Lloyd Webber (Houwelling, 1992).

Although Waters did not sue, he took revenge with his pen, as he composed this little ditty.

> We cower in our shelters, with our hands over our ears
> Lloyd Webber's awful stuff runs for years and years and years
> An earthquake hits the theatre, but the operetta lingers
> Then the piano lid comes down and breaks his f**king fingers
>
> *It's A Miracle* – Roger Waters

Self-Borrowing

Biographers Michael Walsh (1989) and Michael Coveney (1999) both describe Lloyd Webber's habit of taking songs from one musical, re-working them, and using them in something else. In some ways, that is admirable. If a show is not a hit, use the song somewhere else (e.g., some of Lloyd Webber's score for the *Odessa Files* found its way into *Evita*), as Snelson notes.

> Indeed, self-borrowing is one Lloyd Webber technique that needs considering in relation to the more general questions of musical borrowing his work has provoked (e-page).

Generally speaking, self-borrowing isn't plagiarism. In the academic world, the practice is frowned upon and is called "self-plagiarism." Frowning aside, it's not illegal. As Walsh points out, Lloyd Webber often improves the song, and "there is no law against stealing from yourself" (Walsh, 1989, p. 14). Walsh provides many examples of tunes written by Lloyd Webber with lyrics by Tim Rice. A song called Kansas Morning became I Don't Know How to Love Him. A song from *Jeeves* became a song in *Variations*, and later into the "song" part of *Song and Dance*. So far, this isn't a problem.

Lloyd Webber's self-borrowing became a problem was when he took melodies from one musical that already had lyrics, discarded the lyrics, and used the melody somewhere else. He's done this in at least two cases that biographers have documented. Once with Tim Rice, and a second time with Trevor Nunn.

Tim Rice and *Cricket*

Rice collaborated with Lloyd Webber on a short musical called *Cricket* for the Queen's 60th birthday. Once they collaborated on this project, the music and lyrics joined together and became a new product. It was "theirs," not "his." And once the music and lyrics were in tangible form copyright law applied.

However, Lloyd Webber took most of the melodies composed for *Cricket*, which I'm sure he thought of as "his," and re-used them in *Aspects of Love*, with another lyricist. This is possibly an intellectual property violation. The key issue would be whether the author could profit from his work. Once Lloyd Webber reused the melodies somewhere else, Rice's lyrics essentially became worthless. In other words, he could no longer profit from his work because of what Lloyd Webber did. Rice was, understandingly, very upset by Lloyd Webber's casual snatching of the melodies, but probably never realized that he may have had a legal case. He simply stopped collaborating with Lloyd Webber.

According to Walsh, Lloyd Webber "raided" *Cricket* for tunes and used them in *Aspects of Love*, much to Rice's "extreme annoyance." Lloyd Webber claimed in a program note for *Aspects* that "all of the principal melodies" were written in his collaboration with his new lyricists. Not true, according to Rice, who recognized four or five melodies from *Cricket*. *Aspects of Love* destroyed any chance Rice had of using his work. Lloyd Webber's actions didn't surprise Rice any more, but he hoped things would be different this time.

Whatever hopes Rice had of someday staging an expanded *Cricket* were destroyed; gone too was any likelihood that any of the *Cricket* songs, with Rice's original lyrics, would be covered by other singers on records. *Cricket* was a total loss, and Rice felt hurt and betrayed (Walsh, 1989, pp. 220-221).

Trevor Nunn and *Aspects of Love*

Amazingly, he did the same thing to Trevor Nunn, who had collaborated with him on the first version of *Aspects*, which pre-dated *Phantom*. Trevor Nunn wrote the lyrics for *Aspects* and Lloyd Webber took the melodies and used them in *Phantom*. Nunn learned about the swap when *Phantom* was presented in workshop form at Sydmonton. The melodies were,

> now recycled with completely different words, without even a by-your-leave. So that was how Lloyd Webber fired people: so much for Nunn as lyricist for *Aspects*. It was a hard lesson to learn, and a hard, brutally public way to learn it (Walsh, 1989, p. 176).

Nunn later described it as a bitter pill. Still, he stayed involved with the project, hoping Lloyd Webber would let him be part of it.

Nunn was brought in to direct *Phantom* after Hal Prince was fired. It didn't last long, according to Walsh, and some of the issue may have had to do with the way Lloyd Webber casually discarded his lyrics. Lloyd Webber and Nunn finally had a major falling out, which almost came to blows. Some thought it had to do with the "artistic wasteland of *Starlight Express*." Or it might have been about "Nunn's resentment over the cavalier way Lloyd Webber had treated their songs for *Aspects of Love*, summarily snatching the music out from under Nunn's words and reusing them in *Phantom*" (Walsh, 1989, p. 178).

The process of Lloyd Webber taking back his music meant that Nunn's lyrics also became worthless. Given what we know about fair use, both Rice and Nunn may have had a case. Their intellectual property became worthless after Lloyd Webber did a runner with the melodies. At the very least, it's a genuinely crappy way to treat collaborators. Lloyd Webber's behavior could also be legally actionable, although it may fall within one of the gray areas of fair use.

Summary

When I first started researching this chapter, I assumed that the various lawsuits that came up against Lloyd Webber were bogus. Why would someone in his position take the risk? After reading through the documents cited in this chapter, however, Roger Waters appears to have a legitimate case. Whether Lloyd Webber's intentionally used Waters' song is impossible to say. But the similarities are undeniable, and unlike Repp's music with a more niche audience, Lloyd Webber was quite likely to have heard Echoes at some point in his life.

In addition, applying copyright law to the Rice and Nunn's lyrics suggests that Lloyd Webber's action had direct negative financial impact on them. At the very least, they were entitled to some compensation for their labors. Had they felt so inclined, they may have been able to pursue their cases in court.

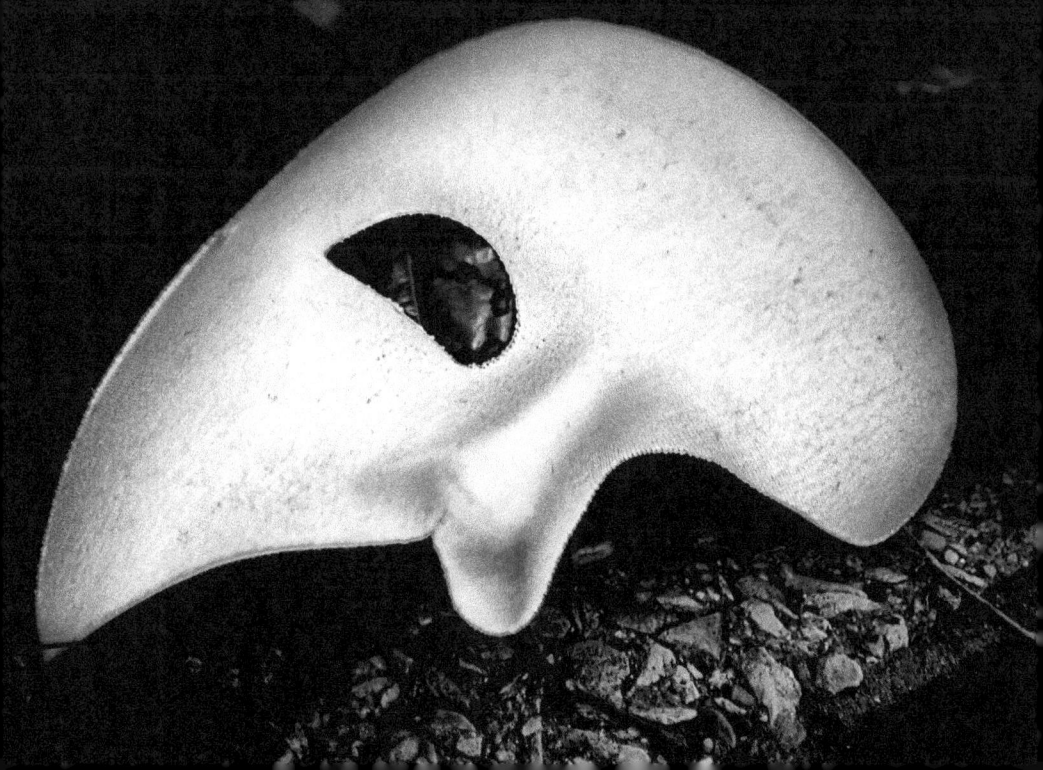

SECTION II
Phantom on Film

CHAPTER 10

Phantom Goes from Stage to Film

The film version of *Phantom* came out amidst controversy and fanfare in 2004, 18 years after its introduction on the London stage. The production of the movie was delayed, partly due to the split up of Lloyd Webber and Brightman. Lloyd Webber said it was "too painful" for him to continue, a somewhat surprising statement considering that Lloyd Webber initiated the break up of his marriage. Another factor was concern that the film would impact ticket sales of the live production. Lloyd Webber's production company needn't have worried about the film hampering sales. Ticket sales for the Broadway version of *Phantom* increased by 30% after the film came out (Dezell, 2005).

Fans were particularly concerned about what Joel Schumacher would do to their beloved story. Protestors also wanted to see Sarah Brightman and Michael Crawford in the roles that they had created. Alas, it was not to be.

Postponement

A film version of *Phantom* was originally slated to come out in 1991. Another 13 years elapsed before it was released. In a September 10, 1990 article, David Fox writes about a postponement of the film. The headline of the article was "Lloyd Webber postpones filming of *Phantom*: The composer says Sarah Brightman will still star." The couple had broken up the previous July. The announcement of postponement led to speculation Brightman would be dropped from the lead. The composer claimed that that would not happen. Lloyd Webber's longtime associate, publicist and friend, Peter Brown, told *The Times* that the movie will indeed be delayed, but he insisted that Brightman would be in the film singing the role that Lloyd Webber wrote "expressly for her." Brown said that Lloyd Webber "emphasized that neither he nor Sarah Brightman would wish the breakdown of their marriage to, in any way, affect their continuing professional relationship" (Fox, 1990).

The article noted that there were "a number of commercial issues" that needed to be worked out between The Really Useful Group and Warner Bros, but that they were confident that they would be, and that shooting could commence during the Summer of 1991, with the original cast.

> The cast, he stated, means Michael Crawford repeating his starring role as the Phantom and Brightman as opera singer, Christine Daae, the woman of the Phantom's desire.

Not exactly how it played out. The movie was not released until 2004 (Fox, 1990).

One of the first decisions that Lloyd Webber made, after the first deal with Warner Brothers fell apart, was to regain the full rights to the film version. In earlier talks with film executives, there was some concern that a film that was 99% singing would not work. Lloyd Webber felt that it would since it had worked so well on the stage. Lloyd Webber wanted to maintain full creative control over the film version of *Phantom*.

The Michael Crawford Phantom Movie Campaign

Surprisingly, *Phantom* fans (or Phans, as they came to be known) generated most of the controversy about the film version. Phans launched an Internet campaign designed to persuade studio executives at Warner

Brothers to cast Michael Crawford in the role of Phantom in the film version. According to *The LA Times*, the fans were told to trust the judgment of the studio.

> "Trust their judgment?" the fans ask incredulously. After waiting all these years only to hear that the filmmakers are thinking the unthinkable: casting a "box-office draw"— Antonio Bandera is the most frequently mentioned—in place of Crawford? How dare they? (Welkos, 1999).

This led fans to form the Michael Crawford Phantom Movie Campaign. This group used several means to voice their outrage, including rallies outside of Warner Bros, and paid advertisements in trade publications, such as *Variety* and *Hollywood Reporter*. In 1998, they launched the fan-operated website: www.phantommovie.com.

Diane Flogerzi, a program analyst for the FAA (Federal Aviation Association), launched the site when she heard that Crawford might not be cast in the role. She immediately started getting emails from people asking what they could do. To raise money, they have sponsored Internet raffles, and they sold tote bags and shirts with slogans like "Anyone for President—Michael Crawford for Phantom." In *The Los Angeles Times*, Crawford said:

> It's very flattering, but it's also slightly embarrassing, not just for me but for the other people mentioned about playing the role. I'm happy that people would like for me to do it, but I'm not on the campaign myself.

> I've done the performance, people have seen it, and if I'm asked to play it again, I'll be more than delighted to do it. But I still say, if I'm meant to do it, I'll do it. And if I don't, the world will go on and it won't matter to me.

> To be historically associated and identified with a role such as the Phantom, in a way that, say, Rex Harrison and Yul Brynner are remembered as Henry Higgins and the King of Siam, is tremendously gratifying, and quite enough in itself.

Crawford graciously offered to provide the voice track for the film.

I love playing the Phantom. And if it meant that just my voice was allowed to be there still, that would make me happy. Because I loved creating the role, I have an enormous amount of love for the character, and the love is still there, every time I sing his songs (Heckman, 1999).

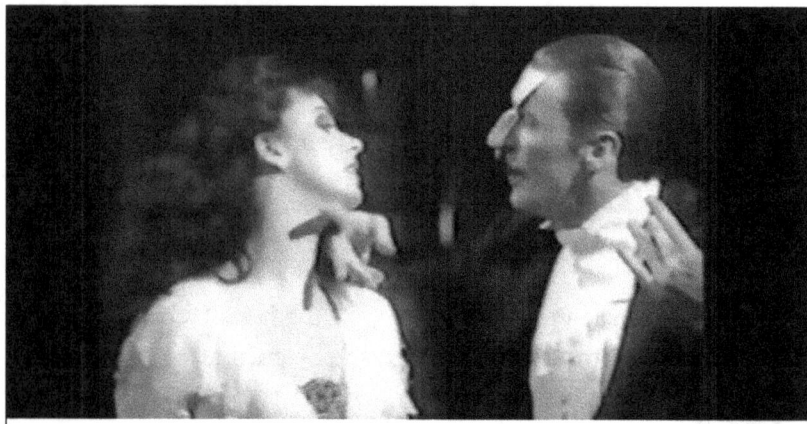

Fans lobbied hard to have Michael Crawford as Phantom in the film version. https://www.youtube.com/watch?v=oZDcSrODALQ

Some of Michael Crawford's fans have taken their obsession with him to an almost frightening level. This is part of a post that one "Phan-girl" wrote about the characteristics of a Michael Crawford Phan. Out of 41 points, there is some serious vitriol directed towards the 2004 movie in general, and Gerard Butler as the Phantom, in particular. She uses the term "Gerik" as a contraction of Gerard and Erik, the name of the Phantom in the original novel. MC is Michael Crawford. Although much of this is tongue-in-cheek, some is downright stalkerish and scary, even happily anticipating getting restraining orders (LePhantomessa, 2010).

♦ Every time someone brings up Gerik, you curse angrily and/ or fly completely off the handle, praising MC almost to the extent of Godliness and cursing Gerik as though he was evil Incarnate who just stole your ice cream and gave it to Dario Argento's Phantom.

♦ You have been involved in huge flame wars on forums, websites, and Youtube, lasting dozens of pages, over which Phantom is better: MC or GB.

♦ You typically win these fights b/c the Gerik Phans just leave to go to another site on which they can gush about him, and not worry about being scarred for life by your Gerik-bashing comments.

♦ You have hosted your own private burning of the DVD of the 2004 movie, and cackled madly over it, "burn, BURN! Let's see your sunburn ruin POTO now, bitch!"

♦ You didn't even mind when you got a ticket for unlicensed garbage burning because you burnt the DVD on a huge pyre in your backyard.

♦ You have written angry letters to Gerard Butler cursing him for ever taking the role of Phantom, and may or may not have gotten a restraining order because of your threats to "strangle his stupid sunburn right off his face."

♦ If you DID get a restraining order, you have hung it up on your wall proudly.

♦ Every year on MC's birthday, you send him a birthday card, or maybe some of your hair, as a declaration of love.

♦ When you got *his* restraining order as well, you cried at first, and then threw GB's restraining order in the trash and framed MC's R.O. and hung it on a wall.

One of her last comments was interesting, particularly in the light of the *Love Never Dies* controversy.

♦ There are some nights in which you ponder (while using some stolen morphine, from Kay Erik, of course) if *Love Never Dies* would have been at all good if Michael had been the Phantom.

♦ When you wake up the next morning with an awful hangover, you decide that even Michael Crawford, in all his glory, could not have saved that musical from being so awful, and beg forgiveness from the little MC shrine you have in your closet for contemplating such thoughts.

Joel Schumacher as Director

Lloyd Webber discovered Joel Schumacher when he went to see the vampire film, *The Lost Boys*, while still married to Brightman. He loved Schumacher's "vision" and "rock sensibility." He said to Brightman, "this is who is going to make our movie."

Schumacher was interested in the *Phantom* project because he liked the story and because it gave more people an opportunity to see it.

… there were two main things that appealed to me about *Phantom:* firstly, it's a beautiful and profoundly tragic love story, and secondly there are millions of people in the world who can't afford to go to the legitimate theater, either because tickets are too expensive, or because it is too expensive a production to play where they live, and those things combined and gave me a huge motivation (Film Companion, 2004, p 48).

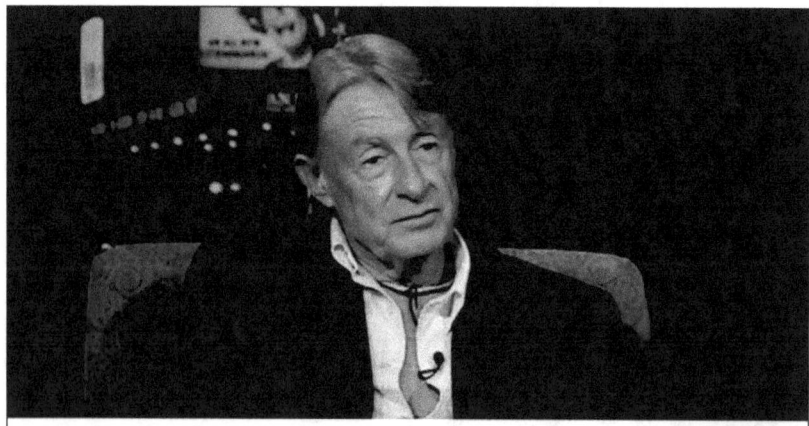

Joel Schumacher was chosen as director for the film version of *Phantom.* https://www.youtube.com/watch?v=FVrmARNTIVA

The objections to Schumacher as director of *Phantom* were long and loud, and focused on two main things. First, many thought he was the "King of Schlock." They felt his movies were gaudy and over the top, but in some ways, that was a good fit for a movie version of *Phantom*. Second, when he directed *Batman and Robin*, he put nipples on the eponymous heroes' costumes. I can't really explain that one, but it seems to be the go-to punchline for people who don't like his work. An article in the *Irish Times* (Clarke, 2004) had an interesting commentary on Schumacher's love-hate relationship with the critics.

> Poor old Joel Schumacher. Though some of his films have been well reviewed, *Falling Down*, *Tigerland* ... he remains, Michael Bay notwithstanding, the critics' favourite whipping boy. He's 65 now. He's made a lot of money, and launched quite a few careers (that of Colin Farrell, for one). Doesn't he deserve a break?

> "But, you see," he [Schumacher] reasons, "when journalists, like you, say I have been unfairly kicked around then they are themselves demonstrating that I am appreciated." Well, yes, but then I'm really just being polite (I don't say). In fact, like most people who have met Joel Schumacher, I find myself wishing his films were a little better. He is so funny, so nice, so entertaining. The former window-dresser and production designer, his shirt collar open across a tobacco-coloured turkey neck, comes across like a deliciously camp Native American retiree. It's a shame that somebody so endearing should be responsible for such unlovely projects as *The Lost Boys* and *Batman and Robin*.

> Andrew Lloyd Webber, unlike Joel, rarely celebrated for the warmth of his personality, has had a similarly torrid time with the critics. So, in some perverse, sod-you sense, Schumacher was the ideal candidate to direct the big-screen version of His Lordship's theatrical phenomenon, *The Phantom of the Opera*.

> Schumacher still seems energised by new challenges. But having, after two decades of furious activity, just joined the bus-pass generation, perhaps he should slow down a little. He

looks astonished. "But I get all these wonderful opportunities. What would I do with myself?" Well, it would, at least for a while, get him out of the eye-lines of ill-spirited critics such as myself.

"Oh, I think I'm treated fairly," he says. "I have caused a lot of trouble with my movies on purpose. But people love my movies. They connect with them. I think I am one of the luckiest people on the planet."

Lloyd Webber and Schumacher Get Together

Lloyd Webber sought Schumacher out, they became friends and were going to produce the film version of *Phantom*. That project eventually fell apart, but the friendship was sustained even after the project faltered. More than a decade passed. In the end, it was Lloyd Webber's wife, Madeline, who talked Schumacher into reviving the project (Portman, 2004). In an interview for Theater Talk, Lloyd Webber and Schumacher described how the deal collapsed and when it came back together.

> **TT:** Quite a delay in getting it to the screen. What were the obstacles?
>
> **ALW:** Well we met, Joel and I, in 1988, and I very much wanted Joel to be the director because I'd seen *The Lost Boys*, which I thought had a fantastic use of music, and the visuals, and the whole thing combined with a rock-and-roll sensibility. We were going to go with the movie very quickly, but as you would know, it was rolling out in the theater, and all my theater collaborators were getting very nervous, the production in Germany and the production in Japan said they wouldn't go if there was a movie. So, in the end, we decided to put it on ice.

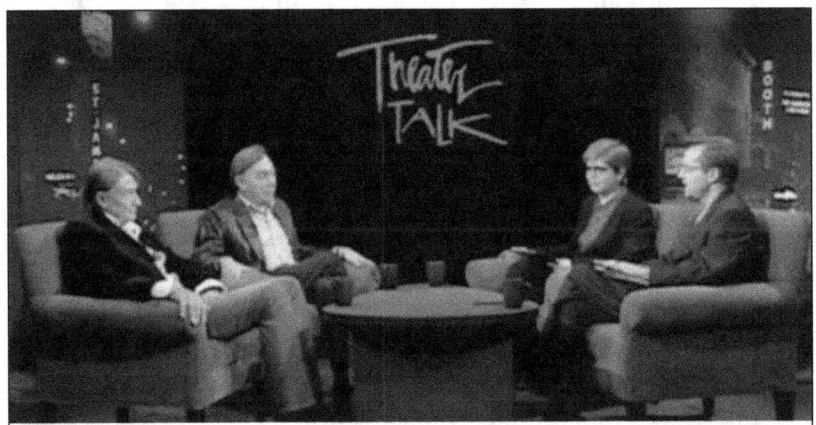

Lloyd Webber and Schumacher describe the *Phantom* film on Theater Talk. https://www.youtube.com/watch?v=FVrmARNTIVA

Watching the interview with the two of them together was interesting, as they really seemed to be working together as equals. Lloyd Webber clearly has a lot of respect for Schumacher, and Schumacher feels lucky that Lloyd Webber "plucked [him] from the chorus." Lloyd Webber gave Schumacher complete creative control over the project, which is quite unusual for him. As someone reputed to be a notorious control freak, sometimes to the detriment of the final product, Lloyd Webber's trust in Schumacher is astonishing. By all accounts, it appears to have been a good working relationship. Schumacher, in turn, ran things like final casting decisions, by Lloyd Webber for approval. This is how they described their relationship for Theater Talk.

TT: What's it like working with Andrew? Andrew is generally the boss of everything.

JS: Because Andrew plucked me out of the chorus. Talk about luck. That he saw this little teenage vampire movie that I did early in my career, and then said to Sarah Brightman, "this is our director." I don't know how he even stumbled into the movie theater.

Although we didn't make the film in 1990, we did become very close friends by that time, and with Andrew's wife, Madeleine. We had a 16-year friendship before we decided to do it again. We had lots of short hand. We also had a relationship that had been tested, including canceling a movie when we had worked hard on it, which some relationships don't. And we always saw each other when we were in each other's cities. That's good news, bad news. And the bad news is that I wouldn't want to fail him after all this time. That's an added pressure. But fools rush in....

Schumacher describes how Lloyd Webber gave him complete creative control.

... and I have to say this, on Andrew's behalf. He doesn't pretend to know anything about film. So the visual part of the film, the actors, the storytelling, really that was left to me. Of course, I would show Andrew everything and he was very supportive. And he did this brilliant job of re-orchestrating the music, and more importantly, he encouraged these young people who were very nervous about working with him, every day. I never saw him criticize them, I never saw him put them down, He always came to the set and told them how great they were doing. And they needed that, where the music was concerned.

Music as Dialogue

Phantom was unique, even among other musicals that have been adapted to film, because there is almost no dialogue. That was one of the issues when they talked about making the film 16 years earlier. The studio was worried that it wouldn't translate well to film and be a commercial success (Theater Talk, 2014).

JS: All the music is our dialogue, basically our script. It moves the plot along.

ALW: That was the biggest worry that all the Hollywood lot had, that you couldn't have something that is through song. In fact, you forgot that it was through song.

JS: That's why Andrew bought that rights back. And did you know that he and his company raised all the money? It was financed by Andrew and his company. Therefore, it was just us.

TT: That's why you didn't want a Hollywood studio?

JS: They were worried about the music.

ALW: Very worried.

Since Lloyd Webber now completely owned the rights to his creation, he was able to make a film version that was quite true to the version on stage, but even bigger—he had more than 110 musicians at his disposal.

Recording the Soundtrack

The way the soundtrack was recorded was also unique. Rather than record the whole thing in the studio, they recorded it on set and repaired it later in the studio. That approach added to the narrative. The orchestra followed the lead of the actors.

JS: So if they cry, or pause, or speak a word, or whisper, or do anything, it's all there.

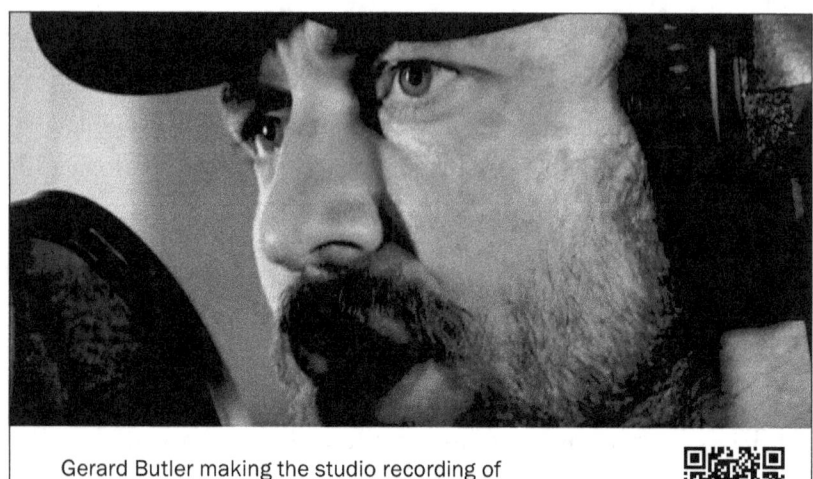

Gerard Butler making the studio recording of Music of the Night. https://www.youtube.com/watch?v=1mPW16cWaoI

Schumacher asked Gerard Butler to wait to stop smoking until after they finished filming, as they didn't want his voice to change. Emmy Rossum's voice also changed as they continued filming, which also coincided with her going from girl to young woman. She was 16 when they started and turned 17 while they were making the film.

> **JS:** Exactly. It's brilliant. And she's a girl in the beginning and she's a formidable young woman by the end of the piece. Well, she's been through a lot (Theater Talk, 2014).

Schumacher Re-Envisions the Show

Rather than simply filming a version of the stage play, Schumacher described how he had to "completely remake it" for the screen. Creatively, that was somewhat risky. It meant veering away from a formula that was clearly working and venturing into new territory. It also meant stirring up the ire of the most ardent fans who wanted nothing changed in their beloved *Phantom*. Schumacher stayed close to the original script, and to the general look, but re-envisioned it as a movie (Theater Talk, 2014).

JS: It's always important when you're dealing with a famous novel, or anything that has a life of its own, you want to keep the essence of it, so what's made it great still exists, but then you have to totally rethink it because, of course, it's a cinematic experience. You want to create the same type of excitement for a movie audience with a different language.

TT: How influential was Hal Prince's production?

ALW: Because we were thinking of this as a movie, we really didn't consider what was on stage … we really did approach it as if it were a completely new venture, a completely new staging of it, and I if hadn't done that, all we would have done would be a filming of the stage show, and I really hoped we hadn't done that.

Schumacher describes his process in an interview for *CanWest* (Portman, 2004).

I analyzed the structure. I took the music, the sets, the costumes and all the obligatory glamour and romance, and put that aside. I thought: what story am I telling? … So I said: "Andrew, they've got to be really young. If they're famous, fine. If they're unknown, that's fine. I just don't want anyone that's not right for the story, or else I can't make it work for you." He said: "You can have anyone you want, but they have to do their own singing." I said: "That's fair!" We shook hands, and that was the deal (Portman, 2004).

Transition from Stage to Film

The movie was quite true to the play in basic storyline. The look and feel were also quite recognizable, even with a different designer. Interestingly, some of things that critics chortled at the loudest about were either part of the stage show, or were part of the book. For example, in real life, there is a lake under the Paris Opera House, with several stories below the main floors. It's not hard to see where Gaston Leroux got his idea.

Some critics howled with mirth about Christine being on horseback when being taken to the Phantom's lair the first time while singing The Phantom of the Opera. The first time I saw it, my reaction was, "where did he get the horse?" The horse, however, was in the book.

Also, the pure Gothic spectacle of it all—the organ, the lit candles coming up out of the water, the punt, the elaborate costumes—caused a lot of critics to snicker. Indeed, all of the elements in the film are faithful to the original stage show. Chances are, if you didn't like this in the movie, you probably didn't like the original on which it was based. But that really wasn't the movie's fault, as film critics, such as Roger Ebert (2004) were quick to point out.

The Heart of the Story

At its very core, Lloyd Webber's version of *Phantom* is a love story, and the whole script is leading up to the final kiss, as Schumacher described.

> My job is just to be a storyteller. And if you take away the glamour, and the sets, and the costumes, and the horses, and the chandelier, at the essence of it is the very tragic young love story. And that's the reason to tell it. Her kissing him at the end is the whole reason to do the whole movie. The whole movie is leading up to that (Theater Talk, 2014).

Schumacher also had a score he loved, and said he wouldn't do another musical unless he felt passionately about the music.

> I had the greatest score in the world. Not all musicals have that (Theater Talk, 2014).

CHAPTER 11

Changes in the Story
from Stage to Film

For the most part, the film version of *Phantom* is faithful to the original stage show. However, in the process of making the film, Schumacher made a number of small changes in the storyline. For the most ardent fans, these changes were sacrilege. For other viewers, the film filled in some gaps in the story that were missing or didn't make sense in the play, making the storytelling more coherent.

Opening Sequence

The opening sequence was one place where a bit more of the story was offered in the film, and in fact, this is one of its most visually compelling sequences. The auction scene is filmed in black and white. Then when lot 666 is sold, the famous chandelier rises to the opening overture. As the chandelier rises, viewers are taken back in time. Suddenly, the *Opera Populaire* is not laying in wrack and ruin. As the light raises over the Opera House, the film goes from black and white to full color. The cobwebs and dirt are swept away, and suddenly everything is clean and bright, with sumptuous excess. The theater is restored to its former glory, while a rich instrumental version of *The Phantom of the Opera* theme plays.

During the opening sequence, we also see quite a bit more of what is happening behind the curtain, as the camera pans over the dancers and wardrobe mistresses, singers, and stage crew. You get a quick overview of what is involved in putting together a production at the

Opera Populaire, bustling about getting ready for a dress rehearsal. The opening overture is longer, and Lloyd Webber added some new segues, allowing time to sweep through the backstage shots.

Chandelier Crash

The biggest single change to the movie script was to have the chandelier crash at the end of the film rather than at the end of the first act. That was a good change and made more sense in terms of the story. The chandelier crash destroyed the theater, and the Phantom got away. The Phantom did it because Christine unmasked him and he needed to create a distraction to be able to drag her off. It made for a better climax to the story at the beginning of the finale. Schumacher described this change for Theater Talk (2014).

> **TT:** [The movie] tracks fairly closely to the stage show with some key changes. The chandelier comes down at the end of the first act [in the stage show].

> **JS:** That was Andrew's idea, and that was our biggest structural change was to burn the theatre down. And of course, if I'd done that in the middle of the movie, I'd have to rebuild it for the next act.

Lloyd Webber elaborated further in an interview for *The Atlanta Constitution* (Longino, 2004).

> It's quite a big change. In the stage show it's a gesture against Christine at the end of Act 1. In this, he's destroying his own world because he's so humiliated. I think it's a much more powerful moment.

During the filming, Schumacher said they rehearsed and rehearsed the chandelier scene. The actors were told that they had to get it in one take—and they did. It makes more sense in the movie, a catastrophe that brings down the whole Opera House.

"Christine Daae Can Sing It"

Another small change in the film, but one that made more sense in terms of the story, was changing the identity of who told Firmin and Andre that Christine could sing. In the stage show, it is Meg who speaks up and says "Christine Daae could sing the part. She has a great teacher." Then Madame Giry speaks up and confirms what Meg says. However, when Meg identifies Christine as a possible substitute singer for their opera, the next line that Meg sings to Christine doesn't make sense.

MEG

Where in the world have you been hiding? Who is your great tutor? I only wish I knew your secret.

Why would she ask that if she knew Christine had been taught by a secret tutor?

The film corrected that (although the original version still stands in the stage play). In the film, Madame Giry is the one who volunteers Christine to sing. That makes more sense in terms of Madame Giry's relationship with the Phantom. And it makes more sense in terms of the story and when Meg sings: "Who is your great tutor?"

The Phantom Backstory

The backstory of the Phantom, and how he came to be living underneath the Paris Opera house, is included in both the musical and the film—and in neither place does this story quite make sense. In both cases, Madame Giry tells this story to Raoul after the Phantom's appearance during the Masquerade Ball. Phantom has just told Christine, "Your chains are still mine. You belong to me!" and disappeared through a secret passage in a cloud of smoke. Raoul suspects that Madame Giry knows more than she is willing to share and asks her to tell him the story. Reluctantly, she reveals the tale. In both cases, she has seen the Phantom in a cage at a traveling freak show.

Stage Version

The Phantom was a young adult, and had formerly been an architect for the King of Persia. If that was true, how had he ended up in a cage at a freak show in France? I realize that disability laws were not exactly enlightened at the time, but seriously, what happened? Conversely, Madame Giry said he was a musician, composer, architect, inventor, etc. If he had been held in a cage in a freak show, how had he managed to accomplish all of that? He would have needed access to something: books, materials, possible teachers. Those skills can't come completely out of nowhere. Also, how did he get away from the freak show and end up underneath the Paris Opera House?

Film Version

In an apparent attempt to make the Phantom's backstory a bit more coherent, Schumacher changed it for the film. In this version, Madame Giry sees him in a cage at a freak show as a child, not an adult. After being abused, once again, by his handler, the Phantom gets the drop on his handler and chokes him to death. Even if we assume that a skinny (probably malnourished) child could choke a grown man to death, and that would be an extremely difficult way for him to kill him, how did he get away? Further, why were the police so quick to investigate the handler's murder, but turned a blind eye towards the imprisonment of a child? And how had this poor little kid living under the Paris Opera House have even survived, let alone become some sort of prodigy? He'd need to learn from somewhere. How had that happened?

The Engagement Ring

Christine's engagement ring has special significance in both the stage show and the film, but they are different in the two versions.

Film Version

In the film, Christine is wearing an engagement ring around her neck. Here is the dialogue from the screenplay.

CHRISTINE

Look at us, a secret engagement, me your perfect bride.

RAOUL

Why is it secret What have we to hide?

CHRISTINE

Promise me, Raoul, please promise me.

RAOUL

It's an engagement, not a crime. *Christine, what are you afraid of?*

CHRISTINE

Let's not argue. You will understand in time.

And they swirl off on the dance floor.

The Phantom then makes his entrance during the ball. He comes down the stairs and gives them the score to *Don Juan Triumphant*. He stops and says something to Carlotta, Piangi, and his managers. Then he sings to Christine how she's good but could still learn more if her pride would let her return to her tutor.

PHANTOM

As for our star, Miss Christine Daae ... (slow and sinister). *No doubt she'll do her best—it's true her voice is good. She knows, though, should she wish to excel, she has much to still learn, if pride will let her return to me, her teacher, her teacher ...*

Magically, the lights dim, isolating the PHANTOM and CHRISTINE. Spellbound, the guests below watch as CHRISTINE and the PHANTOM descend their respective staircases, united by their music, moving ever closer towards each other until they arrive face to face on the mezzanine. She is mesmerized by him. The PHANTOM reaches out, grasps the chain that holds the secret engagement ring, and rips it from CHRISTINE'S throat. RAOUL jumps between them. The PHANTOM turns on him furiously (Film Companion, 2004, pp. 114-115).

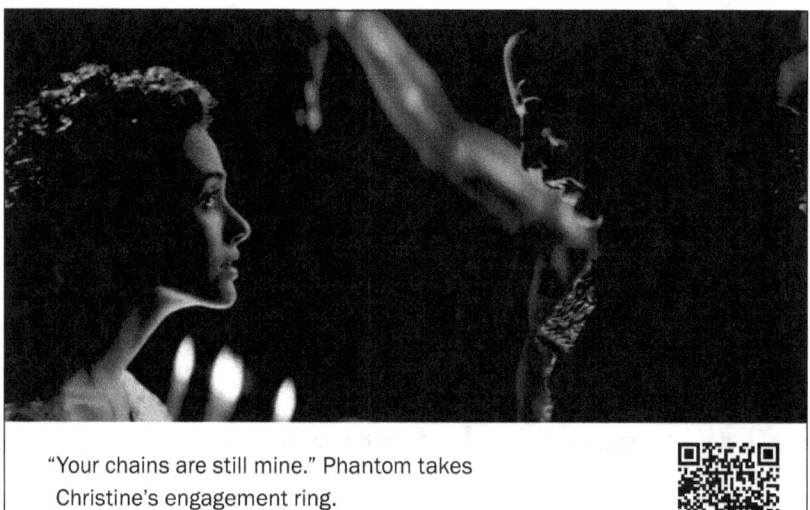

"Your chains are still mine." Phantom takes Christine's engagement ring.
https://www.youtube.com/watch?v=mON5dbdm63M

In the film, Phantom and Christine stare at each other. Playing in the background is an instrumental version of one of the new song Lloyd Webber wrote for the film: Learn to be Lonely. The Phantom spots the ring Raoul gave Christine, and yanks it off, breaking her necklace, and says:

PHANTOM

Your chains are still mine. You belong to me.

He then disappears down a trapdoor.

Stage Version

In the stage show, the Phantom does not talk to Carlotta, Piangi, or his managers. He sings that bit later when he is off stage. He doesn't take

Christine's engagement ring from around her neck or break her necklace. But he points to her and says, "your chains are still mine. You belong to me," but doesn't touch her. So then we have to ask: "What chains?" Most people probably chalked them up to metaphorical chains. He then throws a fireball and disappears.

In the stage version, during Point of No Return, the Phantom removes his pinky ring and slides it on Christine's finger, like an engagement ring. In the film, he uses Raoul's ring after he has abducted her.

Significance of the Ring

The source of the ring takes on an added significance in the finale, when the Phantom has dragged Christine down to his lair and Raoul has come to rescue her. In the stage show, it's the Phantom's ring. In the movie, it's the one Christine received from Raoul.

In the movie, as Christine is singing "pitiful creature of darkness ...," she is taking Raoul's ring and voluntarily sliding it on her finger—willingly giving herself to the Phantom, out of compassion—and to save Raoul.

After the Phantom releases them, Christine returns to give the Phantom the ring. In the play, Christine returns to give the Phantom back his ring. It's a touching scene, but she is basically just returning his property. In the movie, she is giving *her* ring to him. It's a much more meaningful gesture than simply returning his own ring. And this whole segment spins off of what happens in the Masquerade segment when the Phantom first takes her ring. Without that, he has to use his own ring.

The Rose

The symbolism of the single red rose also changed between stage show, film, and the sequel. In early posters for *Phantom*, and in many of the graphics, the rose is prominent. In the sequel, Christine says that Raoul always used to give her a single red rose. That was also true in the 25th anniversary of the stage show, that Raoul was the one who gave her the flower.

In the film, however, the Phantom is the one who gave her the rose, in this case, tied with a black ribbon. Madame Giry gives her one from Phantom after her first performance. He also sends her one before she goes on to perform in Il Muto. That is the one she is carrying as she runs to the roof with Raoul, and the same one she drops in the snow when she is singing All I Ask of You. The Phantom then picks it up after they leave and sings his reprise of All I Ask of You.

During Point of No Return, Christine is also wearing a rose in her hair.

At the very end of the film, when Raoul visits Christine's grave to drop off the monkey music box, there is a single red rose tied with a black ribbon and holding her engagement ring.

So in the film, the red rose is the Phantom's. But by the time Lloyd Webber produces the sequel, the rose is back to being something Raoul gives.

Graveside and Sword Fight

The graveside scene is where there was some added symbolism. First, having Raoul chase Christine as she was going to the graveyard. Raoul riding bareback on a conveniently available white horse. In the middle of a city like Paris, that seems a very odd thing to do, especially for a Vicomte. Patrick Wilson, the actor who play Raoul, later commented on how uncomfortable that was, and how sore he was afterwards (not surprisingly).

Also, amidst the swirling fog was a stag running in the forest. Schumacher was pretty heavy-handed on the symbolism there. In the both stage and film, there is a lovely song, Wishing You Were Somehow Here Again. And then there is the creepy bit in Wandering Child where the Phantom is pretending to be her father, but also wants to be her lover.

Schumacher added another bit that had many of the critics chortling: a sword fight in the grave yard. Phantom jumps down from on top of the sepulcher, sword in hand. The Phantom and Raoul have a sword fight over Christine. Raoul has the Phantom down on the ground at sword point and can kill him. Christine begs, "Raoul, no, not like this." A strange thing to say. How, then, should he kill the Phantom?

Point of No Return

Besides the Chandelier crash, the other significant change was in Point of No Return. Schumacher's version streamlined the story. Point of No Return is the brilliant cat-and-mouse game that the Phantom and Christine play. Schumacher's version made it better in several ways. First, he cleaned up the storyline for this scene. Christine shows that she's scared, but also is trying to be deliberately provocative. Second, Schumacher combined the Phantom's reveal with the Chandelier crash. There is only one reveal, so it's a better *denouement* of the scene, and it makes more sense about why the police didn't rush the stage.

Stage Version

In the stage version, Christine comes out, sits, and immediately spreads her legs—a surprisingly tarty move. She slurps from a big goblet of wine and wipes her hand on the back of her hand. The stage version also unmasks the Phantom twice: once to remove his cowl and show his face with the mask, and a second time to remove his mask. Why didn't the police come after the first reveal? They were so keen to catch him. Did they decide to wait for him to finish his song?

Some of the relationship between Christine and the Phantom is also strange in the stage version of this story. They are often standing apart from each other, especially when he finally starts singing to her. There is also the bizarre bit with the Phantom wearing a bag over his head. What's that all about? Is Christine's character seriously contemplating having sex with a guy wearing a bag on his head?

Surprisingly (given Schumacher's propensity to sex up every scene), Christine shows more innocence in the film version than in the stage version of this scene. She is sitting, looking scared and is modestly dressed. It's more effective, and surprisingly subtle.

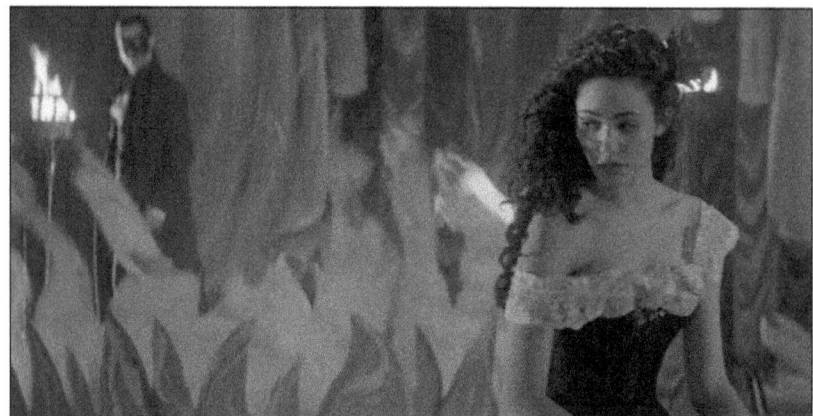

Phantom and Christine play a cat-and-mouse game in Point of No Return. https://www.youtube.com/watch?v=TFZrM38mf7Y

Christine is singing that she is defensive and silent, and she has both sleeves up. As she starts singing, "I've decided, decided," first one sleeve drops, then the other. She's still modestly dressed, but it is a great bit of tease. Then she sings with more boldness, as she says, "our passion play has now begun," and heads for her side the scaffold.

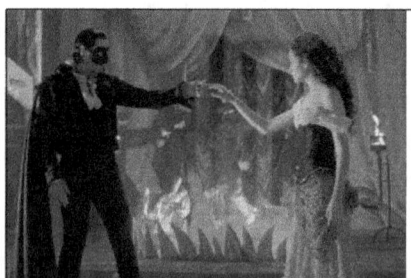

Phantom and Christine headed to the scaffolding in Point of No Return. https://www.youtube.com/watch?v=TFZ-rM38mf7Y

She stands on the bottom stair, and sings across the stage to the Phantom, "how long are we to wait until we're one." She's deliberately toying with him through her character. As they both reach the top, she asks, "when will the flames at last consume us." Then they sing together, "past the point of no return," as they are walking towards each other. The Phantom reaches for Christine and turns her so he is hugging her from behind; "the bridge is crossed, so stand and let it burn, we've crossed the point of no return."

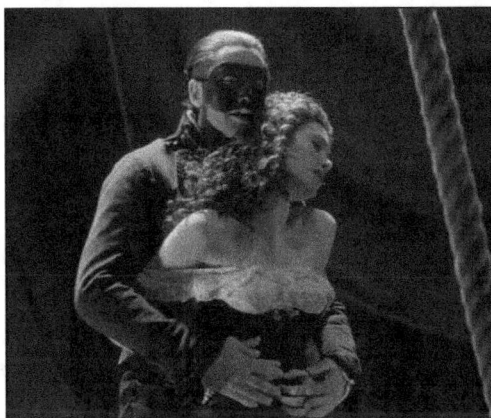

Climatic moment in the Point of No Return. Many believe this moment to be one of the best in the film. https://www.youtube.com/watch?v=TFZ-rM38mf7Y

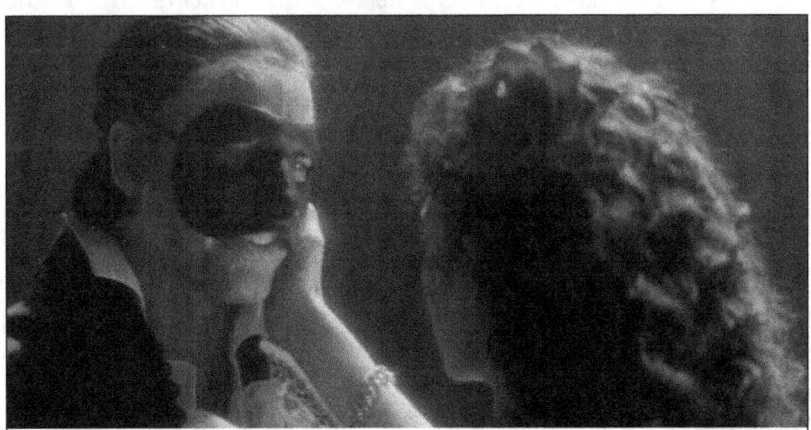

Christine touches Phantom's face before unmasking him, an action that leads to him dropping the Chandelier. https://www.youtube.com/watch?v=TFZrM38mf7Y

The Phantom is embracing her from behind when he sings, "say you'll share with me one love, one life time, say the word and I will follow you," asking her to save him from his solitude. They are facing each other, and he is caressing her hand, "Christine, that's all I ask of you." They stare at each other, and then Christine fully unmasks him. He stares at her with hurt and bewilderment, then anger, as he cuts the cord for the Chandelier and brings it down. He then pulls a lever on the scaffold, and Phantom and Christine drop all the way through to his lair.

Schumacher did decide to sex up the Phantom's outfit, with an open, ruffled shirt. He also wore that in the finale in his lair. Interestingly, Lloyd Webber ended up adopting this costume for the Phantom in the two early versions of the sequel, *Love Never Dies*. In the Australian version, the Phantom is back to being more buttoned-up in his appearance.

Schumacher couldn't seem to resist adding another sexy element not in the original play. He had background dancers in very suggestive poses, with the male dancers groping the female dancers' waists and breasts. They are grossly made-up, with burning flames around them. This part was annoying because the camera's kept cutting to them instead of the main characters. But overall, Schumacher's version improved on the original.

CHAPTER 12

The Casting of Phantom
Schumacher's Most Controversial Choice

Throughout the filming of *Phantom*, Schumacher made many controversial decisions. None proved more controversial than his selection of the then-unknown Scottish actor, Gerard Butler, to play the Phantom. Butler has since gone on to become an A-list star, but when *Phantom* was filmed, he was largely unknown, particularly to American audiences. It was his subsequent film, *300*, that made him famous.

Butler struck many as an odd choice given that there were so many available actors who could sing. Antonio Banderas and John Travolta had been short-listed for the part. Why go with an unknown? And why pick someone who was not a singer? In some ways, a choice like this wasn't unusual for Schumacher. He was known for spotting talent in up-and-coming actors and giving them a break. But this time, there was much hue and cry over his choice for this beloved part.

Who is Gerard Butler?

Unlike many of his contemporaries, Gerard (pronounced GER-ad) Butler is quite well educated. He trained as a lawyer at Glasgow University, and was president of his law society. He was working for a major law firm in Glasgow, but was miserable in his job. He hated his work, was drinking heavily, and as a result, was frequently late to work. He became an alcoholic and was fired a week before he qualified as an attorney. (In some interviews, he said he quit, and in others he said he was fired. It sounds like they mutually agreed for him to leave.)

As Butler described in an interview for *Canada AM* (Thomson, 2005).

> There's a lot of the tortured soul in me. When I was training to be a lawyer I'd say I was manically depressed, and scarily lonely and miserable, yet no one would have known.
>
> A large part of me is very sensitive and can live in darkness. I find it easy to access that.

While he was in law school, he was part of a band called Speed with several of his law-school buddies. Around the time the film was launched, much was said about his previous experiences singing in a "garage band." The press fixated on this, perhaps trying to justify, in their minds, why Butler got the part. Butler downplays this, as do Schumacher and Lloyd Webber in an interview with Theater Talk (2014).

> **TT:** And Gerry Butler had sung in a rock band in Edinburgh.
>
> **ALW:** Allegedly.
>
> **JS:** I think he shook the tambourine and picked up girls.

Butler also downplayed his previous experience singing in a band.

"Was I a rock star in Scotland? Definitely not" (Mitchell, 2004). His substance abuse also affected his participation in this band, as he described to the *Herald Sun* in Melbourne, Australia (Mitchell, 2004).

> I was twice thrown out of my own gigs. I was ejected from the clubs. Once it was because I ran out on to the street with the microphone and I was still singing. Everyone in the club could still hear me. Another time it was the biggest gig we ever did. There were 10,000 people at the Edinburgh Festival. The band got pissed off because I got smashed before the gig. I forgot all my words and I was having such a laugh with the

audience, but I was using abusive language. The police ended up on stage. Our guitarist was saying to the police, "Arrest him, arrest him." He was so angry at me (Mitchell, 2004).

Getting fired from the law firm because of his alcoholism turned out to be a good thing for Butler, for through it he discovered acting. He started doing some work on the stage, being cast in major roles in *Coriolanus* (later made into a movie that he starred in), and the stage version of *Trainspotting*. Butler stopped drinking and went into recovery.

> ... if it wasn't for alcohol, I may have been a lawyer, but living a miserable life, and never would have achieved this happy life as an actor. So that was not such a bad thing (Lyons & Bennett, 2005).

How He Got Picked for Phantom

Butler's journey to *Phantom* began by chance. Schumacher was out of town and wanted to see a movie. He had seen all of the movies at the multiplex, except for the almost-unwatchable *Dracula 2000*, so he decided to give it a try. Butler's performance caught his eye.

As for Butler, he first became interested in auditioning for *Phantom* when he read the script. He wept at the end and he knew then that he wanted to play the part. Not being a singer, he knew the odds were against him, as he described for Paul Fischer (2004) from femail.au.

> **Fischer:** You must be very thankful for *Dracula 2000* if you believe the press notes, apparently was that movie that Joel Schumacher saw.

> **Butler:** There were six films in the cinema and he'd seen all of them, so he said, "Oh, shit, we might as well go see *Dracula*." He tells me the story anyway. It just goes to show you that it can be one character, one movie that somebody sees that inspires them.

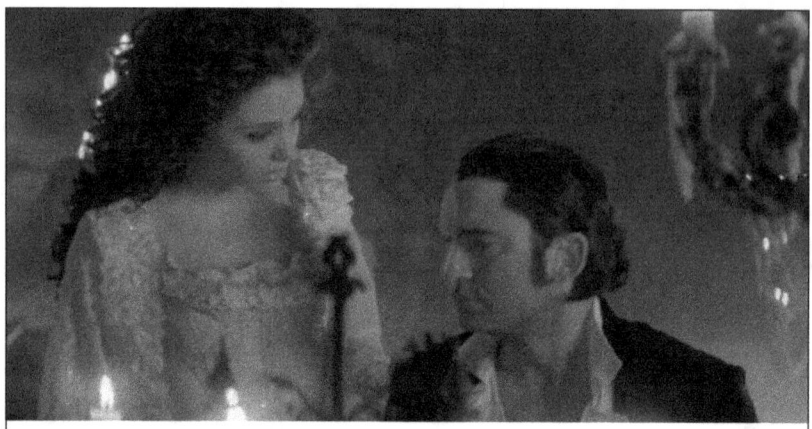

For many fans, Gerard Butler was an odd choice for the role of Phantom. https://www.youtube.com/watch?v=hgEVVCBu6EU

According to Schumacher, Butler got the part because he demonstrated that he "got" the character. He brought something to the part, besides being "younger and hotter." In a press conference, Schumacher said, "Gerry has a strong screen presence and he personally connects with the loneliness of the Phantom. It's palpable on screen. When he was talking to us about the character, he broke down." Butler also described the script's impact on him.

> I'd read the script. I'd listened to the music from the stage show because I had never seen it. I didn't even know the story properly because I had never seen the musical—and I'm glad because it was completely fresh to me and therefore had a much bigger impact.
>
> It's so romantic and so tragic and so painful. It touches people because they identify with something ... the secrets we have inside ourselves, the fears we have. You see the Phantom suffering like that and you think, at the end of the day ... that he's just a lost unfortunate creature who wasn't given the opportunity so many of us take for granted—companionship,

just to have somebody there to love and to care for, somebody to look out for you. That really touched me. I'm a hopeless romantic at heart (Portman, 2004b).

What Butler brought to the part of *Phantom* was the ability to show a range of emotions on his face. The most affecting scene was after the first kiss. His face shows the confusion and surprise from the gesture. The second kiss—the lover's kiss—devastates him. He sends Christine and Raoul away, and sobbing, sings a broken and desperate version of Masquerade.

Then Christine returns. When he sees he, he chokes out the words, "Christine, I love you." When she hands him her engagement ring, his face reflects, at first, hope that she has come back for him, and then despair when he realizes that this is truly goodbye. That whole sequence is much harder to show in a stage production, and it's where film really has an advantage.

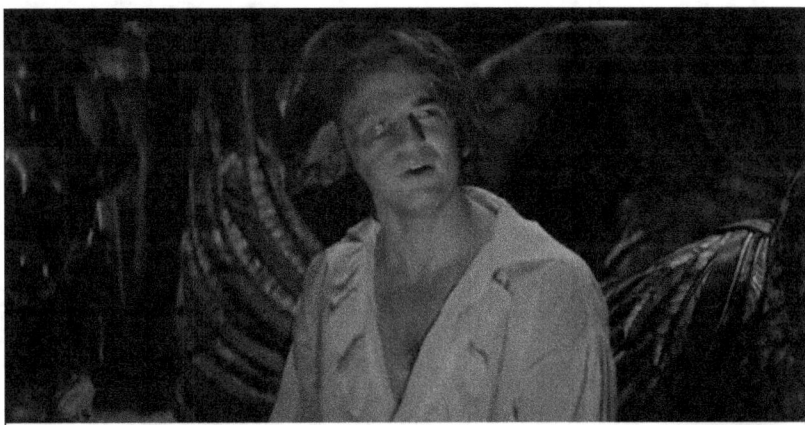

Phantom tells Christine that he loves her in one of the most-affecting scenes in the film.
https://www.youtube.com/watch?v=hgEVVCBu6EU

Even His Mom Was Surprised

Butler himself describes how his friends and family were shocked when he announced that he had been cast in the role of the Phantom.

> When I phoned to tell my mom I was auditioning, she said: "But Gerard, can you sing?" and my friends all asked if it was the non-musical version of *Phantom* (Hobson, 2003).

He was preparing for his audition while filming *Tomb Raider 2*.

> I was singing on set between takes, and in my car on the way to and from the set. When my driver would phone to confirm the time for my next pick up, he'd leave singing messages on my machine telling me I'd never be the Phantom. That I couldn't sing. Now that he's learned I got the part he's leaving messages asking if he can be my driver and I'm telling him just where he can go for having so little faith in me (Hobson, 2003).

In an interview with Paul Fischer, Butler describes a bit more about why he was cast in the role of the Phantom, and what it was like to step into a role that Michael Crawford made famous.

> I was very surprised when they first came to me with this, because I'm not a singer. I can sing, but I never had a singing lesson in my life. When they approached me, I had sung for fun in a rock band when I was training as a lawyer. But that was about as good as it gets. ... So, I was surprised until I read the script and what I connected with, I could see. ... I think it's all the more heartbreaking for the Phantom because he's a man in the prime of his life. Therefore, he's denied sexually, intimately. I think it's more heartbreaking when you know he's already had his story, so he's already been through a lot of that pain, but here he still has so much to offer in every way, but this love is not for him, which killed me in every way (Fischer, 2004).

Butler Auditions for Lloyd Webber

Schumacher wanted him for the part and had Butler audition for Lloyd Webber. During the audition, Butler was so nervous that he couldn't stop his leg from shaking. Schumacher was sitting nervously behind Lloyd Webber.

> I wondered what I'd subjected poor Gerry to. Then he sang. When he finished, Andrew rose from his chair, went over to Gerry and shook his hand. Gerry is incredibly sexy, but he is also vulnerable and can be menacing. And he can sing. Boy, can he sing! I knew we'd found our Phantom (Hobson, 2004a).

Butler also described for Paul Fischer his experience of auditioning for Lloyd Webber.

> I wasn't nervous until I stood by the piano and the enormity of what I was trying to achieve (struck him), and my mind went, "No, this isn't an interesting, independent movie. This is *The Phantom of the Opera*, probably the biggest musical of all time." And then I'm singing Music of the Night, one of the most famous songs of all-time ... in front of the composer, one of the most famous composers of all-time. All those things went through my mind and then my legs started shaking. Simon Lee was playing the piano, and he was (Butler imitated his gasping). It was like a comedy act, he was telling me to breath, but he kept (again gasping). I kept singing, and, of course, I'm my own worst critic. I thought I'd sung terribly, but Andrew really dug it (Fischer, 2004).

Lloyd Webber described Butler's voice as "rock tenor" when interviewed at the London premiere. Interestingly, Lloyd Webber and Schumacher both felt that Butler's less-refined voice was contributed to his character, and contrasted to the smooth tenor of Patrick Wilson's voice, who played Raoul. Lloyd Webber and Schumacher described why they chose Butler in an interview on Theater Talk (2014). They knew from the start that he was not a singer, but they felt that he brought something unique to the role.

ALW: I could see exactly what Joel meant. I mean you've got this incredible presence. I could see he had this amazing connection with the idea and the part.

JS: The passion of the character. He owned it.

ALW: With such passion. It was extraordinary. I was sort of praying when he opened his mouth. He absolutely had a rock tenor voice. It was there. Very raw, but there.

JS: And you loved the counterpoint to Patrick.

ALW: Yes, you've got the sort of Irish Lyric tenor, on the one hand, if you like, and you've got this other voice that's much more dangerous. ... It's not me who's the musical director. It's not me who's going to bring the artist through ... in this case, it was Simon Lee. ... I said to Simon, I defer to you. I think he's terrific, but you're the one who's going to have to bring him through. Simon went away and worked with him, and came back and said, "I can deliver this."

TT: You do detect the rock quality to his voice, but also a melliferous quality to his voice. It's big.

JS: And sexy.

Butler described for Paul Fischer some of his challenges with the role.

I think a lot of my jobs as an actor have been tough. ... But this was the most difficult because of the emotional journey factor. The actors that do it on stage, God love 'em, eight times a week. But the emotional breakdown for six weeks, 15 hours a day, I was going insane, screaming, and crying. I was really in that space. I was a bit of a basket case by the end of it. So there was emotional rollercoaster that I knew I was going to have when I started the job, and then, of course, there was the singing, which was an added pressure. In fact, sometimes it become harder, because the tireder you'd get you were still always recording. I was filming all day, and then I was still working on songs and recording. It was getting worse because my voice was getting tireder.

Yeah, there was so much I wanted to say through the voice. ... I knew the voice was probably the main means of communication, so I wanted to become as technically good as I could. Honestly, I wanted to hear his life story in every note. ... I always felt, even through Music of the Night, that even in his more seductive moments it was tinged with pain. Like he always knew this wasn't going to be for him. ...

Maybe it was too much, but it was my instinctive feeling when I first read it I would think, "This is so sad." Joel would say, "but this is so sexy." Somewhere along the way, we managed to get them both in there. That's one of the most exciting things. If you can do Point of No Return, which is so heartbreaking, and so fuckin' sexy and sensual and lusty, and yet tragic, and yet when you can feel both those things at the same time, they are almost like warring emotions (Fischer, 2004).

The Critics Weigh in on Butler

Many critics argued that the Phantom was supposed to have a lovely voice, one that enchanted Christine. Having Butler in the part violated, in their opinion, a fundamental part of the character. Both Lloyd Webber and Schumacher were confident in their creative vision (including their choice of Butler), so they ignored the controversy. The critics were relentless in the negative assessments. Movie critic Eric Snider (2004) got the ball rolling.

Take, for example, the role of the Phantom himself, the mad, disfigured genius who lives beneath the *Opera Populaire* in 1870s Paris, where the story is set. Schumacher has cast Gerard

Butler, bland star of such loud, dumb films as *Dracula 2000*, *Timeline*, *Reign of Fire*, and *Lara Croft Tomb Raider: The Cradle of Life*. Where in all of that did Schumacher see in Butler the potential to play a sensitive, wounded man who obsesses over a singer?

He didn't like Butler as an actor or a singer.

Butler's singing voice is too lightweight for a man with as much built-up passion and anger as the Phantom. It is not an especially good voice, either, growling some of the lower notes and sounding far too modern and pop-ish for a character whose only musical influences have been opera. (Wouldn't a man who lived under an Opera house sing more like Pavarotti and less like Michael Bolton?)

There were also a surprising number of listservs where singers discussed Butler's voice at considerable length. There was a spirited, middle-of-the-night discussion about this among singers on Broadwayworld.com. As you can see, opinion was sharply divided on Butler, and Butler's ability to play this part. They all posted anonymously. Singer number one weighed in.

I had a funny conversation with my mom about his voice. My mom is a HUGE *Phantom* fan, and I am as well, since my parents were always playing the album when I was little. My mom heard the soundtrack and automatically didn't like Gerard's voice, and then went, "Well ... maybe he's not SUPPOSED to sound good! Who says the Phantom should be a good singer?" Which made me laugh. Who says Nubian princesses are supposed to be good singers? Vietnam soldiers? Crack addict strippers? IT'S A MUSICAL! I AM a fan of Crawford's voice, but I like the gruffness of Gerard's voice. I think he's overshadowed by Patrick and Emmy though.

Half an hour later, another singer totally disagreed.

I don't like it. The Phantom's voice is supposed to be sublime—he is Christine's teacher, after all. But it seems here that the Phantom is the one who needs training. I don't find Butler's rock rawness authentic, either—he sounds like he's *trying* to sing rock, but doesn't succeed. My favourite Phantom is Colm Wilkinson, whose ethereal voice adds to the allure of the character. A Phantom with a good voice is a mysterious ghost; a Phantom with a bad voice is just a creepy guy living under an opera house.

Twenty minutes later, another reader posted his thoughts.

Gang, his voice is horrible. Simple. Period. You don't cast someone who cannot sing in one of the most popular roles written for a man on the stage. No doubt Schumacher got excited at the sight of Butler's good looks at the auditions, and that clouded his less-than-stellar artistic faculties. Patrick Wilson can sing and act his role quite well. Butler cannot do much of either. Seriously, wait until you see it. He is terrible. He moves without grace or cunning. Like a poor man's Batman, actually. (Thanks again, Schumacher.) And whenever he embraces Christine, the lack of passion is astounding.

Another member of this list was more sanguine.

You know ... I don't even know why people are still discussing this. Sir Andrew Lloyd Webber, the *composer* and *maker* over this show obviously loved him and thought him perfect for the part. Same goes for Emmy. And bitching about it won't do any good. The movie is made and being released all over the world. If you don't like him, fine. If you love him, great. :) But there's nothing we can do to change anything.

It's now 2 a.m., and people are still posting.

... Another quote from ALW about Butler's voice (from an interview): "It's absolutely crucial as the film is nearly all sung through. Emmy Rossum, who trained with the Metropolitan

Opera (New York), was just 17 and has got a fantastic voice. Patrick (Wilson) is one of the great natural lyric tenors from musical theatre. And Gerry (Butler) has a great rock tenor voice. That balance vocally was very important because for the Phantom, we needed somebody who's got a bit of rock 'n' roll sensibility in him. He's got to be a bit rough, a bit dangerous, not a conventional singer in a sense." Well, he got what he wanted in that Butler looks dangerous and sounds rough.

Another member asked and answered his own question.

Why has every Phantom in every show been trained as anything other than a rock singer? Because he changed his mind before the show was staged. Now, it seems he has changed it back—at least in the casting of Butler.

Someone else weighed in, with a decidedly anti-populist bent.

Right you are. It has an operatic flavor although the only characters who *have* to be able to sing operatically are Carlotta and Piangi. Singers with operatic training have played the Phantom ... They have all had at least "theatrical voices," except Steve Harley (before the show was staged), and now Gerard Butler. My theory is that ALW didn't want a theatrical tenor. Some of the non-theater lovers he hoped to attract tend to think that men with smooth, high voices are somehow sissy and effete. I think he cast Butler to attract the fangirls (and some of the fanboys), and the "unwashed," theatrically speaking. He kept the film fairly close to the show for all the rest of the fans, let Schumacher use all of the elaborate sets and costumes he wanted to dazzle everyone, and is sitting there, admiring his paintings and hoping that the mix works.

So, if someone likes Butler, they are "unwashed, theatrically speaking?" Another forum member didn't think Butler's performance was bad, but did note some problems with his breath work.

I saw the film a second time, but nothing seemed out of place or wrong to me in the acting. But then I'm not an actor, so some of the finer points of the craft would not be apparent to me. As for them rewriting the notes, since Butler's voice is a baritone, would it not have made sense for them for the songs to be transposed into a key suitable for his range? To the poster who said he was flat all the time, I disagree. I had some concerns about his singing because I knew he hadn't had any vocal training prior to this role, but I didn't hear anything off key when I listened to the highlights for the first time. When I read comments elsewhere about him being flat, I went back and listened again—I still didn't hear it. I've sung in choruses for several years, and I would certainly know a flat note if I heard one. The breathing is another issue. I do hear him take breaths in places where a more experienced singer would not.

It's now 5:22 a.m., and they are still debating this. Another reader responded to the previous post.

There was very little diaphragm support (which is frequently found with poor breathing as the singer has to "snatch" breaths, which leaves them more prone to shallow breathing, and therefore less support from the diaphragm). I can't remember what else. I'll have to have another listen and get back to you. I do remember hearing him struggling with the low notes in AIAOY [All I Ask of You]. Those are definitely at the bottom of his range!

But if you don't believe me, watch it again and count how many unmotivated gestures Butler has throughout the picture. This man was clearly out of his element with this genre. Schumacher is out of his element with every film, but at least I was expecting that going in...

And one final comment. I had no problems with Butler's acting. I thought there was a lot of passion between the two especially during Point of No Return. I liked his singing as well ... he's not a perfect singer, but I didn't hear any off-key notes. I did wonder about the casting when I first heard about it, but I kept an open mind when I finally heard the highlights CD. I liked what I heard, and I like it even more now that I've seen the film.

In the End, Butler Did His Best and Was Pleased with the Result

Despite all the controversy, Butler was pleased with the job he did and the finished product. Butler described his take on the final movie.

> I wanted to do MY Phantom for better or for worse—just to try and make it different. And I hope and think that we have, that at the end of the day it is something that is more human and more emotionally complex, and therefore more moving to an audience, because now you're closer to the hearts and souls of the characters (Portman, 2004b).

In his interview with Paul Fischer (2004), he also reiterates that he was pleased with how the movie came out and why it appeals to the next generation of fans.

> I'm an actor. I do something because it touches me and then you'd expect to understand why something is, in terms of the public. If I were to offer something up, it would be the same reasons it touched me. We are all at heart romantic and passionate, and there is nothing like a dark romance to stir us up, no matter what age you are. On top of that, this movie has everything. It has a lot of old Hollywood, and it feels like an old musical, but at the same time it's vibrant and alive and beautiful and lush, it has a great energy because that's what Joel is great at getting.

Butler describes why this film appeals to people.

> Cinematically, it's a treat. The music appeals to all ages. When I walk past *The Phantom* here in New York, I can't believe

how many kids are going to the theater. So it's obviously their story, and it appeals to everyone. And the movie makes it more accessible because of the cost. A lot of kids don't go to the theater because of the cost, but now they can go see it in the cinema and claim it. This movie has recreated the world of the Phantom, of the Paris Opera House in a dark, luscious (way). And you can claim it and abandon yourself to a romantic, tragic love story.

Fischer asked if he was pleased with the final product.

I'm blown away by it. I always felt like we were doing something special, but even I didn't know the extraordinary amount of vision and talent that had gone into it. I thought when I saw it, "When did he do that? Where did he do that?" And I loved that, because when I finish a film and go see it, I almost wish I wasn't in it because you get too caught up being too vain about your performance. I loved this movie so much I thought, "I wish I wasn't in this film, because I could relax and enjoy it" (Fischer, 2004).

CHAPTER 13

The Phantom Was Not
Ugly Enough

B utler's voice was not the only thing critics complained about.
Butler's Phantom was too pretty. Roger Ebert (2004) called him
"the Fashionably Scarred Stud of the Opera." The critics considered
it prima facia evidence for why the film had no credibility. By making
the Phantom attractive, it was not faithful to the central premise of
the book: The Phantom was considered too ugly and deformed to
have normal social interactions.

> The Phantom calls himself a "loathsome gargoyle," but, unmasked,
> he looks more like a guy with a bad sunburn, or maybe a seafood
> allergy (Debruge, 2005).

The choice to make the Phantom attractive was not something that
started with the film. It started when Lloyd Webber decided to
emphasize the romance, rather than the horror angle. The Phantom
in the stage version had a deformed face, but was charismatic. In fact,
many left the theater convinced the Christine had chosen the wrong
guy. He is also physically powerful, as seen in the way that he effortlessly
carries Christine when she faints, and the way he overpowers and
strangles both Fouquet and Piangi.

Schumacher amped-up the attractiveness factor. The Phantom
was only deformed only in the portion of his face that was covered
by the mask. Everything else was attractive. That was too much of
a departure from the original character for many fans of the original

book, and of the stage production. The Phantom in Leroux's book not only had a horribly deformed face, described throughout the book as a "death's head," but he is so thin that he resembles a skeleton. His hands were bony, cold, and smell of death. In freak shows, he was known as *le mort vivant*—the living dead.

> He has no nose; eyes that are sunken so deep that all is seen are two skull-like eye sockets except when his golden eyes glow in the dark; skin that is yellow and tightly stretched across his bones; and only a few wisps of ink-black hair behind his ears and on his forehead. (His mouth is never described in as much detail, but is referred to as a "lipless, dead mouth" by Christine ...)

Many consider Lon Chaney's 1925 silent film, *The Phantom of the Opera*, to be the most faithful to the book.

> Erik's face resembles a skull with an elongated nose slit and protruding, crooked teeth. In this version, Erik is said to have been deformed from birth. Chaney was a master make-up artist and was considered *avant garde* for creating and applying Erik's facial makeup design himself. It is said he kept it secret until the first day of filming. The result was allegedly so frightening to the women of the time that theaters showing the movie were cautioned to keep smelling salts on hand (Wikipedia, 2017b).

Phantom's Face in the Stage Show

Although Lloyd Webber emphasized the romance of the story, the Phantom's face still showed clear deformity, even though his physical presence and his music were alluring. Christopher Tucker designed Michael Crawford's makeup. Because Tucker designed the makeup for *The Elephant Man*, they were thinking of something distorted, "something like maybe an injury or so."

You know when people have strokes and things like that, one side of their face is maybe paralyzed, so they try and straighten, you know, when they're talking to you, they try not to look paralyzed. They're trying to work against the deformity. Well I thought it I could make his lip, pull his lip up, by some ligaments that have contracted like that, like it would in, say, a major burn. This will give him something to work against. ... I wanted something that was going to register right up in the back, so we made a great big crater with the bone showing (*Behind the Scenes at the Phantom of the Opera 25th anniversary*, part 2, 2011).

Michael Crawford's Phantom

Michael Crawford's makeup was quite involved. The deformity only involved half of his face, but makeup and prostheses covered his full face. His look had to be exaggerated so that even people sitting in the back rows of the balcony could see it. Up close, his makeup looks cartoony and quite improbable. The deformity includes a gash on the right side of his partially balding head with exposed skull tissue, an elongated right nostril, a missing right eyebrow, swollen lips, different colored eyes, and a wrinkled, warped right cheek. It is covered by a white half-mask and wig. This makeup originally took four hours to apply. When the show went to Broadway, make-up artists reduced the time to three hours. The process is now closer to 45 minutes.

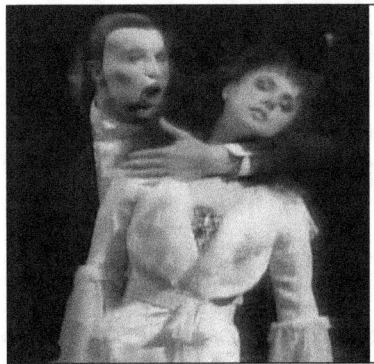

Michael Crawford with Sarah Brightman in the original production.
https://www.youtube.com/
watch?v=oZDcSrODALQ

According to the former official *Phantom of the Opera* website (no longer online),

> ...the prosthetics are made individually for each actor playing Phantom. Chris Tucker, who devised the original make up with Maria Bjornson, still makes each of the pieces for the London production. "He begins by taking a head cast [of the actor]," Tanya Noor explains, "then he sculpts the deformity onto the head, and then makes the foam latex pieces from it." The head cast, complete with the applied pieces, is then supplied to Bob Saunders who makes the mask to fit over the cast and prosthetics.

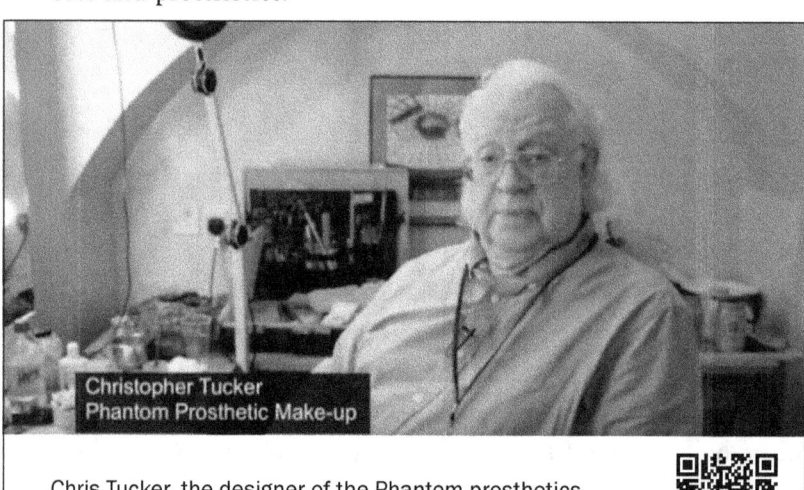

Christopher Tucker
Phantom Prosthetic Make-up

Chris Tucker, the designer of the Phantom prosthetics.
https://www.youtube.com/watch?v=aodCiOjyZgE&t=88s

The prosthetics were complicated to make and were used just once. The make-up articles were first made with a mixture of acrylic paint and glue, which then dries and are individually painted. The process takes a couple of hours. The staff likes to keep a stock of prepared pieces for both the lead actors and the understudies. They couldn't make them too far in advance because the paint fades. Michael Crawford didn't want his pieces premade. He wanted them painted on him, which is why his makeup took so long to complete. The final piece added was the lip prosthetic. Even with premade pieces, it is a time-consuming process.

Hugh Panaro as Phantom

Hugh Panaro played the Phantom on Broadway. He invited Broadway. com to come backstage and see how the Phantom got his look. Panaro has played the Phantom for about 2000 performances at the time of this interview. He likes to apply most of his own makeup. He said he imagined dressing up the "good side" of his face to look like Rudolph Valentino.

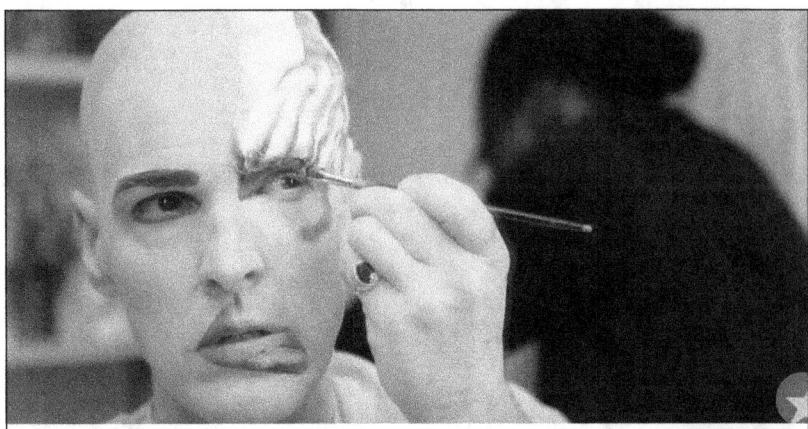

Hugh Panaro applying his Phantom makeup.
https://www.youtube.com/watch?v=7ADiLSQid9M

The Phantom makeup involves a bald cap, and then the prostheses for the deformed part of the face. The actor then wears two wigs: an "alopecia" (thinning hair) wig, and a wig with a full head of hair.

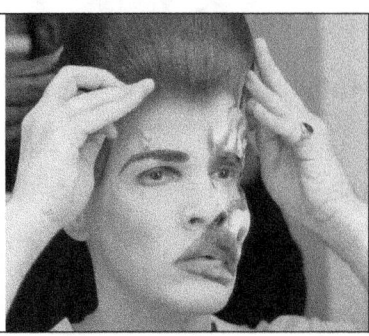

The second wig is the one he shows to the world. Here, Panaro applies the second wig. https://www.youtube. com/watch?v=7ADiLSQid9M

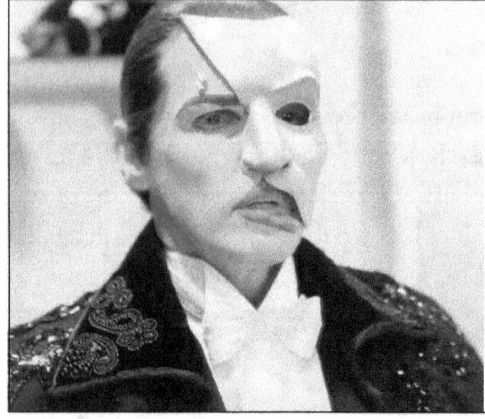

Panaro in full costume, with the mask. https://www.youtube.com/watch?v=7ADiLSQid9M

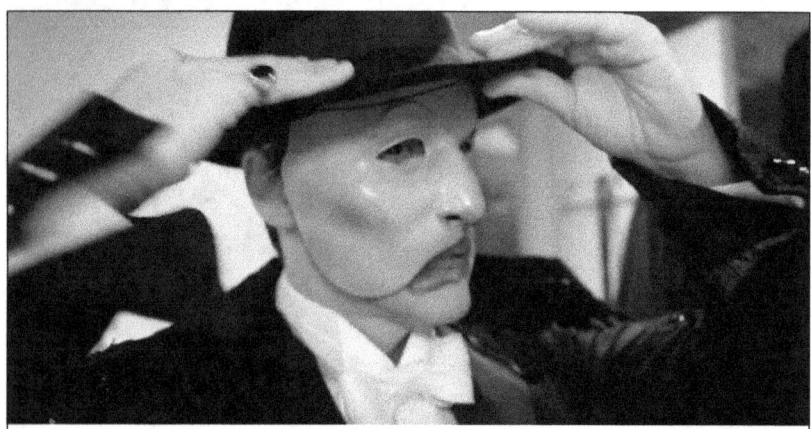

Hugh Panaro in final costume. https://www.youtube.com/watch?v=7ADiLSQid9M

Ramin Karimloo for the 25ᵗʰ Anniversary

Chris Tucker, who designed the original Phantom makeup, designed the makeup for Ramin Karimloo to wear for the 25ᵗʰ anniversary celebration. It is a simplified version of the makeup worn by Michael Crawford. For example, the Phantoms no long wear different colored contact lenses. Karimloo does not wear as much makeup on the non-deformed part of his face.

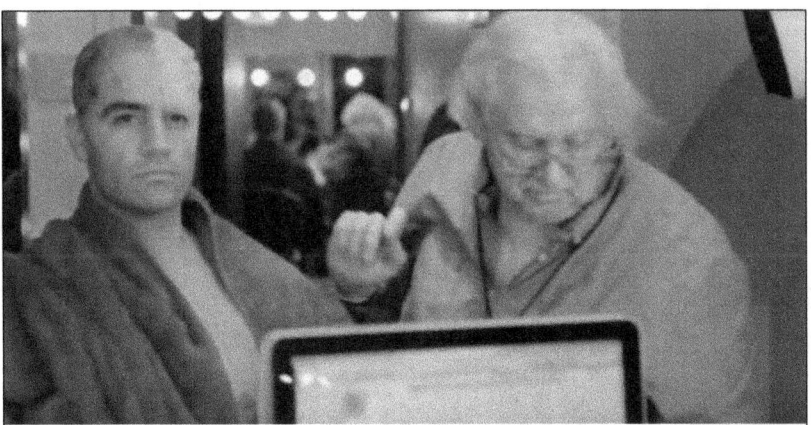

Ramin Karimloo with Chris Tucker preparing for the 25th anniversary performance. He's wearing the first layer of prosthesis.
https://www.youtube.com/watch?v=SInA5s-XyEl&t=182s

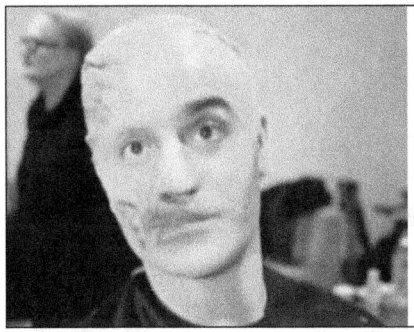

Front view of full prosthesis.
https://www.youtube.com/
watch?v=SInA5s-XyEl&t=182s

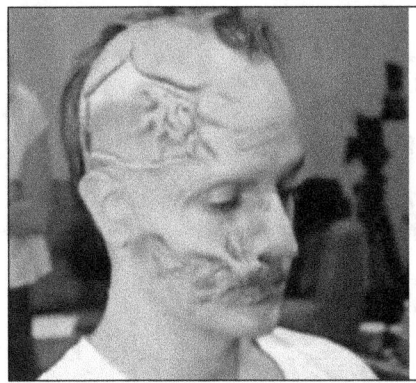

Sideview of Karimloo with the full prosthesis and alopecia wig.
https://www.youtube.com/
watch?v=SInA5s-XyEl&t=182s

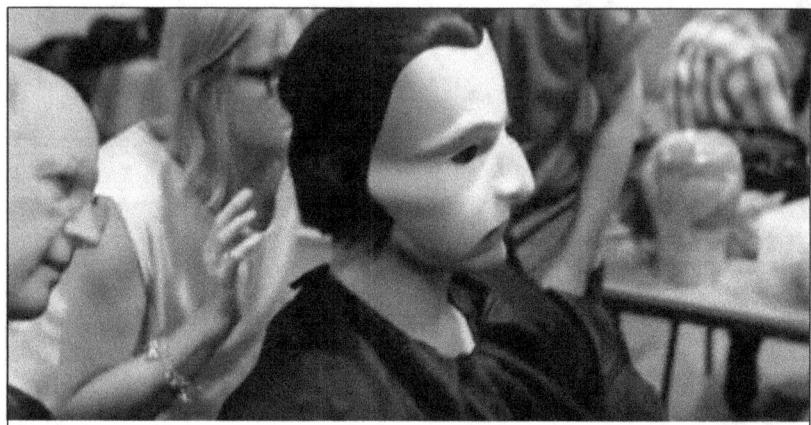

Karimloo with second wig and mask.
https://www.youtube.com/watch?v=SlnA5s-XyEl&t=182s

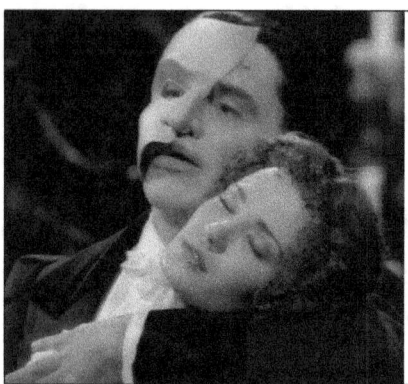

Karimloo in full costume. The non-deformed part of his face has less make up than previous Phantoms. https://www.youtube.com/watch?v=ymclu8ZktrU

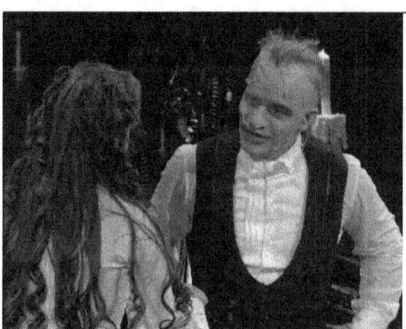

Karimloo in climatic scene after removal of his mask and second wig. His microphones are clearly visible. https://www.youtube.com/watch?v=dBf_08aO7nA

Ben Lewis in *Love Never Dies*

In the Australian version of the sequel, *Love Never Dies*, the makeup was even more simplified. The actor doesn't wear a deformed lip, and there are no prostheses on the non-deformed part of the face. In fact, in this version, they never show the Phantom's deformity. He's either facing away or the lighting drops. He has the two wigs, but not the prostheses.

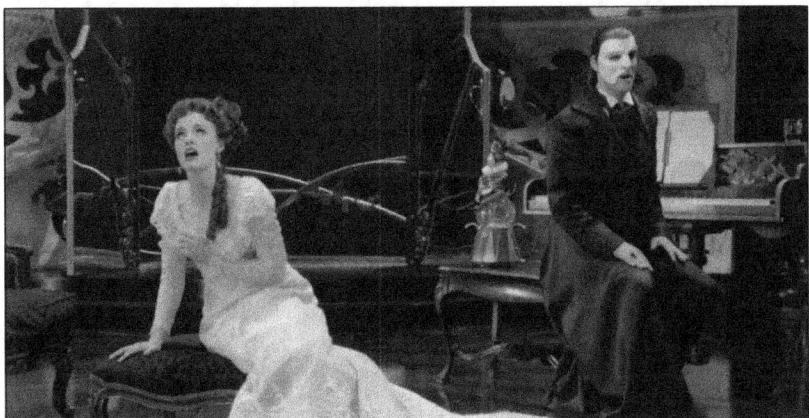

The Phantom with both wigs and mask for Australian *Love Never Dies*. He is not wearing a lip prosthesis. https://www.youtube.com/watch?v=iimYZM8Z-0M

Facial Deformity in the Film Version

The challenge for the film was to make a deformity that was more realistic and could actually exist. For example, it's unlikely someone would have a hole in their scalp, exposing their skull, and still live—especially in the 1800s. Further, the stage version of the makeup would look way too cartoony in a film. Yet, this more realistic looking makeup was deemed "not ugly enough" by many of the critics of the film—especially since the rest of his face was handsome.

In the 2004 film adaptation of the musical, Erik's makeup was made to look much less gruesome than previous adaptations of the story. Instead of a skull-like face, his disfigurement resembles that of a mildly malformed face, which he covers with the mask (Wikipedia, 2017b).

Roger Ebert (2004) reiterates that the Phantom was too good looking.

In the Lloyd Webber version, now filmed by Joel Schumacher, the mask is more like a fashion accessory, and Phantom's "good" profile is so chiseled and handsome that the effect is not an object of horror, but a kinky babe magnet.

Ebert contrasts the pathetic Phantom of the 1925 classic with Lon Chaney to the current movie Phantom.

The modern Phantom is more like a perverse Batman with a really neat cave. ... In this version, any red-blooded woman would choose the Phantom over Raoul, even knowing what she knows now (Ebert, 2004).

Toni Ruberto (2005) of *The Buffalo News* makes a similar point, and also discusses differences between the film and stage version in terms of the Phantom's face.

Director Schumacher took full advantage of Butler's good looks and acting talents—teary eyes, trembling lips—to play up the dichotomy of the Phantom and increase the emotional ties with other characters. And focusing on his face—the tragic element that sets the story in motion—is something the film medium can use to full advantage. After all, that masked face tells both sides of this Phantom's story: He's broodingly handsome, yet under his mask is an ugliness that festers down to his soul.

In the stage musical, the Phantom is a caped figure flying around the stage. But you're not focused on his face unless you have really good tickets or are using opera glasses. In the film, you could see Christine's face, you could see his face up in close-up repeatedly for two hours. I found it moving. It evoked emotion.

Critic Eric Snider (2004) found that Butler's attractiveness took away from the story, and told a very different tale.

> Butler may have been cast because he is handsome—which is actually a liability for this role, since the Phantom is supposed to be disfigured to the point of being shunned by all society. The way Schumacher and his makeup artists have rendered him, the Phantom has three-fourths of a perfectly good, enviably attractive face, marred only by what appears to be a burn scar around his right eye. For this he was put in a circus freak show? He ought to be uglier. But of course, people wouldn't go see a movie with an ugly man as the romantic lead.

Yet, Schumacher's explicit goal was to make the Phantom attractive, as blogger bookwrm17 (2010) also describes.

> The casting director's choice to favor looks over singing ability is indicative of this adaptation's priorities: The Phantom is to be made as attractive as possible. His half-face deformity from the stage version is reduced to the point where it resembles a bad sunburn, and his masks leave large portions of his face exposed. In this modern interpretation, sexuality hardly seems scary at all; on the contrary, it is extremely attractive and desirable. Raoul, on the other hand, is made even more effeminate and portrayed as naïve and foolish, showing that chaste love has lost much of its appeal (bookwrm17, 2010).

Butler as the Phantom

Jenny Shircore designed the prosthetic for the Phantom movie. The deformity had to look realistic. Audiences, who had grown up with multi-million dollar special effects, are more sophisticated than they were in 1925, when Lon Chaney's makeup made women pass out from fright.

Butler described the process of developing and applying his Phantom makeup. For him, it was the worst and most tedious part of playing the Phantom, and there was a lot involved with developing the right look for the movie. The first time they put Butler in full Phantom makeup, it took 9 hours. He commented in several interviews on how much he hated the process, including having a piece of dental floss that pulled down his bottom eyelid, or needing to start the process by 4 a.m. for that day's filming. They eventually got the process down to 3 to 4 hours.

> My [lower] eyelid was glued down and then held in place with a piece of string, which went around my face and down my back. I wore a bald cap and that had to be painted and glued down. Makeup got into my eyes and they used alcohol to get it out. By the end, I was screaming (Backstage.com, 2005).

In an interview with *The Western Mail* (Driscoll, 2004). Butler made some similar comments.

> They finally got it down to about 5 and a half hours, and I hated that with a passion. You've got two or three people poking your eye, your face, your nose. You can't move, so, to me, it's the closest version of torture you can have.

> It also meant very early mornings, getting up at 3 o'clock. There was one period of filming when I had to do that six days back to back, so I wasn't getting to bed until 10:30 at night, and wasn't really getting to sleep, as I was so wound up.

> So it was all about going on set and screaming and crying and breaking my heart all day. Then going to bed for a few hours, and getting up and going through it all again, and thinking "I never want to act again!" (Driscoll, 2004).

Butler made virtue of necessity, incorporating his physical distress into the performance (Butler, 2005).

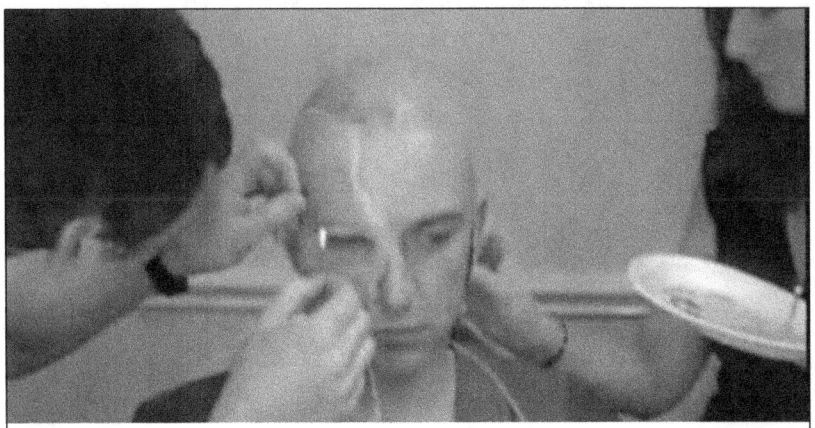

Jenny Shircore applies the prosthesis to Butler's face.
https://www.youtube.com/watch?v=w92cSr4Ezpw&t=5s

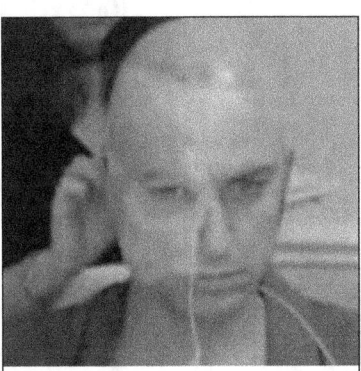

Dental floss was
strung under the
prosthesis to pull
Butler's eyelid down.
https://www.
youtube.com/
watch?v=w92cS-
r4Ezpw&t=5s

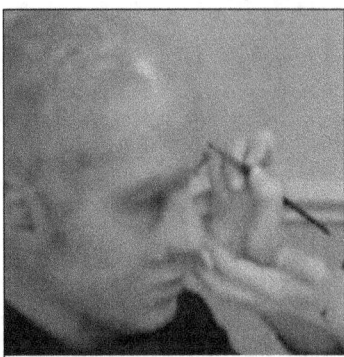

Applying makeup to
Butler's non-deformed side.
There was no prosthesis on
the non-deformed side of his
face. https://www.
youtube.com/
watch?v=w92cS-
r4Ezpw&t=5s

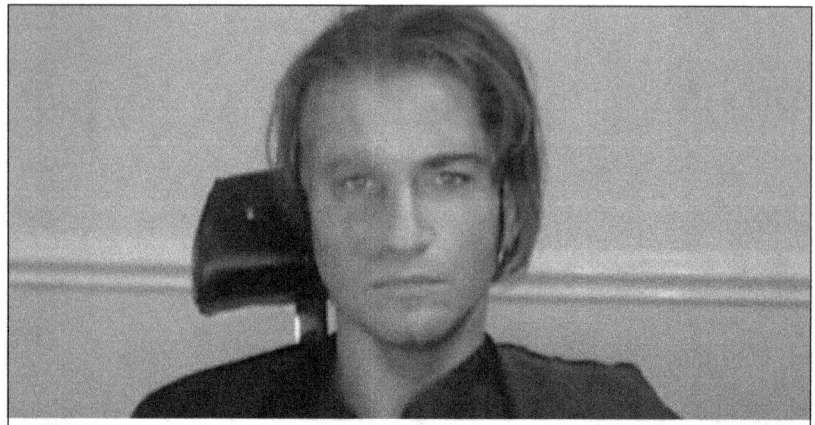

The alopecia wig had considerably more hair than the alopecia wig for the stage performances, so he still looked pretty good.
https://www.youtube.com/watch?v=w92cSr4Ezpw&t=5s

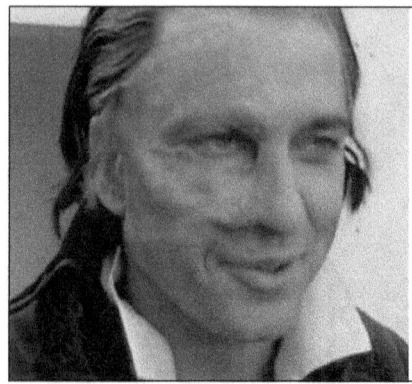

Butler was miserable in his Phantom makeup.
https://www.youtube.com/watch?v=w92cSr4Ezpw&t=5s

Look into my eyes and you can tell how comfortable this is. I was up at 10 past 3 this morning, I was picked up at quarter of 4. We started at 4:30 and I think we finished up at 10:30. ... This whole story is about what's hidden under that mask. We needed to find something that was both repulsive, yet human. But I hated it! (Butler, 2009).

The Origin of the Half-Mask

Part of the Phantom's look is his famous half-mask. In the earliest days, the Phantom is singing in a mask that covered both eyes. The Phantom half-mask was designed for a couple of practical reasons. First, director Hal Prince noticed that a full mask didn't allow Michael Crawford to express himself emotionally. Second, the mask had to allow microphones to fit under it (Wikipedia, 2017b).

The half mask is famous, but all the Phantom logos and advertising show a mask that covers both eyes. The reason for that was timing. By the time Prince and Maria Bjornson had designed the half-mask, the posters for the show had already been printed with the mask that covered both eyes. This remains the most-recognizable logo for *Phantom*.

Designer Bob Saunders made the mask for the 25th anniversary special. He describes the practical considerations and its important symbolism of the mask. Not only does the mask need to fit exactly over the makeup, but it also needs to fit over his microphones. The mask was also designed to make the Phantom look good.

> It also has to enhance Ramin's face in that the idea is that the Phantom has tried to make himself look extraordinarily attractive and masculine and handsome. And so, his way of doing it is the mask. And the original concept of this, which came from Maria Bjornson, is that because of the period, he actually made it out of fine porcelain, although technically we don't use it that's the overall image of thing, that he's made this mask particularly to hid this gruesome distortion in the rest of his face (*Behind the Scenes at the Phantom of the Opera 25th anniversary*, part 1, 2012).

Unlike the makeup prosthetics, the masks can be used multiple times. The mask has changed little over the past 30 years. According to the former official *Phantom* website, masks can be used for several performances, depending on how gentle Christine is when removing the it.

The basic shape of the mask has never changed, but sometimes if there are lighting changes, the mask may require slightly different shading or "tweaking."

As long as the masks don't get dropped or trodden on – some of the Christines are more gentle with them than others! – they can last for each Phantom's entire run. (web page no longer online).

The Mask for the Film

A new mask was designed for the film. Butler described the design process.

We looked at hundreds of masks. I can't tell you the thought that went into every decision about the mask, and I tried on countless masks for camera tests. That alone was a five-week process (Driscoll, 2004).

Butler also described the purpose of the mask.

The mask had to be beautiful, but also ominous. They literally created hundreds of masks of different sizes, shapes, and materials, eye shapes, and expressions before we got one that was the right texture, physical expression, and size (Hobson, 2004a).

After designing the mask, they still had the problem of how Butler would keep it on his face. The week before filming was due to begin, panic set in.

I asked Joel Schumacher how it was going to stay on my face. During the fittings, I just held it on with my finger.

Make-up and prosthetic experts scurried about their shops, finally settling on a two-sided tape similar to the tape used to secure wigs, hairpieces, and costume pieces.

It behaved wonderfully in the makeup trailer, but because the opera house sets were so dry, the tape would fuse to my skin. I'd bruise my skin taking it off.

The opposite happened when Butler had to perform in the sets for the Phantom's underground lair.

Because of all the water in these sets and the hot lights, the air would be so moist the mask kept slipping off (Hobson, 2004b).

More Difficult Than Meets the Eye

Trying to sing with the mask, and to make sure it stayed on, contributed to the general discomfort created by his costume. Butler joked that the problematic mask helped immensely with portraying the Phantom's inner angst. I suspect few people know how difficult the Phantom makeup can be for the actors who must wear it. In the film version, in particular, it's amazing to hear how so many dismiss it as "nothing" once they learn about all that goes into giving the Phantom his "look."

CHAPTER 14

Sex and the Phantom

In *Phantom's* many film adaptations, different directors have emphasized varied elements of the story. The classic 1925 Lon Chaney film, for example, emphasized the horror part of the story. Lloyd Webber's take on *Phantom* emphasized the love triangle between the Phantom, Christine, and Raoul. Lloyd Webber described his first encounter with the book and his decision to emphasize the romance aspect of the story (Theater Talk, 2014).

> What I was unprepared for, it was also a high romance, with a bit of Svengali in it, of course. And when Phantom is exhumed for some reason, they find Christine's ring on his finger... and as luck would have it, I also met Hal Prince that night [at a Tony nominee's cocktail party] ... I said, "Hal, said let's get out of here. I said I've found this book on *The Phantom of the Opera.*" I said I wanted to do a high romance, and Hal said, "so do I."

There is also the element of danger with the Phantom. He kills people and he abducts Christine, as Schumacher described in this interview with Theater Talk (2014).

> Raoul's appearance triggers some violence in him, and ultimately a murderous rage. And that leads to all the destruction that follows, and that makes it impossible for her to really be with him. Because he's actually become someone who's become quite mad. The tragedy of it is another time, another place, they could have been lovers, and of course, a lot of people in the theater want her to stay with him.

Because people do suffer. And people do suffer with longing. And having worked with some of most famous objects of desire, they don't think of themselves that way. No one thinks of themselves as "the one that everyone wants them."

As it turns out, the creators were not just thinking romance. They were thinking, explicitly, of sex. There's a surprising amount of chatter about the Phantom's supposed sex life. Director Hal Prince referred to *Phantom* as being about the "sexuality of freaks" (Walsh, 1989). Musicologist John Snelson (2004) also noted the sexual elements of the show.

> The story revolves around a young and immature woman, unable to let go of the emotional ties to her father, now deceased, and repeatedly prevented by demonic forces from embracing fully her lover. Thus, the entire tale can be viewed as a metaphor for Christine's sexual awakening and maturing, as she is pulled unwillingly from the adolescent relationship of parent-child (the Phantom as Angel of Music substituting for her dead father) to that of adult lover with Raoul.
>
> ... For the first time, she must actively choose between, on the one hand, her father, the Angel, and *music itself as sublimation of and substitute for sex*, or, on the other, her lover, adult romance, and mature sexuality: she must choose between her past world and her future one. ...
>
> Ultimately, she knows her place and so rejects the overturning of society's rules that the Phantom personifies, turning instead to the societal conventions offered through romance and Raoul [emphasis added] (Snelson, 2004, e-page).

And an interesting last line—not unlike the dilemma Brightman faced in real life.

It's the old dilemma of having your man or your career.

In Schumacher's Version, Even the Building was Sexy

One of things that caused critics to jeer at the film version of *Phantom* was Schumacher's stated intent to "sex up" the plot. Schumacher took the implied sexuality of the stage version and amped it up with more attractive actors. He also inserted sexuality into the storyline, through his cast, lines he added to the original, and the costumes. In Schumacher's version, even the building was sexy.

> Not the Paris Opera, it's our own. It's the *Opera Populaire*. Partly because of the scale. You'd have to shoot it so far back. So, we thought of the Opera house as a beautiful woman, hence all the nudes (Theater Talk, 2014).

In an interview around the film's launch, the interviewer on *E!*, who described Butler as "humble, hot, and hilarious," said "It's ironic that such a good looking guy is playing the disfigured Phantom. Gerry says the director tried to capitalize on that." Butler himself describes Schumacher's instructions to him.

> When we were filming, he was much more about "make it sexy," but I was like "it's so sad." "Yeah, I know it's sad, but make it sexy." "But it's so sad" (E! Network, 2008).

In the 25th anniversary volume, Schumacher was quoted as follows regarding the plot.

> Andrew's music is lush and searingly romantic, and the story is a great love story. But it's also dark, it's got a Gothic horror side to it, and that appealed to me. I think above all Andrew's version makes the Phantom much more of a tragic lover—a sensitive romantic, not just a creature of horror and fear. Christine's relationship with Raoul is really her romantic awakening as a teenager. But I think that her pull towards the Phantom is a very sexual, very deep soulful union (Heatley, 2011, p. 111).

175

Schumacher used many opportunities to insert sexuality into the movie that were not there in the stage play. The sexuality shows up early in the story. Schumacher added this bit to the movie version when the new owners, Andre and Firmin, were leering at the chorus girls. Although it likely reflected the real-life vulnerability of young women in the theater at the time, it is an example of a superfluous sexuality that was added to the screenplay. None of this dialogue is in the original libretto. The slave girls' costumes during this segment are also considerably more revealing than those in the stage play. Below is the text from the screenplay, starting with the stage notes.

The BALLET CORPS, including MEG and CHRISTINE, dressed scantily as slave girls, begin their dance, sure to be a crowd pleaser. ANDRE and FIRMIN move closer—they are almost hanging over Mme. Giry, leering at the ballet girls.

MME. GIRY (to FIRMIN)

Monsieur

We take particular pride here in the excellence of our ballets, Messrs.

ANDRE

I see why. Especially that little blonde angel? (indicating MEG)

MME. GIRY

My daughter: Meg Giry

ANDRE has an "oops" moment as FIRMIN leers on ...

CHRISTINE becomes prominent among the DANCERS.

FIRMIN

And that exceptional beauty? No relationship, I trust?

MME. GIRY

Christine Daae. Promising talent. Monsieur Firmin, very promising.

ANDRE

Daae, did you say? No relation to the famous Swedish violinist?

MME. GIRY

His only child ... orphaned at seven when she came here to live and train in the ballet dormitories ...

They admire Christine's dancing and revealing costume.

FIRMIN (salivating)

An orphan, you say ... ?

MME. GIRY (hands off again)

I think of her as a daughter also. Gentlemen, if you would kindly stand to one side?

They turn their attention to a flirtatious, toothy BALLET TART, as the ballet continues to its climax and ends. The CHORUS resumes.

Their diva, Carlotta, also notices their leering attention to the dancers, and it causes her to throw a tantrum. This bit was also added to the movie.

CARLOTTA is getting angry ... CARLOTTA steams because the new managers pay no attention to her. ... Furious, CARLOTTA almost screams her final note in their faces.

CARLOTTA

All they want is the dancing!

ANDRE, suddenly aware of CARLOTTA'S rage, elbows FIRMIN, who is all over the BALLET TART, and they applaud loudly.

CARLOTTA

I hope he is as excited by dancing girls as your new managers ... because I will not be singing! (Film Companion, 2004, pp. 68-69).

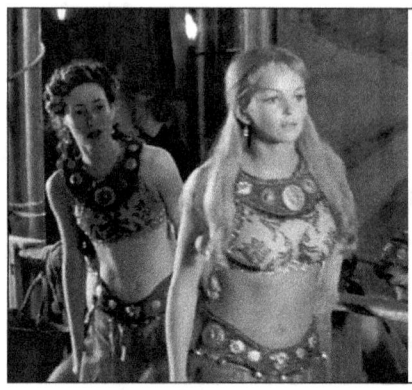 

The dancers in the film version had more revealing costumes than they did in the stage production. https://www.youtube.com/watch?v=N-3mL-s-kGw4

Stage Version

Compare this version to what is in the published libretto for the stage show. The scene has a completely different feel. No "toothy tarts" in this one.

LEFEVRE

We take particular pride here in the excellence of our ballet.

(MEG becomes prominent among the dancers)

ANDRE

Who is that girl, Lefevre?

LEFEVRE

Her? Meg Giry, Madame Giry's daughter. Promising dancer, M. Andre, most promising.

(CHRISTINE becomes prominent. She has absentmindedly fallen out of step)

GIRY

You! Christine Daae! Concentrate, girl!

MEG (quietly, to CHRISTINE)

Christine ... What's the matter?

FIRMIN to LEFEVRE

Daae? Curious name.

LEFEVRE

Swedish.

ANDRE

Any relation to the violinist?

LEFEVRE

His daughter, I believe. Always has her head in the clouds, I'm afraid.

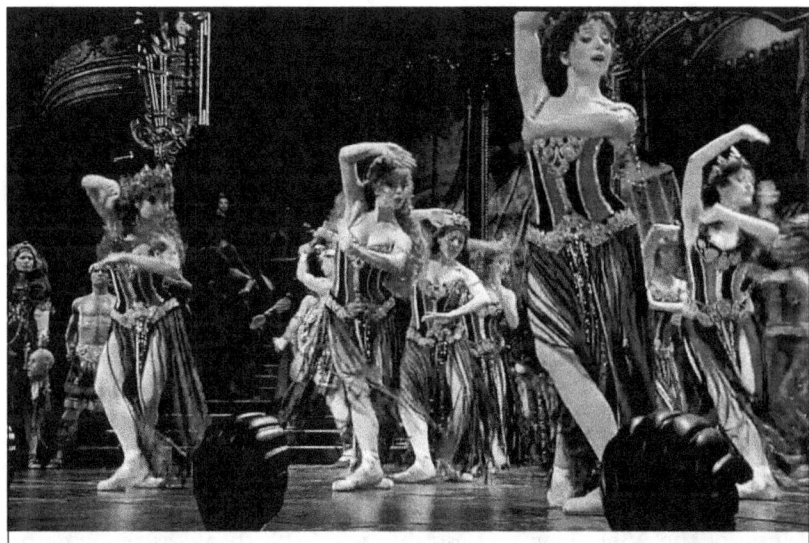

The dancers in the stage production had less revealing costumes than their film counterparts. https://www.youtube.com/watch?v=lXojdzgJA2c

The Music of the Night

Although Schumacher made an explicit decision to amp up the sexuality of the movie, sexuality has always been an underlying theme in the stage production. Nowhere is this more visible than in the song Music of the Night. The BBC documentary, *Behind the Mask*, calls this song "the erotic heart of the show" (part 5). Choreographer, Gillian Lynne, described what was happening in this scene in surprisingly explicit detail.

> The Phantom is deeply into sex. That's what Michael Crawford understood so beautifully. If you don't get from the Phantom that he was this ambitious, cruel man who was thwarted because he was born ugly and maimed, but he's powerful. And through his music he knows how to get into that little girl's mind.

Crawford noted that the Phantom's sexuality was expressed through his passion, so the audience had to recognize that. According to Lynne, Crawford perfected his cat-like movements and thought his hands should be prominent, so he had his sleeves made shorter. When he did:

> ... put his hand in front of Christine and went down the front of her, it was a statement, a big statement, and that added to the sensuality of it.

As he gets Christine into his lair, and drops the gate, he starts singing Music of the Night. Lynne describes what she thinks is really going on. I had to replay the interview twice to make sure I had really heard it correctly.

> He's really, really being powerful with her, and he's desperate, perhaps because he feels like he's not getting it, and he should, and he goes and hangs on the grill in the back, and she brushes up against him, and I've always felt that he must have got an erection, of course, and she'd probably never felt that in her life (*Behind the Mask*, part 5, 2008).

180

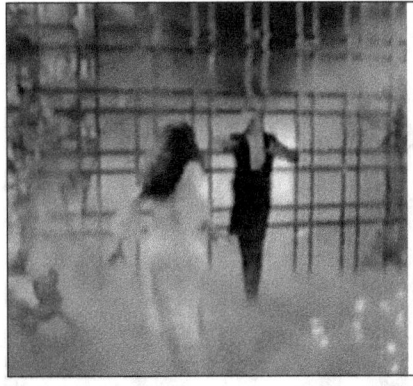

Alleged sighting of the Phantom boner, according to choreographer, Gillian Lynne.
https://www.youtube.com/watch?v=n5dhyiqhR7Y

Whoa, way too much information! Brightman reiterated the implied sexuality of the scenes with the Phantom in a far less-explicit way.

> It was totally sexually charged, the whole thing. From the role of Phantom to Christine, those two parts. That's probably what the root of it was about.

Even though the creators were clear about the sexuality of this story, the notes in the original libretto are pretty modest.

> During all this time [singing Music of the Night], the PHANTOM has conditioned CHRISTINE to the coldness of his touch and her fingers are brave enough to stray to his mask and caress it, with no hint of removing it (Perry, 1986, p. 147).

Biographer Michael Walsh also described the sexuality of the scene in the Phantom's lair, with both Music of the Night and Phantom of the Opera. His description is surprisingly explicit, especially his description of Brightman's high notes.

> The Phantom needs Christine as a singing servant, and his title song becomes a journey of seduction in which she starts vocalizing strangely at his behest. *Sarah Brightman's highest register expressed the weird orgasmic side effects of his bestial act of possession,* summarized in his insistence that she lets her darker side given in to the power of the music that he writes (Walsh, 1989, p. 179, emphasis added).

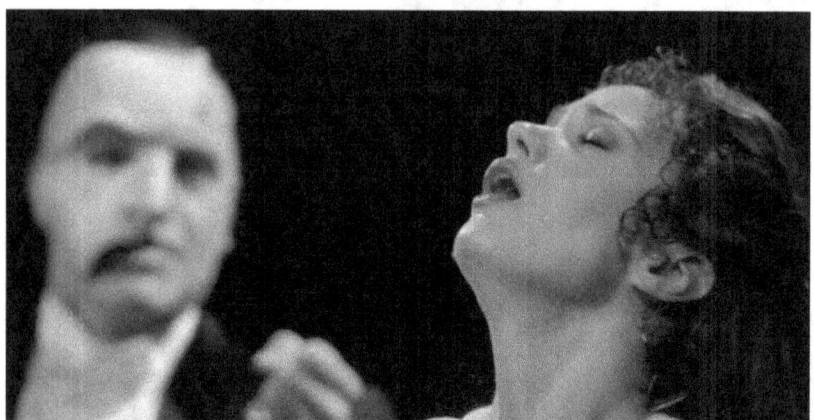

The stage version, the sexuality of Music of the Night is implied, even before Phantom touches Christine. Ramin Karimloo and Sierra Boggess. https://www.youtube.com/watch?v=ymclu8ZktrU

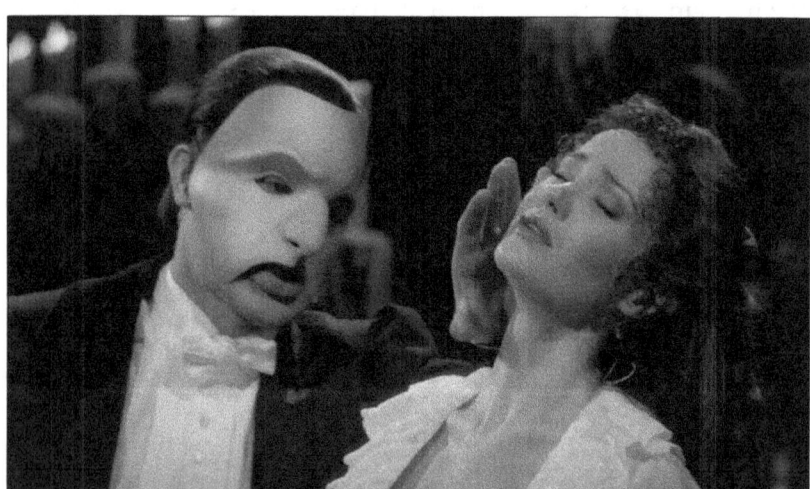

Phantom has Christine under his spell.
https://www.youtube.com/watch?v=ymclu8ZktrU

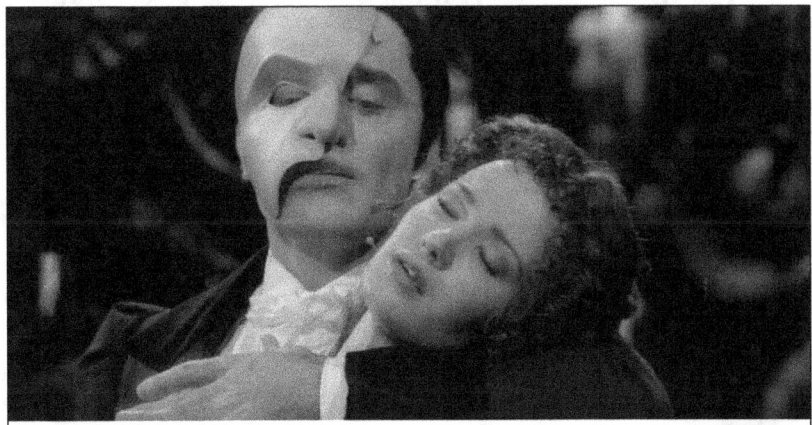

He finally touches her.
https://www.youtube.com/watch?v=ymclu8ZktrU

The Sexuality of the Phantom in Cultural Context

A blogger called bookwrm17 (2010) posted a thoughtful review on the evolving sexuality of *The Phantom of the Opera*. The story of *Phantom* is set in the *Belle Epoque* in France. Historically, she hypothesized that the *Belle Epoque* was an era that was transitioning between Victorian sexuality (where sexuality was feared and repressed), to the beginnings of a sexual revolution. It was a time of dualism and contradictions. Women were viewed as either Madonnas or whores, with no middle ground between the two.

> Erik, then, represents the Victorian idea of sexuality. He is horrifying, repulsive, and overwhelmingly associated with death, and society therefore rejects him and forces him into the underground, subconscious realm. Yet at the same time, there is something fascinating, something irresistibly attractive about him that prevents the other characters from simply being rid of him once and for all. Erik thus embodies perfectly

the dichotomy of Victorian fear of and preoccupation with sex (bookwrm17, 2010).

Describing the love triangle of Christine-Erik-Raoul, she notes that Christine is torn between Raoul, who represents chaste love, safe, but dull; and Erik, who is dangerous, but exciting.

In the 1925 adaptation, starring Lon Chaney, the Phantom's appearance is considered the most faithful adaptation to the book, but the sexual aspects are played down, as Christine is not attracted to him, but terrified. Bookwrm17 (2010) comments on how culture impacted the interpretation of the story. The movie was made in America, which was much more Puritanical than Leroux's France.

... thus even fifteen years after the novel's publication, mainstream American values were still firmly entrenched in Victorian morality.

Bookwrm17 (2010) then discusses the Lloyd Webber version, which veers from the original in several key ways. Lloyd Webber's interpretation is on the other side of the sexual revolution. Erik became simply The Phantom, and only half of his face was deformed, in contrast to the 1925 Lon Chaney film.

... Christine's horror of Erik is played down, and the sexuality of music is further emphasized. The song The Music of the Night describes music in very physical terms as caressing, intoxicating, and tender, and the famous duet between Christine and the Phantom concludes with a series of high notes that sound like a musical orgasm.

Lloyd Webber's Stage Version Wasn't Sexy Enough

The implied sexuality in the stage version of Music of the Night was not sexy enough for Schumacher. In the stage notes for the screenplay, the sexuality of this scene is spelled out in complete detail. Schumacher's screenplay reads like a bodice-ripper novel compared to the relatively tame libretto for the stage play.

PHANTOM

I have brought you to the seat of sweet music's throne ... to this kingdom where all must pay homage to music ... music ... You have come here, for one purpose and one alone ... Since the moment I first heard you sing, I have needed you with me, to serve me, to sing, for my music ... my music ...

The PHANTOM begins to lead the boat gently by a rope around the lair. He is lighting candles as he does so.

PHANTOM

(changing mood) **Night-time sharpens, heightens each sensation ... Darkness stirs and wakes imagination ... Silently the senses abandon their defenses ...**

The PHANTOM lights more candles revealing more of the lair. With the rope, he continues gently to guide CHRISTINE and the boat to shore. She is in a trance. Mesmerized and hypnotized by this stunning sexual master.

PHANTOM

Slowly, gently night unfurls its splendor ... Grasp it, sense it—tremulous and tender ... Turn your face away from the garish light of day, turn your thoughts away from cold, unfeeling light—and listen to the music of the night. Close your eyes and surrender to your darkest dreams! Purge your thoughts of the life you knew before! Close your eyes, let your spirit start to soar! And you'll live as you've never lived before ...

The PHANTOM has stepped into the water and walks towards the boat and CHRISTINE. This is highly sexual. She is completely in his spell.

PHANTOM

Softly, deftly, music shall caress you ... Hear it, feel it secretly possess you ... Open up your mind, let your fantasies unwind in this darkness which you know you cannot fight— the darkness of the music of the night ...

He lifts CHRISTINE out of the boat, her arms are around his neck, and is carrying her towards the shore. Their faces are very close. His love for her has consumed him.

PHANTOM

Let your mind start a journey through a strange, new world! Leave all thoughts of the life you knew before! Let your soul take you where you long to be! Only then can you belong to me ...

They reach the shore and the PHANTOM carries her toward a carved staircase. He lets her caress his mask, his hand reaches out to her face, travels down her neck and breasts. He carries her up the staircase which leads to a second grotto.

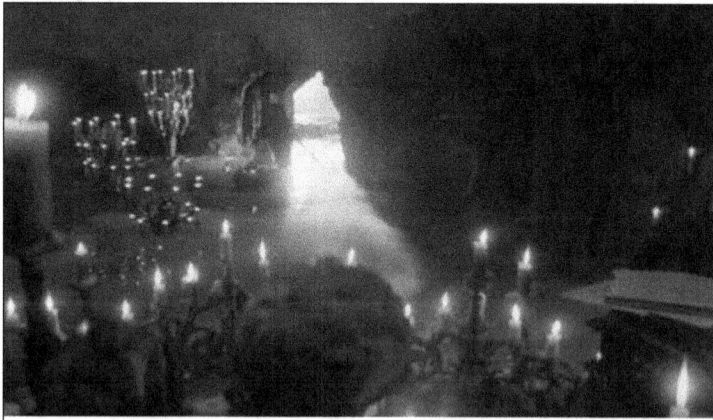

The Phantom's lair in the film, as he brings Christine there for the first time. https://www.youtube.com/watch?v=o1XY_ux5iUl

PHANTOM

Floating, falling ... sweet intoxication! Touch me, trust me ... savor each sensation! Let the dream begin, let your darker side give in to the power of the music that I write—

The power of the music of the night.

They step through into the second grotto. It is dominated by a huge bed in the shape of a black swan. The PHANTOM puts her down. She turns and is confronted by an AUTOMAT. This one is a life-size duplicate of herself in a wedding gown, surrounded by a mirror. It's too bizarre. CHRISTINE faints and falls back into the PHANTOM'S arms. He carries her to the bed where he lays her down, tenderly, and sensuously.

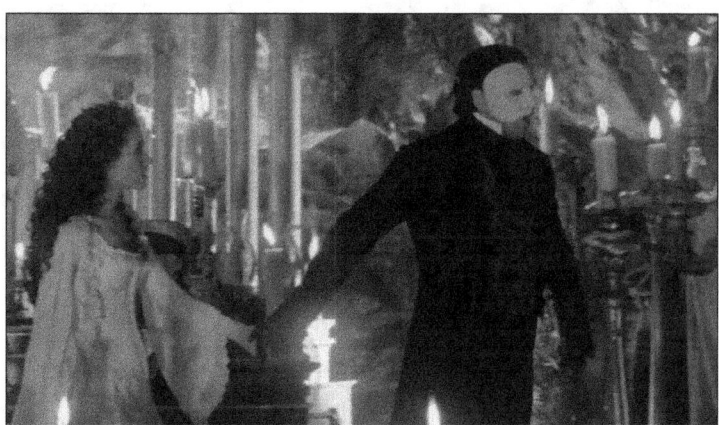

Phantom brings Christine into his lair while singing Music of the Night. https://www.youtube.com/watch?v=TJHMMrVgd-I&list=RDTJHMMrVgd-I

PHANTOM

You alone can make my song take flight—help me make the music of the night ...

The PHANTOM has slowly been drawing a series of sheer curtains around the bed until, as the music resolves, the curtains obscure both him and CHRISTINE and we ...

FADE TO BLACK. (Film Companion, 2004, p. 86)

Christine and Phantom's Sexy Costumes

Christine's costume during this scene is considerably more revealing than it was in the stage play. In fact, she is in her underwear and her robe is open. The play takes place in 1881. Even in the theater world, young women, especially very naïve, innocent young women, would probably not go out dressed only in a bustier and thigh-high stockings. At the very least, she probably would have tied her robe. In the stage version, she is still wearing her costume, and her robe is closed. More on this in the next Chapter.

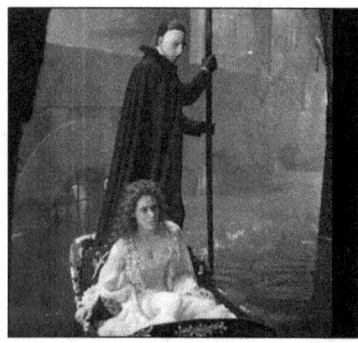

Christine is in her underwear rather than a costume in the film version. https://www.youtube.com/watch?v=o1XY_ux5iUl

We also notice that before Christine walks through the mirror, she is wearing little to no eye makeup. After she walks through, she is wearing quite a bit. According to a note on Amazon, this was not a continuity mistake. Rather, it was meant to reflect her "awakening sexuality."

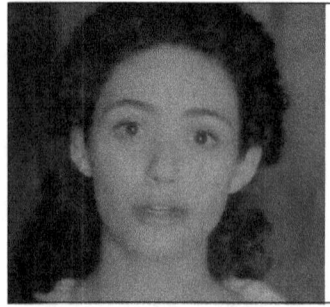

Christine wearing little makeup before she goes through the mirror. https://www.youtube.com/watch?v=yh3_ps50yrg

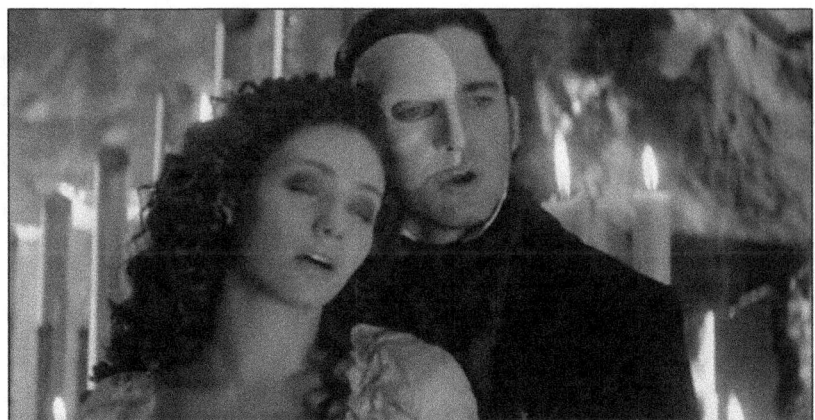

She is wearing considerably more makeup once she enters the Phantom's lair. https://www.youtube.com/watch?v=TJHMMrVgd-I&list=RDTJHMMrVgd-I

The sexuality was also portrayed by the change in costumes for the male leads, particularly the Phantom, as Longino (2004) describes.

> His trademark mask in the movie is white kid leather. His shirt, puffy. And unbuttoned halfway down, revealing the smidgens of hair adorning the chest of *The Phantom of the Opera*.
>
> It's never been this way on the stage. As fans readily know, Michael Crawford, and every other singer who's strutted Broadway as the star of Sir Andrew Lloyd Webber's *The Phantom of the Opera*, have appeared conservatively nipped and tuxed.
>
> But in Joel Schumacher's new $40 million movie version, opening in Atlanta and other select cities today, all bets are off. If the director had his way, that would apply to the men's shirts, too.
>
> "Joel wanted me topless at first," says Gerard Butler, the virtually unknown 35-year-old actor from Scotland selected to portray on film the eerie, disfigured and phantomly "angel of music" (Longino, 2004).

There Are Also Some Disturbing Elements

Unfortunately, along with the increased sexuality—surprising, but tame by many modern standards—were some disturbing elements, which were decidedly neither tame nor acceptable. I'll describe these in the next chapter.

CHAPTER 15

Disturbing Elements in Lloyd Webber's *Phantom*

I would never have embarked on this project if I didn't enjoy *The Phantom of the Opera*. But enjoying something doesn't mean that I take a completely non-critical view. I'm forced to concede that there is also an underlying misogyny and other disturbing elements in Lloyd Webber's version of *Phantom*. The story itself would be called stalking if it took place in modern times. He kidnapped her, held her prisoner, and threatened to kill her boyfriend if she wouldn't marry him. That is not "a great romance." In fact, there is something quite disturbing about how many people think it is. Violence should not equal love. Ever. It's not acceptable to assault (not to mention kill) other people, even if you had a wretched childhood. We obviously sympathize with the Phantom, but that doesn't mean that we should call that behavior "romance." It's the classic excuse that is often offered for partner violence: "He just acts that way because he loves you." "Because he loves you" doesn't make it acceptable.

That's bad enough. Unfortunately, more disturbing elements of this show emerged when I studied it in greater detail. When writing about something like a movie or stage show, you see it differently. In the course of writing this book, I went through scenes frame by frame, I read a lot of online commentaries about different scenes, and I stood back and looked at where *Phantom* fit in the theater world, among the other works of Lloyd Webber, and in the world at large.

Unfortunately, there are elements that condone violence against women, including rape and abuse, and a general disempowering of women throughout. Here are some examples. Surprisingly, this pervasive misogyny starts with the theater building itself.

Disturbing Signs in the Theater

In the course of writing this book, I went to see *Phantom* in New York and in London. (It's lovely when your theater tickets are tax deductible.) At the theater in New York, I noticed that the decoration over the stage clearly showed a terrified woman being pursued and assaulted by some weird, satyr-like creature. "Okay," I thought, "it's just part of the theater, not part of the show." Then I saw the same image over the stage in London. Why was an image that is clearly showing sexual assault hanging above the stage? They did it on purpose! I found the answer in the 25th anniversary companion volume. On the comment of the satyrs grabbing women's breasts, the caption said as follows:

> Director Harold Prince worked with Maria Bjornson on the proscenium design for the original London production, inspired in part by a BBC documentary he had seen.

Prince said:

> I was watching a BBC documentary about people who were physically incapacitated ... and I sensed that the thing that united them all was a very normal, healthy sexuality. And that's what Maria and I wanted to put up there. It affected the design of the proscenium, with its statutes intertwined in some moment of passion which the audience both sees and absorbs (Heatley, 2011, p. 56).

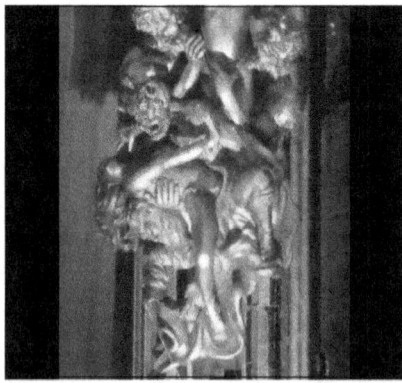

Weird proscenium at Her Majesty's in London. The woman is clearly terrified and pushing the satyr creature away.

Healthy sexuality? Moment of passion? And because someone has a physical disability, they're allowed to act however they want? That statement is not only vile, but it's also quite ableist.

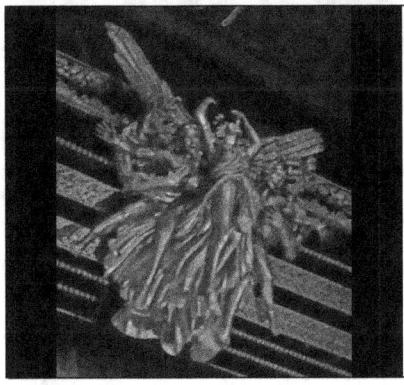

Another weird proscenium at the Majestic in New York. The satyrs are groping women's breasts. The women don't look like they are "caught in a moment of passion." They look like they're trying to get away.

The building also had a role in the movie version. Schumacher characterized the building as "a beautiful woman," so there are many statues of naked women. Naked women are a staple of much art, so that, by itself, is not concerning. What is concerning is when those naked women become a part of a larger schema that objectifies women, which we see in many of his other decisions.

Forcing Christine

Another example of Lloyd Webber's disturbing view of women has to do with kidnapping Christine. In the stage version celebrating the 25th anniversary, during The Phantom of the Opera song, Phantom is supposed to be gently bringing her into his world. Instead, the Phantom is clearly dragging Christine by the wrist. She seems to be fighting him. This doesn't exactly seem consensual. Is this supposed to be romantic?

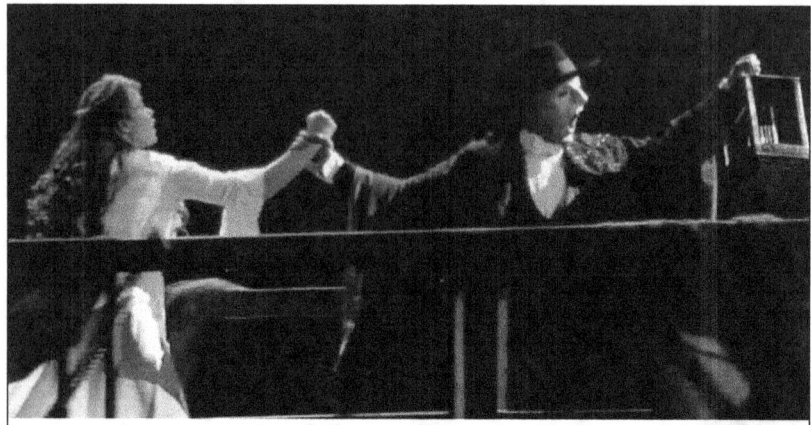

The Phantom is dragging, not coaxing, Christine into his lair.
https://www.youtube.com/watch?v=QVLB_D68Bt8

Fortunately, it's not that way in the movie. He is gently leading her by the hand. She is willingly following him, being mesmerized by his appearance. That seems truer to the intent of the story.

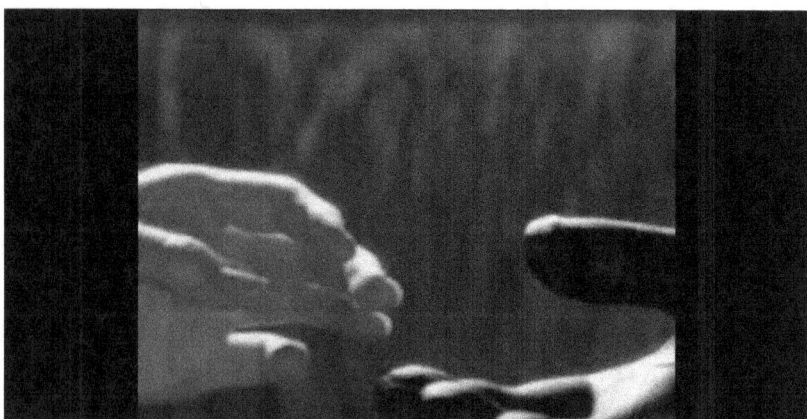

Phantom gently coaxing Christine into his lair in the film version.
https://www.youtube.com/watch?v=-JaeBxYCl9k

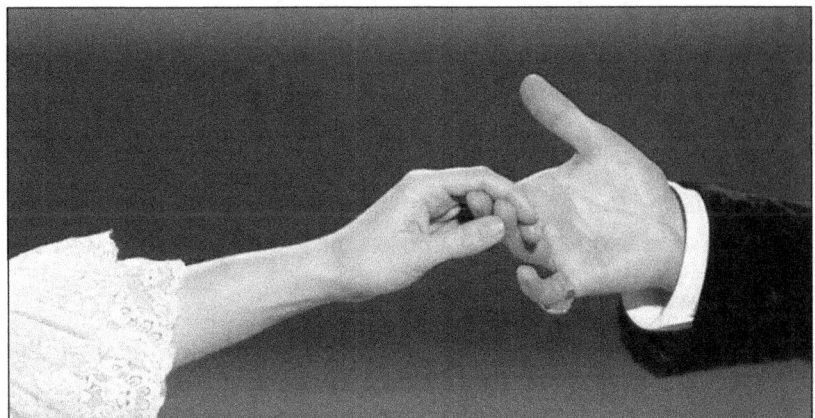

The Phantom is coaxing, not dragging, Christine into his lair in the Russian premiere. https://www.youtube.com/watch?v=QVLB_D68Bt8

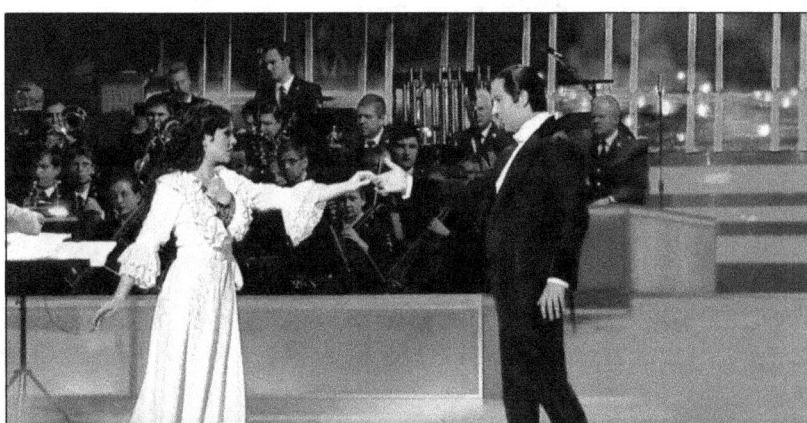

At the Russian premiere of Phantom. Here the scene is quite lovely. https://www.youtube.com/watch?v=I6SWE1gqFF4

Don Juan Triumphant

Yet another example of Lloyd Webber's real distain for women is found in the words for the *Don Juan Triumphant*. Women are there to serve at the pleasure of men. Even innocent young women are not safe from the lascivious Don Juan. I realize that this is part of the character, that he's supposed to be gross and promiscuous. Nonetheless, these lyrics are disturbing.

CHORUS

Here the sire may serve the dam,

Here the master takes his meat!

Here the sacrificial lamb

Utters one despairing bleat!

Sacrificial lamb? One despairing bleat? Sounds pretty awful and non-consensual to me.

CARLOTTA AND CHORUS

Poor young maiden! For the thrill

On your tongue of stolen sweets

You will have to pay the bill—

Tangled in the winding sheets!

Serve the meal and serve the maid!

Serve the master so that, when

Tables, plans, and maids are laid,

Don Juan triumphs once again!

Serve the meal, serve the maid? Don Juan then sings about his brilliant plan to trick an innocent young girl into sleeping with him.

DON JUAN

When you met you word my cloak,

With my scarf, you hid your face.

She believes she dines with me,

In her master's borrowed place!

Furtively, we'll scoff and quaff,

Stealing what, in truth, is mine.

When it's late and modesty

Starts to mellow, with the wine ...

...

PASSARINO

Poor thing hasn't got a chance!

DON JUAN

Here's my hat, my cloak, and sword.

Conquest is assured, if I do not forget myself and laugh ...

Of course, they are supposed to be portraying someone who has a lot of lovers. But generally, those are consensual. Using trickery, and feeling like he has a right to take her virginity, makes the character more ominous, and frankly, disgusting.

The Phantom is Violent When He Doesn't Get His Way

Let's go back to the Phantom character himself. The Phantom is violent with Christine and chokes her when he gets mad. Really not okay! This occurs when Raoul comes to rescue Christine in the 25th Anniversary performance. According to the libretto, there is supposed to be a gate that separates Raoul from the Phantom's lair. There wasn't one when they staged the 25th anniversary performance. So, when Raoul comes to save Christine, the Phantom responds by *choking* her. He's clearly cutting off her air, and he doesn't care.

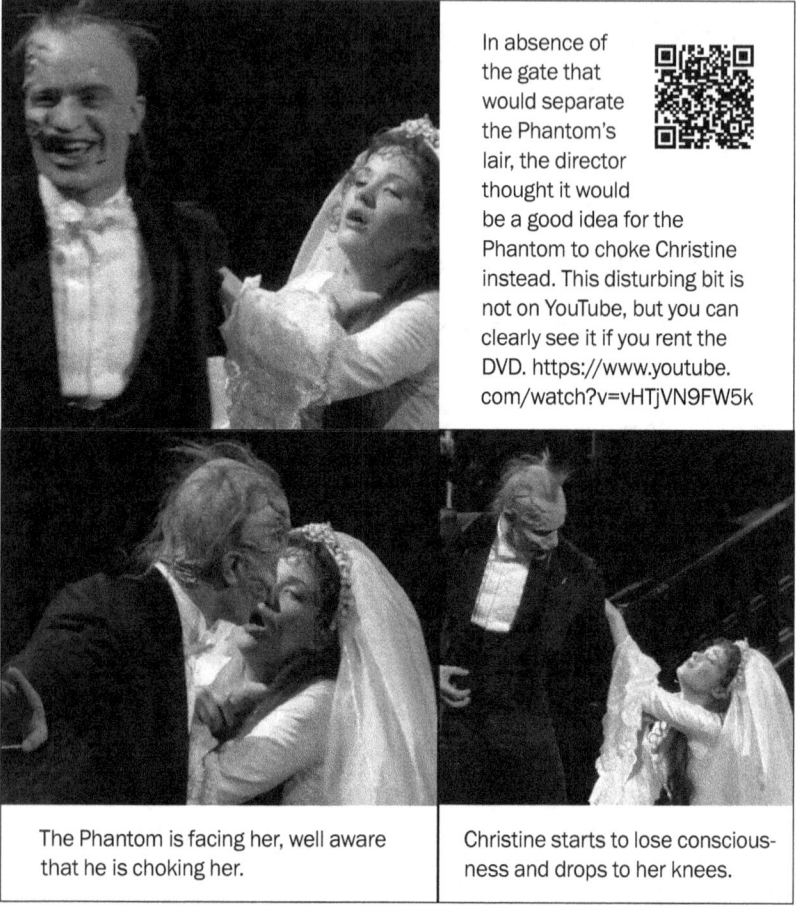

In absence of the gate that would separate the Phantom's lair, the director thought it would be a good idea for the Phantom to choke Christine instead. This disturbing bit is not on YouTube, but you can clearly see it if you rent the DVD. https://www.youtube.com/watch?v=vHTjVN9FW5k

The Phantom is facing her, well aware that he is choking her.

Christine starts to lose consciousness and drops to her knees.

At one point, he faces her and tightens her grip. He keeps singing, and tightens his grip. Clearly, he knows exactly what he is doing.

She eventually drops to the ground and he finally lets go. Then the Phantom oddly sings:

PHANTOM

Monsieur, I bid you welcome!

Did you think that I would harm her?

Excuse me! You just did!

Why would I make her pay for the sins that are yours?

But clearly, he just did. What made the director think that this would be a good idea?

The Phantom Chokes His Way Through the Sequel Too

Choking shows up again in the *Phantom* sequel (played by the same actors, Sierra Boggess and Ramin Karimloo). The Phantom chokes Christine in version 2.0 of *Love Never Dies*. The Phantom has just figured out that Christine's son is likely his. His son screams when he sees the Phantom's face for the first time. (Do you blame him? He's just a little kid.) The Phantom demands the truth about Gustave's parentage. She sings, trying to placate him, and apologize for the fact that Gustave screamed. The Phantom responds by choking her.

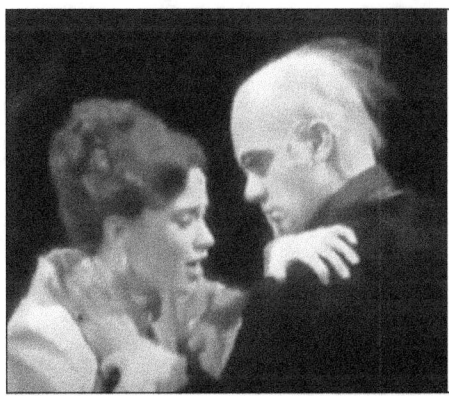

The Phantom sings, "do you have something to confess?" and starts choking her!
https://www.youtube.com/watch?v=-3hLpQPqW28

She keeps singing, saying she's sorry, and trying to placate him. The Phantom responds by tightening his grip. No way he didn't know exactly what he was doing.

Still choking her.
https://www.youtube.com/watch?v=-3hLpQPqW28

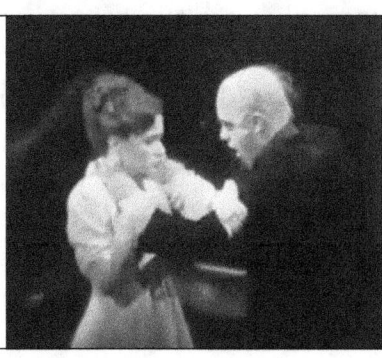

Eventually, she persuades him to stop choking her and *she comforts him*. There is something really off about this scene. It's like it's reinforcing all the classic myths about partner violence, and then setting them to song!

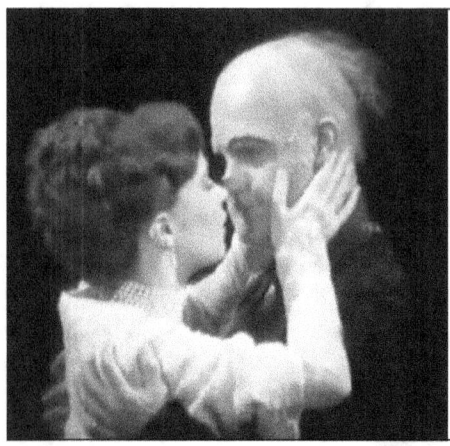

Comforting the Phantom after he is finished choking her!
https://www.youtube.com/watch?v=-3hLpQPqW28

Fortunately, they cut this bit out when they made the much-improved Australian version.

Misogyny in the Movie Version

As I described in the previous chapter, the screenplay for the movie is particularly misogynistic. There are hints of that when you watch the movie, but where you really see it is when you read the background and find out what Schumacher and Lloyd Webber were trying to accomplish, and read the notes in the screenplay. For example, one of the dancers that Firmin and Andre are hitting on is described as a "toothy tart." Because she is a dancer, and "toothy," that makes her a tart? That's not in the original play. Again, there is the assumption that all the dancers, except Christine, are whores. Fortunately, some of these elements were less obvious when the film was made, but the notations in the screenplay do show a certain mindset about women: it's back to that old conceptualization of women as either Madonnas or whores.

Christine is Under Age

In the film, there is another disturbing element not in the stage version: Christine's age. Emmy Rossum, the actress that played Christine, was 16 when she started filming. What I'm going to say now is no reflection on the job Emmy Rossum did in the movie. I thought she was amazing. What was concerning, however, are some of the things Schumacher and Lloyd Webber said in the many interviews they conducted. Again, this reflects a certain mindset.

Let's start with the age difference between the principal actors. Butler was 34. In any other context, a 34-year-old groping a 16-year-old would not be acceptable. In the context of *Phantom*, we call it "a great romance." Think of it this way: what if Christine was a high school junior, and the Phantom was her handsome biology teacher? Would it be okay then? Or would we be calling the cops? Further, most actresses playing Christine on the stage are in the mid-to-late 20s. This show takes on an entirely different feel when the character is a teenager vs. an adult playing Christine. Now according to Rossum, both Butler and Wilson were perfect gentlemen to her. But that doesn't take away from the wolfish intentions of the director and composer.

In the screenplay, the Phantom is supposed to completely tear off Christine's costume after he abducts her during Point of No Return. This action speaks to the non-consensual and violent nature of their relationship. Fortunately, Phantom did not do that in the movie. But its inclusion in the screenplay is disturbing. Schumacher clearly believes that that behavior is sexy.

Christine in Her Underwear

Something else of note. In the film version, Christine sings a surprising amount of songs in her underwear. This was not true for the stage version. For example, in the stage version, Christine is wearing a dressing gown

201

over her costume, and it is tied shut, when she sings Phantom of the Opera and during Music of the Night. In the movie, Christine is wearing an open robe over her very-revealing underwear. These costuming choices indicate relative power in the relationships. If the girl is in her underwear, and all the adults are dressed, it doesn't take a genius to know who has more power in the situation. And oddly, when she ventures into the Phantom's lair, she is wearing no shoes. Why would she go traipsing through the bowels of the Opera House, go on a boat ride, and ride a horse, with no shoes? That doesn't even make sense, and also reflects her powerlessness.

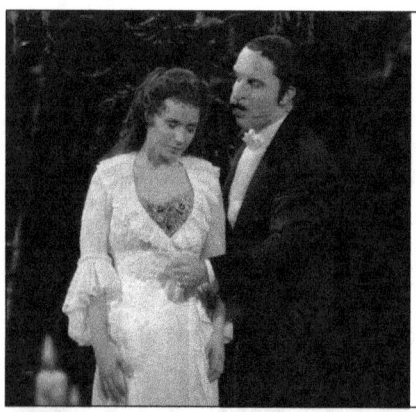

In the play, Christine (usually played by actresses in their mid-20s) is wearing a full costume with a closed dressing gown on top of it. https://www.youtube.com/watch?v=ymclu8ZktrU

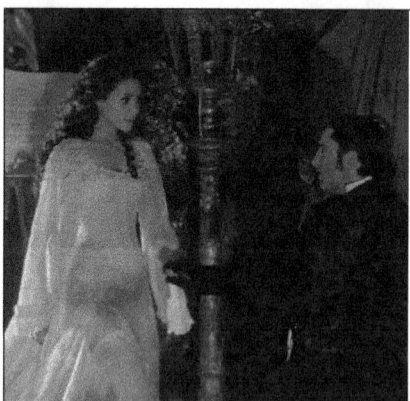

Not so in the film version. Sixteen-year-old Christine is in an open robe and her underwear (a bustier with thigh-highs). https://www.youtube.com/watch?v=TJHMMrVgd-I&list=RDT-JHMMrVgd-I

To make matters worse, when Christine awakens from her sleep, she is missing her stockings. I ran across an online forum that had a great deal of discussion about the significance of that. Was this a continuity error? Or did the Phantom take advantage of her? (I know. Too much time on their hands.) The consensus on the forum was that the Phantom did not take advantage. Either way, she's quite undressed. Given the time when the story happens, and her character's innocence, it seems out of character that she would walk around with so few clothes in front of a strange man. Further, real-life Emmy Rossum would also later complain that having to wear all these corsets warped her growth.

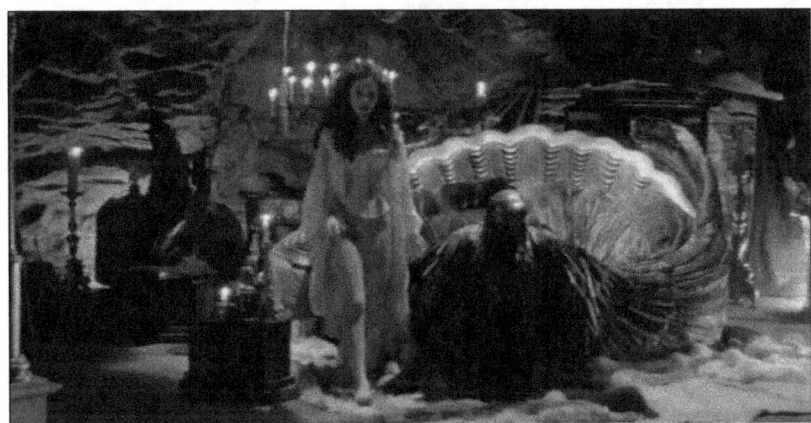

Christine awakens in the Phantom's lair *sans* stockings.
https://www.youtube.com/watch?v=hgEVVCBu6EU

All I Ask of You

Another key place where Christine is in her underwear is when she sings All I Ask of You with Raoul. In the stage version, Christine has a dress on under her cape. In the film version, she's wearing a corset and a slip under her cape—in the snow. Some might argue that she had "no time" to get dressed before she dashed out of the Opera House. Yet, in the stage version, where she arguably has "no time" in real time, she manages to get dressed. In the film, there's no excuse for Christine not being dressed. They literally had all the time they needed. It was clearly done deliberately.

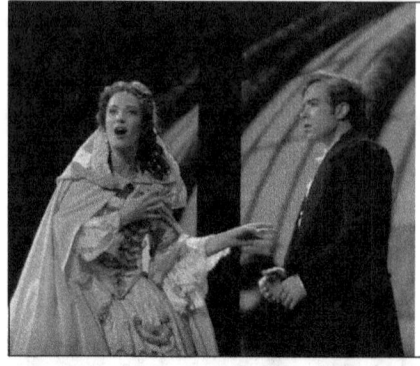

Christine in the stage version, fully dressed.
https://www.youtube.com/watch?v=Yq6NUKNF3LQ

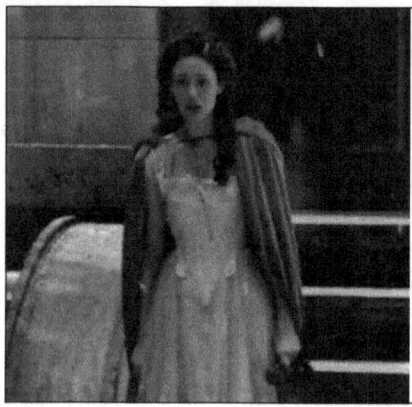

Christine in the movie version, in her corset and slip.
https://www.youtube.com/watch?v=Zy1lWiHHHFY

Christine's Coming of Age

Both Lloyd Webber and Schumacher specifically wanted to cast a very young actress in the part of Christine for the film version. Their reason for this is not nice. In the stage version, Christine is in her mid-to-late 20s. In the movie, she's a kid. Schumacher boiled down the essence of the story. There is something quite debauched in their thoughts behind how they cast this role.

> The story really has to be this very young girl for the first time experiencing this romantic awakening with Patrick Wilson's character. And for the first time experiencing with the Gerry Butler character a darker, more sexual, obsessional, destructive relationship.

At this point, Schumacher apparently paused during the interview, and then said with a wide smile.

You know, the good kind (Longino, 2004).

Of an "obsessional, destructive relationship"? And what kind would that be? Lloyd Webber also weighed in why they needed a younger Christine than what they would have gotten away with on the stage.

> Joel and I have always been pretty clear about what we wanted to do for the film. We wanted to have a young Christine because that's what the original book says, and I think it makes much more sense if she really is a girl from the *corps de ballet*. Of course, we can't do that in the theater because you can't have a 16-year-old do that role night after night (Longino, 2004).

Yeah, the Child Labor Laws would probably kick in. Schumacher further explained his reasons for a young cast in an interview with *Vanity Fair* (Powers, 2004).

> I said I'd only do it with a very, very young cast who are beautiful and sexy. If the person playing Christine is not a teenager, I can't make it work, because her character's so innocent. If she's 35-years-old, I just want to smack her and say, "Grow up."

So, Christine is the problem? *Vanity Fair* explained why Michael Crawford couldn't be in the movie.

> With Rossum cast as Christine, it was no longer possible to have the Phantom played by a 60-something actor like Michael Crawford.

> "You can't have a teenage girl with somebody that old," cracks Schumacher. "It would be Lolita, 1870" (Powers, 2004).

Yet, these two old men drooling over the imminent deflowering of a 16-year-old girl is not? *USA Today* also made reference to the strange incestual undercurrent in the storyline, referring to The Point of No

Return as "the intense duet of fiery desire shared by Christine and the Phantom, *who passes from doting father figure to potential seducer* (emphasis added; Wloszczyna, 2004).

> The studio wanted a PG-13 and was worried about the scary parts. I was more worried about The Point of No Return.

Christine's Disempowerment Continues

Christine's disempowerment continues in the sequel, *Love Never Dies*. She's caught in a vicious triangle between two awful guys. Christine spends a lot of time placating Raoul, who has turned into a drunken lout. The Phantom appears and sings of his undying love. But when Christine doesn't do what he wants, he threatens to kidnap her child and make him disappear. Raoul finds out that she has agreed to sing for the Phantom (not realizing that she has been blackmailed into cooperating), and grabs her wrist while he sings, "I'll deal with you later."

Eventually, Christine, who seems to have no say about anything gets caught up in a triangle between the Phantom, Raoul, and Madame Giry, which eventually leads to her death.

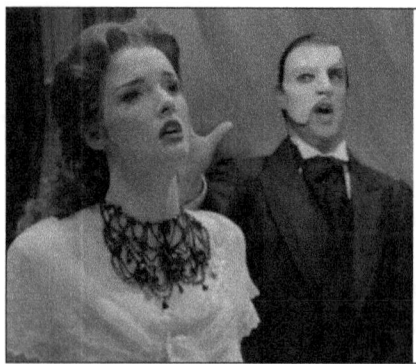

Christine is caught in a vicious love triangle that leads to her death in *Love Never Dies*. https://www.youtube.com/watch?v=_YJY2wRk-PA

At the London press launch of *Love Never Dies*, the Phantom sings, Till I Hear You Sing to an effigy of Christine, who's in an iron cage. It's a great song, but the staging is quite creepy.

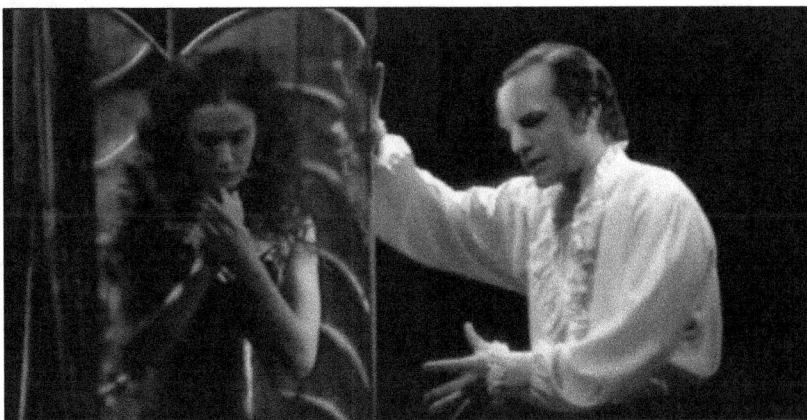

Phantom singing to a caged effigy of Christine at the Love Never Dies launch. The cage is in the London version of the show as well. https://www.youtube.com/watch?v=4Ir-WVfX_JrA

Summary

The view of women in these manifestations of *Phantom* is misogynist. There is no other word for it. Even Christine, the most celebrated character, is worshipped for her innocence, but disempowered by the men in her life. Women who are not identified as "innocent" are portrayed as whores. The view of women reflected in *Phantom* and the sequel suggests that Lloyd Webber has this negative view. His behavior in his personal life is consistent with this viewpoint. (Although, to be fair, he's been awful to some important men in his life as well.) Both Lloyd Webber and Schumacher would argue that they "love" women. But the women that they "love" are cardboard cutouts. They are not real women, who are their own people, and who have control over their lives.

CHAPTER 16

Feel the Love
The Critics Weigh In

Given critics' negative reaction to the stage version, it's not surprising that their reaction to the *Phantom* film was mostly negative. Rotten Tomatoes, a website which aggregates critics' reviews and gives films overall ratings, summarized 167 reviews; the *Phantom* movie received an average rating of 5 out of 10. Fifty-four of the reviews were "fresh" (good), and 113 were "rotten." The overall positive rating was 32%. Rotten Tomatoes summarized the Critics' Consensus as follows:

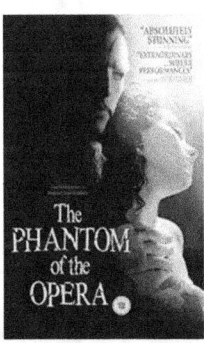

The Music of the Night has hit something of a sour note. Critics are calling the screen adaptation of Andrew Lloyd Webber's popular musical histrionic, boring, and lacking in both romance and danger. Still, some have praised the film for its sheer spectacle (Rotten Tomatoes, 2017).

As it turned out, what many critics really hated was not so much the film, but the musical itself. Given how popular the musical has been, I was somewhat surprised. But I guess I shouldn't have been. *Phantom's* popularity, indeed, may be part of the problem: it's popular, therefore it can't be good. Schumacher had a thing or two to say about critics' elitism in an interview with *USA Today*.

There's this elitist snob thing. If the public loves something, it's not good. If it is some obscure thing the critic loves, that is good.

It's very condescending and insulting. The most scathing critic in Britain wrote my favorite quote about Andrew. Something like, "Let's face it. No one in the world loves Andrew Lloyd Webber but the public." Like my godchild would say, "Duh!" (Wloszczyna, 2004).

The movie gave critics an opportunity to vent their spleens about Lloyd Webber's "big, gaudy spectacle." For critics, it was a dream come true! Add Schumacher, and his reputation for excess (and nipples in costumes!), and wait for the explosion. The critics did not disappoint.

When the reviews came raining in, they were like pennies from heaven in certain portions of cyberspace. Michael Crawford fans chortled, "We told you so," and lovingly posted the reviews on their websites. The amount of *schadenfreude* was amazing; "Ha, ha, ha! It sucks. We told you that it would." Even so, a few critics broke ranks and liked it.

I've summarized a sample of these reviews below. Buckle your seatbelts. It's going to get nasty.

Thumbnail Reviews from Rotten Tomatoes

Several reviewers didn't like it on general principle. Here are some thumbnail versions. A few of the longer reviews are included in the next section. This gives you a bit of an idea about where this is going.

A tedious production made worse by Webber's pseudo-operatic score.

Boo Allen, *Denton Record-Chronicle*

Andrew Lloyd Webber and Joel Schumacher turn out to be a perfect match. Two other people couldn't pull off spectacle this bad.

Jimmy O., *Film Snobs*

Broadway bore comes to the big screen in a movie-musical adaptation that's too little, too late, and too terrible for words.

James Rocchi, *Netflix*

How much you like this movie all depends on whether you like the music; you either love it or you find it repetitive and uninteresting.

Cherryl Dawson and Leigh Ann Palone,
TheMovieChicks.com

Takes everything that's wrong with Broadway and puts it on the big screen in a gaudy splat.

Stephanie Zacharek, *Salon.com*

I didn't see a single fat lady in the entire thing. That must be why it never ended.

Collin Souter, *eFilmCritic.com*

Joel Schumacher's film adaptation of Lloyd Webber's *The Phantom of the Opera* combines fingernails-on-blackboard audio agony with bamboo-under-fingernails physical torture.

Carrie Rickey, *Philadelphia Inquirer*

The movie version of Lloyd Webber's swooning 1986 horror operetta has been directed, by Joel Schumacher, as if Schumacher were the world's hardest-working upholstery salesman.

Owen Gleiberman, *Entertainment Weekly*

Commit one unforced error after another on its way to becoming one of the sloppiest major musicals of contemporary times.

Tim Brayton, *Antagony & Ecstasy*

Without a proper Phantom, the entire enterprise sags monumentally, and, unfortunately, Butler is a disaster here.

David Noh, *Film Journal International*

My own reaction to the current version fashioned by Mr. Schumacher is one of pure stupefaction.

Andrew Sarris, *New York Observer*

Even the most die-hard *Phantom* aficionados might be struck dumb by the sheer level of the crescendo and camp Schumacher achieves here.

Christopher Smith, *Bangor Daily News*

Non-fans will note that Webber's idiom is opera-lite, grafted together with rock, pop, and soap opera. Some of the set-pieces are kitsch allegro ...

Thomas Delapa, *Boulder Weekly*

Some Critics Liked It

It's one of those movies where I spent a lot of my first viewing thinking, "Yes, this is what movies are really all about."

Ken Hanke, *Mountain Xpress (Asheville, NC)*

This is a lavish production best enjoyed at your favorite theater where the full effect of the music and ambiance can be enjoyed. It is also one to be enjoyed more than once.

Vince Koehler, *Entertainment Spectrum*

A spectacular ode to pure romanticism

Fr. Chris Carpenter, *Catholic Sun*

Schumacher has indeed delivered the lavish, lushly romantic film that fans have envisioned for years.

Michael Dequina, *Film Threat*

A visual masterpiece.

Alex Sandell, *Juicy Cerebellum*

Fantastic sets, costumes, great art direction, and imaginative camera work make this a visually stunning film. The musical score, not so much.

Robert Roten, *Laramie Movie Scope*

Damning with faint praise, this was considered a positive review. What does he say when he doesn't like something?

The movie version of Lloyd Webber's smash hit does to the music what the music did to the words and story: It distracts the mind and cajoles the eyes to the point that one doesn't really care that everything the ears are hearing is pure nonsense.

Philip Kennicott, *Washington Post*

A More In-Depth Look at Several Reviews

Critics had a number of issues with the film and the musical itself. Below is a summary of a few detailed reviews. These are in stark contrast to the general fan reaction described in the next chapter. Film critic Roger Ebert (2004) had a particularly interesting review. He liked the movie. What he really hated was *Phantom*.

What I am essentially disliking is not the film, but the underlying material. I do not think Lloyd Webber wrote a very good musical. The story is thin beer for the time it takes to tell it, and the music is maddeningly repetitious.

Yet Schumacher has bravely taken aboard this dreck and made of it a movie I'm pleased to have seen. To have seen, that is, as opposed to have heard ...

He loved the "look" of Schumacher's film, describing it as "great." "...
he creates a film so visually resonant you want to float in it." Ebert
also takes a crack at *Phantom* fans.

> For a decade in London, you couldn't go past Her Majesty's
> Theater without seeing them with their backpacks, camped out,
> waiting all night in hopes of a standby ticket. People have seen
> it 10, 20, 100 times—have never done anything else in their lives
> but see it. They will embrace the movie, and I congratulate them,
> because they have waited too long to be disappointed.

Lloyd Webber thought *Phantom* fans would embrace film, and yet, many
of them hated it. Ebert ends, surprisingly, with a recommendation to
see it, while acknowledging that his review is "nutty." He's recommending
a movie that he "didn't seem to like much."

> There wasn't much Schumacher could have done with the
> story or the music he was handed, but in the areas over which
> he held saw, he has triumphed. This is such a fabulous
> production that by recasting two of the three leads and adding
> some better songs it could have been, well, great (Ebert, 2004).

I like it. Now change everything.

Other reviewers were not so kind. This reviewer, from *The Rocky
Mountain Bullhorn* (Snider, 2004), thought that fans of the original
musical would like this "messy, excessive cinematic adaptation of the
stage musical." Calling Webber's music "bombastic" and his storytelling
"mushy," he warns:

> ... this *Phantom*, with more cluttered production design, clumsy
> camerawork, and incoherent editing than one thought possible
> in a two-and-a-half-hour film,

His recommendation?

> [This musical] is the kind of movie musical that deserves to
> be locked up in a dank, water-filled dungeon and left to molder.

Wow, that's harsh! The reviewer also had a few kind words regarding the director.

> Schumacher, a filmmaker without a subtle instinct in his body, works overtime to drench his film in ornamentation ... It's true that Webber's grandiose *Phantom* lends itself to such extravagance, but the director's visual lavishness is chintzy when it should be luxurious, suffocating when it should be alluring.

In response to "make it sexy."

> Vainly attempting to amplify the play's sexuality, Schumacher has his blandly handsome Phantom (Gerard Butler) bellow and pout like a childish maniac. ... like so much of this odious, overblown opus—merely the stuff daytime soap operas are made of.

Snider is a fan of musicals, in general. He even likes the stage version of *Phantom*, which he insists can be a pleasure, albeit a guilty one. However, he felt that the film gave musicals a bad name.

> Nearly everything that is good about the stage version is lost in the movie version ... [Schumacher] has directed good films, but when he directs bad ones, he directs the hell out of them. I'm thinking of the loud bombast of *Batman & Robin*, or the braying idiocy of *Bad Company*. All of his worst impulses–from bad casting to bad camera angles–are brought to bear in *Phantom*.

He thought Think of Me sounded more like a 1980s pop tune, which made no sense in the middle of a 19th-century opera. He also wondered if Schumacher knew it was a musical.

> A Phantom who can't sing, and who isn't even hideous ... It's as though Schumacher hates musicals, and is trying to sabotage every musical element of the film. ...

Schumacher seems to have had no idea, when he was filming, that there would be music added later, or what kind of music it might be ... regardless of what the texture of the music would suggest he ought to do.

And a few more kind words for the director.

Some of my colleagues have said that a director as shallow as Schumacher is the perfect fit for a musical as shallow as *Phantom of the Opera*, but I think the finished product proves otherwise. ... On screen, what passion and excitement there is in the work has been sucked out; it has become boring (Snider, 2004).

Critic Jeffrey M. Anderson cuts right to the heart of the matter.

If you need to adapt a huge Broadway spectacle to the screen, who better to do it than Joel Schumacher, the man forever infamous for putting nipples on Batman?

Yet, there were a few actual kind words for the director.

And in truth, Schumacher does a remarkable job navigating the film's tremendous sets, floating his camera through rafters and around pillars with great energy.

But not a fan of Lloyd Webber's.

Yet, we have the play itself to deal with ... plagued by Andrew Lloyd Webber's hideous and already dated musical score (parts of it sound like 1980s hair metal; Anderson, 2004)

A. O. Scott entitled his review, "Back with a vengeance: The music of the night." Apparently, not a fan of either Lloyd Webber or Schumacher.

"Far too many notes for my taste," sniffs one of the proprietors of the *Opéra Populaire* in *The Phantom of the Opera*. I quite agree. ... his complaint applies perfectly to the music of Andrew Lloyd Webber, whose relentless bombast afflicts this movie like a bad case of swollen lymph nodes.

Just in case the first paragraph was too subtle, he further illuminates his point.

> Of course, Lord Lloyd Webber's music is the whole point of the film, and Joel Schumacher, the director, does his best to find a visual style to match the vulgarity and pretentiousness of the soundtrack. He succeeds admirably ... to produce nearly two and a half hours' worth of overstuffed tableaux...

> This kind of spectacle might work onstage ... but this screen version, for all its wailing emotionalism and elaborate production design, lacks both authentic romance and the thrill of memorable spectacle.

It really comes down to Lloyd Webber's score, which represents "a victory of pseudo-populist grandiosity over taste."

> ... an act of cultural butchery akin to turning an aviary of graceful swans and brilliant peacocks into an order of Chicken McNuggets.

Surprisingly, he did like the singers, calling both Butler and Rossum "impressive." And good point here!

> Although everyone in the movie is supposed to be French, only Miranda Richardson, as the head of the *corps de ballet*, attempts a French accent (Scott, 2004).

Cole Smithey (2005), who modestly refers to himself as "The Smartest Film Critic in the World," foreshadowed the content of his review by titling it a "musical cheese horror." I think we know where we're going with this. He noted that the film was "monotonous" and "doomed before shooting began."

> ... most audiences will either fall asleep or hit the cinema doors running. There is nothing imaginative in the film's musical arrangements or visual style to deliver the screechy play from its corny trappings. ...

He also mentioned that Miranda Richardson was the only one who bothered with a French accent, but then didn't like the drum machine. (Okay, I really can't defend the drum machine.)

> *The Phantom of The Opera* is a horror story written by Gaston Leroux in 1911. Andrew Lloyd Webber's attempt to convert it into a cotton-candy musical romance is a conspicuous disaster that New Yorkers typically snigger at whenever the musical is brought up in conversation. ...

Of course, they do! Once again demonstrating the populist touch of the New York elite. And a disaster by what metric? Money? Long run? Popularity? Or the approval of a handful of critics? Just curious.

> The most galling thing about Schumacher's relentlessly crappy movie is that audiences who ... will likely fall for its glittery set design. It's full of things like lit candelabras surfacing from beneath the Phantom's watery moat in his lair. ... The director is so intent on reliving the Broadway play ... that the audience gets inundated with Webber's artificiality. There are endless squiggles of blind romance bereft of any real lust.

The Filmsnobs.com review was not at all subtle in their opening sentence. Go ahead. Tell us what you really think.

> I don't know what we're looking at, but one thing is for sure: It's the dumbest, gayest thing I've ever seen.

Isn't that hate speech? And there's more.

> But compared to the works of Sir Andrew Lloyd Webber, most new theater look like weapons of mass subtlety. If most musicals attempt to emulate cinema, Webber aspires the experience of an amusement park ride. Big sets, fancy visual effects, and high concept hope to distract from a complete lack of heart, soul, or substance.

Apparently, not a fan of the stage play.

Webber is a really flat and uninspired writer. All of his dialogue ... sounds like stage direction: "Look, they're falling in love." "Here's that prissy costume mistress. I bet she'll really tell us off." ...

Apparently, it's fare only middle-aged women will love.

... Just a fantasy for soccer moms on the level of TV's *Beauty and the Beast*.

Schumacher and Lloyd Webber are, in his view, the Dream Team of awful.

Most critics have bemoaned the combination of Sir Webber and the director of *Batman and Robin* as a match made in Hell. I personally can't think of a better pair to put together. Sir Lloyd Webber's empty spectacle should be matched by a director who thrives in style over substance in the extreme form that Schumacher normally takes in large-scale films like this.

And of course, Schumacher was not "helped out by his cast."

Emmy Rossum and Patrick Wilson, as Christine and Raoul, commit common crimes like chopping up songs with their wide ranges, but are largely innocent. Gerald Butler as The Phantom simply cannot sing, with a flat delivery and a rough tone.

But the stand-out in overacting is Minnie Driver as diva Carlotta. Sporting a Hispanic accent that would make Al Pacino in *Scarface* cringe ... It survives as the worst performance of 2004. All of Andrew Lloyd Webber's *The Phantom of the Opera* is a total mess (Jimmy O., 2004).

Collin Souter (2004) of efilmcritic.com also weighed in. He starts with his general distain for Lloyd Webber. "A very, very, very, very long, long, long, long, long engagement."

High-profile, over-hyped big-screen adaptations, such as *Phantom of the Opera*, can't be reviewed without first qualifying the opinion, so let's get that out of the way. I'm NOT an Andrew Lloyd Webber fan ... I do like musicals ... I do not get bent out of shape when characters suddenly burst into song. ... I had no opinion of Webber's stage musical prior to walking into the screening. ... Now, I think I know too much.

Phantom is boring.

I went 32 years on this planet unscathed by the music of *Phantom of the Opera*, and was all the better for it. ... If I had seen the stage play, perhaps my reaction would be different, but I doubt it. I can't stand this stuff. It just bores me silly. ... I don't hear any real emotion coming from the songs, just cheesy artifice. I just flat out plain don't get the big deal. ...

He really missed seeing the fat woman sing.

... I remember it started at 7:05pm. Three hours later I looked at my watch and it was only 7:25. I needed a fat lady singing like I've never needed one before. Speaking of fat ladies, I started wondering about the stage performers. Were they really this hot back then? No, seriously. ... Were they really built like this? I've seen pictures of women on vaudeville stages and they look like they have some meat on their bones. They look abundantly nourished. Not fat, just a little more real.

Back to the music.

That's all nice on the eyes, but the ears get something else entirely. This music made me feel as though someone had struck me in the back of the head with a 17th century concrete gargoyle, and I have this feeling that I'm supposed to stay awake so I don't die from a concussion, but yet I'm much more comfortable closing my eyes and drifting away.

This reviewer likes musicals. Just not this one.

> ... I don't want musicals to be bad. I like them. I'm tired of the Musical as being an outcast in today's cinematic climate. ... I don't want *Phantom* and Musicals to be in the same boat. ... I remember being underwhelmed by Alan Parker's *Evita*, but certainly not bored to tears. ... It was all I could do to stay awake (Souter, 2004).

Summary

So, there you have it. The critics tore it apart. That's not terribly surprising. It's been Lloyd Webber's lot from the beginning. Fortunately for Lloyd Webber and Schumacher, the fans (if not the Phans) strenuously disagreed. It's interesting to see the huge gap between the two, as we will in the next chapter.

CHAPTER 17

In Contrast, the Fans
Liked It

Perhaps not surprisingly, fans experienced the movie very differently than the critics. Their responses were so different, that I sometimes wonder if they saw the same movie. Most of the fans liked it. On the film review site, Rotten Tomatoes, a polling of 411,223 fans found that 84% of fans liked the film (compared to 32% of critics), and gave it a 3.7 out of 5 rating (Rotten Tomatoes, 2017). Not dazzling, but not terrible either. The rating of the DVD on Amazon was even higher: 77% gave it a 5-star rating, and the overall rating was 4 ½ stars, based on 3,387 reviews (as of August, 2016; Amazon, 2017).

The fan reaction was also mentioned in the volume celebrating the 25th anniversary of *Phantom*. While not a critical success, the *Phantom* film was nominated for several awards, including best song for the 2005 Academy Awards. The Really Useful Group considered "the film was a resounding success with the only people who really matter—the audience." The DVD was also successful, as the "Phans once again showed their support in large numbers" (Heately, 2011, p. 119).

In this final chapter on the film version of *Phantom*, I share some of the fan reviews. They don't all agree with each other, but they differ markedly from the critics' reviews. I'll begin with a top-rated review of the movie on Amazon (meaning that that the highest number of people identified it as helpful). The author was J. Irwin (posted January 19, 2006). This review was entitled "a visual powerhouse and a musical delight for anyone willing to give it a chance." It was particularly thoughtful, so I have quoted it in detail. The author identified as both "an avid musical theater fan" and a "classically trained singer." This reviewer is not a fan of Michael Crawford, for a variety of reasons, and said the campaign to have him be the Phantom in the movie was silly.

> ... I couldn't picture Michael Crawford as anything other than Cornelius, the wussy shop boy in *Hello, Dolly.* ... Who wants to watch a 61-year old lusting after an older teenager? That is not entertainment, that is just gross ...

Irwin eventually did see *Phantom* in New York (having avoided it in the 80s) and loved it, but especially loved the movie. Things that others distained, Irwin thought were quite appropriate to the genre.

> ... The movie is an absolutely-over-the-top, spectacle in everything (AS IT SHOULD BE, FOLKS!) We're dealing with 19th century, gothic romance and a musical score that is closer to opera than not. Honestly, what else could you expect?

Irwin found the visual aspects of the film to be particularly good, rich and sensual, drawing the viewer into the world of *Phantom.*

> ... From the opening crack of the auction gavel to the end scenes of Phantom disappearing into the emptiness of his life, I found myself ignoring the actors to "let the spectacle astound" me.

Irwin liked the performances of the three principle players, finding Patrick Wilson handled his role well, and "even ups the hero factor." Hated his hair, though. Emmy Rossum was "angelic."

> ... Again, the critics drive me insane with reviews stating her young voice was not polished enough. DUH!!! She was 17. ... Rossum's upper register did sound a bit pinched in a couple of spots, but the quality in general was pure and open, especially during the boat ride to Phantom's lair, as she is essentially vocalizing on an open "ah" that ends on E above High C. Yikes!

Irwin was particularly impressed with Butler's performance, calling it "sublime."

> ... As the critics have said, he's no Michael Crawford. THANK THE GOOD LORD!!! This talented Scot absolutely commands the eye to watch every move he makes. His Phantom is emotionally wrecked, sexy, dark, edgy, tragic, soulful, and ultimately heartbreaking. As others scoff at the frilly costumes, and assume the bared chest shots are purely for female viewers, I feel his vulnerability is made even more apparent by those ruffled shirts which seem to lay wide open his aching heart that waits for someone to take care of it.

Acknowledging some weaknesses in Butler's singing, Irwin felt the rough quality of his voice added to his character (as Schumacher and Lloyd Webber envisioned).

> Butler's singing performance is quite good for someone with so little training. Yes, a couple upper notes seem shouted and/ or strained, but I do not think it detracts from the performance, but rather adds a sense of desperation that he no longer has control over Christine, and his efforts to do so are futile. Butler's performance highlight is, without a doubt, Point of No Return; it is simply mesmerizing. Butler's Phantom is raw sensuality and emotion. He could not possibly be more in love with Christine, and it is heartbreaking to watch him be denied, and ultimately defeated. If you can watch the last 30 minutes without crying, you have a cold, dead heart! Butler is so captivating and convincing that it is inconceivable to me how Christine chooses Raoul over Phantom.

Irwin's final recommendation?

> Do yourself a favor. Get a bottle of good Italian wine, settle in for a couple of hours of shameless romance, and let your fantasies unwind through Gerard Butler's Phantom.

In the comments section, many others agreed with her rating of Butler's performance, and the film in general.

> I so agree with your review of Gerard Butler's role as Phantom. The imperfections in his voice make his character even more amazing, you can feel the anguish, hurt, anger. I've listened to other Phantoms, and although they have better voices, you don't feel the same emotions. Cannot stop watching this movie. So mesmerizing. (Kim D.)

> Ditto-Gerard Butler. Not only is Point of No Return mesmerizing, but also sensual, seductive, and downright erotic. Absolutely beautiful, and in my humble opinion, the standard by which all other Phantoms will be measured. Fell in love with the character, and being a rebellious soul by nature would have said "to hell with Raoul! I want the Phantom." Recently rediscovered the DVD in our library and can't tear my eyes away as I watch again for probably the tenth time this week. (C. Isaacs)

> I got so agitated over the bad reviews of Gerard. He was mesmerizing, handsome, yet disfigured I don't know what the critics wanted. A monster????? I liked the film as much as the play. Get this CD [sic]! You will love it & watch it over & over & over !!!!!! (Serenity)

Not all fans on Amazon agreed, however.

> RE: Crawford, I agree in theory, but not in substance. I can't say I find him appealing in person, BUT he owned that role. I was 3rd row center in Los Angeles for one of his first-run performances. I've never recovered. The staging, the supporting cast, the music. The audience went bananas. Lots of handkerchiefs got worked for all they're worth that night.

Fans Also Pushed Back on the Critics' Reviews

When critics posted their reviews online, fans had an opportunity to give their reactions to what they read. Many strongly disagreed with the review, and with each other. With many reviews being online, readers can now easily comment—and comment they do. Below is one sample of fan comments to Nick Schager's review in *The Rocky Mountain Bullhorn*, which I cited in the previous chapter. Many of the fan comments are quite funny. Some are concerning. They don't all like the movie, but they really wanted to respond to the review. To the extent possible, I left the original punctuation because it adds to the effect of their comments (Schager, 2005).

> I think *The Phantom of the Opera* is the best Broadway musical, and the best movie in the entire world me and my friend ariel watch it like every day and still cannot get enough of it. The top thing on my birthday list which is July 27 is *The Phantom of the Opera* soundtrack!! I can't wait to get it!! i Just wanted to tell ya'll how much ariel and i adore this movie!!! we love Gerard Butler in this movie!!!!!! He has the song of an angel!!!! (The angel of Music that is) also I think all the other cast members that were casted in this movie were absolutely perfect for the part!! Emmy Rosssum did an awesome performance in this terrific movie!!! Katie Beth and Ariel

A fan named Bill weighed in, wanting a happy ending.

> COME ON ANDREW WE ALL KNOW THAT MICHAEL CRAWFORD IS THE ONLY GREAT PHANTOM AND SOME HOW SOME WHERE THAT THE PHANTOM SHOULD WIN THE HEART OF CHRISTINE AND GET MARRIED AND LIVE A HAPPY LIFE TOGETHER. EVEN IF HE HAS TO HAVE HIS FACE FIXED (MY NAME IS BILL).

Nick Schager, author of the original review, couldn't resist responding.

> Oh yeah, a man who's responsible for the death of innocents, a stalker, and an obsessed madman should get exactly what he wants. He lost Christine. He eventually got over it and lived on.

The ending was happy enough, thank you very much! Posted by: Nick

Another fan weighs in

> I TOTALLY DISAGREE WITH THIS REVIEW!!! though we r all entitled 2 our opinions I find it quite rude. i believe it was fantastic! i have seen and heard the stage production, but what really blew me away was this movie. Sure, there are a few mistakes, but blame schumacher, NOT the amazing cast. They did a terrific job, but this is ALW's fault. He is the one who wanted it this way. Posted by: Emmy Rossum # 1 fan

A fan called GreenandCrunchy liked the musical. The movie? Not so much. She described the movie as "painful," hated Raoul's "romance-novel cover ensemble," and the fact that he jumped onto "a convenient white horse." (I actually hated that too.)

> I had to buy my friends a round to make up for inflicting the movie on them.

Then a serious Phan weighed in. She recommended the book and play, and said, "skip this movie." She warned that if you didn't, you'd want to give Schumacher a good, hard slap.

> I'm a huge fan of the book and the musical. I live in NYC, so I see this *Phantom of the Opera* A LOT. I have the soundtrack with Michael Crawford and Sarah, T-shirts, a mask (lol), and posters. I will not even go near the movie's soundtrack. Whoever plays The Phantom (I don't even care enough to say the actor's name, if you call that acting). The worse thing was that [he] had no voice! ... They ruined Music of the Night. I really had to step out of the room, my mom had a pained look on her face during the whole thing. ... Skip this movie, it will just make you want to slap the director and screenwriter across the face. Hard. Oh, and his face was not that bad. They could have done SO MUCH better.

Some Fan Reviews from the Web

The website Christiananswers.net also featured many thoughtful and detailed reviews of the movie. The comments were equally spirited, and viewers' ratings were either positive, neutral, or negative. It was the only site I saw that objected to lingerie and the bare butt when a character mooned Carlotta, but some reviewers surprisingly missed the underlying sexual theme. The reviewers raised many of the same issues as other sites, but this was the only site I found that listed the reviewers' ages. The reviewers under age 18 were the most enthusiastic. Most the reviews were positive.

> I must say this movie sent me to paradise with the music! The cinematography was amazing and the acting stupendous! Full Marks!!! The movie is alluring, yet dark and romantic, but not sexual. There is an underlying sensuality that is continually prevalent throughout the whole movie. The singing is phenomenal and the story fantastic. I never saw this on the stage, but my husband did and he enjoyed it more because it said it helped him understand the story more. ... Overall, this was one of the best movies I have seen in a long, long time. NO SEX, NO FOUL LANGUAGE... this is RARE now days.—*Claire, age 35*

Given Schumacher and Lloyd Webber's explicit designs for the movie, I must disagree that there was no sex, but she's right in that it was not overt. Maria and Dana loved the movie, finding the story and music to be beautiful and transforming.

> Simply the best movie I've seen this year. ... It's a beautiful story of love, compassion, and redemption. The music was enchanting and emotionally charged. It's one of those movies I could watch over and again.—*Maria, age 23*

> A fantastic, must-see movie for any fan of the Broadway musical! The sets are rich and lush, and the acting superb. And of course, the MUSIC! The famous music is powerful and transforming!

I LOVED this movie!! As for decency, the movie shows far less nudity than it could have given the rather provocative plot. ... Some of the scenes between the Phantom and Christine are a bit sensual, but nothing worse than you see on your average television show. ... All in all, everyone over age 16 or so should enjoy this fabulous movie.—*Dana, age 19*

Barry loved the redemption in the story of the Phantom and Christine.

This is a great story of good overcoming evil by wonderful acts of love. Christine loving the Phantom by looking past his physical disfigurement and his sins. Raoul's willingness to die to save his wife to be, Christine. ... This movie does a much better job of telling the story then the musical does.—*Barry, age 41*

Becky loved the compassion in the story.

The Phantom of the Opera is the beautiful tale of love, music, and compassion. Christine, who is young and innocent feels that she loves the mysterious Phantom, until she meets with her childhood sweetheart, Raoul, who shows her that real love is selfless. The Phantom was cruel and wicked if only to get revenge for the way people in the outside world treated him, but Christine still showed him compassion. The music is wonderful in this movie, everyone did a wonderful job. It is visually stunning, and while the acting was pretty cheesy, the music made up for it 100%.—*Becky Martin, age 19*

Jim compares the film to the stage show, and talks about the reaction of the New York cultural elite. He was less impressed with Butler's voice than other reviewers on the site.

One of the pleasures of living in New York for the last 20 years has been the ability to return to see *The Phantom of the Opera* on stage year after year. A musical pilloried by the New York critics (especially *The New York Times*), and snickered at by Manhattan elites, it continues to pack in the crowds because it has a certain something that cannot be defined, something that goes beyond the stirring music, the mythical romantic story and the exquisite stage sets. ... And I agree with the reviewer here—Gerard Butler, though powerful and moving, has a voice that is too often wobbly or distant. Michael Crawford had the perfect tenor voice that floated above the orchestra—it was haunting and heartbreaking at the same time...—*Jim, age 51*

Kirsten, in contrast, loved Butler's performance, and highly recommended the movie.

As a fan of Broadway musicals, I was excited to see this film. I expected it to be good, but it far surpassed my expectations. The music was awe-inspiring, and the cinematography was absolutely amazing. Gerard Butler did a tremendous job of capturing the essence of the Phantom—his love for Christine and his madness. ... Overall, I thought it was fantastic. I would recommend it to everyone—even those who aren't fond of musicals—because the story is a good one and the movie is definitely a must-see.—*Kirsten, age 18*

Lori found that the movie filled in a lot of plot holes that were in the play, but that the movie was not a replacement for the stage show.

I absolutely loved this film. ... Sure, it was sensual, but in a beautiful way. ... I did take my daughter, age 8. I saw the Broadway version in NYC a month ago and was totally enthralled. I came home playing the music constantly. My daughter, a music fan, fell in love with the score. ... I thought this was as good, but not a replacement for the stage show. I wouldn't trade that experience for anything, but this explained and filled in a lot of holes. I think the two complement each other very well. ...—*Lori S., age 33*

Taran loved the movie, especially Christine's compassion toward Phantom.

> I went to see this movie on opening day, and I must say it was my favorite movie all year, and I can't wait to see it again. ... As a Christian, I found many parallels to Christ, especially in the way Christine treated the Phantom, with unconditional love and mercy. ... Indeed, the movie greatly encourages us to love people, even your enemies, as yourself and maybe by doing so, they can change. ... I recommend this movie to everyone! —*Taran, age 18*

Not everyone liked the movie on this site, however. One reviewer found it boring.

> Very beautiful cinematography, this film had some breathtaking shots and sequences... that was the highlight of the film for me. At first, I was certain it had the potential to be "amazing" ... HOWEVER, after only a few minutes I realized that there is nothing comparable to the stage and I found myself quite bored at times. I felt some of the talent was mediocre and that much of the heart of the story on stage was removed and became a bout of melodrama that went on far too long on screen. Overall the cinematography was beautiful at times, and the music so familiar to my heart was beautiful, but I don't think I will devote two and a half hours to seeing this film again. —*M. Wagner, age 28*

Another reviewer objected to the violence and sexual content of the film, rating it "extremely offensive." Her review was definitely in the minority, but she was correct about the underlying sexual theme.

> I found the dances to be very sexual. There is violent and scary content. This film is not for anyone under the age of 17. It should have got an R rating. —*Amy R, age 35*

Kids Weigh In: Reviews from the Under-18 Set

Some critics have speculated that only middle-aged women like *Phantom*. Judging by these reviews, I'd say that's not even close to true. Many of the teens and tweens who wrote these reviews weren't even born when the stage play launched in 1986. Based on their reviews, they were clearly enthralled. All of the comments in this section were positive, and many of them commented that the movie made them want to see it on Broadway. These reactions also give some insight into why this show continues to be popular, even 30+ years after its initial launch.

I am speechless. This is definitely one of the BEST movies I've ever seen. ... I'll put this movie among the ranks of *Spiderman 2* and above. The acting was wonderful; I felt as if I were a part of the movie. ... I am still speechless about this movie, wow, and now want to go see it on Broadway! —*A.I., age 13*

Wow, this movie was absolutely amazing!! I loved every minute of it. If nothing else the music is amazing, the acting is spectacular. It is well worth your time and money. —*Tiffany, age 17*

I really enjoyed this movie. The actors had awesome voices. People keep saying that the Phantom was a disappointment, but I think he fit the character of the Phantom perfectly. ... Another reason why I love this movie is because it shows that you shouldn't judge someone by their appearance before you get to know them. The Phantom showed so much hatred because that's all he ever received; people made a freakshow out of him because he was so distorted. My point is, you can have so much hatred for one person just because of the way they look. But, once you break a barrier that has never been broken you realize that that person has feelings and just wants to be loved like everyone else. I feel like *The Phantom*

of the Opera demonstrates this well. I love this movie!!
—*Briana, age 15*

Beautiful! Spectacular! Absolutely, positively breathtaking!
What an outstanding performance by all cast members! I loved
every moment of it. ... Not recommended for all viewers, but
all that aside, what an amazing movie! The performances
were stupendous...—*Anne, age 16*

I thought that *The Phantom of the Opera* was phenomenal.
It had breathtaking talent with acting and singing. It was very
sad and I was so close to crying. When you see this, I guarantee
you will want to see it again. It was absolutely, positively
outstanding! In my opinion, it should get at least five Oscars ...
—*Nicole, age 11*

Summary

The *Phantom* film inspired quite a few fan comments. They weren't
always positive. As Schumacher said in his interviews, the critics
may hate it, but most audiences loved it. Opinion among the fans
was mixed regarding Gerard Butler as the Phantom, but he clearly
has a strong fan base. And as we now know, he went on to become
an A-list star. One recent review implied that Butler would now be
embarrassed by his performance in *Phantom*. "Gerard Butler may
have hoped we've forgotten about this, but I *never* will" (Coates,
2014). At the time the film was released, he seemed pleased, in spite
of many negative reviews. However, in a recent interview, he seemed
to wince when the interviewer brought up *Phantom*, so it's hard to
say what his current views may be. He's certainly gone on to do
much more work.

Love it or hate it, *Phantom* continues to inspire passionate discussion.
And that passionate discussion continues. Both the stage and film
version raised the possibility of Christine choosing the Phantom over

Raoul. Did she make the wrong choice? That was a question Lloyd Webber decided to address—in a sequel.

The controversy about the film was minor compared to what happened next.

The *Phantom* Sequel

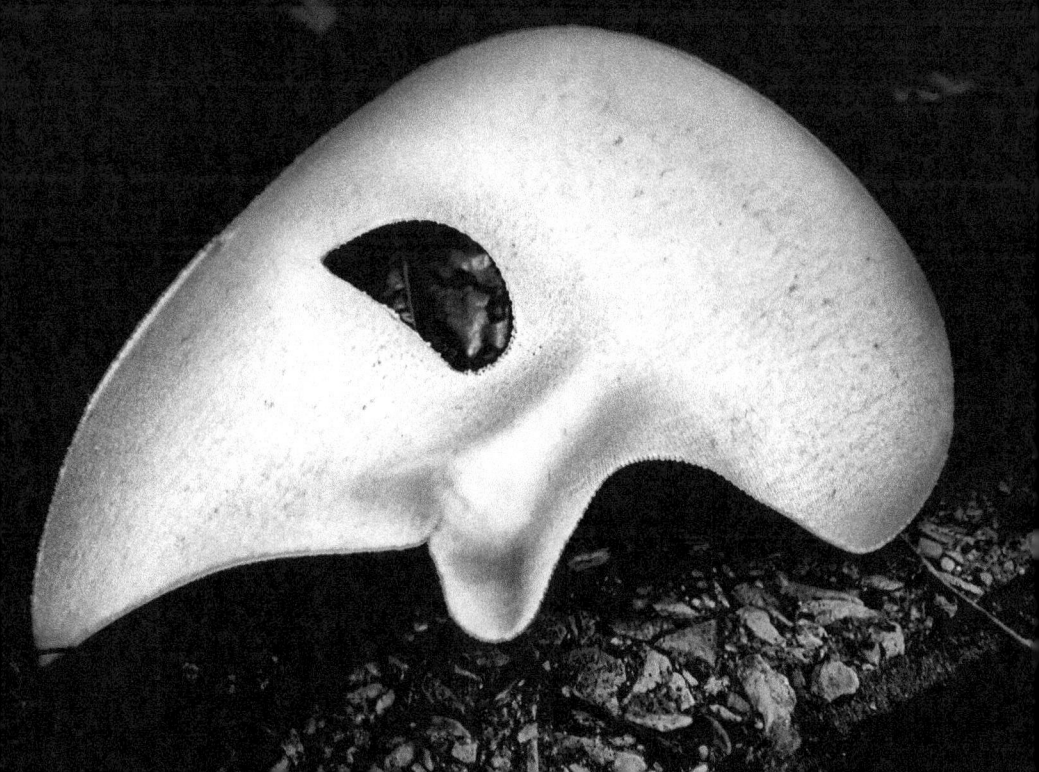

CHAPTER 18

Introduction to the Sequel

*L*ove Never Dies, the sequel to *The Phantom of the Opera*, opened with fanfare on London's West End on March 10, 2010. *The Telegraph* reported that Andrew Lloyd Webber and the show's stars received a standing ovation. The audience included luminaries, such as Sir Michael Caine, Sir David Frost, and Gerard Butler, who played the Phantom in the film version. David Frost, who had seen *Phantom* eight times, said *Love Never Dies* was "terrific."

> It has some of Andrew's greatest ever music. The great advantage is that even if it was half as successful as *Phantom*, it would still gross 1.5 billion and be a mega, mega hit anyway. I think the prospects are great (*The Telegraph*, 2010).

Long before it opened, however, there was controversy and evidence that not everyone was happy with a *Phantom* sequel. In fact, there was a vigorous social media campaign designed to keep the musical from even opening. This final section is the story of the *Phantom* sequel, the novella, the social media campaign, and inevitable pushback from Lloyd Webber. Through the process, as annoying as it was to Lloyd Webber, the musical improved. Lloyd Webber's score for *Love Never Dies* is really quite good. The storyline, however, continues to be a problem.

Hell-Bent on Telling this Story

Andrew Lloyd Webber was a man on a mission. He was determined to produce a sequel to *Phantom*, and he had certain plot elements in mind: he wanted Christine and Phantom to get together, which was central. He wanted Phantom to be in New York, and he wanted Phantom and Christine to have a child. Lloyd Webber talked about this project for years, mentioned it in numerous interviews, and was even talking about it before the movie came out in 2004. When *Love Never Dies* was finally launched, Lloyd Webber described it as a project that was 20 years in the making.

The story of the production of *Love Never Dies* reminded me of an old joke about a dog food company worried about its lagging sales. The executives got together and said, "We just don't understand it. We have the catchiest advertising jingles, and the fanciest packaging. Why aren't we selling more?" Finally, one of their minions speaks up and says, "The dogs won't eat it." And therein lies the rub.

Lloyd Webber presented a package to the public that had all the bells and whistles, and every possible advantage. Had it not been a *Phantom* sequel, all these advantages might have been enough to ensure a decent run. Lloyd Webber was sure that the *Phantom* fans would just gobble it up. The problem was that the "dogs" wouldn't eat it.

Lloyd Webber's single-minded focus caused him micromanage the first production. He had a creative vision and that was what he was going with. Anyone who disagreed was fired or replaced. Jack O'Brien, the director he fired after the first version bombed, said that Lloyd Webber wouldn't listen and wouldn't allow him to change anything, so essentially, his hands were tied. It was not a happy relationship.

Lloyd Webber was shocked by the negative reaction to the first version of *Love Never Dies*. I'm shocked that he was shocked. A couple of Google searches would have revealed the potential problems, long before the social media campaign, and long before production began. The truth is that he didn't care about the negative feedback. His single-minded focus also caused Lloyd Webber to ignore a lot of warning signs, and that refusal to listen cost him over £5 million pounds.

What Happens When Unlimited Resources Meets Hell-Bent Desire

Lloyd Webber had nearly unlimited resources at his disposal. He had bags of money. He had purchased back control of his production company, and co-owned the theater where it opened. He also had the very talented Sierra Boggess and Ramin Karimloo as Phantom and Christine. In fact, Lloyd Webber said Boggess was the best Christine he had ever heard—even better than Sarah Brightman. High praise, indeed. He had a splashy premiere, with many A-list celebrities singing his praises.

Lloyd Webber's advantages didn't end there. He persuaded a bestselling and accomplished author to write a piece of fanfiction for him. Fanfiction, or "fanfic"—a genre most accomplished writers distain. Frederick Forsyth went out on a considerable limb for Lloyd Webber. I suppose that when Andrew Lloyd Webber asks you write something, the temptation is too great to resist. The result was a novella called *The Phantom of Manhattan* (Forsyth, 2007).

The reviews of *The Phantom of Manhattan* were relentlessly bad, and that should have been Lloyd Webber's first warning. Many wondered what had caused Forsyth to sell-out and write, in their opinion, a reprehensible piece of crap. Forsyth was willing to put his considerable reputation on the line to write this story. In the end, Lloyd Webber abandoned almost all of the original story of *The Phantom of Manhattan*, so Forsyth's sacrifice was for naught.

In fact, Lloyd Webber and his team had considerable problems with the book for *Love Never Dies*; that's apparent from the number of co-authors. Judging from the number of edits and major changes to the story, I'd surmise that they were having trouble making the story "work." In storytelling, you need a credible way to get from Point A to Point B. You can see they struggled with that mightily throughout the writing process. For example, how can you have Christine and Phantom get together in a way that doesn't make Christine look like a cheater (or slut)? (We're supposed to be rooting for her.) She, supposedly, married

Raoul the *very next day* after she slept with Phantom. One way to do that is to turn Raoul into a jerk. Similarly, Phantom needs to be appealing, and not a creepy, obsessive stalker.

The "Dogs" Speak Out

The problems with this show were far beyond the adamant protest of the hardcore fans. The fans merely highlighted the problems. Lloyd Webber claims that the social media campaign "turned" public opinion—and the reviewers—against him. That is unlikely. The social media campaign was, by far, the noisiest branch of the public, but it was not the only one. And the critics made a point of distancing themselves from the fans.

Long before the show launched, the protest was loud and long on websites, such as Goodreads and Amazon. Lloyd Webber owns an entire production company. Surely, one of his minions could have monitored this discussion and reported back to Lloyd Webber. Perhaps some of them did.

"The Focus Groups Loved It"

Lloyd Webber claims that he presented to idea of a sequel to focus groups—and they loved it. According to his focus group "research," *Phantom* fans were just waiting for a sequel. If the average *Phantom* fan was clamoring for a sequel, where were they? There are millions of fans of the original. If they wanted to see the production, they would have. Controversy is generally good for ticket sales, not bad, such as how banned books often become bestsellers. Clearly the results of the focus groups did not reflect the sentiments of the general public.

The problem with focus group research is that it is remarkably easy to skew the findings to get the results you want. That's why, when you conduct this type of research, you need be strict with your methodology and carefully monitor who's in your groups. In this case, it would have been easy to fill groups with Lloyd Webber sycophants who said that they would love a sequel. After all, Andrew Lloyd Webber was asking for their opinion. They were probably so in awe, that they were going to say nothing but, "genius, sheer genius." The researchers conducting the focus groups might have also been Lloyd Webber sycophants who did not want to give him a negative answer.

In the end, Lloyd Webber's focus-group researchers did not do him any favors. If this had been an academic study, rather than research for hire, the results would have been more balanced. The groups would have contained those who thought a sequel was a good idea, and those who didn't. Lloyd Webber would have gotten a more accurate read on public perception, and perhaps would have been able avoid some of the mistakes in the earlier versions.

Editing Made It Better

So, what are we to say about the critics and social media campaign? What did they accomplish? That question interested me. An artist produces something. The public comments, and in this case, comments and comments. Lloyd Webber indicated that he felt victimized by the social media campaign. But what was the end result? Did the criticism lead to a better product? I think it did.

Although critics have often been the major voices in earlier musicals, *Love Never Dies* is unique in showing the major input of fans throughout this process. Social media has forever changed the role of fans. Fans are no longer mere consumers of musical theater; they also have a voice and are now players in this process.

The story of *Love Never Dies* is an interesting case study of the interaction between creator and fans, and how fans, armed only with a website and Facebook page, were able to significantly alter the course of a major musical. Ultimately. *Love Never Dies* went through two major revisions, resulting in three versions. Examining those three versions gives us some insight into how a musical is edited and changed throughout the process. As a result, we get a front-row seat to the creative process. This is how it all began.

CHAPTER 19

The Phantom of Manhattan
Forsyth's Sequel to *Phantom*

*L*ove *Never Dies* is loosely based on Frederick Forsyth's novella, *The Phantom of Manhattan* (Forsyth, 2007). Readers had many objections to this story. The first objections occurred before people even read it: *The Phantom of Manhattan* is fanfiction, and fanfiction is bad.

That's not necessarily true. After all, there have been several decent spin-offs from popular movies and TV shows. For example, two great series have spun off of the popular and beloved *Inspector Morse* series (*Inspector Lewis* and *Endeavour*). A quick spin through Amazon reveals that *Phantom* has inspired many books where the Phantom gets the girl. So why was this one picked? Frederick Forsyth is an established novelist, with many well-written books to his credit, including *The Odessa Files* and *Day of the Jackal*. So, you have to wonder why he decided to write a piece of fanfiction. It turns out that he didn't just wake up one day and decide to write *The Phantom of Manhattan*. Lloyd Webber asked him to (Tapper, 2007).

Forsyth did what he could with the material, and created a half-way interesting story, with a whole new list of characters. His story may have been contrived, but the characters were more consistent with the original than they were in *Love Never Dies*. Although *The Phantom of Manhattan* was directly solicited, Lloyd Webber basically decided it wouldn't work, discarded the entire story, and came up with one of his own. This was partly because Forsyth's story was too complex to tell in musical form. Lloyd Webber said *Love Never Dies* was based on the novella, *The Phantom of Manhattan*, but they used almost none of it. However, Forsyth was listed as an author on *Love Never Dies*. This is how the story development was described in the *Phantom* 25th anniversary book.

> Forsyth developed the ideas and published his own version as a novella, *The Phantom of Manhattan*. By then, Lloyd Webber had moved on to other projects because although he sensed the seeds of a story for a show, he couldn't make the plot work for himself as a composer. Nonetheless, he found it very difficult to leave the story alone (Heatley, 2011, p. 95).

Storyline from *The Phantom of Manhattan*

The Phantom of Manhattan opens where *The Phantom of the Opera* leaves off. After the Phantom destroyed the Paris Opera House, he escapes France and eventually makes his way to New York, where he becomes part of the freak-show population on Coney Island. There were many freaks there, so he did not stick out. As in Gaston Leroux's book, the Phantom has a name, Erik, that is used throughout the story. Erik is a mechanical genius and soon devises many devices for ticket sales and ride admissions that earn him a great deal of money. Foreshadowing Donald Trump, he buys real estate in Manhattan, becomes even more wealthy, and soon owns many sizable holdings.

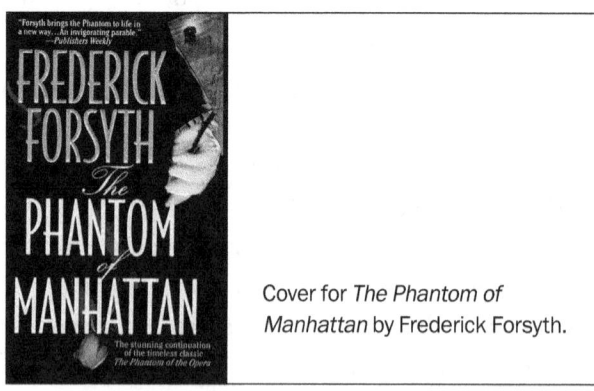

Cover for *The Phantom of Manhattan* by Frederick Forsyth.

Alas, he is still disfigured, and it is 1905, an era with a very unenlightened view on disability. He realizes that he needs a front man to transact his business, so he takes on a business partner. This partner is a shadowy character who handles all the business transactions, which leads to him becoming fabulously wealthy while fronting for Erik. Eventually, the Phantom buys an opera house, partnering with Oscar Hammerstein. Missing Christine, and obsessing about her, he asks Oscar Hammerstein to invite her to America to open his new opera house in Manhattan.

Christine, in the meantime, married Raoul, and has a 13-year-old son named Pierre. She has been singing ever since her Paris Opera days, and has had a dazzling career in Europe. She is still best friends with Meg, who accompanies her on her trips as her assistant. Pierre is tutored by an interesting and highly educated priest, who accompanies the family on their trip to the U.S. During the trip, he is inspired to aid the plight of the poor he meets while in New York. Raoul is still a good guy who supports Christine's singing career. He also accompanies her on the trip.

The storyline switches to Madame Giry, who, one day, happens upon a soldier who was mugged and severely injured. She comes to his aid, and ensures that he is taken to the hospital, where she goes to visit him. She learns that he will recover from his injuries, but he was injured in a rather inconvenient place. He will never have a child.

Before Christine marries Raoul, she finds out that she is 2 months pregnant with Erik's child. Raoul knows this and agrees to marry her. Christine knows that Raoul is conveniently sterile, so there is no question about paternity. Raoul knows who Pierre's real father is, but raises Pierre as his own. We never learn when Christine and the Phantom had sex, but we get the sense that it was more frightening than romantic.

Phantom is behind the scenes when Christine and Raoul arrive in America. Pierre receives a toy from the Phantom, but doesn't know who it is from. Apparently, he has inherited his biological father's mechanical genius, shown when he takes apart the toy, reverses a gear, and it plays a melody that Christine recognizes. She hears it and is terrified when she realizes that Erik is nearby. She is afraid to see him, another indication that the story is more creepy than romantic. If their relationship was consensual, and a great passion, we would expect that she would not be so afraid.

In the meantime, Erik has composed an opera for her to sing, which is set during the American Civil War. She plays a nurse. Her love interest is a soldier who gets wounded in the face. The injured soldier doesn't want Christine's character to feel like she has to be with him. Christine's character recognizes his voice. During the performance, Erik slips into the part of the injured soldier and sings a very moving duet with her, his face obscured with bandages. The applause went on and on.

In the meantime, Erik's business partner has become jealous of the Phantom's attachment to Christine and plots to kill their son, Pierre. Christine never gets together with Erik in this story, because when they have a meeting in a park, the partner ends up killing Christine by accident, and Erik kills him in retaliation.

In the process of this, Pierre finds out that Erik is his biological father, decides to stay with him in New York. Raoul lets him stay (pretty astonishing since Pierre is only 13, and Raoul is the only father he has ever known). The Phantom hires a bunch of real soldiers who have had facial injuries to work in his house, and stops hiding behind a mask. Pierre's tutor, the priest, starts working with the urban poor in New York City and has a secret benefactor, so that he is never short of money. Raoul returns to France alone.

Forsyth managed to create a somewhat interesting story here, even if silly (I kept reading). It was clear, however, that the storyline was too complex for a musical. Even before Lloyd Webber and his crew modified the story, readers weighed in on the storyline. They had a lot to say, and some were downright *offended* by the shear silliness and improbability of it all.

248

Readers React to *The Phantom of Manhattan*

Lloyd Webber might not have been surprised by the negative reaction to *Love Never Dies* if he had listened to the feedback on *The Phantom of Manhattan*, as reviews were popping up on Goodreads as early as 2008. This is a site for readers, and they gave a lot of negative feedback long before there was a social media campaign or reviews from critics.

Much of what these readers reacted to was Forsyth deviating from the Gaston Leroux's original book. In fact, *The Phantom of Manhattan* made the list of "Books I Regret Reading," and was listed at number 226 out of 1,647. Other luminaries on this list included most of the *Twilight* series and *The DaVinci Code* (Goodreads, 2017).

Leroux Got the Character Wrong?

The critiques started with Forsyth's introduction, where Forsyth argued that Leroux got the story wrong! Many reviewers bristled at the arrogance of that statement. As Gemma noted, how could LeRoux have gotten his own character and story *wrong*?

> Forsyth actually has the nerve to insist that Gaston Leroux— without whom none of this would even exist—got his own story wrong! Oh, hell to the NO! ... If an author falls to belittling another person's work in such a manner, it's best to just drop the book and forget it completely. Sadly, my stubborn streak wouldn't let me off the hook so easily, and I kept reading.

Christina was also not impressed with the "arrogant, conceited preface."

> ... in which the author has the gall to insist that Gaston Leroux did not understand his own characters and that Andrew Lloyd Webber corrected these errors. The preface is truly the only remarkable prose in this novel as it is completely unnecessary and is riddled with fallacies in logic in the author's attempts to justify the novel's existence ...

Lin made a similar point, with the comment that Forsyth was engaged in some serious pandering to Lloyd Webber.

> Never in my life have I chanced upon an unauthorized "sequel" to a classic ... that insults the original within the first five sentences. That is impressive! And it continues, page after page, scoffing at Leroux's original novel and pointing out how unremarkable it was for most of his life, arguing the most inane points against it, that seem to miss the point of dramatic effect entirely. Claiming something is true in a work of fiction is a literary device, yes, but it does not, to my mind, restrict the author to pure realism. His complaints are as inane as they are nitpicking as they are strange! Is this book seriously going there? The sheer ego! Not only that, but it continues on with some bizarre and excessive Andrew Lloyd Webber ass-kissing that holds him up as the only man to ever truly "understand" the important parts of the story, better by far than that gross old Leroux who invented the damn characters!

Is a Sequel a Good Idea?

Other readers questioned the wisdom writing a sequel at all, as Christine, a self-identified PHANATIC, described. Being a fan of both the stage play and the book, she wondered how Lloyd Webber could even consider doing a sequel. Again, another early clue that fans were not necessarily going to eagerly embrace *Love Never Dies*.

> Curiosity gave in and I got a hold of this book. I was disappointed before reading it, I was pissed after reading it, I was upset for the author writing it, and I was furious Webber spawned *Love Never Dies* from it! I knew from the moment I read the preface that it was all downhill for this tale. Forsyth begins by saying that Leroux's novel is garbage and that he misunderstood the character of the Phantom, getting his facts wrong. Leroux CREATED the characters! ... It is a work of FICTION so how can the author get everything wrong when he is its creator?!

For someone who is copying someone else's work, he has a lot of nerve.

Jennifer hated what Forsyth did to Raoul.

The first error the author made was a cheap shot at Raoul by having him castrated. This seems to be something so many phan phiction writers like to do to poor Raoul. Everyone seems to forget that although a tragic, somewhat romantic character, the Phantom, is a PSYCHO KILLER with some serious emotional issues. No need to pick on Raoul so much.

Isn't Phantom Supposed to be a Musician?

Lin noted that the story both lacked genuine passion and was not built around the music, and that without the Gothic aesthetic, it was just a "two-old-lovers-come-back-together-again narrative." Her biggest critique was its absolute lack of passion.

Music is incidental, and seems to be involved in the plot only because it's impossible to separate the Phantom mythos from music. There's no interest in artistry or creativity, and this is only highlighted by the Phantom's new occupation as a businessman, the head of his own corporation. ... And that's maybe an apt description for the whole thing. It feels like a corporate cash-in, and not anything written out of a genuine creative spark. ...

Problems with the Story and Book Itself

Many readers hated the story on general principle. They found many aspects of the story were just not credible. They were also angry at Forsyth for writing it, as Sharon noted.

Honestly, I think Frederick Forsyth should be ashamed of himself for writing such absolute tripe. He clearly is unfamiliar with Leroux's original novel and casts Erik in a humiliating

light that the original character would never countenance.
To be avoided at all costs.

Gemma provides more detail about her angst, noting that she could
not recall "ever hating a book outright" as much as this one. On a
more positive note, she preferred Forsyth's "much-abused" Raoul to
Lloyd Webber's gambling alcoholic version.

> So this is what regret feels like.... Against my better judgment,
> and the advice of everyone I've heard mention this atrocity,
> I went to the library and borrowed The Phantom of Manhattan.
> Thank God, I didn't actually waste money on buying it!
> I ended up reading it as fast as I could—not because it was
> any good at all, but just to get it over with as soon as possible.
> And I still have no clue how I managed to keep from throwing
> the stupid thing across the room in disgust. Unless I was
> paralyzed by aforesaid disgust.

> ... No wonder the musical bombed in London, based off this
> garbage!

Lin had no kind words about the text itself, calling it "amateurish"
and boring, with flat dialogue, not enough diversity in narrator voices,
and nothing in the text to urge readers to continue reading. Jennifer
was more to the point.

> Do not waste your time nor your money on this piece-of-crap sequel.

Alexandra calls this, "bad fanfiction before I knew what bad fanfiction
was," noting the common theme where Christine and Erik get a happy
ending.

> I blame the people who feel Erik is the perfect man, despite
> the fact that Christine is terrified of him throughout the
> course of the musical, in which he hurls a chandelier at her
> after she professes her love to Raoul.

Christina wasn't impressed with the story.

... one marvels at how mediocre the story is, how ignorant, crude, and beyond salvation the characterization is; and how forced, clumsy, and tasteless the historical allusions are... Its only saving grace is its length: it's short ...

She worried about the impending sequel. *Love Never Dies* premiered three years later.

Incidentally, as of 2007, I am sad to report that Andrew Lloyd Webber's ego was so effectively inflated by Forsyth's toadying in the preface that a musical based on the novel's premise is now on its way to the West End.

Overall, the rating was bad. Readers particularly didn't like Forsyth's description of the two main characters, as Christina describes.

I thought he was not true to the characters I loved from Leroux's book and the POTO [*Phantom of the Opera*] musical. The original leads you to believe that Christine, traumatized by everything that happened, is happy to marry Raoul and retire to quiet life in the country ... Erik, as tragically wonderful a character as he is, is deeply flawed. He's an obsessive stalker who is willing to commit murder to have what he wanted. He doesn't deserve a happy ending! Do not waste your time or money reading the pompous pages of this supposed sequel. I will not waste any on Andrew Lloyd Webber's *Love Never Dies*!

"What the Hell?"

To this reviewer, the story didn't make any sense, and listed several "WTH" (What the Hell?) moments, especially with the ending. While Pierre watches his mother bleed to death, Christine explains to him that Erik is his real father. Raoul confirms this and tells Pierre that he must decide whether to stay in the U.S. with Erik, or to return to France with Raoul.

The boy takes off Erik's mask, sees how horribly deformed he is, and decides to stay. WHAT???

WTH No. 1 Is the moment a young boy is watching his mother bleed to death in front of him really the time to tell him his father is not his real father??

WTH No. 2 Furthermore, is it really the time to tell him to decide whether to stay with his father or go off with a perfect stranger who is his biological father?

WTH NO. 3 The characters talk more than once about how kind Raoul is, and how good he is to his family. What kid, after losing his mother forever, would willingly leave the only father he's ever known—a GOOD father, who has raised him as his own—to live with a man he's never met before?

WTH No. 4 and personal gripe. Raoul tells his son, about Erik, "He loved her too, in a way I never could." Seriously? Yeah. I mean, Raoul never kidnapped Christine, or lied to her, or manipulated her, or threatened to kill those she loved, so I guess the Phantom did love her in an entirely different way. More of a Creepy Obsessive Stalkery sort of way. I wouldn't necessarily say that's a good thing. Or maybe he means in a physical way, since Forsyth made sure Raoul couldn't do any of that?

Another reader also objected to the ending and Pierre needing to choose between Erik and Raoul.

The idea of forcing a 13-year-old child, who has just witnessed his mother shot and killed, to choose between his father and the man he has just been told is his REAL father is absolutely absurd and cruel. That he would pick Erik, a physically deformed stranger, is even more bizarre. The ending is completely devoid of any understanding of human emotion and psychology that it's easily the worst part of the novel. ... I can't believe I'm saying this, but *Love Never Dies is better!*

A Few Readers Actually Liked It

Although most of the reviews were negative, not everyone hated it. In fact, a few readers really liked it, as Patrick described. Amazingly, he agreed with Forsyth's critique of Leroux.

> You don't tend to think of Frederick Forsyth, master of such spy-and-international-intrigue thrillers as *The Fourth Protocol, The Dogs of War,* and *The Day of the Jackal,* to write a sequel to *The Phantom of the Opera.* But he did. And it's great! The conceit is that Gaston Leroux ... was a bad journalist. He told the "true" story of the deformed man who lived in the cellars of the Paris Opera house, but his research was faulty, resulting in numerous plot holes. Here, what Forsyth offers is the real story...

Isn't this *fiction?* Patrick continues, clearly holding the minority view.

> The worst thing about the book is that it ends too soon, and far too abruptly. The story is moving along at a crackerjack pace when suddenly—boom!—it's all over and everyone goes home.

Renee had mixed feelings about *Love Never Dies,* and was curious about the book. She liked *The Phantom of Manhattan* more, and that it was "not as bad as Phans made it out to be."

> And it really wasn't. The main thing is that you can't come to it looking for the same sweeping romance of Webber's *Phantom,* and I think this is what fans of the musical found so disappointing. This is written very much in the style of the original Gaston Leroux novel ... telling the story of Erik's post-*Phantom* American exploits ... There's little romance about it, and what's there is somewhat overblown and unconvincingly depicted; all in all, the book had the feeling of more of an intellectual "what if" exercise, rather than (as

255

LND felt) like something born from a yearning to give Christine another shot at choosing Erik over Raoul. The narrative did get slow in some parts, and I found at least one coincidence (Mme Giry tending a wounded young Raoul when he was a soldier) a little *too* convenient to swallow. Overall, though, it wasn't horrible, simply as another perspective on the original story.

Summary

As you can see, the *Phantom* sequel inspired a great deal of passionate response. I agree with Renee's response (cited above) that the story in *The Phantom of Manhattan* was truer to the original characters than *Love Never Dies* (i.e., they didn't undergo major personality changes). But while reading *The Phantom of Manhattan*, I, also, had many "oh, come on!" moments. Even people who were not particular fans of the original didn't think that the story of *The Phantom of Manhattan* made a lot of sense. Unfortunately, the Really Useful Group didn't listen to this very clear feedback from their target audience—fans of the original. Things went downhill from here.

CHAPTER 20

The Phantom of Manhattan
Becomes
Love Never Dies

A s I described in the previous chapter, *Love Never Dies*, is based loosely on Frederick Forsyth's novel, *The Phantom of Manhattan*. Many story elements changed on its way to becoming a musical. Some of those changes are due to the nature of musicals themselves. Some were based on Lloyd Webber's preferences. Unfortunately, the revisions did not improve the story. They made it worse.

Storytelling in Musicals

From a storytelling perspective, musicals are the slowest way to get a story across. With a movie, you can use more visuals that tell the story in an instant. Dialog then moves the story along. With a musical, you may need several minutes to make the same point. Because of this, the storyline of a musical needs to be simple, otherwise the musical would be 4 hours (or 4 days!) long.

Because musicals have simple storylines, you can't expect a deep plot. The storyline of many (if not most) musicals is silly, and some are even downright stupid. Despite this, if the music is good, musicals usually work. In the worst of the genre, there is no real plot; they're simply words stuck between musical numbers. Better musicals have a coherent story they tell via song.

In addition, when seeing a musical, you need to suspend your normal disbelief and realize that in the musical universe, it's perfectly normal to burst into song when you are trying to say something, that music swells and no one turns around to see where it is coming from, and that complex problems can be resolved in only 2 hours. Fans of musicals know all of the above and are willing to play along. Even so, *the story needs to make sense.* Within the fictional universe created for the story, the actions of the characters need to show some consistency, and there has to be logic in their actions. When the story doesn't make sense, even in a fictional context, fans get upset.

Continuity Issues Between *Phantom* and *Love Never Dies*

Storyline was the single biggest issue for the *Phantom* sequel, particularly the lack of continuity between the stories of *Phantom* and *Love Never Dies*. In the writing world, this lack of continuity is known as a plot hole. Fans who are invested in a story feel that they "know" the characters. If these characters change in a fundamental way, there must be a reason. This type of reader reaction is not unique to the *Phantom* universe. There are many recent examples of this. For example, readers were very upset when Atticus Finch turned about to be an old racist in *Go Set a Watchman*, the purported sequel to *To Kill a Mockingbird*. People have been inspired by Atticus in *Mockingbird* for decades. I heard one attorney on TV say that he became a lawyer because of Atticus, and I suspect his character inspired a whole generation of attorneys. These attorneys, and many other readers, were let down with the new rendition of Atticus, and they reacted by rejecting the book.

Another example is people's fanatic devotion to *Star Wars*, *Star Trek*, and *The Lord of the Rings*. Some devoted fans even go so far as to learn the fictional languages. They go to conventions dressed as their favorite characters, and they know when parts of the story don't add up. It's one of the reasons that Peter Jackson had to ship black-faced sheep to New Zealand when filming *The Lord of the Rings* rather than simply relying on white-faced sheep that were native to his country: black-faced sheep were in the book and the fans of the trilogy would know.

What is true with other genres is also true for *Phantom*. The Lloyd Webber version is a story people invested in. If not that, they turn to the original book. Many thought Lloyd Webber's *Phantom* was perfect as it was, and didn't want to see what happened next.

Love Never Dies Storyline

In *Love Never Dies*, the creators eliminated most of Forsyth's story, partly because it had too many characters and was too complex to convey in a musical. The only thing that they seemed to have kept was that the Phantom was in New York, and that he and Christine had a love child.

Thirteen-year-old Pierre becomes 10-year-old Gustave (there were probably more things that rhymed with 10 than 13, but I don't understand why they changed his name too). Raoul, instead of being a nice, conveniently sterile guy, turns into a complete jerk, who has bankrupted his family, was jealous of Christine's singing, and kept her from it. I think they did this so that you didn't feel bad that Christine cuckolded him bigtime, and then eventually chose the Phantom over him. Raoul's been raising a child that wasn't his. If Raoul was nice, we'd be less likely to be sympathetic towards Christine. And if he was a good dad, we'd not really like it when Gustave decides to stays with the Phantom.

A couple of other things that don't quite add up. In *Phantom*, Christine had a couple of performances in the Paris Opera 10 years ago. It's highly unlikely she would be "famous" after that, especially in the U.S. How would Hammerstein have even heard of her? And building a whole show around her? And all the reporters waiting for her ship to arrive? All of that seems unlikely after a couple of performances in an obscure opera house, with no Internet and no social media.

That part only makes sense if she has been singing all along and is famous in Europe, as she had in the Forsyth novel. But not singing for the past 10 years and famous? I don't think so. Also, is she going to perform without rehearsing? Not even once? That also seems unlikely. I would imagine that she's a bit rusty.

One bit that I would have loved to have seen was the song that was in the original Forsyth story: the duet between Phantom and Christine, where he was the wounded soldier and she was the nurse. With the story set in the Civil War, that was quite a bit more American than the song that she ended up singing. In fact, the eponymous song was one that Lloyd Webber originally wrote for New Zealand opera star, Kira Te Kanawa, to sing for his 50th birthday celebration. Lloyd Webber originally decided to put it in another show, *The Beautiful Game*, but then decided that it didn't work, and used it as the title song for *Love Never Dies*. It's Christine's signature song for the show, but it doesn't do much to establish a sense of place. The story doesn't feel particularly American, even though it is set there.

Gustave's age is another detail that shows that this story was clearly written by a bunch of guys. They forgot to factor in something that most women would know: you need to include time for gestation. If Christine and Phantom's liaison was 10 years ago, it's unlikely that Gustave is also 10. Yes, if he was conceived at the beginning of the year, and the story happens towards the end of the year, it's possible, but the odds are against it. Women would have known this. The men clearly didn't think of it.

In the meantime, Madame Giry and Meg have come to New York with the Phantom and helped him set up his businesses. Meg seems to have a serious thing for the Phantom, and is dying for the Phantom to notice—and he never does. Madame Giry is upset that Christine is coming to New York and hopes she stays far away from them. Instead of still being friends with Christine, as they are in the Forsyth book, they are jealous of her and how she "fled from the Master yet fled with his heart."

The Phantom sends his carriage for Christine and her family, and brings them to his property. It is here that he makes his big reveal, and Christine finds out that he is not dead—and she is pissed. They sing Beneath the Moonless Sky. It is in this song that we learn of their liaison. He left her because he couldn't face her seeing him in the morning light. Christine went ahead with her wedding *that same day*, and her big secret.

When the Phantom meets Gustave, he's intrigued. Gustave is fascinated by Coney Island and wants to see more. The Phantom offers to be his guide and Gustave is thrilled. Christine is less thrilled. When she says that she doesn't want to sing for him, the Phantom threatens to make her son disappear on Coney Island. The whole encounter makes her weep.

The next day, they go over to "Mr. Y's" theater (owned by the Phantom), where we learn a few things. ("Mr. Y" is supposed to a contraction of "mystery." I know I'm not the only one who didn't get it.) Raoul learns that Christine is singing for the Phantom and that Madame Giry has been working for him all along. He's furious, especially when he learns that Christine most likely knew that the Phantom was still alive. It doesn't matter that Christine has been blackmailed into it. Her husband is not supportive and hurts her arm. Raoul says, "I'll deal with you later." Meg learns that Christine will be singing in the same show, overshadowing her "lucky break," so she's upset. And Madame Giry wonders what this will mean for her and Meg.

The Phantom takes Gustave on a tour of his world of freaks and is thrilled to learn that Gustave loves his world. When Gustave plays a melody on the piano, he says "he sounds like me," and then he does the math. He is 10 years old. 10. Years. Old. That's when he realizes that this child might be his. He dares to show his face to Gustave, who flees in terror.

The Phantom confronts Christine, who admits, yes, it's true; Gustave is his. The Phantom is broken by the news, but then sings about giving his son all that is his. Madame Giry overhears the song, and is afraid the she and her daughter are about to be cut out of his fortune, which sets things in motion for the tragic ending.

In the end, Christine chooses the Phantom over Raoul during her *Love Never Dies* song. The Phantom and Christine finally kiss. Then they finally realize the Gustave is gone. After a frantic search, they realize that Meg has taken him—planning to drown both him and herself. Phantom and Christine run to the dock and are able to talk Meg into letting Gustave go. He runs to his mother. Then Meg pulls a gun. There is no mention of where she was hiding this big gun in her outfit, and why she brought a gun when she was planning to drown herself, or where she got it in the first place. Even in 1905, New York City was not the wild West: guns were not thick on the ground.

The Phantom tries to get the gun away from Meg. It is in his hand when he makes the mistake of mentioning Christine. Christine, hearing her name, walks towards them. The gun goes off. Christine falls to the ground, mortally wounded. Christine tells Gustave who his real father is. The kid is having none of it, even after Christine sings a rather nice deathbed song to him. He runs off to find Raoul. Christine dies in the Phantom's arms after giving him one last kiss. Gustave comes running back with Raoul in tow to lie on the lap of his now-deceased mother. The Phantom gently hands Christine's body back to Raoul and staggers to the end of the pier, where Gustave comes after him. In the end, Gustave removes his mask and touches the Phantom's disfigured face. The light fades.

Analysis of the *Love Never Dies* Plot

The storyline for *Love Never Dies* went through two major revisions, resulting in three versions. I'll describe these changes in detail in Chapters 24 through 26. For now, I will use the final version, version 3.0, as the basis for this discussion. Lloyd Webber and his collaborators had trouble converting the story to musical form. Lloyd Webber kept adding co-authors. Eventually, there were five authors of "the book."

The challenges of the story were also described in the book commemorating the 25th anniversary of *Phantom*.

> It was in 2006, after producing several new musicals, revivals, and pioneering casting for theatre by television, that Andrew seriously decided to look at the story again. He discussed it with several writers and directors to no avail until he outlined the problems he had with the plot to his old friend and colleague, Ben Elton. ...
>
> It was Elton who found the way through the roadblock. He pointed out that the first thoughts for a new plot contained several new characters and suggested that any continuation of the story must be about the protagonists of the original show. So, the new characters were axed and Gustave, Christine's son, is the only new principal character in *Love Never Dies*. Come the autumn of 2007, Elton had shaped a story outline that Lloyd Webber felt could be made to work (Heatley, 2011, p. 96).

Adding co-authors likely did not help. In fact, it muddied the storyline.

Difficulties Getting from Point A to Point B

Many of personality changes in *Love Never Dies* had more to do with the expediency of the current story than the continuity between the stories (e.g., Christine cheating on Raoul with the Phantom seems less awful if Raoul's a lout, which he is in *Love Never Dies*). The problem is getting from Point A to Point B. What explains these changes?

These changes between stories raise some significant questions. Some viewers never got past them. I admit that these bothered me a lot when I saw *Love Never Dies* for the first time. They distracted me enough that they took away from some of the enjoyment of the show. I was not alone. Viewers have been quite vocal in their objections to the plot holes in the sequel. I've outlined a few of the key questions they raised below.

1. What made Raoul turn into such a whiny loser when he had been a heroic figure in the first show?

Raoul is a bit dense in *Phantom*, but basically a good guy. Remember, he was the one who ran straight into the Phantom's lair to rescue Christine, which was pretty damn brave. So what caused him to suddenly turn into someone who gambled away his fortune, and becomes a bully to his wife and son? It's not consistent with who he was in *Phantom*.

2. They have a child? When did they have sex?

Normally, I wouldn't care. It's none of my business. But they have a kid? In *Phantom*, we pretty much saw every minute that they were together. So when did they do it? This question bugged me a lot the first time that I saw *Love Never Dies*. I finally decided that it wasn't important. Interestingly, in reviewing the older versions of *Love Never Dies*, I learned that this detail was edited out in what came to be the final version. More on that in a bit. But kind of important, guys.

3. How did she know Gustave was the Phantom's child, in the days long before DNA testing?

Another important detail. How does she know Gustave is Erik's child? In the text that was edited out, we learned that Christine came to the Phantom *the night before her wedding*. In Beneath the Moonless Sky, we learned that that they did three times. (I know. Way too much information.)

"And I took you."

"And I begged you."

"With a need to urgent to deny. Again and then again, beneath the moonless sky."

While Christine slept, Phantom slipped away. Since the Phantom decided to leave, Christine went ahead with her wedding *that same morning*. If Christine slept with the Phantom and Raoul on the same day, there really was no way for her to know for sure who Gustave's biological father was. This action also gets back to the issue of Christine's character. Under most circumstances, a woman sleeping with one man and marrying another the very next morning, would be monstrous and a huge betrayal of her husband. Yet, we are to take this behavior in stride.

Another issue is if she was so in love with the Phantom, how could she marry someone else so casually? Again, her unfaithful behavior doesn't seem consistent with what fans think they know about Christine.

There were other things that didn't seem to really add up.

4. Meg Giry was in love with the Phantom? And he was ignoring her?

It's not like he has lots of other choices, so that is a strange plotline. Also, Meg's super jealous of Christine? Since when? They were best friends in *Phantom*, and that continued in *The Phantom of Manhattan*. It's not to say that that couldn't happen, but it seems like a leap without something to explain it. In *Love Never Dies*, the continuity between these plot points is sadly missing as well.

Summary

There were significant continuity problems between *Phantom* and *Love Never Dies*. *The Phantom of Manhattan* may have been silly, but at least the characters seemed truer to the original than *Love Never Dies*. Objections to these plot points appeared early, once fans had a chance to hear the concept album. The story for the version 1.0 was apparent for all to see. The story was clearly on a collision course with *Phantom*, but Lloyd Webber was not going to be deterred by the opinions of a few fans. He was determined to move forward with his project, sure that the fans would fall into line.

CHAPTER 21

Love Never Dies 1.0
The Flop

*L*ove *Never Dies* opened with fanfare on London's West End. *The Daily Mail* reported that "Andrew Lloyd Webber was in defiant form last night at the premiere of his *Phantom of the Opera* sequel, which has come under fire from fans of the original."

> So-called "Phans" have panned *Love Never Dies* after watching the preview, a Facebook campaign has been set up to voice its animosity and a critic on one website said the show was so bad it should be retitled "Paint Never Dries." (see below for that review; Todd & Glass, 2010).

[Just to clarify, the *Paint Never Dries* label was not from the Facebook campaign, but the bloggers calling themselves the West End Whingers (2010).]

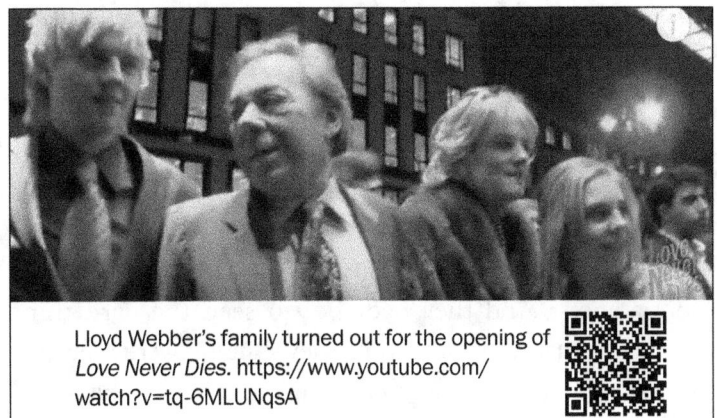

Lloyd Webber's family turned out for the opening of *Love Never Dies*. https://www.youtube.com/watch?v=tq-6MLUNqsA

The Critics Weigh In

Even in the face of Lloyd Webber's defiance, it wasn't long before the critics weighed in. Most of the news was bad, and it wasn't from just a few "mental" *Phantom* fans. The negative reaction came from established theater critics, many of whom specifically distanced themselves from the Facebook campaign. For example, Scott Matthewman, assistant editor of *The Stage*, posted on his Twitter account:

Love Never Dies=Shit Never Flushes. Just Awful.

Although *The Daily Mail* was mostly positive opening night, and describing how Lloyd Webber was determined to enjoy his big night, they noted that the critical reaction was largely split (Todd & Glass, 2010). Ben Brantley (2010), of *The New York Times*, described some of this controversy even before the show opened, describing *Love Never Dies* as a "big, gaudy new show," and noting that the rejuvenated *Phantom* "might as well have a 'kick me' sign pasted to his backside."

> Surely no stage show has ever been as widely and severely prejudiced as this belated sequel from Andrew Lloyd Webber.
>
> You see, Mr. Lloyd Webber's original *Phantom of the Opera* ... has developed a stark raving fan base since it opened ... in the late 1980s. When the news got out that there was to be another show about the Phantom ... a few of those fans took to their cyber-soapboxes to cry sacrilege.

Fans started contacting the theater critics, who wanted nothing to do with them.

> Soon theater writers (including me) were receiving e-mail messages from *Phantom*-ites lamenting the show's rank inappropriateness. And they hadn't even seen the darn thing. Once the musical went into previews, many were reporting in chat rooms and blogs that their darkest fears had been confirmed. Of course, bad advance word on the Internet has

sometimes proved false. (Ever hear of *Avatar?*) And I would be delighted to tell you that's what happened here ... but how can I, when, at every opportunity, Mr. Lloyd Webber's latest sets itself up to be knocked down? ... this poor sap of a show feels as eager to be walloped as a clown in a carnival dunking booth.

He also noted the plot holes described in the previous chapter.

Friends of *Phantom* will recognize these characters, as they are all (except Gustave) recycled— and in some cases, changed beyond recognition—from the earlier show. ... And its plot is so elaborate and implausible it makes the libretto of *Il Trovatore* read like a first-grade primer. If you don't know the first *Phantom,* you will be very confused; if you do know the first *Phantom,* you will also be very confused.

He separated himself from the fans, but also actually agreed with them.

Ian Shuttlework (2010), critic for *The Financial Times* had also heard from enraged fans about the sequel to *Phantom,* but formed his own opinion.

In recent weeks, I have received e-mails and Facebook messages from fans of *The Phantom of the Opera,* outraged that Andrew Lloyd Webber and his collaborators should have written a sequel at all, never mind one that travestied the original characters and relationships.

They're not entirely unjustified. It's possible that heroine Christine's beloved Raoul, now her husband, might turn out to be a wastrel and a drunkard; less conceivable that her single kiss with the Phantom 10 years ago should have borne a son. ... Enough liberties, then, to provoke high dudgeon in devotees, but not necessarily to irritate newcomers seeing this musical on its own terms.

The Whingers Weigh In

Bloggers calling themselves the West End Whingers (2010) provided a thoughtful, yet often funny and snarky review. Before launching into their review, they did recount the story of not being able to get comp tickets "due to the extremely high demand and a strictly limited ticket allocation." The producers made a mistake there. It started the Whingers off in a negative mood.

They started with the title, which they noted had been ripped off from a James Bond movie. They did give the producers good marks for managing to get both love and death into the title, but they pointed out that it was total "bollocks" that love never dies. Of course, it does. All of the time.

Overall, they found the production to be a bit gloomy and dark, and noted the "po-facedness of it all." They noted the same plot holes. "If Raoul is a drunken gambler, doesn't that rather pull the rug out from under those who loved the original and went away thinking it had a happy ending? Ben Elton should have thrown away his key." They also noted that the Madame Giry was "channeling Mrs. Danvers," another apt comparison. And they really hated the set.

> The scene in the Phantom's Aerie at the top of what looks like a Blackpool Tower and which is dress with freakish oddies, such as a Medusa like singing chandelier and a half woman-half skeleton walking hostess trolley (the Whingers really liked that), all played out to an appalling rock-ish music score. It's the most fabulous overwrought mess currently on view on the West End stage ... wrings the worst excesses of Art Nouveau to produce the bastard child of sexual congress between a peacock and an owl in a Notting Hill antique shop.

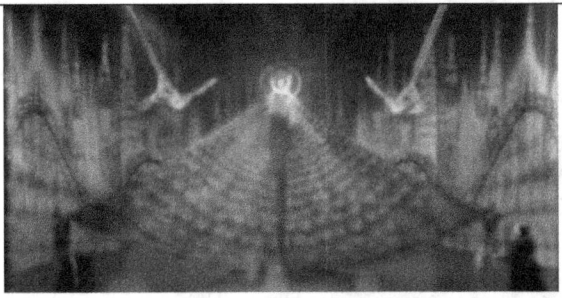

The opening Coney Island segment. The effects are actually pretty cool.
https://www.youtube.com/watch?v=6QgmLTya9_Q

And it was boring.

The Phantom's lyric "time keeps moving on" had Phil looking at his watch. Was the Phantom sure? Surely it had stopped.

Also, the "big moments" lacked any kind of intensity.

The first appearance of the Phantom, his first meeting with Christine, the Phantom's unmasking. All thrown away. Christine's surprise suggested that the Phantom had bought a new pair of trousers since she last saw him rather than the fact that a disfigured kidnapper she thought was dead was in her bedroom.

They also commended Joseph Millson, who played Raoul, for going on and not "pulling a sickie every night. We would have." They ended their review with the following verdict. And it was a name that stuck with the show.

Verdict: Dull. Like watching paint dry, and as we all know, paint never dries.

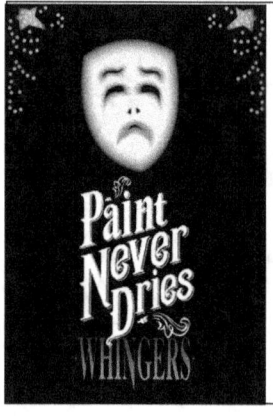

Parody of the title from the West End Whingers (2010).

More Critics Weigh In

The review from *Time Out, London* (Marlowe, 2010) was worse, calling it an "interminable musical monstrosity." The reviewer noted the "sickening swirls of video imagery, pointless plot, and protracted, repetitive songs," and found the overall effect to be "punishingly wearisome."

> *Phantom* oozes overblown gothic romanticism, fatally, that's replaced by soapy banality in this mongrel creation, collectively by composer Lloyd Webber, Ben Elton, Frederick Forsyth, and lyricist Glenn Slater. ... Phantom's freakshow sidekicks look like refugees from *The Rocky Horror Show*. Similarly, the act one finale sees Lloyd Webber's score, otherwise comprised of Richard Rodgers-esque waltzes and lachrymose opera-lite arias, take a ludicrous nosedive into guitar-bristling 1980s cock rock. It's an excruciating low-point in an extraordinarily ill-judged show. Ghastly (Marlowe, 2010).

In contrast to much of the mostly negative reviews, Michael Billington (2010), of *The Guardian*, offers a more tempered review, but notes that most of the problems with the show are because of the book.

> There is much to enjoy in Andrew Lloyd Webber's new musical. The score is one of the composer's most seductive.

He also liked the sets—something many other reviewers took issue with.

> Bob Crowley's design and Jack O'Brien's direction have a beautiful kaleidoscopic fluidity.

But here is the issue.

> The problems lie within the book, chiefly credited to Lloyd Webber himself and Ben Elton, which lacks the weight to support the imaginative superstructure.

He also discusses the role of the Phans and difficulties between the stories.

> But there is a crucial difference between the two shows. The hero of the *Phantom* was a crazed Svengali prepared to murder, and send chandeliers crashing, to further the career of his beloved Christine. In *Love Never Dies*, set 10 years later, he has become "Mr Y"—the mysterious owner of a Coney Island pleasure ground who lures Christine back for a well-paid gig. Romantic obsession may be common to both shows, but where one may feel sympathy for a doomed outsider, it is hard to feel much for an omnipotent impresario.
>
> What the show lacks, in a nutshell, is narrative tension ... In short, the show has much to commend it and the staging is a constant source of iridescent pleasure. But as one of the lyrics reminds us, "diamonds never sparkle bright unless they are set just right." Although Lloyd Webber's score is full of gems, *in the end a musical is only as good as its book.* With a libretto to match the melodies, this might have been a stunner rather than simply a good night out. [emphasis added]

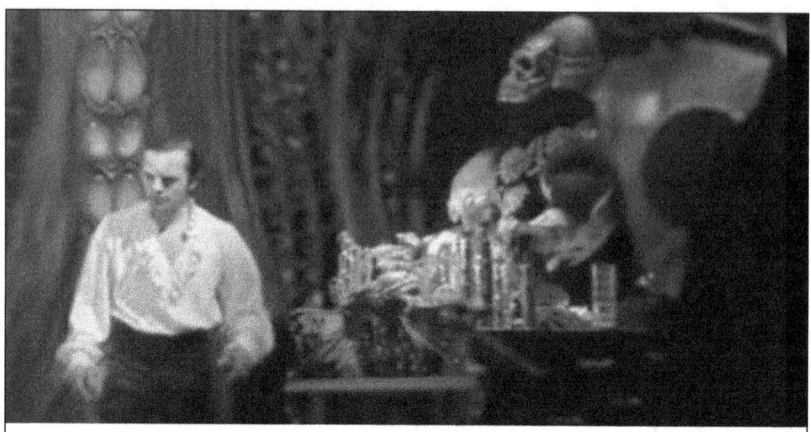

The freak show in Beauty Underneath.
https://www.youtube.com/watch?v=Ndl36IBLfHQ

Quentin Letts (2010), in *The Daily Mail* says, "Stodgy Phantom sequel not quite a hit ... but Lloyd Webber's operatic music lifts it to a higher plane." Among the problems he notes are an overly long beginning, describing it "as slow to motor as a lawnmower at spring's first cut. It doesn't really smoke into life until the 20th minute, and even then it splutters for a while."

In an interview with Charles Spencer (2013), Lloyd Webber discusses his career, and notes some of the problems with *Love Never Dies* that critics raised.

> **CS:** What do you think when you look back over your career?
>
> **ALW:** What strikes me is that there's a very fine line between success and failure. Just one ingredient can make the difference.
>
> A really good example of that is *Love Never Dies*. The London production didn't have any consistency of style, so it would go from say Art Nouveau to Art Deco to straightforward, old-fashioned Broadway showbiz. The Australian production [which has been very successful]

had its own language. It was more like Maria Bjornson's original design for *Phantom* or the original design for *Evita*, it was at one with the piece.

In the face of negative reviews, Lloyd Webber closed *Love Never Dies 1.0* to re-tool it. The result was *Love Never Dies 2.0*, which re-opened at the end of 2010.

CHAPTER 22

Love Never Dies 2.0
Different, but
Not Different Enough

Taking the critics to heart, *Love Never Dies* closed briefly to be revamped. It re-opened December 21, 2010, and Lloyd Webber attempted to revise every aspect of it. He fired his director and choreographer. Patrick Marion, of *The Daily Mail*, noted that Lloyd Webber was attempting to "stem the tide of seats flipping up and tickets reportedly going for as little as £3." *The Stage* critic, Mark Shenton, noted that *Love Never Dies* "suffered from a series of production miscalculations," and noted Lloyd Webber's "hubristic" plan to simultaneously open the show on three continents (Sharp, 2011).

Lloyd Webber asked critics to give version 2.0 another chance, partly because they were about to open on Broadway. Some of the key scenes had been reworked, as well as the opening and closing scenes. Madame Giry (whom several critics called Mrs. Danvers-esque) no longer had a long opening soliloquy, which *Variety Magazine* called "lumpen." They brought in Charles Hart, the original lyricist on *Phantom*, and a new choreographer and producer. They now opened with their strongest song, Till I Hear You Sing.

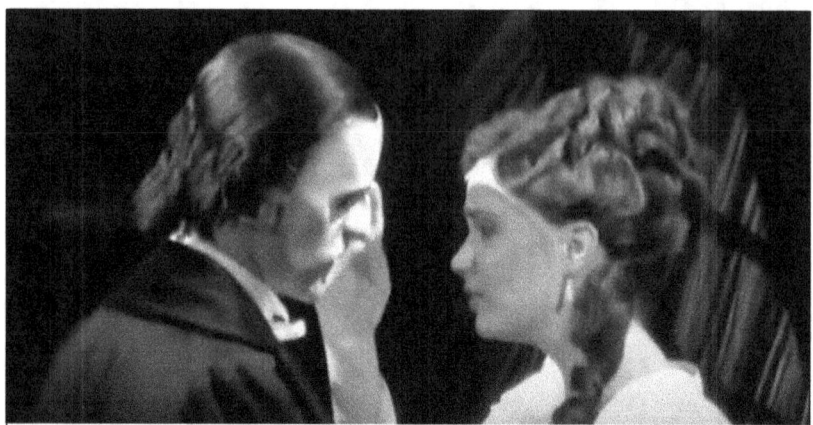

Phantom and Christine sing to each other in
Beneath the Moonless Sky in version 2.0.
https://www.youtube.com/watch?v=1jAtShinhUo

Even with these revisions, the show didn't quite work. The critics mostly agreed with each other. The revamped version was improved enough to pick up seven Olivier award nominations, but did not win any (Sharp, 2011).

As with the previous version, the key problem with was the story. *Variety* noted that although the audience is happier now, since it heard a good number upfront, the overall play lacked dramatic tension (Benedict, 2010b). The staging, although streamlined, was still a problem and lacked credibility. Marion noted the following in his review in *The Daily Mail*.

> Alright, musicals are licensed to be flimsy, but this one's got no real oomph to get it going. It also has little at stake to sustain it until well into the second half—long after the Phantom's beloved Christine has been lured to his den in the fairground of Coney Island.

> Lloyd Webber's music fares better, but broods and toils with violins sighing and straining as it yearns to give the story a shove. Instead it merely heaves away, experimenting briefly with prog-rock. And all the stringy melodramatic romanticism merely proves it to be a musical out of time.

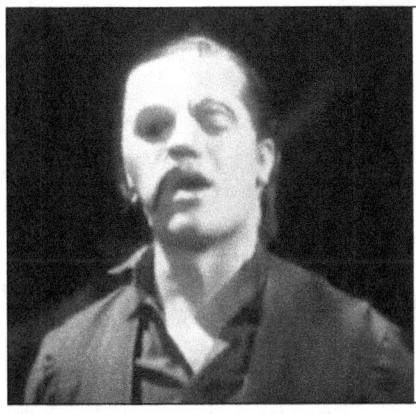

Version 2.0 now opens much stronger with Till I Hear You Sing. https://www.youtube.com/ watch?v=4lrWVfX_JrA

Henry Hitchings, of *The Evening Standard*, noted many significant improvements in version 2.0, but still referred to it as a "lachrymose companion to *The Phantom of the Opera*." He noted that the new version is was "now more fluid and coherent, as well as more emotionally satisfying." But there were still problems: "it is still repetitious, lacks real suspense, and suffers from the fact that several key characters seem one-dimensional."

Hitchings noted that Charles Hart "adjusted the cadences of the original clunky lines written by Glenn Slater." He praised the work of both Ramin Karimloo and Sierra Boggess, but raised the issue of plot holes.

> Yet the relationship between the new work and the beloved old one proves problematic. Although we are emphatically told that 10 years have elapsed since *Phantom*, the principal character seems a good deal younger than in that show. And we're never given a convincing explanation of how he's ended up in Coney Island—a setting that, for all its vivid realization, appears incongruous.

Time Out London gives another negative review, from a different critic, Nina Caplan (2011). Again, a critic mentions the weakness of the storyline as one of the central problems.

> *Love Never Dies* has seen some frantic revamping of late ... but despite some improvement, the new mask does little to

hide the ugliness beneath; the problems are integral. ... Ramin Karimloo as the Phantom and Sierra Boggess as Christine both have lovely voices, but they aren't given anything to say. The producers have exchanged the Paris Opera for an American theme park, and the swap is not a happy one.

Bad Blood Over *Love Never Dies 1.0*

The London *Evening Standard* (Hitchings, 2010) was the first to report what other outlets had hinted at: that there was lots of bad blood between Lloyd Webber and Jack O'Brien, the original director. Lloyd Webber closed the show to create *Love Never Dies 2.0* and fired O'Brien, bringing in Bill Kenwright and choreographer Bill Deamer. O'Brien said:

> It did not end happily. I found Andrew Lloyd Webber impossible to work with. It's either his way or there's no way.

Noting that there were problems and imperfections, The *Evening Standard* asked him why he didn't fix them.

> He would not let me. I'm finished with it.

"Love Never Dies ... But It's Hurting"

In May 2011, Baz Bamigboye, of *The Daily Mail* noted that *Love Never Dies* had lost more than £4 million, money, which it was unlikely to recoup. At that time, there were no plans to close the show. In the meantime, the opening of a completely new version, *Love Never Dies* 3.0, was scheduled to open the next day in Melbourne, Australia.

> "There is no decision to close the show in London," an executive involved with *Love Never Dies*, ... For a show that should have been a sure-fire hit, it has been beset by some of the bloodiest behind-the-scenes shenanigans seen in the West End.

> The Nederlander Organisation is the co-owner of the Adelpi, with Lloyd Webber's production company, the Really Useful

Group. The Nederlander Organisation wanted to close *Love Never Dies* and replace it with something that what would make them some money. In a report to *The Daily Mail*, an executive involved with the *Love Never Dies* production in London wanted to tell Scandalios (who runs the theatre production) "not to close *Love Never Dies* because the Melbourne version is previewing very well."

According to *The Daily Mail*, Lloyd Webber was happy with the Australian version and wanted to bring it to London, but that would mean shutting it down again and giving it new sets, costumes, and cast (Bamigboye, 2011). It never happened. People involved with the London production blamed Lloyd Webber for the problems with the show and its failure to take off.

> They insist that during rehearsals and previews last year the impresario refused to allow a single note of his score to be cut, which meant that there could be no changes to the show's structure. It's easy to understand why Lloyd Webber wouldn't want to cut his score—it's one of the most beautiful he's ever written.

> But his recalcitrance caused mayhem behind the scenes and led to director Jack O'Brien, designer Bob Crowley, and others asking lawyers to intervene (Bamigboye, 2011).

After losing £4 million, the producers weren't allowed to raise any more funds, so the Really Useful Group funded it itself for months. They slashed their costs by £15,000 per week. The producers admitted to their investors recently: "All of us are devastated that a project so full of promise has come to this pass. It's hard to explain fully."

> Really Useful claims they can afford to keep *Love Never Dies* running because it's "haemorrhaging peanuts" rather than haemorrhaging to death (Bamigboye, 2011).

Love Does Die After All

These changes were not enough to keep the show afloat. *Love Never Dies 2.0* closed August 27, 2011. A spokesperson for the Really Useful Group announced the closure and refused to comment further.

The reviews on the reboot were better, but still not good enough to overcome the initial stigma following the first round of reviews. The narrative was clearer in the second round. *The Telegraph* noted that it was nearly impossible for the production to overcome the stigma of the label Paint Never Dries (Malnick, 2011). In responding to questions about the production, Lloyd Webber admitted that he was "not on the case" during the time that the first production was released. (According to his director, Jack O'Brien, he may have been too much "on the case.") In June 2011, Lloyd Webber revealed that he was suffering from prostrate cancer when *Love Never Dies 1.0* was opening, which prevented him from properly overseeing it. He admitted that he should have put off the opening of the show until he felt well enough to fully participate in overseeing production of the show (Malnick, 2011).

> I had a unique issue because I got cancer in the middle of all of it. With hindsight, we should have said, "Let's put the whole thing on hold until I'm 100 percent again." Frankly, I wasn't feeling very well.

The Stage critic, Shenton (2011) said:

> I can hear the gloating already from the mad "Love Should Die" lobby of *Love Never Dies* detractors, who have run their disgraceful campaign of intimidation and aggravation, lies, and deceit around the show since before it even opened. But now they are finally getting their wish.

Lloyd Webber reported that he loved the new Australian version of the show, noted that it "cannot be improved upon." This version had more positive reviews and is coming to North America in 2017.

It is fabulous to look at and they completely understand what I'm trying to get at with the score. It has momentum that is wonderful.

Lloyd Webber described what happened with *Love Never Dies* and the controversy surrounding it in an interview with Playbill.com (Shenton, 2011):

PB: *Love Never Dies* has had a checkered history, hasn't it? You originally announced plans to open this sequel to *The Phantom of the Opera* on three continents simultaneously ...

ALW: Thank goodness, we didn't!

PB: So, what happened?

ALW: A couple of things went extremely wrong there, and I think one was that due to dates, Jack O'Brien got involved in the workshop of *Catch Me If You Can*, so we got shunted around; and then, of course, I got cancer. At the time, I thought I was going to be able to control the show far more than I did, but whatever anybody may say, you can take a while to recover from these things. And although I'm in the clear completely now ... I was not on peak form throughout. That's probably the best thing to say about it; if I'd had Bill [Kenwright] there as a producer from the word go, he'd have said there are certain things we can't go ahead with. But we'd recorded the album, and it had been very well received; a lot of people thought it was right up there with the others. I think it was a combination of me not being very well, the team perhaps underestimating what it needed, and perhaps everybody thinking it was going to be far easier thing to do than in fact it was.

PB: But it has been overhauled now ...

ALW: Yes, I said to Bill, "I knew the order's not quite right," so he went in and did this extraordinary work on it, with no pay. It's completely transformed, even though for me as a musician it wasn't a big job to do. Some of them are thoughts that were going to happen for Australia anyway, but Bill has given me the most fantastic blueprint for it now to be got right around the world.

PB: So, what's happened to Jack O'Brien and Jerry Mitchell (who directed and choreographed the original West End premiere)?

ALW: They're not involved in the next production planned in Australia, which Simon Phillips from Melbourne Theatre Company is directing. But Bill is a great friend of Jack O'Brien's, and a great admirer of his, but it got to a point where everyone was very close to it, and an outside mind was a good idea. ... If the Australian production is phenomenal and everyone is extremely pleased with it, then that might be the production that then goes to America. ... But it's a show I'm very confident about. I'm not remotely worried about it. Even though things have been slightly altered order-wise, I've always thought that the score to it will outlive me easily. That's all one can really think about. There are certain pieces of mine that might not: unless somebody can find a way of finding a better end to *The Woman in White*, for example, that piece ain't going anywhere! ...

PB: But musicals often have their own momentum and challenges, don't they?

ALW: When you look at *Cats, Phantom,* or *Les Miserables*— and let's face it, those three are the big ones of the 80s—one throw of the dice slightly the wrong way and any one of those could have been derailed. For example, *Les Miserables* opened to awful reviews—anybody who thinks *Love Never Dies* had bad reviews should read the *Les Miz* ones ... It's all about the throw of the dice—what if, for example, we'd done *Phantom of the Opera* with the *Cats* team? That could have happened; and if it had, would we even be talking about *The Phantom of the Opera* now?

CHAPTER 23

Love Never Dies 3.0
The Much-Improved Australian Version

The Australian version of *Love Never Dies* opened May 2011 at the Regent Theatre in Melbourne. *Love Never Dies 3.0* was completely reworked from the ground up, with an all-Australian cast. Tim McFarlane who ran the Really Useful Group Asia Pacific, approached Lloyd Webber to see whether he would consider a new production of the show. Lloyd Webber was finally willing to listen to feedback, and gave his blessing. McFarlane and his team addressed many of the issues that plagued earlier versions.

> Without hesitation, Lloyd Webber immediately gave the go-ahead and met with Australian director Simon Phillips. ... Impressed by the frank response he received from Simon about the West End production, he had no hesitation in entrusting him with helming a brand-new production of the show. In Simon Phillips' own words, "at our first meeting, Andrew said, 'I want it to be different.'" So that was the brief Phillips worked on with designer Gabriela Tyleson, choreographer Graeme Murphy, and lighting designer, Nick Schlieper (Heatley, 2011, pp. 99-100).

This version is a substantial improvement over previous versions—and is good.

There are still issues with the plot (e.g., the personality changes in the characters, the Phantom and Christine's love child, and Christine's purported fame). However, they are less glaring in this version. You almost have to think of this as a new show, and not the sequel to *Phantom*. If you can do that, you may enjoy it. Lloyd Webber's score is excellent, and it's a shame that it's attached to a show that has had so many problems with the story.

In this version, the staging is crisper. The actors' actions seem more purposeful, and they aren't simply milling around the stage. Phantom and Christine seem to be thinking about what they are singing, so that the song lyrics become dialog. (In earlier versions, they might have been singing about their grocery lists for all the passion they exhibited.) The actors used the stage more effectively, and so were not simply confined to a small spotlighted area. Also, key scenes, such as the finale, were edited so that they had more power.

The Really Useful Group decided to record a live performance in Australia, which they released on DVD. The video techniques that they used make it seem like we are seeing something that was made for video rather than a live performance. This helped the Really Useful Group relaunch the show in other countries, including the U.S., and to create some positive buzz. The criticism of 3.0 has been far less harsh than it was for the earlier versions.

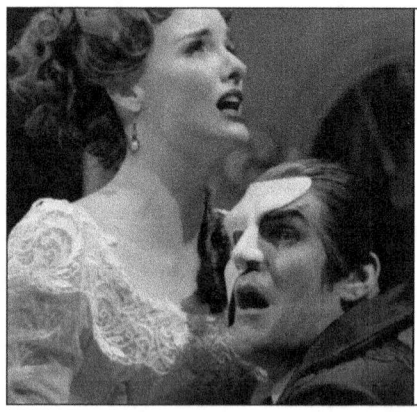

Ben Lewis and Anna O'Byrne play Phantom and Christine in *Love Never Dies 3.0*.
https://www.youtube.com/watch?v=iimYZM8Z-0M&index=1&list=RDiimYZM8Z-0M

Controversy Followed Them

Even with these substantial changes, controversy still plagued *Love Never Dies 3.0*. *The Herald Sun* reported that there was a campaign afoot to discourage audiences from seeing the show (Platt, 2011). When the social media campaign took place in London, Lloyd Webber characterized this group as a bunch of "nutters." When Love Should Die went after the Australian version, team Lloyd Webber tried a different tactic. They characterized this campaign as an "attack on creative freedom."

> I find it amazing that they can take it on themselves to say, "We have the right to decide what should be done with the Phantom," he said.

> Surely that's Andrew's call. He's the composer, the creator, and he's upset and bewildered as to why a small group of people would want to try to stop him doing what he does.

Technically speaking, Lloyd Webber is the creator of *a version* of *Phantom*. Leroux is its actual creator.

> The campaign, which came from the UK, are trying to keep the original *Phantom* as a "one-off."

McFarlane, the CEO of the Really Useful Group Asia Pacific, said:

> To try and stop a creative interpretation of this relatively useful new show is perplexing when this is such a fantastic opportunity for all the people involved.

Regarding "the *Love Never Dies*-haters," he described them as "archaic people who don't want change."

> How strange others want to judge something that hasn't even been born yet.

In the end, he concluded the following.

> At the end of the day, the public should have the right to decide whether they want to go to it or not. If you disagree

with it, well don't go. Don't come out and say we're going to censor other people, including the composer himself, from working with his music (Platt, 2011).

Public Response to the DVD on Amazon

Not surprisingly, reviewers of the DVD raised many of the same concerns regarding plot as they did with *The Phantom of Manhattan*. They gave *Love Never Dies 3.0* 4 out of 5 stars: mostly positive reviews, and likely better than the previous two versions would have received in the same format. But only 55% gave it a 5-star review, which shows a more mixed response compared to the *Phantom* movie. Below are some of the excerpts from Amazon reviews.

Love Never Dies in Sydney Australia

Outside of England, to my knowledge, Australia where I live, is the only other country to have *Love Never Dies* currently showing, that finished in Melbourne just before Christmas and is about to open in Sydney. I have seen the show twice now. *The Phantom of the Opera* I saw 5 times, and it is my favourite Musical. ... There is drama, love, and sadness as there was in the original *Phantom of the Opera*, and throughout *Love Never Dies*, there are a few subtle references back to the original show through the music score, When Christine sings her signature song, the scene took my breath away. If you loved *Phantom of the Opera*, you will love, *Love Never Dies*.

He recommended that viewers keep an open mind, even in the face of the negative reviews. He noted that Aussies tend to ignore reviews and decide for themselves.

I too had read negative reviews when the show opened in London. Perhaps us Aussies do not pay much attention to other's views, and would rather see it for ourselves before passing judgement. I have no regrets spending my money to see this show. It was fantastic. Enjoy the DVD. Feel the beautiful music score and enjoy the show (Ozboy).

Another reviewer called it "Stunning," and was actually at the performance when it was filmed.

> This is a must have for any DVD collection. ... The sets are amazing, something new to see every time you look. Ben Lewis and Anna O'Byrne give memorable performances ... The score is one the best Andrew Lloyd Webber has written, and the vocal talents of the cast blend beautifully with it. My personal favorites are Till I Hear You Sing and Beneath the Moonless Sky (K. Imlach).

Still another reviewer noted that "It's meant to be different," and to not try to directly compare *Phantom* and *Love Never Dies*.

> ... both VERY amazing/awesome/phantastic, even if the story is different from what some people think should happen. It's still a masterpiece and deserves to be recognized for its own music and story and actors, not for its prequel. The music is amazing. The cast is amazing in both productions. It's worth buying. Keep an open mind and you'll be amazed (kathrynannabelle).

But not everyone approved of the new version, for many of the same reasons outlined in earlier versions. This review was titled, "Atrocious, Skip It."

> ... I don't recommend this if you're a fan of the original. It's very rare for me to find fault with Andrew Lloyd Webber, but this was atrocious. It takes everything that was good and pure about *Phantom of the Opera* and destroys it. The story of the Phantom, by Gaston Leroux, is so much more dark and disturbing. Webber took that story and created a brilliant musical that touched hearts through the music. What happens in this completely undermines everything beautiful about *Phantom*.
>
> I have always viewed the Phantom as the dark soul that didn't understand love, only obsession. He was the stalker who only

at the end of his life realized his mistake. Raoul was the light in the dark for Christine. He was literally the sun in the dark world the Phantom had trapped Christine in. To turn around and try to convince the audience that Christine regretted her choice and ran back to the Phantom to sleep with him that very night is wrong. It was much like Stockholm Syndrome in that regards, which it really is if you've read the novel and know how dark it is.

Not to mention the Phantom running away because he was scared is completely out of character. He would never have done that. He wanted Christine at all costs. He would never have run away if she came to him willingly, especially then. Then there's the child he conceived with her, the drunk and gambling Raoul, and the utterly horrific carnival music. I was extremely disappointed in this musical and have decided just to pretend it doesn't exist for the sake of my own sanity.

Reviewers Weigh in on Goodreads

Goodreads, the site that posted reviews of *The Phantom of Manhattan*, also published reviews of the DVD of *Love Never Dies 3.0*. The comments take place from October to December, 2014. Below are excerpts from a spirited middle-of-the-night discussion. These comments reiterate problems cited earlier, including various plot holes. This discussion also gives a real sense of the passion people have over *Phantom's* story. These reviewers are not associated with Love Should Die, yet they voice many of the same concerns. It gives some idea why *Love Never Dies* encountered the problems that it did, even though version 3.0 was a big improvement.

Here is the discussion question one reader posted:

I haven't watched *Love Never Dies*, but I want to know what people think of it. Is it worth watching?

The first reader responds.

It is an interesting movie, but hardly a valid sequel. This is not what you would expect to happen to characters in the future.

And at points I was thinking "these actions are so out of character for these people. This would never happen, or even be appropriate for people of class at that time period." It was a good movie, but I did not like it as a sequel.

Another reader, loved the music and sets, but also agreed that it wasn't a good sequel.

One can argue if it's a good SEQUEL, but the music and setting are phantastic! And Anna O'Byrne as Christine is just brilliant. I recommend it! See it as a show on its own, if you don't like it as a sequel.

Another argued found it impossible to ignore that it was a sequel because the overall storyline was too upsetting.

Yes, I agree the music is fantastic, but the actual plot and story are so wrong and upsetting, in my opinion. I will see it sometime though, and I'll try to think of it as an individual show.

Still another reader did not find the storyline to be as improbable as people claimed.

I think a lot of it fits...

1. Meg as a show girl. People always think Meg has to be a super innocent little ballerina. But people don't understand, that ballerinas and show girls had basically the same social status. A very low one, indeed. Same goes for opera singers. The thing is, a ballerina could find more spotlight as a leading show girl, especially one who also has some singing abilities, which are not enough for opera, but perfect in addition to her dancing. Being a show girl was just the right chance for her to become famous on her own, which would never work in the opera ballet.

2. Raoul is an alcoholic. Alcoholism is a genetic problem and, being aristocratic, genetic defects are very likely. His whole family could be related.

Ah, blame those upper-class recessive genes! Bit of a leap of logic here, but okay, let's go with it.

> And he always was a weak person. It just makes sense that he needed some "help" and didn't get out of it, especially after his brother's death.

Do we know that?

> 3. Christine sleeping with Erik. Well, some people love that idea! Most people, actually. There are so many ideas of them having a child. Of course, it's matter of opinion.

As middle-of-the-night social-media rants, this one is pretty entertaining. Keeping in mind that these are *characters*, not real people, these readers seem to have some pretty definite ideas. Yet another reader weighs in.

> Okay, I don't really have a problem with the whole Meg thing, but Raoul's story line is the problem, and Christine's child with Erik. No offense taken, it just upsets me!

> First, Raoul loved Christine. Look what he did to win her. Besides, there is no reason for him to become an alcoholic; his relationship with Christine was fine, so he obviously wasn't depressed. ... If he was getting too obsessed with alcohol, he would have cared enough for Christine and their relationship to get better and accepted her help getting over it.

We hope.

> Now Erik and Christine's child, WHAT RUBBISH. ... There was no chance for them to have slept together. In the Point of No Return, the Phantom wanted to sleep with Christine for the first time. That was the whole point: he desperately wanted her. Yet nothing happened, and no there was no chance for the child to have been conceived. AND Christine was not a slut. She loved Raoul and wouldn't have been with Erik; in the final scene—the Final Lair—you can see how the idea repulsed her. So that's my opinion! Sorry, I'm getting quite worked up about this! :)

Don't get worked up. It's only Fanfict! Nevertheless, it was quite upsetting for yet another reviewer.

> No, I see your problem. I'm not too fond of that idea either. Still, I find it silly when people scream "IT'S RUINED PHANTOM FOR ME!!!" while it's just a mediocre (not even bad!) piece of fanfiction. Still, everything does kind of make sense—except that it doesn't mean one would like it. Anyways, you should give it a try. Just see it as a stand-alone musical, where people for some reason have the same names. ;).

Another discussion was raised. This one had to do with why Raoul's character changed so much.

> When Raoul found out that the Phantom obviously wanted Christine, it's not like he chickened out and got another girl, which would suggest a weak character. He had to love Christine, surely, to fight for her. ...

> Also, Raoul was a member of the aristocracy, and Christine just a broke chorus girl. He didn't have to marry her. He could have made her his mistress (the fate of many actresses/singers at the time), or just tossed her aside when she proved too much trouble. He was by no means perfect, but I think his heart was in the right place.

Some wondered if Raoul really loved Christine. If he did, what happened to him? This reviewer agreed with the previous comment about Raoul's heart being in the right place, which made her more upset about the changes in *Love Never Dies*. She offered a theory about why Raoul changed.

> ... Obviously, things got too much for him. I feel that maybe in *POTO*, definitely by the book, that maybe Raoul was broken by the end ... As a (maybe) spoiled young man this was all too much and completely new. He just hadn't been brought up ... to face all of this that life had to offer, especially the challenges he faced in *LND*. So yeah, blame his parents :). I just feel that in *LND* Raoul was obviously struggling from perhaps a

miserable childhood? Raoul simply wasn't equipped for all of this, but he loved Christine despite everything.

Raoul with PTSD? Maybe getting a bit beyond the plot here. Another reader had not seen *Love Never Dies*, but still had objections.

> I've never seen *Love Never Dies*, but I know enough of the major plot to have an opinion. And just the idea of it makes me want to lose hope in humanity. Christine would never cheat on Raoul with the Phantom. Let's not forget that she was utterly terrified of him for most the play, and was kidnapped and harassed by this man who so-called loved her. And even if she did love him, she was a good and honorable person. Don't get me wrong, I'm completely obsessed with *The Phantom of the Opera*. But no, Webber should have stopped tampering with the original story. It completely contradicts everything that happened in the first. Ugh.

It's all about the plot. The problem persists.

> Yeah, I also looked up the major plot line, so I also have an opinion now! Yes, Sarah, I agree with you completely. The way Raoul and Christine acted together in *POTO* proves they would never fall apart in their relationship. Look what he did to try win her! And the way she saved his life! And the Phantom is a murderer! I am also ADDICTED to *The Phantom of the Opera*, but I agree with you Sarah, Webber SHOULD NOT have tried his luck with a sequel. And so true, it does contradict everything. I mean, I felt sorry for the Phantom in *POTO*, but I was all for Raoul and Christine. Now they spoil everything in the sequel.

A final comment on *The Phantom of Manhattan*.

> I still think the major flaw lies with Frederick Forsyth's *The Phantom of Manhattan*. It was simply an awful book. It read like a Mary Sue fanfic. So if you're using that as your basis for a musical sequel, then you're doomed from the start. I

know the author is established, but the book was just so amateurish and showed that he didn't understand what made the original novel and the musical so special.

It's All About the Story

In the end, it all comes back to the story. If it makes sense, the fans will follow you to your musical parallel universe, where people sing instead of talk. If the story doesn't make sense, they will turn on their heels and walk away, even when presented with a possible sequel to a much-beloved original story.

The first time I saw *Love Never Dies*, I had problems with the plot holes. My questions took away from my enjoyment of the show. So, my reaction the first time I saw it was "Meh."

Then I decided to give it another chance. I approached it as a separate show, not as a *Phantom* sequel. When I did that, I got totally hooked. I love the music, and there are many great moments that I have replayed multiple times. (I'll describe why in more detail in Chapters 24 to 26.)

My recommendation on *Love Never Dies* is to give it a chance. Put the plot holes aside (if you can), and consider it a separate show. I know that is asking you to make a leap, but if you do, I believe it will be worth it. It's not at the level of *Phantom*, but it is an enjoyable show. See what you think.

CHAPTER 24

Pivotal Scene I
Phantom Reveals Himself to Christine

*L*ove *Never Dies* is unusual in musical theater because it went through three iterations before it ended up in its final form. The editing itself was not particularly unusual. Several other Lloyd Webber shows have gone through a similar process. What is unusual is that this editing took place in an era of social media. Audience members recorded sections on cell phones and posted them on YouTube, so we now have the "official" version (the DVD of version 3.0 recorded in Australia), but also shots of versions 1 and 2. These video clips give us a chance to observe the editing process in action across versions.

In the next three chapters, I will talk in some detail about differences in three key scenes in the three versions of *Love Never Dies:* the reappearance of the Phantom, the Phantom finding out about Gustave, and the finale. These changes measurably improved the show. Putting aside the issue of plot holes and the improbability of the story for a second, *Love Never Dies 3.0* was a lot better than the previous versions. I've included video links you can see these changes, and how they improved the show, for yourself.

Beneath the Moonless Sky

The Phantom's big reveal is the first pivotal scenes of the show: so pivotal, it forms the central part of the trailer for the DVD. It's one of my favorite scenes. It opens with an instrumental version of the song, Beneath the Moonless Sky. A door flies open and the Phantom appears amidst swirls of smoke.

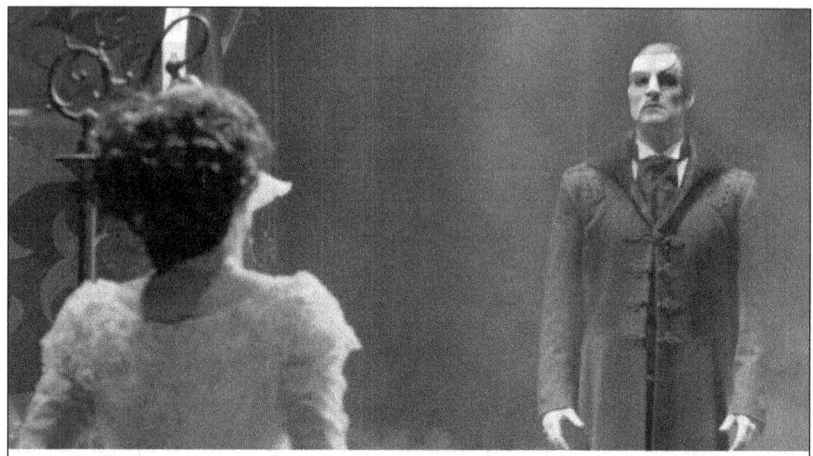

In version 3.0, Phantom enters Christine's room for the Big Reveal. Christine is so shocked that she passes out. Phantom gently carries her to a chair.
https://www.youtube.com/watch?v=iimYZM8Z-0M

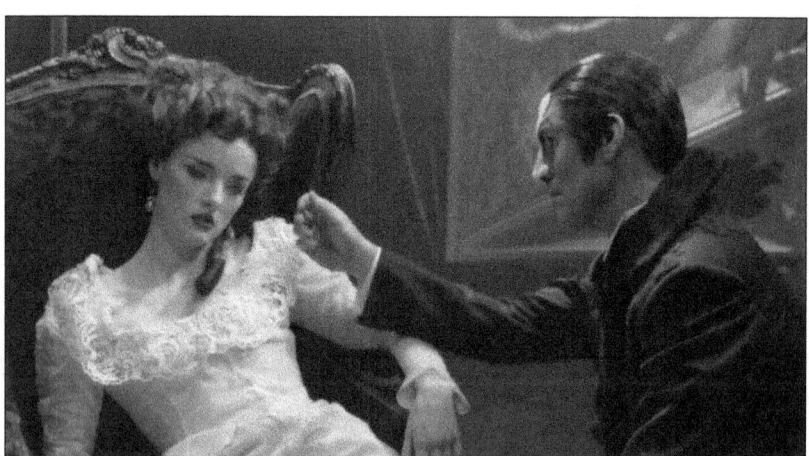

Phantom gently checks on an unconscious Christine.
https://www.youtube.com/watch?v=iimYZM8Z-0M

In versions 1.0 and 2.0, this scene loses much of its power. The blocking and choreography in both versions seemed off. The Phantom and Christine are often apart when they are singing key lyrics. They are supposed to be attracted to each other, but they are often not near, or even looking at each other. Even when they are singing about when they had sex, there is very little heat.

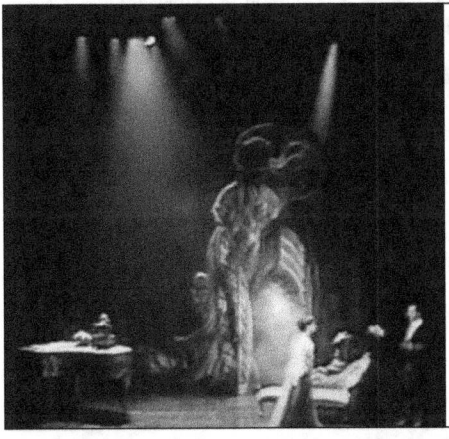

Dark, gloomy staging in 1.0, and Phantom and Christine don't spend a lot time near each other, odd for such a key scene. https://www.youtube.com/watch?v=PwZlOCFNDQs

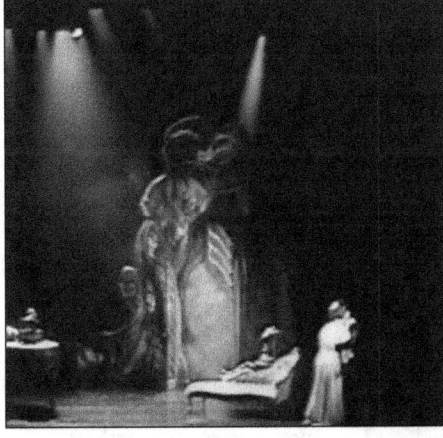

Christine hugs Phantom here and then they chase each other for the rest of the song. https://www.youtube.com/watch?v=PwZlOCFNDQs

This scene improved in 2.0, but version 3.0 is cleaner throughout.

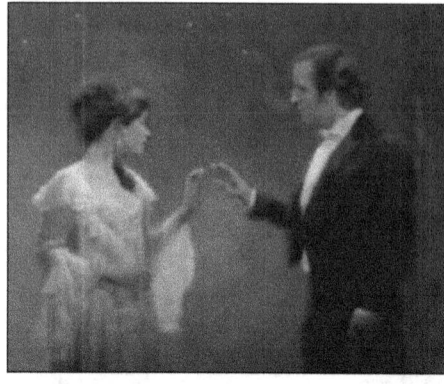

A lovely moment from Beneath the Moonless Sky in version 2.0. At least they are singing to each other in this version. https://www.youtube.com/watch?v=1jAtShinhUo

In 3.0, the director and actors seem to be a lot clearer about their goals for this scene: Christine is both repelled yet attracted to the Phantom. She's mad that he abandoned her, but is also drawn to him. She's also a married woman and does not want to start an affair with the Phantom, yet, she's remembering. So, they frequently come together and then she pulls away.

Versions of The Big Reveal

In version 1.0, the door flies open and Christine turns around. She sees him and backs away. He opens his arms, she runs to him, and they hug. Then she backs away. He grabs her arm to try to stop her. And then they don't seem to touch each other much for the rest of the song. In fact, they spend a lot of time chasing each other around the perimeter of the stage.

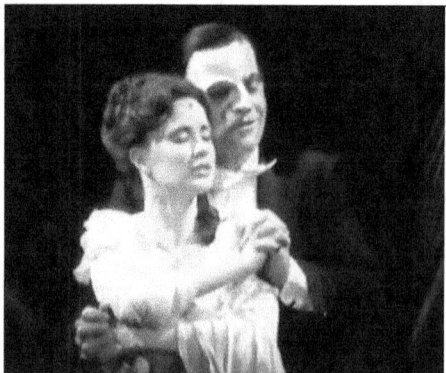

Another lovely moment in 2.0. It's nice that they are touching each other. https://www.youtube.com/watch?v=1jAt-ShinhUo

Version 2.0 tried to remedy some of the problems, by bringing them together more, but then it does something really strange: they play the opening bars, the door flies open, and Christine doesn't turn around. Wouldn't a normal person turn around, at least to hear where the music was coming from? She finally turns when the musical phrase was repeated (about 8 bars). It's quite a long time.

When she sings, "how dare you invade my life," there is no conviction.

In version 2.0, they added the Phantom's line (to explain his long absence): "if you knew the pain I've had, you'd know I had no choice." And in this version, Christine sings the opening to Beneath the Moonless Sky.

CHRISTINE

Once there was a night beneath the moonless sky, too dark to see a thing, too dark to even try.

This is the Phantom's line in versions 1.0 and 3.0.

In 2.0, they are still not touching, but are at least in more proximity to each other and are not chasing each other around the stage. They are also facing each other in this version. A definite improvement. Christine and the Phantom are now close to each other. She reaches up to touch his head, while singing:

CHRISTINE

There blind in the dark, as soul gazed into soul, I looked inside your heart, and saw you pure and whole.

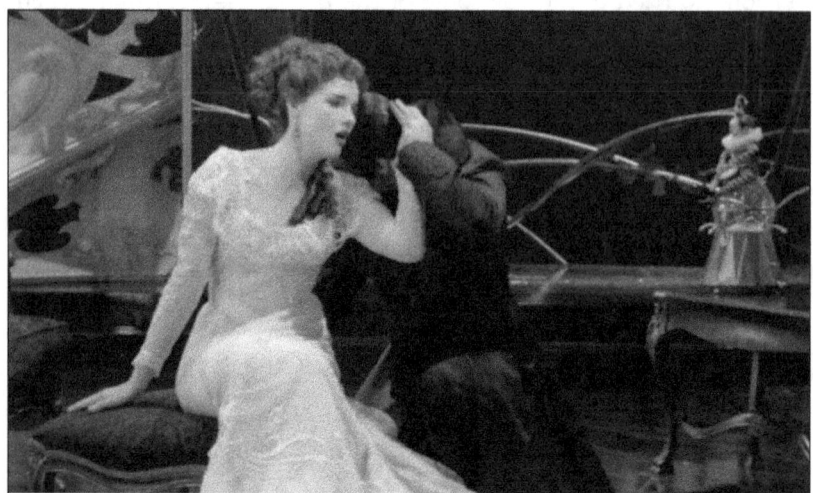

Christine Singing about Phantom being "pure and whole" in 3.0. It's another tender moment. https://www.youtube.com/watch?v=iimYZM8Z-0M

There are some lovely moments in this section, the way the reach for each other, or intertwine their fingers. It seems like they are paying more attention to the lyrics they are singing in this version.

Unfortunately, they still gallop through some key lyrics.

In version 3.0, the door flies open and Phantom stands there. Christine faints after seeing him after all this time, which is understandable. After all, she thought he was dead. He picks her up (from the ground! I worried about Ben Lewis' back). He then carries her to a seat. There's a lot of tenderness in this scene.

What really struck me in version 3.0 was the excellence of the choreography. Every move is accounted for. Even the way he brushes aside his long coat, reminiscent of a cape, is perfectly timed with the music, as is her throwing her arm over his shoulder when he picks her up after she's fainted. They use the stage well. Every shot seems well-framed, and there's a real precision to their moves.

Editing Helped with the Dialogue

In an earlier version of 3.0 posted on YouTube (before the DVD version), Christine's opening phrase is a lot wordier. Editing made it more concise. Christine says her last two lines with a lot of anger and then defeat. Here's the earlier (pre-DVD) version of 3.0 (Ben Lewis and Anna O'Byrne Sing Beneath the Moonless Sky, 2011).

CHRISTINE

I should have known that you'd be here
I should have known it all along
This whole arrangement bears your stamp
You're in each measure of that song
How dare you try and claim me now?
How dare you come invade my life?

The Phantom immediately launches into:

Christine, my Christine.

In that time when the world thought me dead.

And here, we get an important bit of plot information.

My Christine, *on the night just before you were wed.*

Ah, Christine. You came and found where I hid.

Don't you deny that you did. That long ago night.

This bit of information is also in version 1.0.

PHANTOM

My Christine, on the night just before you were wed. You came and found where I hid.

That answers the important (and crucial) plot question: They have a love child. When did they have sex? That line was cut on the DVD version of 3.0, and it's a problem. It's a point a lot of critics (and fans) raised.

Christine's opener in the DVD of 3.0 is more concise. She wakes up from her faint, and she is *pissed.*

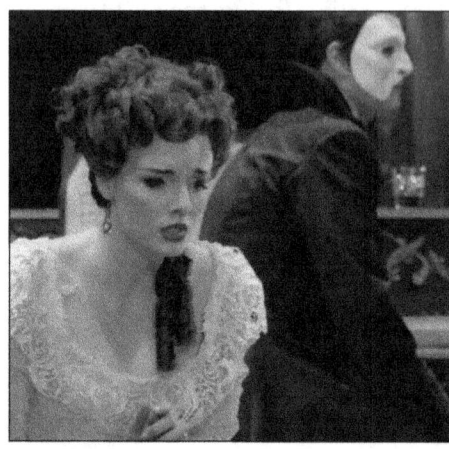

Christine was unhappy to see Phantom. She is torn by her anger and attraction to him. https://www.youtube.com/watch?v=iimYZM8Z-0M

CHRISTINE

So, it was all an empty lie.

One final lie to fool us all. To make us think your story's end. That put your life beyond recall.

She stands and confronts him, and she's really mad.

CHRISTINE

***How dare you* come and find me now! Invade my life, ensnare my voice!**

In version 3.0, there is more of a segue to explain (kind of) why the Phantom hasn't been seen for the past 10 years.

PHANTOM

If you had known the pain I've known, then you would know I had no choice.

The Phantom reaches for her. These lines were added and show her fighting back.

PHANTOM

Oh Christine, my Christine.

CHRISTINE

"Your Christine." She bats his hand away.

I was yours one brief night long ago. Long ago, with a man that I no longer know.

PHANTOM

Oh, Christine, you came and found where I hid. Don't you deny that you did, that long ago night. (Phantom hits a lovely high note.)

From a lyric standpoint, this is a lot cleaner. The music was also simplified, so it no longer sounds like the characters are tripping to get all their words out. But they left out a crucial bit of plot information: when!

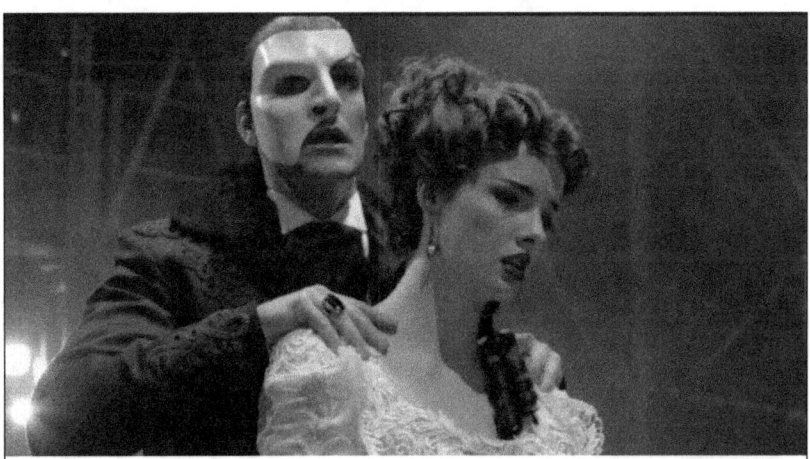

Phantom begins to sing Beneath the Moonless Sky to Christine. https://www.youtube.com/watch?v=iimYZM8Z-0M

In 1.0, he's standing clear across the stage while singing this song. It doesn't make sense, considering what they are singing about.

In 3.0, he comes behind her and takes her shoulders as he sings, "that long ago night." This launches them into the Beneath the Moonless Sky, as he runs his hands down her arms.

PHANTOM

Once there was a night, beneath the moonless sky. Too dark to see a thing. Too dark to even try.

Christine pulls away.

CHRISTINE

I stood by your side, tormented by my choice. I couldn't see your face, but trembled at your voice.

In 1.0, although they are still across the stage from each other, Christine is at least looking at the Phantom, but he's singing the song to the audience, not her. This is another way there seems to be a substantial disconnect in this number. Both sing it very well, however.

CHRISTINE

I felt no longer scared.

PHANTOM

I felt no longer shy.

BOTH

At last our feelings bared, beneath the moonless sky.

CHRISTINE

There, blind in the dark, as soul gazed into soul, I looked into your heart, and saw you pure and whole.

In version 1.0, the Phantom and Christine just stand there and sing through those lyrics and don't sound like they are understanding them. They just sing the lyrics without acting them. I think they had little choice. It's hard to emphasize a note or phrase when the orchestra keeps barreling away.

He finally walks over to her when singing,

BOTH

We said things in the dark, we never dared to say.

He stands behind her and they raise their hands. Then they separate again, as they are singing:

PHANTOM

And I caught you.

CHRISTINE

And I kissed you

BOTH

And the world around us fell away.

Oddly, the word they both emphasize is "And. I." This is underscored with a very loud French horn and timpani. They are way across the stage from each other, and sing all of those notes equally, without emphasizing the content, so they just float over each other.

They Slept Together?

The key thing we need to take away from this scene, in terms of plot, is that they slept together. In version 1.0, you need to be playing very close attention to the lyrics to get that. They sing it, but with not much conviction. They are standing on opposite ends of the stage. And they don't emphasize any of the lyrics. You don't feel any of the passion they supposedly have for each other. They're singing about the one time they got together, and they don't touch each other. Their actions and words don't match up. Also, by not emphasizing words, some of the important bits get lost.

PHANTOM

And I took you.

CHRISTINE

And I begged you.

BOTH

With a need to urgent to deny.

They don't sound particularly urgent here. In fact, it doesn't even seem like they are singing about having sex. They might as well be singing about their grocery list.

Phantom: I bought oranges.

Christine: And bananas.

Both: And a juicy plum or two or three.

After their "urgent need," they do get more together on the next line.

BOTH

Again, and then again, beneath the moonless sky.

By way of contrast, in 3.0, the words that are more meaningful in the sentences are emphasized, so they sound like dialogue. They've also been changed slightly to work more efficiently with the music.

She is sitting on a couch and the Phantom is on a piano bench. As she sings, he comes and kneels next to her and puts his head on her shoulder. She touches his head. You start to see her attraction to him. Up until then, it has been all him. They move so that he is touching her hand and they are facing each other.

CHRISTINE

There blind in the dark, as soul gazed into to soul, I looked into your heart and saw you pure and whole.

PHANTOM

Clothed under the dark, with nothing to suppress, a woman and a man, no more and yet no less.

In version 3.0, Christine is doing a good job of showing both her attraction to him and her anger at him appearing in her life once again. He slips his arm around her waist.

PHANTOM

And I *kissed* you.

CHRISTINE

And *caressed* you.

BOTH

And the world around us fell away. We said things in the dark, we never dared to say.

They stand, with their arms around each other.

PHANTOM

And I *took* you.

Tight hug.

CHRISTINE

And I *begged* you.

Christine grabs his lapels.

BOTH

With a need to urgent to deny, again and then again,

Okay, three times, then.

BOTH

Beneath the moonless sky.

311

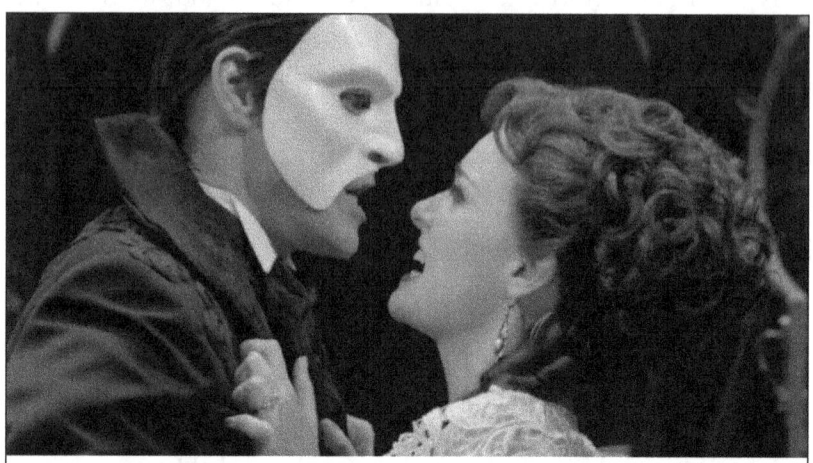

Version 3.0 has a lot more passion in this scene, "and I took you." "And I begged you." https://www.youtube.com/watch?v=iimYZM8Z-OM

There were also some important lyric changes here in version 3.0. There's a bit more lead up to "and I took you." The Phantom sings that he kissed her. She says she caressed him. They confided in each other. Then it goes to "and I took you," with one important addition: Christine's "and I begged you," making it sound much more consensual. "And I begged you" was in some versions of 1.0, but not others.

After their night of passion, the Phantom leaves a sleeping Christine and slips away before morning.

PHANTOM

Then, when it was done, before the sun could rise, ashamed of what I was. Ashamed to see your eyes. I stood while you slept and whispered my goodbye, and slipped into the dark, beneath the moonless sky.

This news seems very hard for Christine to take and she is visibly upset by it.

CHRISTINE

And I *loved you*, Oh, I *loved you*. I'd have followed anywhere you led.

She's really pissed now.

I woke to swear my love, and found you *gone* instead.

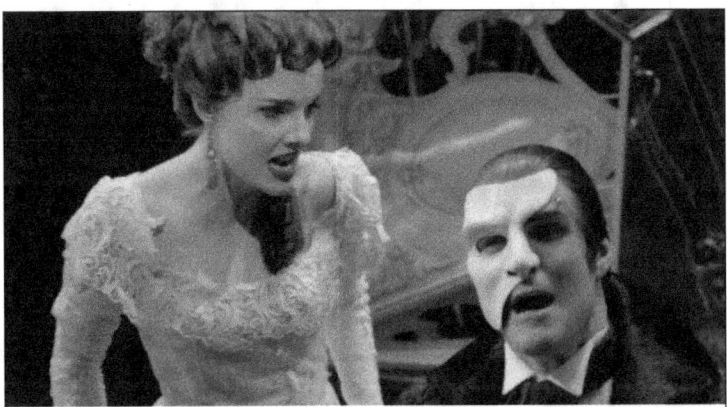

Christine is very upset that Phantom slept with and then abandoned her.

Phantom explains that it would have never has worked for them to be together.

PHANTOM

And I loved you, and I left you, and I had to, both of us knew why.

CHRISTINE

We both knew why.

BOTH

And yet I won't regret, from now until I die, the night I can't forget, beneath the moonless sky.

By now, they are standing and facing each other.

PHANTOM

And now?

CHRISTINE

You can talk of *now*? For us, there is no now!

The song segues in Once Upon Another Time, the song that describes how they both made choices they need to live with. It also says how their moment has passed. It is another lovely song. Unfortunately, Phantom screws it up the very next scene by threatening to kidnap her child if she won't sing for him.

CHAPTER 25

Pivotal Scene II
The Phantom Finds Out He's a Dad

Pivotal scene II is when the Phantom finds out that he has a son. I'm still not sure how they would know for sure, but let's just go with it. As we learned from Beneath the Moonless Sky, Christine slept with Phantom the night before her wedding. Technically speaking, Raoul could also be the father. But let's assume she knew for sure. The next pivotal scene is when Phantom figures out that he could be Gustave's father. He confronts Christine.

Version 2.0 had one of the most appalling bits in the whole show, as I described in Section II. This scene definitely changed for the better in the Australian version.

Phantom Shares His World with Gustave

This scene begins when the Phantom takes Gustave on a tour of his strange, Coney-island world. Phantom's circus-freak sidekicks escort Gustave to meet "the Master." Gustave sees a piano and asks if he could play it. When Gustave plays the piano, the Phantom asks what he is playing. Gustave sings,

Just a song in my head.

Phantom urges him to continue. The Phantom listens and says, "he plays like me." He does the math and realizes that Gustave is 10, and it's been 10 years since he's seen Christine (ignoring gestation). Could Gustave be his?

Phantom discovers that Gustave loves all the weird things in this world and sees the "beauty underneath" (the name of the song they are singing). Phantom takes a chance, and removes his mask and wig to show his real face. Gustave screams and runs to his mother, saying "it's horrible, horrible." Not a surprising reaction from a 10-year-old who's just seen a hideously deformed face. In the London version (versions 1 and 2), Christine immediately apologizes to the Phantom.

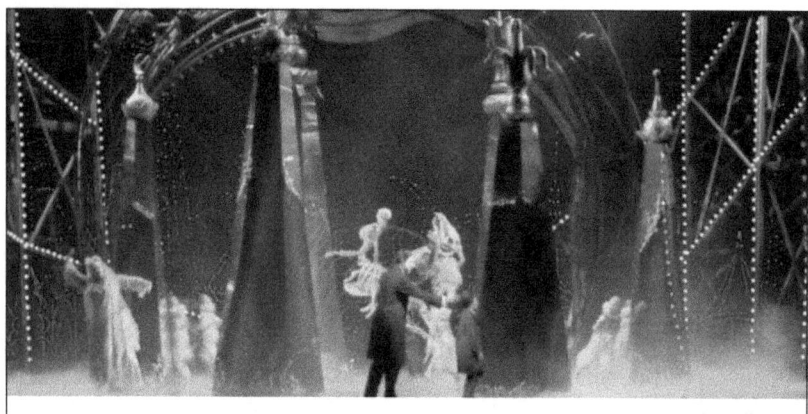

Phantom shares his weird world with Gustave in Beauty Underneath. https://www.youtube.com/watch?v=0rmC2ouWtfw

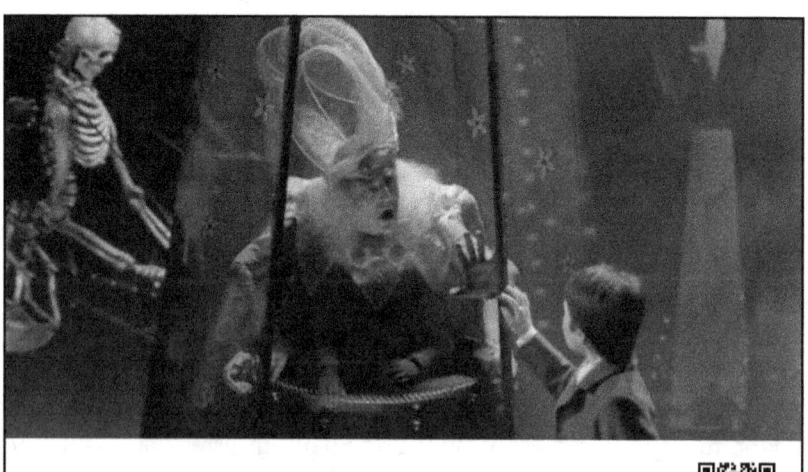

Gustave is captivated by it. https://www.youtube.com/watch?v=0rmC2ouWtfw

CHRISTINE

I'm so sorry. Please **forgive him. He meant no harm.**

PHANTOM

How could you think I wouldn't guess? How could you think I wouldn't know? Do you have something to confess?

And here is the previously mentioned most appalling bit in the whole play. The Phantom runs towards her and chokes her while singing,

I want the truth right now, is all.

Christine's tone is placating, even as she is *being choked.*

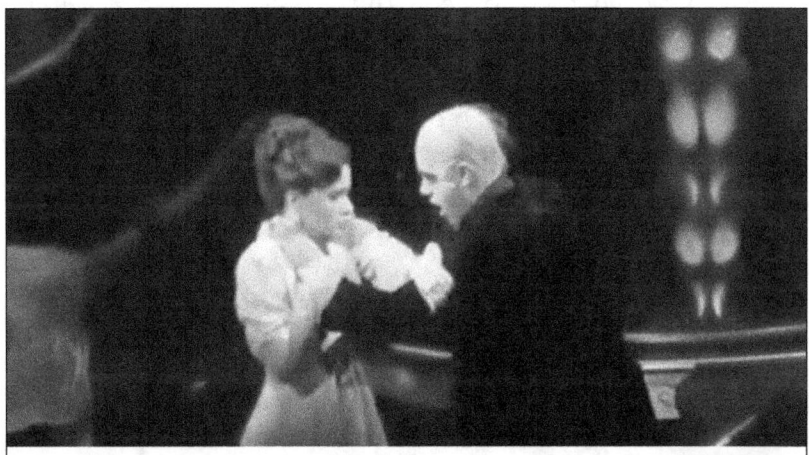

Phantom confronts Christine about Gustave's paternity—by choking her in version 2.0. https://www.youtube.com/watch?v=-3hLpQPqW28

What the hell? Still being choked, she starts singing to him.

CHRISTINE

Once upon another time you loved me and left me alone.

317

The Phantom tightens his grip on her neck. *What the hell?*

CHRISTINE

But that's not all you did. You left me with a son.

The Phantom finally loosens his grip. He walks away, and finally seems moved. Christine sings that she will sing his music. They turn and face each other, and she suddenly reaches for the Phantom's face with both hands, comforting him, and they end in an embrace.

Okay, so let me get this straight. The Phantom knocks her up, and leaves her, at a time in history when it could have ruined her (did anyone see *Les Miserables?*), lets her think he is dead for 10 years, and *he's* pissed? *Seriously?*

And why did the producers think that Phantom assaulting Christine is sexy? It isn't. Ever. It's a character flaw. My sympathy for the Phantom instantly evaporated. I'm glad they cut this bit in 3.0. In fact, this same scene in 3.0 is touching.

This scene also shows some confusion about what they were trying to do with the character of Christine. The point that 3.0 was much clearer on was that Christine really didn't want to get back together with Phantom. Yes, she was attracted to him, but she was also *married* and realized that they had missed their moment. The director did a better job of communicating that in 3.0.

Version 3.0: Story Without Abuse

The Australian version used exactly the same lyrics in this section, but staged it entirely differently. The Phantom figures out that Gustave is his son and takes the risk for show him his face. As in versions 1.0 and 2.0, Gustave screams and says it's "horrible, horrible." The Phantom runs off briefly and puts his mask back on. He's still bald, with the wispy gray hairs, but his face is hidden.

He comes back on stage in step with the music.

PHANTOM

Did you think I wouldn't guess? Did you think I wouldn't know? Do you have something to confess? I want the truth right now is all.

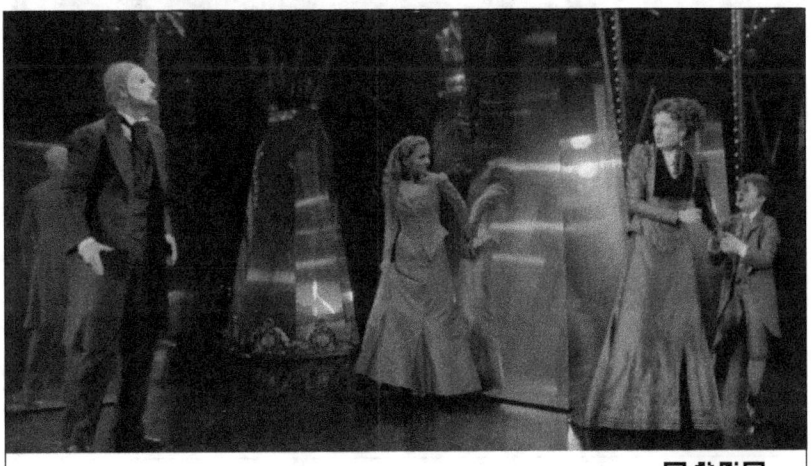

Phantom confronts Christine, but does not choke her.
https://www.youtube.com/watch?v=b5kVtREuzJU

He is across the stage from Christine, and is pointing. But there is some distance between them. He's certainly not choking her. And Christine is not apologizing.

CHRISTINE

Once upon another time, you loved me and left me alone. But that's not all you did. You left me with a son.

The Phantom staggers backwards, bowled over by the news.

CHRISTINE

Ever since that other time, I wish you could have somehow have known.

I kept the secret hid, a secret my marriage forbid, what else could I have done?

No kidding! The Phantom drops to his knees and stares at his hands.

PHANTOM
A son. My son.

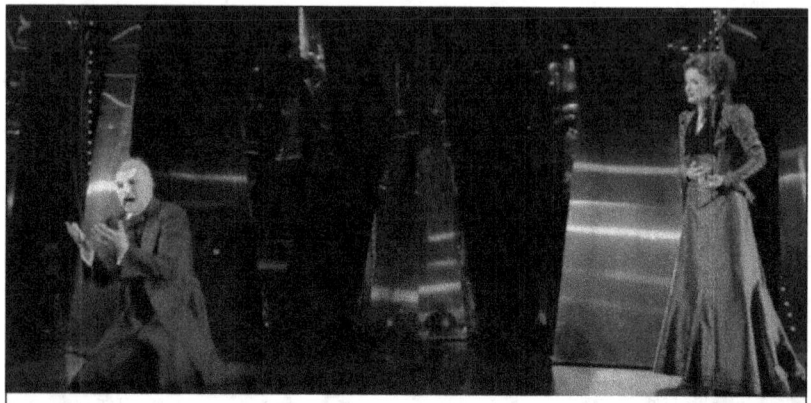

Phantom is overwhelmed by the news about being a father.
https://www.youtube.com/watch?v=b5kVtREuzJU

Christine walks over to him and puts her hand on the top of his head. The Phantom takes her hand, holds to his face, and says, "Christine, forgive me."

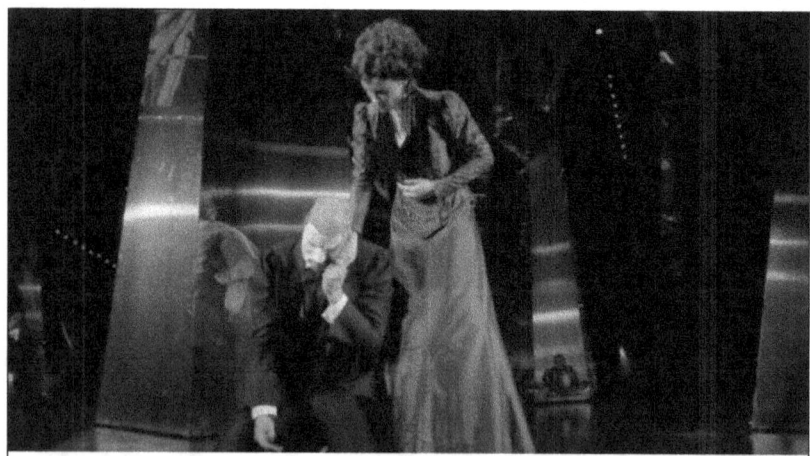

Phantom asks for Christine's forgiveness for abandoning her.
https://www.youtube.com/watch?v=b5kVtREuzJU

PHANTOM

He sees me and shuns me, as you did once. Take him, take him now and go.

Christine starts to walk away.

PHANTOM

Go now. Be free. But swear one thing to me. He will never, ever know.

Christine turns back to him.

CHRISTINE

I swear it. Believe me. You know you have my word.

She picks up the score and walks back towards him.

CHRISTINE

And I swear your music won't remain unheard. This music, your music will live again. One more time just as I soar.

BOTH

And soar once more, we will once more be whole.

PHANTOM

When I hear you sing.

The Phantom reaches to touch her hands holding the score. She pulls away.

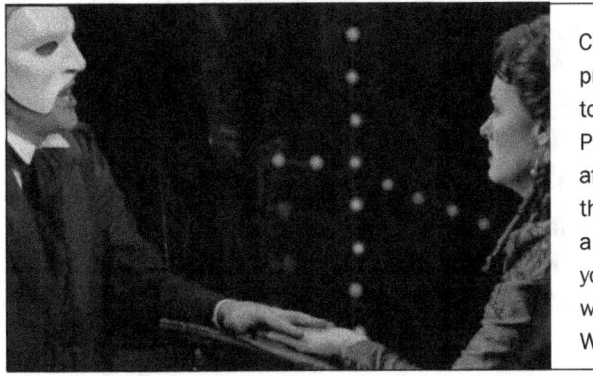

Christine promises to sing for Phantom after he's broken by the news that he has a son. https://www.youtube.com/watch?v=OrmC2ou-Wtfw

CHRISTINE

Once more.

Christine runs off the stage.

The Phantom stars into a mirror, while taking off his mask. The lighten drops on the deformed side of his face so that the audience never sees it.

PHANTOM

From out of ugliness, such light. From out of darkness, such a flame. In him, my wrongness is made right. And yet he loathes me just the same. So let him shun me in disgust, let him flee this cursed face. If I must hide from him, I must. Yet he shall be my saving grace.

For Christine, my Christine, if it's true, he's my reason to live. Ah Christine, and our son shall have all I can give. Ah, Christine, all I create on this earth, all that I'll ever be worth, all shall be his.

Madame Giry overhears him singing, and thinks her and Meg are about to be cut off. She sings a few demented verses, which set the tragic events of the final scene into motion.

Summary

This scene of Phantom confronting Christine dramatically demonstrates the difference that good direction makes. The music is essentially identical, with just a few small changes. However, the scene in 3.0 has an entirely different feel to it than earlier versions. In the version 2.0, the Phantom is an abusive jerk. Christine placates and enables him, in a way that is similar to the way she placates and enables Raoul. I feel for her. That may reflect the reality women faced in 1905, especially once married. But as I mentioned earlier, partner violence certainly should not be part of a story that's supposed to be "a great romance." It's not necessary and it's appalling.

In fact, here is a note to producers and directors everywhere: assaulting women is not sexy. It's a felony. Please stop including assault in storylines that are supposed to be romantic. You're just reinforcing rape and partner violence myths. Thank you to the team in Australia who cut this part of the story.

By cutting the abusive bit, and making the Phantom's demeanor less angry and aggressive, 3.0 made him a much more attractive and sympathetic character. It was also moving to see him overcome with the news about being a father. Christine feels compassion for him, and he's apologizes for abandoning her. It changes the whole tone of the scene. Christine's dilemma of being drawn to the Phantom, but not wanting to violate her marriage vows, also comes across clearly in this scene.

CHAPTER 26

Pivotal Scene III
The Finale

The final scene of a show should be its most memorable. After all, it's the part that brings together all the threads and leads to the climax of the story. If done well, it's the part people remember. In the original stage show, and the film, the Phantom is crushed and broken, weeping and telling Christine that he loves her. Most audience members were moved by that, which is the way a finale is supposed to work.

Unfortunately, that did not happen with the first two versions of *Love Never Dies*. In fact, the critics had a field day with it. When there is a death scene, and critics are saying "die, already," it's safe to say that the scene is not working. One critic said that it even raised the possible debate about euthanasia. Rather than moving the critics, the final scene seemed to merely annoy them.

So what were the problems? And how did the Australian team fix them?

The Problems with the Finale

The first objection critics raised to earlier versions of the finale is that it dragged on for a very long time. There was a recapping most of the major songs, impressive when someone is dying. And it simply didn't work.

The second objection had to do with its visual appeal. In 1.0, the staging continued to be gloomy: just overly lit characters with fog swirling around. There was not much else to the set. The blocking was also really off. For example, many of the characters, the Phantom included, had their backs to the audience for significant lengths of time. The young actor who played Gustave looked like he really had no idea where he was supposed to stand. It was like watching a bad high-school version of *Our Town*.

The video is not as clear on YouTube as it is with some other segments, so it might be easy to miss things. But the big strokes were still quite apparent. The choreography is definitely less crisp compared to 3.0. It is also less interesting visually.

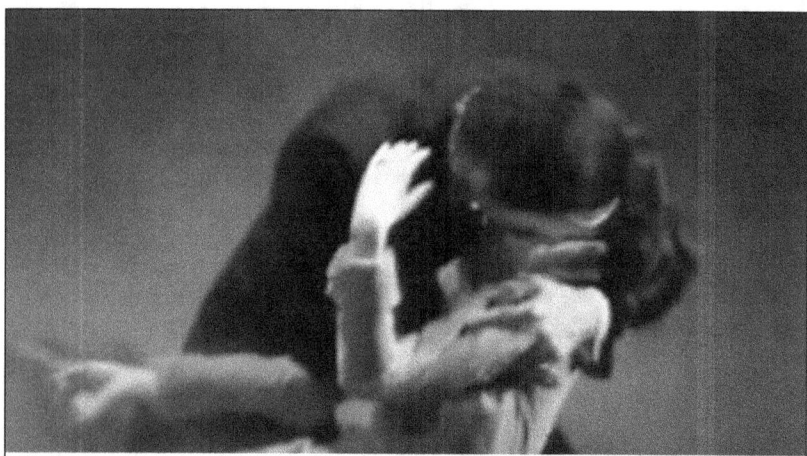

In the finale, Phantom cradles Christine after she's been shot. They are sitting on the ground and there isn't much else on the stage. https://www.youtube.com/watch?v=8WL-4b7uZZPg

The Action in This Scene

In the finale, Meg is upset because she feels the Phantom has rejected her and replaced her with Christine, thanks to the poisonous suggestion of her mother. To even the score, Meg plans to drown herself and Gustave. That's kind of big. Most people do not respond to rejection by drowning a child! Phantom and Christine realize Gustave is missing at the end of the show. They find out Meg has taken him and rush through the carnival to find Meg at the end of the pier. The Phantom finally talks her into releasing Gustave, who runs back to his mother.

Not be outdone, Meg pulls a huge gun out of the pocket of her dress, and holds it to her temple. Phantom tries to talk her into giving him the gun, and acknowledges that he's probably been a bit of an ass. He might have been ignoring her in ways that he shouldn't have, so tries to make amends.

PHANTOM

Diamonds never sparkle bright, if they aren't set just right. Beauty often goes unseen.

And then he makes a big mistake.

PHANTOM

We can't all be like Christine.

Meg pulls apart from the Phantom upon hearing Christine's name, turns towards her, still waving the gun. In version 1.0, she sings the original "Christine, Christine," from *The Phantom of the Opera*. It looks like she draws her gun and shoots Christine on purpose.

Christine drops to the stage. From the time she drops to the stage, until she dies, 8 and a half minutes elapse. That may not seem like long, but in musical-death-scene time, it's forever. It's like that old joke: Are you living longer, or does it just seem like it?

Phantom holds a dying Christine. While bleeding in his arms, they need to take care of the next bit of plot information: she needs to tell Gustave who his real father is. Christine reveals this and then immediately launches into the next song:

CHRISTINE

Look with your heart, and not with your eyes. The heart understands. The heart never lies.

It's a bit of a non-sequitar. Gustave hasn't rejected the Phantom, so why is she telling him not to reject him? The song seems out of place. Then Gustave continues the song.

Together, they sing quite a bit of the song.

And then Gustave finally shouts, "No," and runs off.

Why is he saying no? What is that in reaction to? That Christine is dying or that Phantom is his dad?

The Phantom and Christine are alone on the stage. She is lying on the ground. The Phantom holds her, and sings some of the more moving lyrics in the show.

PHANTOM

Once upon another time, our story had only begun. I had a taste of joy, the most I ever knew.

Now there isn't any time, and somehow our story is done.

And what about the boy? What am to I do?

CHRISTINE

Just love, just live.

PHANTOM

I'll give all that I can and take what little I deserve.

Throughout this scene, the Phantom is sitting in what looks to be a terribly uncomfortable position. He is sort half squatting, and then leaning over Christine, which is an example of when the blocking and choreography distract from the story. We shouldn't be wondering how the Phantom is managing to stay upright in that position.

As the Phantom and Christine move into the climax of the scene, the music swells with a reprise of Till I Hear You Sing. At the apex of the phrase, Christine sings:

CHRISTINE

Kiss me one last time.

They kiss and she dies in the Phantom's arms. This happens 6:46 minutes after Meg draws the gun. The Phantom rocks and holds her, before setting her down on the ground.

On the ground?

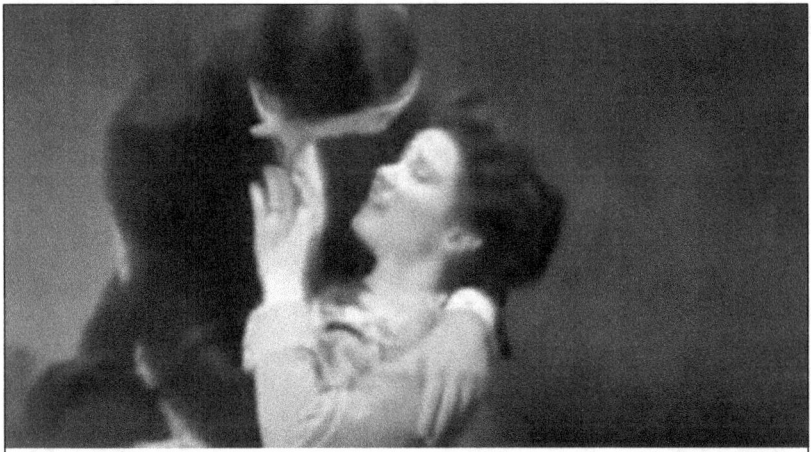

Christine is saying goodbye to Phantom in version 2.0.
After she dies, he sets her on the ground and goes to comfort Meg.
https://www.youtube.com/watch?v=8WL4b7uZZPg

A single flute plays Beneath the Moonless Sky. Phantom covers her with his coat, and then goes over to Meg and puts his hand on her shoulder. He comforts *Meg?* He seems oddly unmoved by this chain of events.

The next bit is where things get really weird. Gustave, who has just seen his mother shot and bleed to death, walks over to the Phantom and reaches out to lift his mask. The Phantom grabs him hard by the forearm to prevent this, a lovely way to treat a little boy who has just seen his mom die.

Phantom, recognizing that he's probably been a jerk, then kneels in front of Gustave and removes his own mask and wig. Gustave reaches to touch his face. The West End Whingers had a lot to say about this bit. In fact, I think it was one of their favorite parts. Gustave put his fingers in the crater on the Phantom's skull. Yuck! West End Whingers made a crack about a bowling ball.

Gustave then draws back, and then hugs the Phantom. The Phantom resists at first, and then hugs Gustave back. The scene fades to black. The story is over.

This scene did not seem to change substantially from versions 1.0 to 2.0.

Overall, even with all of these issues, I still find this final scene to be moving. The music is good, and it is sad. Unfortunately, the scene doesn't quite have the power it needs, as the critics relentlessly observed. Version 3.0 improved it substantially.

Editing Made It Better

The finale was probably the scene most changed for the Australian production, and it works a lot better as a result. One immediately apparent change is the set. Rather than simply being on the ground, with the characters lit (or overlit), the production used a set. It is simple, but they are not on the ground. It is an elevated platform that is supposed to be a dock. It is also tilted at an angle, making it visually more interesting and allowing for more movement among the characters. The lighting was subdued, but the entire stage was included, giving it a more polished appearance.

Second, Gustave's character was more effective. He wasn't just milling around and seemed to know exactly where he was supposed to be. Gustave was also well integrated into all the events of the final scene. The actor who played Gustave was better overall, and appeared less gangly and awkward in his movements.

Next, the scene was shorter, and the music had been edited throughout. It still covers the same songs, but in a shorter form. The movement between songs was also crisper and more efficient. These edits dramatically improved the overall flow. Starting with the point where Meg drew a gun, the Phantom sings the same song as in the earlier version.

PHANTOM

Give me the gun, Meg. Give me the hurt and the pain, and the gun, Meg. ... Give me the chance to see you clear at last. ...

Then he heads into what will turn out to be the fatal line.

PHANTOM

Diamonds never sparkle bright if they aren't set just right. Beauty sometimes goes unseen. We can't all be like Christine.

Meg simply says, "Christine" only once. They cut the whole "Chris-tine, Chris-tine" phrase from *The Phantom of the Opera*.

Christine, hearing her name, leaves Gustave on the dock and walks towards Meg. The Phantom tries to wrestle the gun away from Meg, but it goes off. Christine suddenly drops to the ground. It's an accident.

Meg tries to go to her, but the Phantom yells and tells her to "get away" from Christine. That reaction is more understandable. He also yells to Madame Giry to get help. Madame Giry grabs Meg and they hurry away.

The Phantom holds Christine. Gustave comes to her and says, "Father, I must find Father."

Christine, hearing this, says:

CHRISTINE

Your Father. Your real Father.

PHANTOM

No, Christine.

CHRISTINE (to Phantom)

I know I promised, but you are all he has now. He has to know the truth.

CHRISTINE (to Gustave)

Your father, your real father is here.

331

The Phantom lifts his head away from Christine to look at Gustave. Gustave is having none of it. He says, "No. *No.*" This prompts Christine to hold his hands and sing:

CHRISTINE

Look with your heart and not with your eyes. The heart understands. The heart never lies.

GUSTAVE

Noooooo!

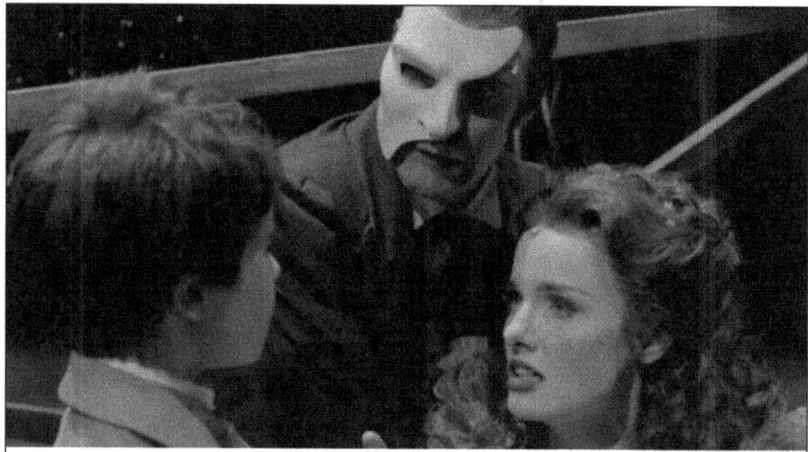

Dying Christine tells Gustave who his real father is.
https://www.youtube.com/watch?v=nJEOQ6ecHb8

The song makes considerably more sense in this context than it did in the earlier version. She's singing it in response to Gustave's reaction. It is also quite a bit shorter.

Gustave runs away. Christine attempts to run after him and falls back onto the stage. The Phantom holds her to his chest and they sing the same moving song.

PHANTOM

Once upon another time, our story had only begun. I had a taste of joy. The most I ever knew. Now there isn't any time, and somehow our story is done.

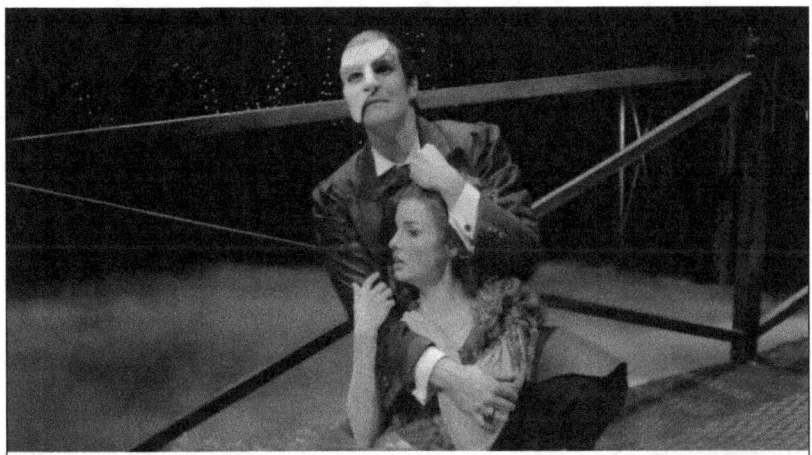

Phantom sings Once Upon Another Time while sobbing.
https://www.youtube.com/watch?v=nJEOQ6ecHb8

The Phantom looks off in the distance to where Gustave ran off to, and sings with anguish. As the Phantom is singing, he is sobbing. I've always found this quite moving.

PHANTOM

And what about the boy? *What am I to do?*

CHRISTINE

Just love, just live. Just give what you can give and take the love that you deserve.

BOTH

Just love, just live.

The Phantom promises to take care of her child.

PHANTOM

I'll give all I have to give and take what little I deserve.

Dying now, Christine sings.

CHRISTINE

Come closer, I beg you.

The Phantom shifts to hold her closer.

CHRISTINE

Closer still.

The Phantom shifts again, while gently holding her across his lap.

CHRISTINE

... Kiss me one last time.

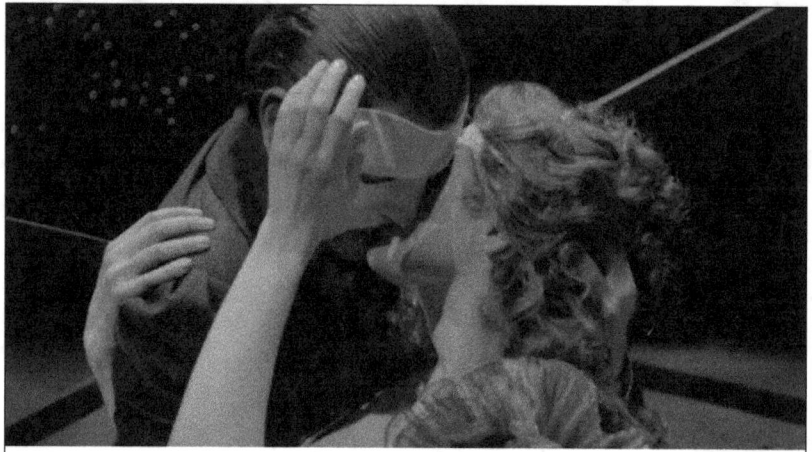

Phantom and Christine's last kiss.
https://www.youtube.com/watch?v=nJEOQ6ecHb8

He gently kisses her, while her hand rests on his mask. In the midst of the kiss, her hand drops and she dies in the Phantom's arms.

Here again is another significant difference between 1.0 and 3.0: what happens at the ark of the phrase. In 1.0, the Phantom kisses Christine. In 3.0 as the music is swelling, a beautifully orchestrated version of Till I Hear Your Sing, Christine dies near the climax of the phrase. Just as the phrase reaches its apex, the Phantom lets out a primal yell of grief— "NOOOO"— as he holds Christine's body in his arms.

It is one of the most affecting moments of this entire show.

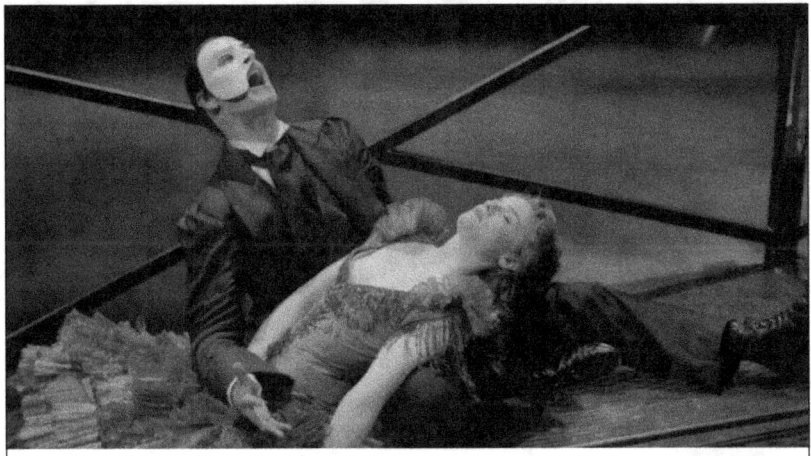

Phantom is overcome with grief and just keeps yelling "No," while rocking her body. https://www.youtube.com/watch?v=nJEOQ6ecHb8

He then rocks her in his arms while sobbing and yelling, "NO, NO." It has a lot more power than the earlier versions. He cares that she died. He's holding her body in his arms and rocking her. He didn't set her on the ground.

Gustave runs up with Raoul in tow. When Gustave realizes that his mother has died, he lays his head on her lap and cries. Phantom is still cradling her in his arms. He reaches down to gently touch Gustave's head, showing real tenderness. There is no grabbing of Gustave's arm.

Then looking up, the Phantom realizes that he needs to give Raoul a chance to say goodbye. The Phantom gently hands Christine's body to Raoul and staggers up the dock ramp, overwhelmed by grief. He falls to his knees at the end of the dock. Gustave walks up to him and gently puts his hand on the Phantom's back. The Phantom turns, faces him, and sings the last song of the show.

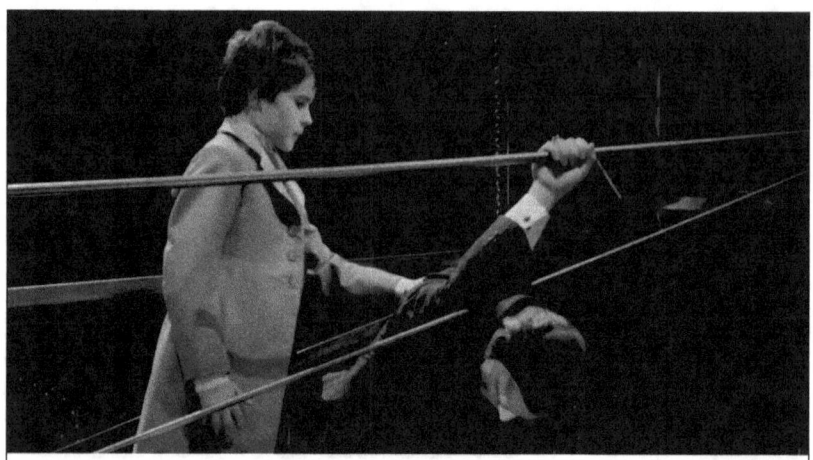

Gustave goes to Phantom, who is overwhelmed by grief and has staggered to the end of the pier.
https://www.youtube.com/watch?v=nJEOQ6ecHb8

PHANTOM (acapella, with a faltering voice)

Love never dies. Love never falters. Once it has spoken, love is yours.

PHANTOM (stronger, with orchestra)

Love never dies, love will continue.

The Phantom reaches for Gustave and pulls him into a hug. He clutches Gustave while continuing to cry. The Phantom and Gustave draw back from each other. The Phantom is still on his knees, so he is the same height as Gustave.

Gustave reaches out to touch the Phantom's mask. The Phantom flinches and moves slightly away. Then he holds still and lets Gustave remove his mask. Gustave stares at the Phantom, and then gently reaches out to touch the disfigured portion of the Phantom's face with the back part of his hand. The Phantom is clearly moved by this simple gesture of acceptance from Gustave, and brings his hands to his heart.

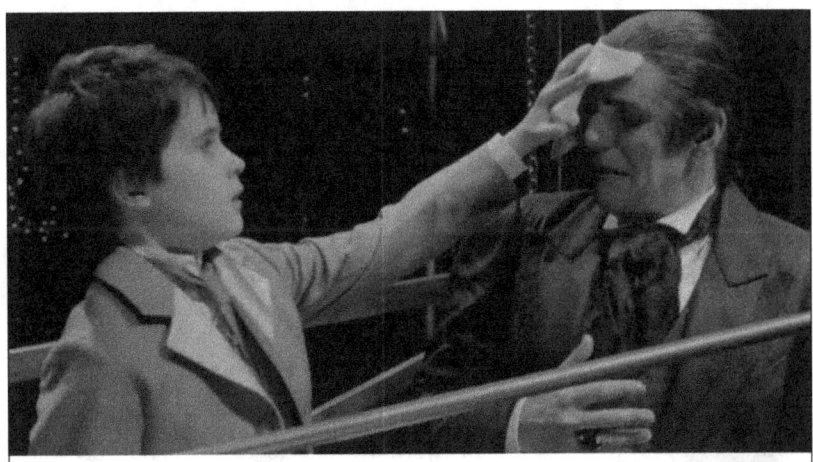

Gustave reaches for Phantom's mask.
https://www.youtube.com/watch?v=nJEOQ6ecHb8

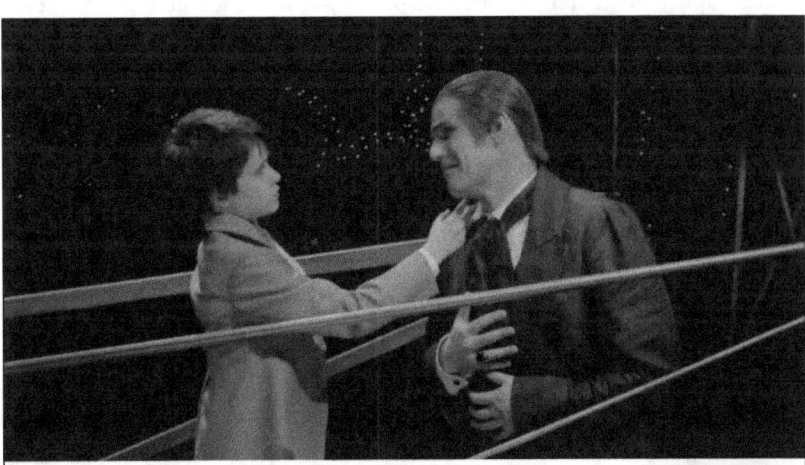

Gustave touches the deformed part of Phantom's face.
This simple act of kindness completely overwhelms Phantom.
https://www.youtube.com/watch?v=nJEOQ6ecHb8

With that, the stage fades to black, and the show ends.

Summary of Changes to This Scene

There were two changes in the production that made this scene work so effectively. First, throughout the 3.0 production, we never see the Phantom's face. In the confrontation scene, we see his bald head, but the deformity is implied. It is never shown. When the audience sees the Phantom, the deformed side of his face is always facing away. This decision moves away from the sometimes cartoony makeup that characterizes the stage performances. It also gets away from the ghoulish moments of 1.0 where Gustave sticks his fingers in the crater. I'm sure that the West End Whingers (2010) were not the only one who noticed how genuinely weird that was. Those types of details can be super distracting and take the audience out of the story.

Second, the revised score used primarily one song throughout the scene—Till I Hear You Sing. There was a bit of Look with Your Heart, Once Upon Another Time, and Love Never Dies at the very end, when the Phantom briefly sings to Gustave. The effect of using primarily one song decluttered the scene and was more parsimonious. By cutting out the clutter, the whole finale felt crisper and more cohesive. It worked a lot better and really moved the audience. That was what the final scene was supposed to do. The final scene, in particular, demonstrated that editing really did make it better.

CHAPTER 27

Should Love Die?
The Social Media Campaign

In the story of *Love Never Dies*, many were blamed for its premature demise: the directors, authors of the book, choreographer, and bloggers. Yet no group was as demeaned, threatened, and bullied as the 12 plucky "nobodies" who took on the Lloyd Webber juggernaut— and prevailed. Their goal was simple: they didn't want a sequel to their beloved *Phantom*. They especially balked at the publicity the Really Useful Group was churning out, saying that *Phantom* fans were "eagerly awaiting" this sequel. They wanted it on the record that this statement did not represent their views. They wanted Lloyd Webber to listen. He wouldn't, and in fact diligently tried to shut them down. The problem was they were not breaking any laws, so he went after them in the media.

The Controversy Begins

The controversy over *Love Never Dies* was not the first time that a Lloyd Webber show caused protest, but it was the first time that the protest produced results. The website was a pun on the name of the show. Instead of *Love Never Dies*, it was Love Should Die. Love Should Die also had a Facebook page that eventually grew to about 1,400 followers. This campaign was so effective that Lloyd Webber attributed the failure of his show to this group, whom he sensitively referred to as "mental." Lloyd Webber and his production company were very irked by these people. Who were *they* to challenge him?

The Really Useful Group said many untrue things about Love Should Die in the press. Therefore, I think it's important to let Love Should Die speak for themselves. They were very clear on their goals and posted them on their website. They have not been active since 2012, but they left their website up for posterity. It was a treasure trove of information about the controversy, some of which I will share in this chapter.

What Love Should Die Hoped to Accomplish

According to their site, Love Should Die's goal was as follows.

When the "Love Should Die" Twitter account was originally set up, it was intended as a harmless joke among a small number of fans of The Phantom of the Opera who considered the sequel a preposterous concept at best.

Almost two years later, with a Facebook group globally recognized by the media, "Love Should Die"—its creators and its followers and fans—has managed to transform completely the ignorant perception of the wider world and the media concerning the attitude of Phantom fans in relation to Lloyd Webber's ill-conceived sequel Love Never Dies.

In their more detailed mission statement, they elaborated further.

Now that previews for Love Never Dies have started in London, the Love Should Die community has suddenly attracted a huge increase in attention. Critics of our "campaign," as they call it, have condemned Love Should Die as ultimately pointless, because it is, of course, delusional to think that an Internet community with a niche common cause will close down a multi-million pound global entertainment product.

For this reason, the team of Love Should Die thought we should clarify our position and our objectives.

Let it be known here that Love Should Die does not aim to bring about the closure of Love Never Dies. It doesn't need to.

The show is dreadful enough to close itself. Nor do we wish any harm upon the cast or creative team of this completely unnecessary and tasteless venture.

As stated on the "information" page of our Facebook, our goal is to provide a platform for the many devoted fans of *The Phantom of the Opera,* in all its previous incarnations, to voice their feelings in condemnation of *Love Never Dies.*

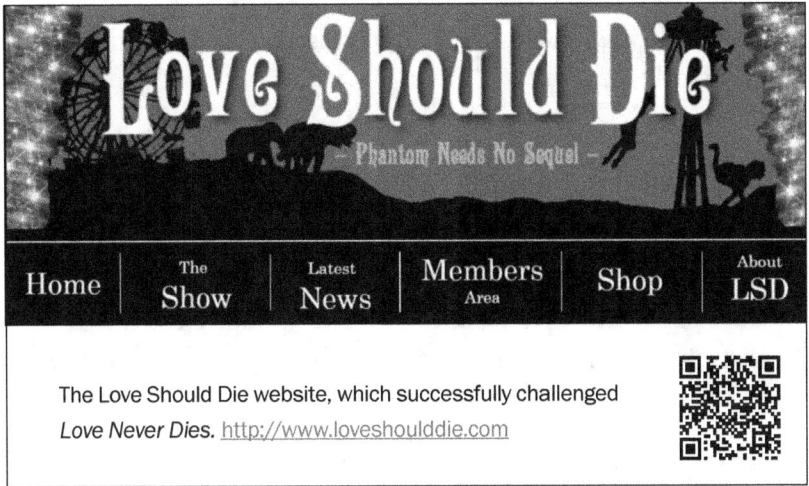

The Love Should Die website, which successfully challenged *Love Never Dies.* http://www.loveshoulddie.com

Love Should Die encouraged followers to print out leaflets to bring to performances of *Phantom,* and let people know that a sequel was in the works. When they closed the site, in 2012, they issued this final statement, thanking their many supporters.

Our mission at Love Should Die was very simple and consisted of two basic elements:

♦ To provide a platform for *Phantom* fans to speak out against this illogical sequel.

♦ To alter completely the image perpetuated by the Really Useful Group and the world press that *Phantom* fans have been eagerly awaiting this sequel since the publication of Frederick Forsyth's *The Phantom of Manhattan.*

In both, we have succeeded. Love Should Die will remain open and will welcome anyone who maintains this project should have never been given the green light. Feel free to use it to discuss the story of the *Phantom* and what it means to you.

Concerning the second point, our efforts have most certainly not been in vain. Having originally declared that *Phantom* fans could not wait for the sequel in October 2009, Lloyd Webber's The Really Useful Group can no longer use this completely false image to promote *Love Never Dies*. All over the world, papers have been reporting *Phantom* fans' discontent with the sequel.

At the heart of LSD's discontent, was what Forsyth and Lloyd Webber did the original story. It all comes down to plot holes (again!). For Love Should Die, protest started with the novella.

When Forsyth's flop novella, *The Phantom of Manhattan*, was first published, they read it, despised it, and rejected it. By default, they have done the same with this sequel, as, despite the claims of Lord Lloyd Webber, it has always been clear that the story of *Love Never Dies* was to be based—however loosely—on Forsyth's ridiculous plotline, and indeed this week this fear was confirmed.

They wanted to protect the story.

Furthermore, it would not have mattered what the story of *Love Never Dies* was: the fundamental point is that any sequel to *The Phantom of the Opera* inherently diminishes the emotional power and impact of the original story, in particular, its conclusion.

Their goal was not censorship, but protesting the storyline, and also, protesting the characterization of *Love Never Dies* as something that *Phantom* fans would enjoy.

There is, however, one small correction we feel the press should acknowledge: fans' outrage is not caused by delusions of possessiveness. It is not possessive in the least to object to stories that have no legitimate basis, merely sensible. Protective may be a better word, but there are not delusions of "ownership" in play here.

They noted that by giving fans a forum, eventually the world press noticed. As a result of their campaign, the press realized that not all *Phantom* fans were onboard with this latest story. As it turns out, *Phantom's* audience was not as easily led as people thought.

> That the aforementioned newspapers have recently begun to take notice of those fans who do not support *Love Never Dies*—even if this is at the cost of being labelled "diehard fanatics," which perhaps some of us are—assures us that our efforts have not been in vain. Our mission is thus already successful. But there are still many false perceptions yet to correct, and as long as they exist, we will continue to speak out (Love Should Die, 2010a).

Lloyd Webber Was Angry

Lloyd Webber's opinion was not so sanguine. He couldn't believe that the group he thought would be the core audience for *Love Never Dies* had the temerity to challenge him. He described Love Should Die as a "sad culture of people who live only by the old *Phantom of the Opera*" (Todd & Glass, 2010). According to *The Daily Mail*, Love Should Die was "irksome."

> Most irksome is, without a doubt, the Facebook group called Love Should Die, set up as a platform to voice animosity (Todd & Glass, 2010).

The Investigation: Who Are the Masterminds Behind this Campaign?

The Daily Telegraph identified Jeff and Rebecca Timmons, a couple from Toronto, as the masterminds behind the plot. Jeff Timmons had seen *Phantom* 126 times. He told *The Daily Telegraph*,

> My life has been *Phantom*. My wife and I met at *Phantom*. We developed a relationship through *Phantom*. We had a *Phantom*-themed wedding. Rebecca dressed as Christine and I was the Phantom, but it was much more than that. We had fog and a church organ playing the title song. The wedding was hugely popular with Phans. It was a big thing to us.

> Each time we hear the words *Love Never Dies*, and the story behind it, it feels like we're getting slapped in the face by Lloyd Webber and his creative team.

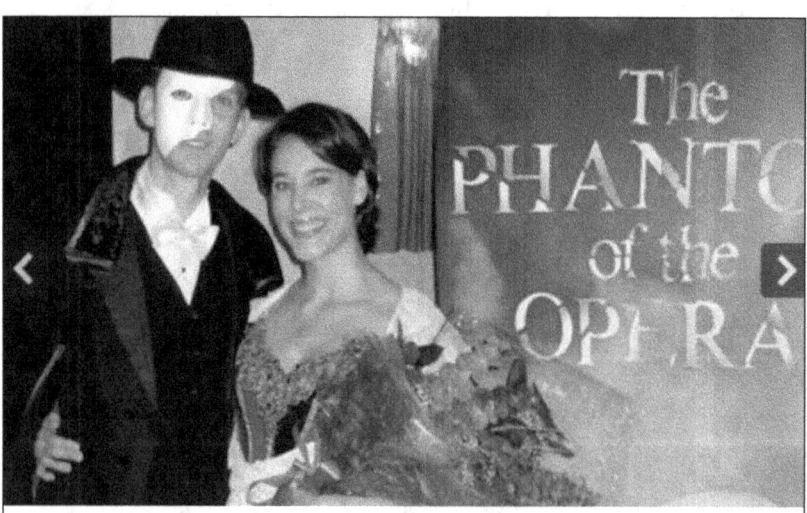

Jeff and Rebecca Timmons, the Canadian couple who were the alleged masterminds behind Love Should Die. In reality, all they did was purchase the domain name.
http://www.telegraph.co.uk/culture/culturenews/7822526/Unmasked-the-fans-haunting-the-Phantom-sequel.html

The "investigation" consisted of finding out who had purchased the LoveShouldDie.com domain name. (Finding out who owns a domain name takes about five seconds and consists of typing in the domain name into WHOIS.) The article was entitled, Unmasked: The Fans Haunting the *Phantom* Sequel. The author, Anita Singh, notes that the Love Should Die site is linked to 4,000 other sites, including many theater sites. According to Singh,

> The couple initially denied founding Love Should Die, which is administered by anonymous character call "the Real Phantom," saying they are only supporters. However, the website is registered to them.

Team Lloyd Webber used their considerable media clout to publicly shame this couple through their social media accounts. Lloyd Webber admitted, in an interview with Playbill.com, that he instigated the investigation (Shenton, 2011).

PB: Of course, *Jeeves* suffered from its reception by the critics, but *Love Never Dies* has had to deal with something else: hostility in the blogosphere.

ALW: That was quite extraordinary. Obviously, you can't stop people who've genuinely come to see a show and don't like it; that's fine. But, as it was discovered in the end, *a lot of the stuff posted on the net was completely fake*—three months after it opened, we discovered most of those reviews that were put up couldn't possibly have been written by anybody who had actually seen the show. But it duped enough journalists, including *The Times*, and it came down to a couple who lived in Toronto and were mental *Phantom* fans, and just did not want anything else to happen to the Phantom. But it took everyone in, and it is a bother, because it was a highly professionally done operation. *I gave the dossier to Daily Telegraph who found what happened and published an article exposing it all,* but damage had been done by that time [Emphasis added).

But somebody said to me the other day what *Love Never Dies* is *Madame Butterfly*—Puccini thought it was going to be the big one, but opera claque booed it off the stage and it was taken off. He then re-wrote a bit of it, it was re-staged and brought back. And an organized opera claque is the "Net"—it's a modern-day version of it.

This is an interesting version of the story. Let's summarize what Lloyd Webber said.

♦ A lot of the reviews posted on the site were fake and couldn't have been possible written by anyone who had seen the show.

How would that be possible? There were reviews from major papers and entertainment websites posted on Love Should Die, with the reviewers' names. The Love Should Die site is still up. Some of the reviews are no longer online, but I tracked down quite a few that still existed on their original sites. Love Should Die quoted them exactly.

In addition, most news organizations keep zealous track of the way their names are used, looking for copyright infringement and other issues. Is it likely, or even possible, that none of them noticed the "fake" reviews? That seems unlikely, especially since the reviews had quite a few details about the show itself that seem to accurately describe it compared with the video clips available on YouTube. Wouldn't it be strange if two reviewers from say, *The New York Times*, had something posted? Theater critics are usually not short on ego. I'm sure they would have noticed if someone was posting a fake review in their name, or the name of their publication. Is it likely that the real theater critics would not have noticed that there were fake reviews?

♦ It [the fake reviews] duped enough journalists, including *The Times*.

346

Then shame on *The Times* for lazy reporting. This statement seems strange to me. Why would an actual journalist report on a show without going to it? I can't imagine any journalist worth his or her salt who would write an article on a new show by only going to a site that was dead set against it. In fact, mainstream critics made a point of separating themselves from the cyberfans, as Michael Billington (2010), of *The Guardian*, noted.

> I should say that I have no truck with those ghoulish groupies who've seen *The Phantom of the Opera* 852 times, and regard any sequel as equivalent to painting a moustache on the Mona Lisa. No masterpiece has been besmirched.

♦ It all came down to a couple in Toronto, who were "mental *Phantom* fans."

As you will see from the discussion below, this was not true. They were members of the group, but not the masterminds behind it. And that's a disrespectful way to refer to a member of your core fan base, just because you disagree with them.

♦ It took everyone in because it was a highly professionally done operation.

They did all of this without being in the country and with just a website? Then he ought to hire them. They're awesome!

♦ I gave a dossier to *The Daily Telegraph*, who found what happened and published an article exposing it all, but the damage had been done by that time.

This is where the story gets creepy. Lloyd Webber compiled a dossier? And just happened to give it to a newspaper in Toronto? Seriously? This is a man with nearly unlimited resources at his disposal. Are you going to tell me that he hadn't already tracked down this couple, the owners of the domain name, and then selected a newspaper in their home town who would "uncover" it all? It's interesting that he gave the dossier to the second-tier paper, not the major paper in Toronto, *The Globe and Mail*.

The Really Useful Group's Statement to the Newspaper

Andre Ptaszynski, chief executive of the Really Useful Group (RUG), and the show's producer, made the following statement in Singh's article. I'm quoting it here because this public statement contradicts, in tone and content, what he said in a private letter to Jeff Timmons.

> Love Never Dies has been extremely well received by the audiences with a standing ovation every evening, but its success has not been helped by the hostile Internet campaign.
>
> Of course, we appreciate the fantastic support and loyalty that so many fans of The Phantom of the Opera have shown over the years. We would like to thank them for their contribution to the worldwide success of the original show, and we'd love them to continue supporting it.
>
> However, we are disappointed that a group of them have become part of what appears to be an organized Internet campaign in North America and Europe to smear Love Never Dies. They are creating the illusion that audiences aren't enjoying the show, yet we know that the vast majority of audiences that flock to see the show at the Adelphi love it.
>
> It is an unfortunate use of the Internet when it is used to damage any show, especially when many of those involved do not seem to have seen the show they write about.

Love Should Die Weighs In

After the Timmons were outed in the press, Love Should Die posted a statement on their site. They defended the Timmons and reiterated that the Timmons were not the masterminds, but had simply purchased the domain name for the group.

> Oh, what a circus, oh, what a low. Really Useful has gone to town over LSD [Love Should Die].

This is a quick response from the LSD team to the article from today's *Daily Telegraph* that the Really Useful Group has chosen to bring the attention of its followers via Facebook and Twitter.

We, firstly, would like to state categorically that Mr. and Mrs. Timmons are no more the founders of LSD than any of our other team members. They were, in fact, the most recent additions to our team. The LSD team has nearly a dozen members living in Europe, N. America, Central America, and Australasia. There is no way any one person would be able to manage our operations (how else, for example, could we monitor our Twitter in every time zone?). It is, and has always been, a team effort. Mr. Timmons kindly volunteered to pay for the domain www.loveshoulddie.com. It is through the domain that *The Daily Telegraph* got in contact.

Mr. Timmons has informed us that Anita Singh has misquoted him (as can be expected) and Mrs. Timmons, and has deliberately omitted considerable information in order to paint a picture of an obsessed lunatic, which we know our readers are intelligent enough not to fall for. This is merely an extension of Lloyd Webber's previous comments that fans against the sequel are "sad," in order to argue that their opinions cannot possibly be taken seriously.

Lloyd Webber probably picked *The Daily Telegraph* to be the recipient of his dossier because they had written an earlier article bashing "mental" *Phantom* fans.

We have reason to be suspicious of *The Daily Telegraph*. ... In this article, he claimed the fans against the sequel were, in effect, "emotionally vulnerable" housewives who led short lives induced by heart attacks coming from the strain of seeing the original too many times, always in costume, and always "buying another ticket on the way out." We needn't comment further on how ridiculous a picture this is.

They also noted another potential conflict of interest in the Lloyd Webber often writes for *The Telegraph*, characterized as a "right-wing" newspaper that shares his views. He had recently guest edited the Sunday supplement for the paper.

> This "supplement" amounted to no less than an entire magazine devoted to promoting *Love Never Dies*, in which his noble Lordship claimed that Glenn "empty as a tomb" Slater was the best lyricist he had worked with since Tim Rice (!), and that the original *Phantom* story was "the biggest piece of hokum ever written," in a bizarre attempt to disparage the original show in order to present *Love Never Dies* as a much worthier alternative.

Timmons knew he was likely to be smeared, and that "his views and character would be completely misrepresented to feed the monster that is the publicity machine for *Love Never Dies*." The Really Useful Group then shared this description of the Timmons on their social media pages.

> The result is what you would expect: a howling chorus of *Love Never Dies* fans condemning Mr. and Mrs. Timmons as (we quote verbatim), "sad," "pathetic," "idiot losers." Of course, we doubt they would be saying this had the article described the Timmons promoting *Love Never Dies* instead of criticizing it. *This is quite possibly the first time we have ever heard of a producer actively inciting hatred and insulting comments to fans of its own shows in order to counteract disappointing sales.* The RUG has endorsed this comment can only be interpreted as a very uncivilized "faux pas" by an organization that has more than enough problems with its image in how it deals with its fans and promotion. (emphasis added)

Hardly a fair fight. There's a name for this kind of behavior: cyberbullying.

> We will not react as they may wish us to by denouncing the fans of *Love Never Dies*, even though there is ample material with which to work ... They have every right to like the sequel,

just as those who follow us have every right to dislike it. Love Should Die's comments have always been directed at the material of the sequel itself—in particular, its abysmal book—and not at those who are fans of it.

It is perplexing that a show that would apparently be seen to be doing so well (the article in question states it plays to "packed houses") feels the need to condemn publicly those who do not support in order to generate yet more publicity and, moreover, dismissively marginalize dissenters' opinions. Could it be that LSD actually does have an effect on ticket sales? We have no information, but the article in question claims that ticket sales are 20% below what had been estimated, amounting to a £8 million loss. How a show that plays to "packed houses" every night can also suffer damaged ticket sales is beyond us. Perhaps this theory makes sense to an organization who claim that 1907 is ten years after 1881, and that only "four or five" people writing on the Internet do not like *Love Never Dies*, rather than the 1,400 fans of this Facebook page, not to mention the theatergoers who post on message boards throughout the Web. We perhaps would even be flattered if we were responsible for the full extent of this damage, but we doubt it.

Our aim was never sabotage, and in any case, how can a small group of fans with a niche interest seriously contend with a multi-million-dollar international corporate entertainment venture?

True. How can they?

Apparently enough to frighten the powers-that-be to resort to such shameful and tasteless smear tactics. ...

By the way, it may interest you to know that the journalist who wrote this magnificent piece of propaganda also claimed not to like *Love Never Dies*. Could it be that it is not any one Internet campaign that is the cause of poor ticket sales, but just the plain simple fact that people, in general, do not wish to see *Love Never Dies*?

Would that RUG spent more time thinking about what is wrong with their show than attempting to expose those who do not like it to unwarranted ridicule.

If you are appalled by these tactics, we urge you to write to RUG and *The Telegraph* (Love Should Die, 2010b).

The Timmons Get in Touch with the Really Useful Group

The Timmons wrote to the Really Useful Group about being smeared in the press, and received a surprisingly peevish letter back from RUG Chief Executive, Andre Ptaszynski, dated June 30, 2010. Keep in mind that this is the head of a multi-million-dollar organization up against an ordinary couple, "a couple of nobodies," from Toronto.

Dear Mr. Timmons.

I received your letter following the publication of the article about Love Should Die in *The Daily Telegraph,* and I was rather shocked by your admission that you were hurt by the "insulting" nature of some of the comments made about you and Love Should Die on sites under our control.

I should make it clear to you that *we are not responsible for the Telegraph article* (emphasis added)

Not involved? That's not what Lloyd Webber said when he bragged about giving them a dossier.

[A]nd we were reluctantly brought into a press investigation which initially involved a number of newspapers.

Reluctantly? And besides *The Daily Telegraph,* which other newspapers were involved?

Our decision not to take down the remarks on our sites has obviously offended you. Well, in the words of the great American comedian Bill Hicks, "be offended then."

Take that!

> Like us, you'll just have to get used to it. We are, you may be surprised to hear, not faceless, corporate granite. We are people who love and have chosen to work in the theatre. We have families, friends, mortgages, problems, and good times like everyone else.

Mortgages, problems, and good times? Really?

> Over two hundred people like that worked on the three-year project to bring *Love Never Dies* to the stage. We are committed to it and love the idea of keeping our company profitable by putting on a show (this is what we do) which suggests that the Phantom and Christine met again.

Is he seriously equating their huge team to the Timmons?

> The storyline and its conclusion is highly personal to Andrew who has composed what many feel to be his best score ever.

Lots of problems with the storyline, but it is a good score. Very good, in fact.

> Focus-group work on the show says a hefty ninety-seven percent of audiences love it.

A very strange statement. Focus groups are, by definition, small—in the 8-to-10 people range. How many focus groups did they conduct? Enough to be a full-audience size? Dinner-theater size? As I pointed out previously, there was enough protest, completely independent of Love Should Die, on sites like Goodreads and Amazon, to argue with this statement. Ninety-seven percent of whom?

> We are all very proud of that and we equally respect that percentage of the audience who feel that we have failed them and are disappointed.

Really? They're not being very respectful.

But it is our livelihood, our lives. And now we have had to accept the offence caused to us by people who haven't seen the show.

A single couple, in another country, did all this? Impressive!

From early previews, it became clear that the activities of the LSD site and others were going to do their best to stop our endeavor having a fair reception. The malicious attacks on our new show from people who had not even seen it seemed unfair and hurtful. The online commentary began to be picked up by the mainstream press and skewed our attempts to get positive word on the show into the public domain.

One website did all of that? Since when has the press listened to a single website?

You talk to me about "negative" and "offensive" remarks. How does that sit with what you have been hitting us with for months:

"Are you one of the unfortunates who have seen Love Never Dies? *Are you a fan who will never waste their time or money seeing* Love Never Dies? *If so, why not make a video review and upload it to YouTube. We'll add it to our fan videos page!"*

"Be sure to visit Amazon.com, Amazon.ca, and Amazon.co.uk, and add a review for the preposterous Love Never Dies *soundtrack. Be sure to rate the product and leave a review. This is the only way the Amazon star rating will bring the ratings down. A review must be left."*

"Write to your local newspaper theatre desk and tell them what you think about Love Never Dies—*A musical monstrosity that bastardizes the original story by Gaston Leroux and Webber's smash hit musical,* The Phantom of the Opera."

"Are you seeing The Phantom of the Opera *on tour? Broadway? London? If so, be sure to download and print our LSD Campaign Flyer to distribute at the show. If you're shy, just leave a bunch around the theatre lobby, bar, brochure/advertisement stands, and public mingling areas. Or if you're really vocal, you can hand these out before and after the show, during intermission...you get the idea. Just hand them out and let the reader make their own choice."*

"The more we get the word out, the faster we can put a stop to this lunacy!"

Keep in mind, that this was not just the work of the Timmons. They live in *Canada. Love Never Dies* did not come to North America.

I can't be bothered to go on. This campaign is waged by people who have not even seen a show that two hundred of us have spent months and months on.

Isn't that their job?

It is nasty, negative, and hurtful without the validity of the completely proper criticism and word of mouth we may get—good and bad—from people who have seen it. For Andrew, unfortunately, the campaign came hard on his recovery period following his operation from prostrate cancer which, frankly, make it more upsetting to bear, particularly in the light of his total emotional commitment to the music.

On behalf of us who thought we were just trying to put on a good show, nothing could be further from my thoughts than to offer you an apology after what you and your associates have done to us.

It's interesting that Ptasynski equated criticisms of the show, story, and plot to the *personal* attacks they waged on the Timmons. Love Should Die never attacked anyone personally (although the Really Useful Group took it that way). Imagine what it was like for the Timmons. Their idol, Andrew Lloyd Webber, is calling them "mental" in the international press, and inciting his many followers to do the same. Hardly a fair fight.

> Your letter was personal to me, as is my reply to you. I would prefer not to read it subsequently on the Internet, but that is in your gift, not mine.
>
> Yours sincerely,
>
> Andre Ptaszynski

The Timmons did indeed post it online, which is why we all get to read it.

The Timmons Respond on Love Should Die

After being outed and subjected to vitriol from around the world, all for the crime of purchasing a domain name and being part of a group that challenged Lloyd Webber, the Timmons issued a statement on Love Should Die.

> The LSD Campaign is, and has been, the collective effort of a global team to which we were the most recent additions. We'd like to reiterate the intention of the group was to counteract the perception ... that all *Phantom* Phans around the globe were waiting with breathless anticipation of the new sequel. It was never the intent of the team to dismantle the show. ...
>
> We have never targeted members of the cast or *LND* fans. In fact, in speaking with the reporter, we made particular effort to mention that we thought the cast were very talented, hard-working, and we wished them all the best—a point that was conveniently ignored for the article.
>
> Although we've been painted as the poster boy and girl for the LSD campaign, we are not the masterminds—we were simply the only members of the team the reporter was able to track down. We had donated funds to the team to assist in the creation of the LoveShouldDie website.

The fact that the *Love Never Dies* team had posted the article immediately on their Facebook page was disappointing. For a large organization (RUG) to reduce themselves to targeting loyal Phans (of the original *Phantom of the Opera*) of their own production, is simply regrettable (Love Should Die, 2010b).

At the One-Year Anniversary of Love Should Die

Love Should Die existed for far longer than they expected to. At their One Year Anniversary, they noted that they were not celebrating, and were, in fact, sad that they had to exist at all. They then summarized what they had accomplished in that first year.

> Over the last 12 months, we have *Love Never Dies* cancel their Broadway opening twice, watched theatre critics and audience members publish crippling reviews, observed the relationships amongst the creative team fall apart while the production changed its ad campaign several times, and more recently watched the show struggle with ticket sales by constantly offering free tickets and discounted ticket offers. Not to mention, the LSD Campaign hit major newspapers around the world, allowing fans' voices to be heard despite multiple attempts to have the campaign shut down. The Love Should Die team and campaign has been said to have created an £8,000,000 dent in profits for the production.

They also indicated that the Really Useful Group was trying to shut them down, claiming copyright infringement. In a contest that Love Should Die sponsored, they asked participants to be mindful of this.

> While we very much appreciate and encourage all contributions, please ensure that no image posted contains a production image of *The Phantom of the Opera, Love Never Dies,* or any other image that is copyrighted by the Really Useful Group. *We, unfortunately, have to insist on this as RUG tried to shut our account down citing*

breach of Intellectual Property Rights as their justification (emphasis added) (Love Should Die, 2010c).

Mission Accomplished: Love Should Die Says Goodbye

Love Should Die finally closed-up shop once they felt that they had completed their mission. They thanked their many supporters and said goodbye. This is their final statement (Love Should Die, 2011).

> *The Phantom of the Opera* has been billed since 1999 as the most successful entertainment venture of all time, its gross revenues having surpassed any other production in history, theatre, film, or otherwise. It is a ubiquitous cultural product that has broken national boundaries and that has become a classic musical. Like it or loathe it, it has long been acknowledged—even by its producers, Cameron Mackintosh and the Really Useful Group—that a huge factor in its success is the loyalty of its audience, its fans who have supported the show since its beginnings, and who continue to support it now.
>
> When the press launch of *Love Never Dies* took place on October 8, 2009, the producer, Lloyd Webber's Really Useful Group ... used the above statistics to boast about *Phantom's* success and use it, quite understandably, as a marketing bedrock for promoting *Love Never Dies*. It was quite clearly targeting the fans who had made *Phantom* a huge enduring success as its potential audience. Hours later, videos appeared on YouTube with vetted "Phans" proclaiming their excitement about *Love Never Dies*. Press coverage supplemented this image with claims, such as "fans of *The Phantom of the Opera* have been hoping for a sequel since 1999" (*The Daily Telegraph*), and "fans happy with *Phantom* sequel" (*Associated Press*).
>
> Even before the press launch, it was well-established that longstanding fans of *The Phantom of the Opera*—those who understood its characters and story, in addition to those who

were fans of Gaston Leroux's original novel from 1910—were extremely concerned about this ill-conceived sequel, not least because Lloyd Webber had originally tried to go through with the idea in the 1990s, using Frederick Forsyth's abysmal *The Phantom of Manhattan* as its basis. These fans did not agree that they could not wait for a sequel. Neither did they agree with the press comments that they had been hoping for a sequel since they fell in love with the original. These press comments were inaccurate, empty hype.

Once "Love Should Die" took off—something entirely unplanned; indeed, its popularity took its creators by surprise—it was obvious that the fans attracted to it should unite to counter these ridiculous claims. ... Fast forward four months following the sequel announcement, and the press had changed its tune ... and now acknowledged that those they term "diehard Phans" are categorically against *Love Never Dies*. Majority of these articles, we would like to add, are newspapers that previously claimed said "Phans" had an insatiable appetite for everything *Love Never Dies*-related....

You will note that many of the articles make explicit reference to "Love Should Die" and/or its supporters. We have come a long way from the press mindlessly repeating the hype of the Really Useful Group that "the Phans can't wait."

What does this mean? Essentially, that we have successfully accomplished the mission we set ourselves. ...

Our efforts, of course, have not been appreciated by everyone in the fan community. Do we apologize? No. We are saddened by any offense caused, but none of our actions have been deliberately malicious. ... We also know that some don't quite get our sense of humor. Too bad. But given that everything we have done has resulted in the press turning 180 degrees in their coverage of the fans' reception of *Love Never Dies* (and has even led the Really Useful Group to completely disassociate itself with the opinion of "Phans," with Lloyd Webber denouncing them as "insane" or "sad"), we regret nothing.

We do not stand for hatred. We do not stand for sabotage. We merely wish our views to be given a public voice and to be acknowledged. And in that, we have succeeded. We'd like to thank everyone for their support. And that, dear friends, concludes our initiative at Love Should Die. ...

We may have earned the wrath of Lord Lloyd Webber, who has publicly "disowned" the very fans who have been lining his pockets ... Once again, we respect everyone's right to like or dislike the sequel. If you wish to see *Love Never Dies*, we cannot stop you. If you are someone who is looking forward to *Love Never Dies*, then go ahead and see it and we hope you enjoy the show, but the show is not one we support.

You can disagree with us. But you can't suppress us. There's room for more than one opinion in this world. Love Should Die is not a hate campaign. It is not a sabotage, in spite of our tongue-in-cheek name. Its purpose is to remind the world that the sequel is not canon and never will be ... Our goal having been accomplished, therefore, it is time for LSD to take a backseat as the hype surrounding *Love Never Dies* begins to wane. Rest assured, we will be vigilant and return when the need arises.

In the meantime, we suggest all fans take a moment to appreciate Gaston Leroux's *The Phantom of the Opera*, and the musical of the same name penned by Andrew Lloyd Webber, Charles Hart, and Richard Stilgoe, and directed by Harold Prince, and remind themselves of just why the original *Phantom* inspires the passions that it does. Our small team—no, we're not just one person, contrary to popular myth—are still around to hear your opinions, particularly as we think everyone could do with a nice break from the negativity surrounding this overhyped show. It is important to remember that, for all the hype—both positive and negative—*Love Never Dies* is just that: only a show.

Yours,

LSD Team

August 27, 2011

http://loveshoulddie.com/LSD/LSD_Conclusion.html

CHAPTER 28

"You Asked Us to Listen"
New Role of Fans in the Age of Social Media

With *Phantom*, the theater world saw the birth of a new kind of fan: ones who saw the show over and over again. (We've seen that phenomenon with a lot of movies, but then again, that's a lot more affordable.) William Langley (2010), writing for *The Telegraph*, noted the following:

> With *Phantom*, that changed. Not only was it a theatrical sensation, racking up 9,000 performances (and counting) at Her Majesty's Theatre and grossing almost £3.5 billion in its various productions worldwide, but it also created a new kind of fan. Hardcore "Phans" aim to see the show as often as possible, often notching up hundreds, even thousands, of performances, and travelling all over the world to see them. When, towards the end of the second act, the orphaned chorus girl Christine sings Wishing You Were Somehow Here Again, the Phans usually are, too.
>
> On any night of the week, you can see them swarming around Haymarket, many in costume. They follow a routine that essentially consists of seeing the show, weeping copiously as the Phantom (today played by David Shannon) lets rip with Music of the Night, and buying another ticket on the way out (Langley, 2010).

Who Are These Fans?

Lloyd Webber had much to say about the hardcore fans during the *Love Never Dies* controversy. He portrayed them a sad little people with no lives. When you look more closely, however, you find that many hardcore fans are just ordinary people, with families and jobs. They "connect" with the story of *Phantom*. It speaks to them. In 2005, theater critic John Moore profiled a Phantom fan named Dick Moore (no relation). John Moore describes Dick Moore's obsession with *Phantom* with both morbid curiosity and a whiff of distain. John Moore, although a theater critic, has scrupulously avoided seeing *Phantom*, so this obsession makes no sense to him. However, he concedes that if you took out the word "Phantom" and substituted "Broncos," this level of obsession would include quite a few others in his native Denver.

> Dick Moore ... has seen *Phantom* 104 times in 38 cities. When the national tour opens its fifth Denver stop tonight, he will be hovering like a phantom in the Buell Theatre balcony for 31 of the 41 performances—all on his own dime. Make that 14,200 dimes, or $1,420, in tickets alone. ...
>
> Moore is an oddity among oddities: he's 67, he's gleefully obsessed with *The Phantom of the Opera*, and yet he's not exactly swinging from the chandeliers. He has spent more than $38,000 on *Phantom* tickets, airfare, and hotels since 1988, yet his friends and family don't worry about him too much. "We'll, not anymore," he said. "They don't have any choice." Yes, when Moore flew to London last year to see the first screening of the Joel Schumacher film adaptation, it was his 10th *Phantom* trip across the pond. Yes, he has a 300-piece *Phantom* collectibles menagerie in his basement, along with every framed Playbill from every production he's ever attended. Yes, he has a huge mask decal covering the hood of his Miata (license plate OPRGOST - for "opera ghost"). And for Saturday's matinee, yes, he will be arriving at the Buell by horse and carriage wearing full *Phantom* regalia.

But Moore is not some independently wealthy eccentric. He's a working stiff who mans the counter for a DIA shuttle service, and just happens to also be an enthusiastic *Phantom* Phreak.

"To me it is exactly like going to a baseball game 104 times," he said. "Every time I see it, it's like seeing it for the first time, and I never get tired of it. Sure, people say I'm crazy, but this is all fun for me. I mean, I don't do drugs, and I don't hurt anybody by doing this."

Dick Moore didn't see *Phantom* until he received a book for his 50th birthday that described the pop culture of *Phantom*. He was intrigued and decided to fly to London to see it. From there, he was hooked.

"It was nothing like I had ever seen before. The music and the staging were overwhelming. It just grabbed me, and I was hooked."

To that point, Moore would describe himself as a major but not fervid theater fan. "But I probably was looking for something to fulfill my life, and this is what has done that," he said.

When *Phantom* came to Denver, Dick Moore went to see 26 performances. He was invited back to meet the star and given a signed poster and tour jacket. When he followed the show to Philadelphia, Kevin Gray, the star he met in Denver, acknowledged him in the audience.

After 17 years, Moore's favorite Phantom remains the original, Michael Crawford, whom he saw in Los Angeles, and his favorite piece of memorabilia (besides his car) is a poster signed by Schumacher and the film's stars, Gerard Butler, Emmy Rossum, Minnie Driver, and Patrick Wilson. His greatest regret is never having seen the original Christine, Sarah Brightman, former wife of composer Andrew Lloyd Webber. ...

For all of us who will be seeing *Phantom* and hearing its Music of the Night for the first time in the next month, Dick Moore has a bit of confident advice.

"You're in for a wonderful night of beautiful music and wonderful theater," he said. (Moore, 2005).

The Super Phans

These superfans are what the Langley calls the "phundamentalist" factions, who "claim the whole *Phantom* phenomenon as their own." And they don't want anyone, including "the saggy-chopped maestro," to mess with it. These are the fans, who often by their own admission, are working extra shifts at Wendy's so they can buy theatre tickets. And they found their tribe online. We saw it first with their banding together over the protest about the movie. And we saw it in the previous chapter with Love Should Die. When the previews for *Love Never Dies* were pending, these hard-core fans predicted a dismal failure.

> The Internet, where the phan community mostly airs its views, is alive with apprehension. "Stand by for a phlop," says a typical posting. Another is more succinct: "Phor ph---'s sake, Andrew, don't" (Langley, 2010).

Phantommania has been going on for years, long before there was a movie, or a sequel. Cashing in this trend, co-producer Cameron Macintosh released a best-selling perfume in the U.S.: *Esprit de Phantom*. Lloyd Webber biographer Michael Coveney shared his thoughts on this venture.

> You too can have the sophisticated fragrance of a hideous misfit who lives in the Paris sewers (Coveney, 1999, p. 76).

Langley suggests that the fanatical fans are mostly women who share a romantic streak. He also says that "psychological research" (none was cited) indicates that they have a tendency towards emotional vulnerability, adding that the late Princess Diana was an early Phan. Langley also described the story of Dan Lehner, a wealthy business man (and notably, *not* a woman). He was America's most fanatical phan. Lehner saw the show at least once a week, met his wife at one performance, proposed to her during intermission of another, and died of a heart attack at age 49.

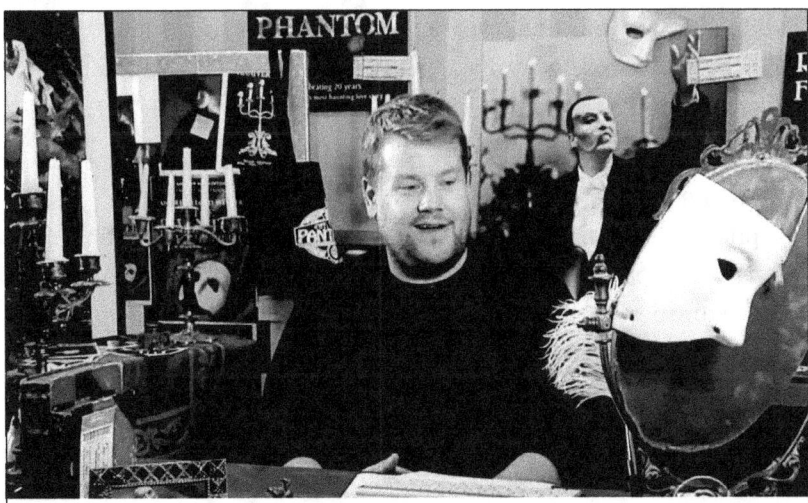

Super-fan and talk-show host, James Corden, does a walk-on appearance in Phantom as "Fop 2." At the end, he pushes the Phantom aside to take an extra bow.
https://www.youtube.com/watch?v=76zXQfOCmGc

The Hard-Core Fanbase is Why Phantom Has Been So Successful

Lloyd Webber has had much to say about the "sad little people" who launched the social media campaign against *Love Never Dies*. To me, Lloyd Webber's distain for his central fanbase is one of the more disturbing elements to emerge from this story. Whatever you think of the central fanbase, they are the ones who have made *Phantom* the enduring show that it is. These fans make personal and financial sacrifices in order to feed their *Phantom* habit. They have also made Lloyd Webber the richest man in musical theatre. Rather than thanking them, Lloyd Webber treats them with contempt. In an interview in 2010, he called the fanatical fans "insane."

There's something very elitist and wrong about his attitude. Lloyd Webber may not understand their obsession with one of his creations, but that doesn't mean that they deserve his contempt. The "repeat audience," as it's known in the trades, has been key to *Phantom's* success. Still, this subculture does make people shake their heads in wonder, as Coveney describes.

> Which makes you wonder whether or not hit shows depend on the kindness of strangers, or just strange people. ... This phenomenon lay at the heart of the Andrew Lloyd Webber success story. No show runs unless people who need people— the funniest people—send in the people. These folks keep the flame alight (Coveney, 1999, p. 329).

Langley (2010) also acknowledges,

> Sad or not, such Phans have helped make *Phantom* both a theatrical powerhouse and a cultural battlefield.

> *At the heart of the current ill-feeling is the issue of who the show belongs to.* Lloyd Webber may have his name up in lights, but the story of the disfigured genius's love for a young soprano has been adapted dozens of times ... Many Phans now consider it a universal story that should belong to the world and be enjoyed by everybody. Preferably, they would argue, without the distraction of phollow-ups [emphasis added].

Who Owns This Story?

This really is the central issue. It's very clear that Lloyd Webber views this story as *his*, so much so that he has also made disparaging comments about Leroux's original *Phantom* story, and indicates that he can't understand why it's so popular. Forsyth clearly shared this view.

Although he's had a phenomenal amount of success in his career, nothing he's done has been even remotely as successful as *Phantom*. It's like Lloyd Webber's annoyed that people haven't responded as positively to his more recent work. For example, *Stephen Ward*, his musical about the Profumo affair, a political scandal in the UK in the 1960s, closed after only 4 months (BBC News, 2014).

Lloyd Webber's most recent venture, *School of Rock*, launched in 2015, seems to be doing well. It opened to decent reviews in New York and London. It will probably have a reasonable run, but it is unlikely to ever top the runaway success of *Phantom.*

Lloyd Webber's attempts to distance himself from the success of *Phantom* reminded me of a book I once read about the life of Judy Garland. Towards the end of her life, when she was struggling mightily with the addictions that would eventually kill her, directors would do many things to make life easier for her, like paint a yellow-bricked road outside her dressing room. These types of gestures made her feel worse. She wasn't too keen on the fact that they were still harkening back to a show she made when she was 16-years-old. I've often wondered if Lloyd Webber feels the same way about *Phantom*. He wasn't 16, but the overarching success of *Phantom* has overshadowed all the other things he's accomplished, before or since. It seems that he has come to resent that.

On Obsessive Fans

Lloyd Webber acts like *Phantom* fans are simply some very strange aberration. Yes, I agree some of this obsession seems strange. But *The Phantom of the Opera* is, by no means, the only show that has inspired this amount of slavish devotion. Consider the fans of *Star Wars* or *Star Trek*; both series' have fans that have seen those shows hundreds, even thousands of times. They know every line of dialogue. They dress in costumes. They worship the stars. They've even learned to speak *Klingon*. Sound familiar?

How about *The Lord of the Rings*? *The Lord of the Rings* books were the bestselling books of the entire 20th century. J.R.R. Tolkien made up languages when he wrote the books, and his fans actually learned to speak them. When Peter Jackson and his crew were filming, fans would simply appear at various locations. Peter Jackson put them to work, and made them extras.

Some *Lord of the Rings* movie locations became places tourists wanted to visit. One is Hobbiton, where scenes from the Shire were filmed. It's a working sheep farm. So many fans were popping by, on a pilgrimage of sorts, that the farm owners asked for, and eventually got the rights to keep up some of the sets. The only thing that kept them from being destroyed in the first place were torrential rain storms that delayed demolition. When my family went to Hobbiton in 2008, there were no signs directing us to it. My friend who lives in New Zealand told me (while eyerolling) to "go to a town called Mata Mata, and turn right at the gas station." Hobbiton is now a major tourist attraction. Since *The Hobbit* movies, the facades were rebuilt, and are now still in place. Even in 2008, Hobbiton was cool to see. And think about all of the people who have had *Lord of the Rings*-themed weddings? Are they all freaks?

Another example of this type of fandom is Comic-Con, a huge convention for people who are fans of comics, anime, wrestling, movies, fantasy, sci-fi, and pretty much every pleasure that was once perceived as nerdy. Those conventions draw thousands and thousands of devoted fans, as well as attracting huge names in their respective industries. Many dress like their favorite characters. I went to our local version, AMA-Con (a much smaller, but still significant convention), with my son, where he had a booth to sell his art. There were tons of people there in costumes (even a few who might want to rethink wearing blue spandex. No, the cape does not completely cover it). Although I couldn't imagine what would possess people to spend two days dressed like anime characters, it clearly was important to them. Not my thing, but my sons insist that people think that it is fun.

A more high-brow version could be fans of *Pride and Prejudice*. I've seen people almost come to blows over which version was better, the BBC version with Colin Firth, or the movie with Keira Knightley and Matthew MacFadyen (I like both, but I liked the movie better). There are also Jane Austen conventions, interest groups, and online forums. And consider all the spins offs. Are all these people odd? And don't even get me started on hard-core opera fans!

370

My point is, if you think about this more broadly, rabid devotion of fans is not unusual. For one group of fans, the subject of their obsession is *The Phantom of the Opera*. There is no rhyme or reason for this, necessarily, but for whatever reason, *Phantom* speaks to them. I think the failure to understand this group, and what they were responding to, led to some unnecessary strife. The fans were invested in the story. Lloyd Webber thought that it was his, and that he could do whatever he wanted to it, a persistent theme throughout his life. The fans disagreed and raised some legitimate points. Had Lloyd Webber listened, he might have saved himself some aggravation—and money.

"You Asked Us to Listen"

In thinking about this fan controversy, and Lloyd Webber's reactions to it, I was reminded of Nick Hornby's book, *Juliet, Naked*. This book is about an online group that is obsessed with the life and works of an obscure rocker named Tucker Crowe. Crowe produced one truly brilliant album, which had become a cult classic. Crowe then disappeared from the scene. Duncan, one of the main "Croweologists," starts an online community where fans come together, share bootleg concert recordings, and discuss the secret meaning behind his lyrics. Tucker Crowe has contempt for these obsessed fans, and it's one of the reasons he has stayed hidden.

Earlier in the book, Tucker had shared with Annie, his love interest in the book, and Duncan's former girlfriend, that the reason he ran away and dropped out of the scene is that the supposed romance and break up behind his most famous album was all a bunch of lies. It's considered the greatest breakup album of all time. However, the woman Tucker broke up with turned out to be a dimwit, and it was no great loss. Tucker can't believe that his fans like that album.

"You're telling me that art is *made up*? My God."

"I'm telling you that my ... art is inauthentic. Sorry. Let me rephrase that. I'm telling you that my rock album is a fake bunch of crap ... See ... it's like I'm a chef, and you're eating in my restaurant, and you're telling me how great my food is. But I know I pissed all over it before I served it up. So, you know, your opinion is valid, but ..."

This is not unlike Lloyd Webber saying in interviews that *Phantom* is the "greatest bunch of hokum."

... "So Tucker Crowe thinks his fans can't taste pee when it's served to them."

That was exactly what Tucker Crowe thought during that tour. He hated himself, but he also despised everyone who had lapped it all up. That was one of the reasons it had been so easy to quit.

Later in the book, when Annie asks Tucker to meet Duncan, Tucker's most avid fan, Tucker refuses.

"Because (a) he's a fucking fruitcake, and (b) I might kill him, and (c) if I didn't kill him, he'd drop dead from the excitement anyway."

"Well, 'c' is a definitely possibility."

"Why do you want me to meet him?"

"Because no matter what you think, he's not stupid. Not about art, anyway. And you're the only artist alive who's made any sense to him, just about."

"The only artist alive? Jesus Christ. I could write you a list of a hundred people better than me off the top of my head."

"It's not about better, Tucker. *You speak to him. For him. He connects. You plug right into a very complicated-looking socket in his back. I don't know why, but you do*" (pp. 334-335) (emphasis added).

Through a series of events, Duncan finally has a chance to meet his idol and he becomes aware of Tucker's contempt for their little online community.

"All I can say in my defense is that … well, *you asked us to listen*. And some of us listened a little too hard...

This will probably sound silly, and not what you want to hear. But I'm not the only person who thinks you're a genius. *And while you might think we're … we're inadequate as people, we're not necessarily the worst judges in the world. We read, and watch movies, and think …* I don't pretend to understand what those songs meant to you, but it's the forms of expression you chose, the allusions, the musical references. *That's what makes it art… I value what you did on that album more highly than, I think, anything else I've heard.* So, thank you" (pp. 356) (emphasis added).

While most of us may not understand the behavior of the most devoted *Phantom* fans, in the grand scheme of things, their behavior is not unusual. For whatever reason, these fans connect with *Phantom*. *Phantom* speaks to them. It plugs into a complicated socket for them, and that is what art does and is supposed to do. Lloyd Webber may think these fans are "crazy" and live "sad, little lives," but they do not deserve his contempt. To Lloyd Webber, they could rightly say: "you asked us to listen." Lloyd Webber should not be upset that they did.

Epilogue

Writing this book has been an amazing journey. It started for me in 2005, when I got curious about the movie version of *Phantom* and went online. I finally decided to write this book two years ago. For the past two years, I've immersed myself in all things *Phantom*. The more I dug into this story, the more interesting it became. When people have asked about why I got interested in this story, it's hard to give them a short answer. There's so much to it.

Writing this book took me in directions I never expected. That's the fun part of writing. For example, I never expected to think that Sarah Brightman got treated really badly. Why did all the male biographers solely blame her for breaking up Lloyd Webber's marriage? They weren't equals, but somehow people thought she had all the power, and lured him with her "musky scent of forbidden fruit." Good God! All she did was sing. I'm amazed people actually bought that. And she was trashed because she wanted to work. Have we suddenly been transported to the 1950s? I've always liked Brightman's music. After knowing her story, I found myself cheering for her personal transformation and success. You go, girl!

I never expected to find claims of plagiarism to have some validity, particularly regarding The Phantom of the Opera theme. Whether those claims would stand up in court is another matter, but certainly a case could be made. I doubt that Lloyd Webber did it on purpose (although I can't say that for sure). The similarities between those melodies, however, are undeniable.

When I first heard about the Love Should Die site, I thought "seriously?" By the time I finished researching their story, I was impressed. I wouldn't have necessarily joined their campaign, but dang! They were effective. Something else that was interesting. Even the Love Should Die folks wanted a scenario where Phantom gets the girl. Jeff and Rebecca Timmons, the alleged masterminds of the plot, had a Phantom-themed wedding, where he was Phantom and she was Christine. I realize Lloyd Webber was frustrated with this group, but he came across as a real bully. Love Should Die did him a favor. His show is now a lot better.

One final thing that I did not expect was the disturbing misogyny of this story. Women had almost no power at so many levels in the actual story, and in its production. The fact that the men behind *Phantom* thought it would be acceptable for Phantom to choke Christine. Or that the proscenium was deliberately designed to show freaks sexually assaulting women. Or that a bunch of old guys would be drooling over the "sexual awakening" a 16-year-old girl. Both Butler and Lloyd Webber have made filthy references to women in interviews that made me feel like I needed to take a shower. I was surprised, and disappointed, by both. Show business continues to be a man's world. I now understand why so many women choose to work outside the system, and produce independent works. The playing field in the entertainment industry is not at all level, and continues to skew white, male.

So now it is time for me to say goodbye. I hope you have enjoyed this social history. It's been my pleasure to bring it to you. *Phantom* continues to be the world's most popular musical. That will likely be true for many years to come.

References

20/20 Phantom Strikes Broadway, part 2. (2010). Retrieved from: https://www.youtube.com/watch?v=aDsiOviHiWQ

Alexandrovics, J. (n.d.). *An analysis of Andrew Lloyd Webber's musical 'Plagiarism'.* Retrieved from: https://www.academia.edu/8237079/An_analysis_of_ Andrew_Lloyd_Webbers_musical_Plagiarism

Amazon.com. (2017). Reviews of *Love Never Dies.* Retrieved from: https://www. amazon.com/Andrew-Lloyd-Webbers-Love-Never/dp/B006GHA9QQ/ref=sr_ 1_1?ie=UTF8&qid=1494818463&sr=8-1&keywords=love+never+dies+dvd

American Psychological Association. (2010). *Publication manual of the American Psychological Association, 6th Ed.* Washington, DC: Author.

Anderson, J. (2004). *The Phantom of the Opera.* Retrieved from: http://www.combustiblecelluloid.com/2004/phantop04.shtml

Andrew Lloyd Webber pays royalties to Puccini. (2014, Sep 20). Retrieved from: http://abcclassic2.tumblr.com/post/98427075196/andrew-lloyd-webber-pays-royalties-to-puccini

Andrew Lloyd Webber and Joel Schumacher on *The Phantom of the Opera.* (2013). *Theatertalk.* Retrieved from: https://www.youtube.com/watch?v=0pfnF9nziPs

Associated Press. (2009, Oct 9). *Phantom of the Opera* fans happy with sequel. *The Sydney Morning Herald.* Retrieved from: http://www.smh.com.au/news/entertainment/arts/phantom-of-the-opera-fans-happy-with-sequel/2009/10/09/1255019601399.html

Audiojunkie. (2012). *Beauty Underneath* (Love Never Dies). Retrieved from: https://www.youtube.com/watch?v=NdI36IBLfHQ

Backstage.com. (2005, Jan 13). *Singers of the night.* Retrieved from LexisNexis.

Ball, M., & Lloyd Webber, A. (2013). *40 Years of Andrew Lloyd Webber, part 2.* Retrieved from: https://www.youtube.com/watch?v=dPw67_2dfiY

Bamigboye, B. (2011, May 27). Love Never Dies ... but it's hurting. *The Daily Mail.* Retrieved from: http://www.dailymail.co.uk/tvshowbiz/article-1391371/Love-Never-Dies--hurting.html?ito=feeds-newsxml

BBC. (2008). *Behind the Mask, part 1*. Retrieved from: https://www.youtube.com/ watch?v=EmPwlfJxSjw

BBC. (2008). *Behind the Mask, part 2*. Retrieved from: https://www.youtube.com/ watch?v=g_BhzOaymx

BBC. (2008). *Behind the Mask, part 3*. Retrieved from: https://www.youtube.com/ watch?v=jgxXSK8nLSo

BBC. (2008). *Behind the Mask, part 4*. Retrieved from: https://www.youtube.com/ watch?v=GBBOcYbXaFU

BBC. (2008). *Behind the Mask, part 5*. Retrieved from: https://www.youtube.com/ watch?v=nRnIU-vbEpE

BBC. (2008). *Behind the Mask, part 6*. Retrieved from: https://www.youtube.com/ watch?v=KZwp9oEKx88

BBC. (2008). *Behind the Mask, part 7*. Retrieved from: https://www.youtube.com/ watch?v=HsVkU2-QrGA

BBC. (2008). *Behind the Mask, part 8*. Retrieved from: https://www.youtube.com/ watch?v=KLErOwvo720

BBC. (2008). *Behind the Mask, part 9*. Retrieved from: https://www.youtube.com/ watch?v=X_jW_Sq2ngs

BBC News. (2014, Feb 25). *Lloyd Webber flop musical* Stephen Ward *to close early*. Retrieved from: http://www.bbc.com/news/entertainment-arts-26336382

Behind the scenes at The Phantom of the Opera *25th anniversary, part 1*. (2012). Retrieved from: https://www.youtube.com/watch?v=SInA5s-XyEI&t=182s

Behind the scenes at The Phantom of the Opera *25th anniversary, part 2*. (2012). Retrieved from: https://www.youtube.com/watch?v=aodCi0jyZgE&t=88s

Ben Lewis and Anna O'Byrne sing Beneath a Moonless Sky from Love Never Dies. (2011). Retrieved from: https://www.youtube.com/watch?v=DtZnadb99_8

Benedict, D. (2011, Jun 17). Andrew Lloyd Webber show to shutter. *Variety*. Retrieved from: http://loveshoulddie.com/LSD/Variety_LND_Closure.html

Benedict, D. (2010, Mar 10). *Love Never Dies. Variety Magazine*. http://loveshoulddie.com/LSD/Variety_Press_Review.html

Benedict, D. (2010, Dec 21). Review: *Love Never Dies*. Version 2. Retrieved from: http://variety.com/2010/legit/news/love-never-dies-2-1117944212/

Bermudez, M. (2013). *Ramin Karimloo* Love Never Dies *Till I Hear Your Sing*. Retrieved from: https://www.youtube.com/watch?v=4lrWVfX_JrA

Billington, M. (2010, Mar 9). *Love Never Dies. The Guardian.* Retrieved from: https://www.theguardian.com/stage/2010/mar/10/love-never-dies-review

Bocelli, A., & Brightman, S. (2013). *Time to say goodbye.* Retrieved from: https://www.youtube.com/watch?v=LWQbuJ24Wzg

Boggess, S., & Karimloo, R. (2013). *Beneath the Moonless Sky. Version 1.0.* Retrieved from: https://www.youtube.com/watch?v=PwZlOCFNDQs

Boggess, S., & Karimloo, R. (2015). *Beneath the Moonless Sky. Version 2.0.* Retrieved from: https://www.youtube.com/watch?v=1jAtShinhUo

Boggess, S., & Karimloo, R. (2013). *Phantom confronts Christine. London Cast.* Retrieved from: https://www.youtube.com/watch?v=-3hLpQPqW28

Boggess, S., & Karimloo, R. (2013). *LND OLC Finale.* Retrieved from: https://www.youtube.com/watch?v=8WL4b7uZZPg

Bookwrm17. (2010). *Evolving views of chastity and sexuality in* The Phantom of the Opera. Retrieved from: http://bookwrm17.livejournal.com/32318.html

Brantley, B. (2010, Mar 9). Same *Phantom,* different spirit. *New York Times.* Retrieved from: http://www.nytimes.com/2010/03/10/theater/10love. html?_r=0

Brightman, S. (2009). *Sarah Brightman Jonathan Ross Interview, part 1.* Retrieved from: https://www.youtube.com/watch?v=F4dQPNWBMzk

Brightman, S. (2011). *Sarah Brightman talks about Andrew Lloyd Webber* (Kennedy Center Honors, 2006). Retrieved from: https://www.youtube. com/watch?v=sTQ4CZxyQxs

Brightman, S. (2013). *Sarah Brightman and Andrew Lloyd Webber on 25 years of* Phantom of the Opera. Retrieved from: https://www.youtube.com/ watch?v=aRdkbMzJJDA

Brightman, S. (2013). *Sarah Brightman on Loose Women ITV.* Retrieved from: https://www.youtube.com/watch?v=qNCAs0Ecjig

Brightman, S. (n.d.) *Biography, 1981-1989.* Retrieved from: http://www.sarahbrightman.com/biography/1

Brightman, S., & Banderas, A. (2011). *The Phantom of the Opera.* Retrieved from: https://www.youtube.com/watch?v=I71jSwn6etw

Brightman, S., & Crawford, M. (1988). Phantom of the Opera *1988 Tony Awards.* Retrieved from: https://www.youtube.com/watch?v=oZDcSrODALQ

Brightman, S., & Harley, S. (2014). *The Phantom of the Opera (promo video).* Retrieved from: https://www.youtube.com/watch?v=AHtLc7JctLc

Broadway.com. (2014). *Character study: Watch Hugh Panaro transform into Erik, aka* The Phantom of the Opera. Retrieved from: https://www.youtube.com/watch?v=7ADiLSQid9M

Butler, G. (2009). *Making the Phantom's disfigurement*. Retrieved from: https://www.youtube.com/watch?v=w92cSr4Ezpw

Butler, G. (2010). *Gerard Butler sings Music of the Night*. Retrieved from: https://www.youtube.com/watch?v=1mPW16cWaoI

Caplan, N. (2011, Jan 5). *Love Never Dies*—version 2.0. *Time Out London*. Retrieved from: https://www.timeout.com/london/theatre/love-never-dies

CBS Morning News. (2012). *Andrew Lloyd Webber on "Phantom" turning 25*. Retrieved from: https://www.youtube.com/watch?v=LgKIjgaCL4Y

Chinese Phantom of the Opera. (2006). Retrieved from: https://www.youtube.com/watch?v=3AQJzxKTocs&list=RDeY_Xs3sXQDg&index=

ClapYo'Hands. (2011). *Lloyd Webber vs. Puccini*. Retrieved from: http://www.broadwayworld.com/board/readmessage.php?thread=1036461

Clarke, D. (2004, Dec 10). Behind the mask. *The Irish Times*. Retrieved from LexisNexis.

Coates, T. (2014, Nov 13). *Do you remember when Gerard Butler starred in* The Phantom of the Opera? *Decider*. Retrieved from: http://decider.com/2014/11/13/gerard-butler-phantom-of-the-opera/

Cottcott123. (2011). *Quello che tacete/The Music of the Night*. Retrieved from: https://www.youtube.com/watch?v=fx1KNRCijCY

Coveney, M. (1999). *The Andrew Lloyd Webber story*. London: Arrow Books.

Craig, O. (2008). Sarah Brightman's Hot Gossip days are over. *The Telegraph*. Retrieved from: http://www.telegraph.co.uk/news/celebritynews/3536240/Sarah-Brightmans-hot-gossip-days-are-over.html

Crawford, M. (2007). *The Music of the Night. Michael Crawford and Sarah Brightman*. Retrieved from: https://www.youtube.com/watch?v=n5dhyiqhR7Y

Debruge, P. (2005). Review of *The Phantom of the Opera. Premiere Magazine*. *Retrieved from: https://www.rottentomatoes.com/critic/peter-debruge/movies?page=19*

Dezell, M. (2005, Apr 24). You've seen the movie, now see the show. Film versions give musicals a lift. *Boston Globe*. Retrieved from Lexis-Nexis.

Driscoll, R. (2004, Dec 8). The pressure truly hit me one second before I sang. I suddenly thought, "Oh, my God, I'm about to sing one of the most famous songs of all time, in front of the guy who wrote it, and the director and producer. No pressure there, then!" *The Western Mail.* Retrieved from LexisNexis.

E! Network. (2008). *Make it sexy … Phantom.* Retrieved from: https://www.youtube.com/watch?v=1A54EF1kGMs

Ebert, R. (2004). Andrew Lloyd Webber's *Phantom of the Opera.* Retrieved from: Http://rogerebert.com/reviews/andrew-lloyd-webbers-phantom-of-the-opera-2004

Film Companion. (2004). *The Phantom of the Opera companion.* London: Pavilion.

Fischer, P. (2004). *Butler's Irish eyes are smiling. Gerard Butler/The Phantom of the Opera interview.* Retrieved from: http://www.femail.com.au/phantom-of-the-opera-gerard-butler-pf.htm.

Forsyth, F. (2007). *The Phantom of Manhattan.* New York: Macmillan.

Fox, D.J. (1990, Sep 10). Lloyd Webber postpones filming "Phantom": Movies: The composer says Sarah Brightman still will star. *Los Angeles Times.* Retrieved from: http://articles.latimes.com/1990-09-10/entertainment/ca-262_1_lloyd-webber

Giggan1. (2008). *Echoes vs.* Phantom of the Opera. Retrieved from: https://www.youtube.com/watch?v=xkx4ia6Th1A

Gliatto, T. (1990, Jul 23). Andrew Lloyd Webber leaves his leading lady—as his aspect of love turns to a woman named Gurtie. *People.* Retrieved from: http://people.com/archive/andrew-lloyd-webber-leaves-his-leading-lady-as-his-aspect-of-love-turns-to-a-woman-named-gurtie-vol-34-no-3/

Goodreads. (2017). *Reviews of* The Phantom of Manhattan. Retrieved from: https://www.goodreads.com/book/show/109513.The_Phantom_of_Manhattan

Griffiths, C. (2010, Dec 6). Lloyd Webber pulls gloomy *Love Never Dies* off West End stage to give it a facelift. *The DailyMail.com.* Retrieved from: http://www.dailymail.co.uk/tvshowbiz/article-1335755/Andrew-Lloyd-Webber-pulls-Love-Never-Dies-West-End-stage-facelift.html

Healy, P. (2010, Aug 31). *Love Never Dies* looking less likely for Broadway season. *New York Times.* Retrieved from: https://artsbeat.blogs.nytimes.com/2010/08/31/love-never-dies-looking-less-likely-for-broadway-this-season/

Heatley, M. (2011). *The Phantom of the Opera: 25th anniversary edition.* London: Pavilion.

Heckman, D. (1999, Aug 13). Crawford unmasks views of "Phantom" film. *LA Times.* Retrieved from: http://articles.latimes.com/1999/aug/13/entertainment/ca-65215

Hitchings, H. (2010a, Mar 10). Review of *Love Never Dies. The Evening Standard.* Retrieved from: http://loveshoulddie.com/LSD/Evening_Standard_Press_Review.html

Hitchings, H. (2010b, Dec 22). Phantom still lacks spirit in *Love Never Dies. Evening Standard.* http://loveshoulddie.com/LSD/Evening_Standard_V2_Press_Release.html

Hobson, L.B. (2003, Aug 9). Opera man. *Calgary Sun.* Retrieved from: LexisNexis.

Hobson, L.B. (2004, Dec 19a). Phantom pain. *Calgary Sun.* Retrieved from: LexisNexis.

Hobson, L.B. (2004, Dec 19b). Mastering the mask: The Phantom's trademark mask was just one more problem for Gerard Butler to overcome. *London Free Press* (Ontario). Retrieved from LexisNexis.

Hornby, N. (2009). *Juliet, Naked.* New York: Penguin.

Hot Gossip. (1978). *I lost my heart to a starship trooper.* Retrieved from: https://www.youtube.com/watch?v=kgW9l7CR1WQ

Houwelling, P. (1992). Who the hell does Roger Waters think he is? *Q Magazine.* Retrieved from: http://utopia.knoware.nl/users/ptr/pfloyd/interview/roger2.html

Irwin, J. (posted Jan 19, 2006, accessed Aug 16, 2016). *Amazon review of* The Phantom of the Opera DVD. Retrieved from: https://www.amazon.com/product-reviews/B002QRWJA4/ref=cm_cr_getr_d_paging_btm_16?ie=UTF8&filterByStar=positive&reviewerType=avp_only_reviews&showViewpoints=0&pageNumber=16

Itzkoff, D. (2010, Oct 22). "Phantom" sequel going underground while changes are made. *New York Times.* Retrieved from: https://artsbeat.blogs.nytimes.com/2010/10/22/phantom-sequel-going-underground-while-changes-are-made/

Jimmy O. (2004). *The Phantom of the Opera.* Filmsnobs. Retrieved from: http://www.filmsnobs.com/www/jimmyo/unfortunate.htm

Kendall-Tackett, K.A. (2005). *How to write for a general audience*. Washington, DC: American Psychological Association.

Krista2Bway. (2013). *Phantom confronts Christine. LND London cast.* Retrieved from: https://www.youtube.com/watch?v=-3hLpQPqW28

Krista2Bway. (2013). Coney Island Waltz LND London Cast. Retrieved from: https://www.youtube.com/watch?v=6QgmLTya9_Q

Langley, W. (2010). *The Phantom returns: Poor show, Andrew?* Retrieved from: http://www.telegraph.co.uk/culture/theatre/theatre-news/7386503/The-Phantom-returns-poor-show-Andrew.html

LePhantomessa. (2010). *The ultimate guide to Phangirls*. Retrieved from: https://www.fanfiction.net/s/6388392/3/The-Ultimate-Guide-to-Phangirls

Leroux, G. (1987). *The Phantom of the Opera*. New York: Harper Perennial.

Letts, Q. (2010, Mar 10). Stodgy Phantom sequel not quite a hit ... but Lloyd Webber's operatic music lifts it to a higher plane. *The Daily Mail.com*. Retrieved from: http://www.dailymail.co.uk/tvshowbiz/reviews/article-1256833/Love-Never-Dies-review-Andrew-Lloyd-Webbers-music-lifts-Phantom-sequel.html

Lewis, B. (2012). *Love Never Dies. Act 1 (Till I Hear You Sing)*. Retrieved from: https://www.youtube.com/watch?v=HOUFfITzYnM

Lewis, B., & O'Byrne, A. (2013). Love Never Dies. *Beneath the Moonless Sky*. Retrieved from: https://www.youtube.com/watch?v=iimYZM8Z-0M

Lewis, B., & O'Byrne, A. (2015). *The Phantom confronts Christine: Love Never Dies*. Retrieved from: https://www.youtube.com/watch?v=b5kVtREuzJU

Lewis, B., & O'Byrne, A. (2012). *Love Never Dies HD*. Retrieved from: https://www.youtube.com/watch?v=nJEOQ6ecHb8

Lewis, N. (2014). *Norm Lewis & Sierra Boggess perform The Music of the Night*. Retrieved from: https://www.youtube.com/watch?v=lCAdkACAH78

London Evening Standard. (2011, May 6). Bitterness lives on over *Love Never Dies*. *London Evening Standard*. http://loveshoulddie.com/LSD/London_Evening_Standard_Bad_Blood.html

London Footage—*Love Never Dies*. (2014). *Trailer*. Retrieved from: https://www.youtube.com/watch?v=PYssEMBrlCM

Longino, B. (2004, Dec 22). Hollywood unmasks two more holiday films: *Phantom* musical bares some skin, adds new scenes. *The Atlanta Journal-Constitution*. Retrieved from: Lexis-Nexis.

Love Never Dies—Phantom Sequel. (2011). *Theatre critics reviews.* Retrieved from: https://www.youtube.com/watch?v=iaDEhylirbo

Love Should Die. (2010a). *Mission of Love Never Dies.* Retrieved from: http://www.loveshoulddie.com/LSD/_Mission_Note.html

Love Should Die. (2010b). *Statement from the LSD team.* Retrieved from: http://www.loveshoulddie.com/LSD/Public_Statement.html

Love Should Die. (2010c). *Notes from the LSD team: Love Should Die One Year Anniversary.* Retrieved from: http://loveshoulddie.com/LSD/Notes_From_LSD.html

Love Should Die. (2011). *Love Should Die conclusion.* Retrieved from: http://loveshoulddie.com/LSD/LSD_Conclusion.html

Lyons, B., & Bennett, C. (2005, Jun 4). Gerry's boozy blessing. *Scottish Daily Record & Sunday Mail.* Retrieved from LexisNexis.

Malnick, E. (2011, Jun 18). Lloyd Webber's *Love Never Dies* draws its last breath. *The Telegraph.* Retrieved from: http://www.telegraph.co.uk/news/uknews/8583939/Lloyd-Webbers-Love-Never-Dies-draws-its-last-breath.html

Mannara, B. (2015). *Beneath a Moonless Sky, Ramin Karimloo Sierra Boggess.* Retrieved from: https://www.youtube.com/watch?v=1jAtShinhUo

Marlowe, S. (2010, Mar 18). *Love Never Dies* review. *Time Out London.* Retrieved from: http://loveshoulddie.com/LSD/Time_Out_London_Press_Review.html

Marlowe, S. (2011, Jan 5). *Love Never Dies* (second review). *Time Out.* Retrieved from: https://www.timeout.com/london/theatre/love-never-dies

Marmion, P. (2010, Dec 21). First night review: *Love Never Dies*, at the Adelphi Theatre. *The Daily Mail.* Retrieved from: http://www.dailymail.co.uk/tvshowbiz/article-1340688/Love-Never-Dies-Adelphi-Theatre-FIRST-NIGHT-REVIEW.html?ito=feeds-newsxml

Mitchell, P. (2004, Dec 20). Rocking the opera. *Herald Sun* (Melbourne, Australia). Retrieved from LexisNexis.

Moore, J. (2005, Nov 4). "Phantom Phreak" will haunt Buell Theatre. *The Denver Post.* Retrieved from Lexis Nexis.

Musicalchannel. (2015). *Before the performance.* Love Never Dies. Retrieved from: https://www.youtube.com/watch?v=_YJY2wRk-PA

Namoweb. (2010). *Andrew Lloyd Webber: Genius or plagiarist?* Retrieved from: https://www.youtube.com/watch?v=wW5wwi4ahLc

Nathan, S. (2011). "She's my angel of music": Andrew Lloyd Webber still has a special place in his heart from ex-wife Sarah Brightman. *DailyMail.com*. Retrieved from: http://www.dailymail.co.uk/tvshowbiz/article-2044960/ Andrew-Lloyd-Webber-special-place-heart-ex-wife-Sarah-Brightman.html

Nestruck, K. (2011, Apr 18). A love-hate relationship with Phantom. *The Globe and Mail*. Retrieved from: http://loveshoulddie.com/LSD/Globe_and_Mail_Interview.html

Nightwish. (2010). *Phantom of the Opera*. Retrieved from: https://www.youtube.com/watch?v=zccEDofeEqQ

Official Theater. (2014). *Andrew Lloyd Webber, Trevor Nunn, & Gillian Lynne interview*. Retrieved from: https://www.youtube.com/watch?v=_m3NqP5gvnQ

Paton, M. (2008). Soprano superstar: How Sarah Brightman turned her life around. *The Daily Mail Online*. Retrieved from: http://www.dailymail.co.uk/home/you/article-533758/Soprano-Superstar-How-Sarah-Brightman-turned-life-around.html#ixzz4Y0ttNd2B

Perry, G. (1986). *The complete Phantom of the Opera*. New York: Henry Holt and Company.

Phantom of the Opera. (2015). *The Music of the Night. 2004 Film*. Retrieved from: https://www.youtube.com/watch?v=TJHMMrVgd-I&list=RDTJHMMrVgd-I

Phantom of the Opera. (2015). *The Music of the Night (Ramin Karimloo). The Royal Albert Hall*. Retrieved from: https://www.youtube.com/watch?v=ymclu8ZktrU

Phantom of the Opera. (2015). *The Phantom of the Opera. 2004 film*. Retrieved from: https://www.youtube.com/watch?v=o1XY_ux5iUI

Phantom of the Opera. (2015). *All I ask of you. 2004 film*. Retrieved from: https://www.youtube.com/watch?v=Zy1lWiHHHFY

Phantom of the Opera. (2015). *The ballet of Hannibal. Royal Albert Hall*. Retrieved from: https://www.youtube.com/watch?v=lXojdzgJA2c

Phantom of the Opera. (2012). *The final lair*. Retrieved from: https://www.youtube.com/watch?v=lNwe3H8tvWI

Phantom of the Opera. (2012). *Masquerade/Why so silent?* Retrieved from: https://www.youtube.com/watch?v=mON5dbdm63M

Phantom of the Opera. (2014). *Point of no return.* Retrieved from: https://www.youtube.com/watch?v=TFZrM38mf7Y

Phantom of the Opera. (2011). *Hannibal rehearsal.* Retrieved from: https://www.youtube.com/watch?v=N3mL-s-kGw4

Phantom of the Opera. (2011). *I remember/Stranger than you dreamt it.* Retrieved from: https://www.youtube.com/watch?v=hgEVVCBu6EU

Platt, S. (2011, Apr 28). Shadow over *The Phantom of the Opera* sequel *Love Never Dies.* Retrieved from: http://www.heraldsun.com.au/entertainment/shadow-over-the-phantom-of-the-opera-sequel-love-never-dies/news-story/3d21b5fe6a14d1012032d4f84a55976b

Portman, J. (2004, Dec 20a). The elusive Phantom: Director Joel Schumacher and composer Andrew Lloyd Webber are fans of each other's work and have been trying to bring *The Phantom of the Opera* to the big screen for 16 years. *CanWest News Service.* Retrieved from: LexisNexis.

Portman, J. (2004, Dec 20b). Behold! A new man behind the mask: Unlikely actor lands prime Phantom gig despite lack of experience. *Edmonton Journal (Alberta).* Retrieved from LexisNexis.

Powers, J. (2004, Dec). A little night music. *Vanity Fair, 194*(12), 239.

Queenan, J. (1998). *Reb lobster, white trash, and the blue lagoon. Joe Queenan's America.* New York: Hyperion.

Ross, D. (1997, Sept 8). Wrapped up in her gift. Deborah Ross talks to Sarah Brightman. *The Independent.* Retrieved from: http://josvg.home.ex4all.nl/cits/sb/intervw.html

Rotten tomatoes. (2017). Reviews of *The Phantom of the Opera.* Retrieved from: https://www.rottentomatoes.com/m/phantom_of_the_opera

Ruberto, T. (2005, Jan 14). The Phantom of Hollywood: A disfigured icon makes his way to the big screen again in the latest adaptation of Andrew Lloyd' Webber's musical. *The Buffalo News.* Retrieved from: LexisNexis.

Rusher Jcat. (2014). *Christine, I love you.* The Phantom of the Opera (25th anniversary). Retrieved from: https://www.youtube.com/watch?v=dBf_08aO7nA

Russian *Phantom of the Opera.* (2014). Retrieved from: https://www.youtube.com/watch?v=I6SWElgqFF4

Schager, N. (2005, Jan 4). *Andrew Lloyd Webber's* The Phantom of the Opera. Retrieved from: http://www.nickschager.com/nsfp/2005/01/andrew_lloyd_we.html

Scott, A.O. (2004). *Back with a vengeance: The music of the night.* Retrieved from: http://movies2.nytimes.com/2004/12/22/movies/22phan.html

Sharp, R. (2011, Jun 18). *Love Never Dies* (but the West End musical has). *The Independent.* Retrieved from: http://www.independent.co.uk/arts-entertainment/theatre-dance/news/love-never-dies-but-the-west-end-musical-has-2299298.html

Shenton, M. (2010, Feb 17). *Love Never Dies* and the curse of the Phantom menace. *The Guardian.* Retrieved from: https://www.theguardian.com/stage/theatreblog/2010/feb/17/love-never-dies-andrew-lloyd-webber

Shenton, M. (2011, Mar 1). Andrew Lloyd Webber talks of *Wizard of Oz, Evita, Love Never Dies,* his health, his next shows, and more. *Playbill.com.* Retrieved from: http://loveshoulddie.com/LSD/Playbill_Interview.html

Shuttlework, I. (2010, Mar 12). Review, *Love Never Dies. The Financial Times.* Retrieved from: http://loveshoulddie.com/LSD/Financial_Times_Press_Review.html

Simon, J. (2005). *John Simon on theater: Criticism 1975-2003* (pp. 145-148). New York: Applause & Cinema Books.

Singh, A. (2010, Jun 10). Unmasked: The fans haunting the Phantom sequel. *The Daily Telegraph.* Retrieved from: http://www.telegraph.co.uk/culture/culturenews/7822526/Unmasked-the-fans-haunting-the-Phantom-sequel.html

SoSoGeRRy. (2010). *Gerard Butler.* Phantom *makeup.* Retrieved from: https://www.youtube.com/watch?v=zVUkZ8GjNMs

Souter, C. (2004, Dec 22). *The Phantom of the Opera,* review. Retrieved from: http://www.efilmcritic.com/review.php?movie=11360&reviewer=233

Smithey, C. (2005). The Phantom of the Opera: *Musical cheese horror.* Retrieved from: http://www.colesmithey.com/reviews/2005/05/the_phantom_of_.html

Snelson, J. (2004). *Andrew Lloyd Webber.* New Haven, CT: Yale University Press (Yale Broadway Masters Series).

Snider, E. (2004, Dec 22). *The Phantom of the Opera. The Rocky Mountain Bullhorn.* Retrieved from: http://www.ericdsnider.com/movies/the-phantom-of-the-opera/

Spencer, C. (2013). Andrew Lloyd Webber: "My greatest regret." *The Telegraph*. Retrieved from: http://www.telegraph.co.uk/culture/theatre/theatre-features/9955003/Andrew-Lloyd-Webber-My-greatest-regret.html.

Stark, F. (n.d.). *Notes to a young director*. Retrieved from: http://www.theatermirror.com/mocrit.htm.

Stirling, L. (2012). *Phantom of the Opera*. Retrieved from: http://www.youtube.com/watch?v=TCL94MsxYc&list=RDeY_Xs3sXQDg&index=26

Tapper, J. (2007, May 27). Frederick Forsyth signed up to write sequel to *Phantom of the Opera*. *DailyMail.com*. Retrieved from: http://www.dailymail.co.uk/tvshowbiz/article-457902/Frederick-Forsyth-signed-write-sequel-Phantom-Opera.html

Theater Talk. (2014). *Andrew Lloyd Webber and Joel Schumacher*. Retrieved from: https://www.youtube.com/watch?v=FVrmARNTIVA

The Telegraph. (2010, Mar 10). Andrew Lloyd Webber and *Love Never Dies* stars given standing ovation. *The Telegraph*. Retrieved from: http://www.telegraph.co.uk/culture/culturenews/7411626/Andrew-Lloyd-Webber-and-Love-Never-Dies-stars-given-standing-ovation.html).

Thomson, B. (2005, Mar 28) Actor jokes about his special no-name characters. *Canada AM*. Retrieved from: LexisNexis.

Timmons, J., & Timmons, R. (2011, Mar 2). *Exposing The Really Useful Group*. Retrieved from: http://loveshoulddie.com/LSD/Exposing_RUG.html

Todd, B., & Glass, K. (2010, Mar 10). Standing ovation shows love for Andrew Lloyd Webber's *Phantom* will never die ... even if critics want to retitle sequel "Paint Never Dies." *DailyMail.com*. Retrieved from: http://www.dailymail.co.uk/tvshowbiz/article-1256707/Love-Never-Dies-world-premiere-New-Andrew-Lloyd-Webber-musical-debuts.html

Walsh, M. (1989). *Andrew Lloyd Webber: His life and works*. New York: Harry N. Abrams.

Welkos, R.W. (1999, Jun 27). They want their Phantom: Michael Crawford fans are waging a determined campaign to see him in the film version of the musical. *LA Times*. Retrieved from: http://articles.latimes.com/1999/jun/27/entertainment/ca-50445.

West End Whingers. (2010, Mar 2). Review. *Love Never Dies*. Adelphi Theatre. Retrieved from: https://westendwhingers.wordpress.com/2010/03/02/review-love-never-dies-adelphi-theatre/

Wigg, D. (2011). I was so ill I thought my career was over: Legendary actor Michael Crawford reveals the very personal reason he is back on stage. *DailyMail.com*. Retrieved from: http://www.dailymail.co.uk/femail/article-1362592/Michael-Crawford-reveals-personal-reason-s-stage.html

Wikipedia. (2016). *La fanciulla del West*. Retrieved from: https://en.wikipedia.org/wiki/La_fanciulla_del_West

Wikipedia. (2017a). *Sarah Brightman*. Retrieved from: https://en.wikipedia.org/wiki/Sarah_Brightman#cite_note-video-31

Wikipedia. (2017b). *Erik (The Phantom of the Opera)*. Retrieved from: https://en.wikipedia.org/wiki/Erik_(The_Phantom_of_the_Opera)#Erik.27s_deformity

Wikipedia. (2017c). *The Phantom of the Opera (1986 Musical)*. Retrieved from: https://en.wikipedia.org/wiki/The_Phantom_of_the_Opera_(1986_musical)

Winker, A.E. (2014). Politics and the reception of Andrew Lloyd Webber's *The Phantom of the Opera*. *Cambridge Opera Journal, 26*(3), 271-287. Retrieved from: https://www.cambridge.org/core/journals/cambridge-opera-journal/article/div-classtitlepolitics-and-the-reception-of-andrew-lloyd-webbers-span-classitalicthe-phantom-of-the-operaspandiv/9371691605B377CB220083DDBD9BC585

Wloszczyna, S. (2004, Dec 15). A night at the "Opera." *USA Today*. Retrieved from LexisNexis.

World Entertainment News Network. (2007). Brightman's heartache over no children. *Contactmusic.com*. Retrieved from: http://www.contactmusic.com/sarah-brightman/news/brightmans-heartache-over-no-children_1034453

About the Author

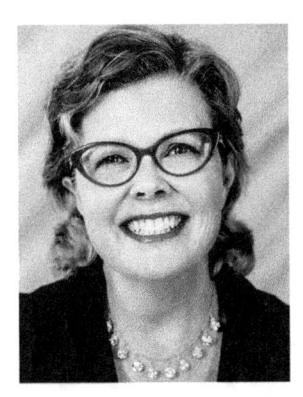

Kathleen Kendall-Tackett, PhD, FAPA, is a psychologist, and researcher, and Clinical Associate Professor at the Texas Tech University School of Medicine.. In many ways, *Phantom of the Opera* is an unlikely topic for Dr. Kendall-Tackett write about, but she never could resist a good story. Dr. Kendall-Tackett is a musician, and is a researcher in health and trauma psychology. She has won multiple awards for her work, including the 2017 President's Award for Outstanding Service from the American Psychological Association's Division of Trauma Psychology. She is a Fellow of the American Psychological Association, edits two peer-reviewed journals, and is the Past President of the APA's Division of Trauma Psychology. Dr. Kendall-Tackett has authored more than 420 articles or chapters. *The Phantom of the Opera: A Social History of the World's Most Popular Musical* is her 35th book.